7-H-6

83.70

RALA

Injeeling

x1/76

D1337116

THE INVASION OF NEPAL

Sir David Ochterlony

THE
INVASION OF
NEPAL

John Company at War

BY

JOHN PEMBLE

CLARENDON PRESS · OXFORD

1971

Oxford University Press, Ely House, London W. 1

GLASGOW NEW YORK TORONTO MELBOURNE WELLINGTON
CAPE TOWN SALISBURY IBADAN NAIROBI DAR ES SALAAM LUSAKA ADDIS ABABA
BOMBAY CALCUTTA MADRAS KARACHI LAHORE DACCA
KUALA LUMPUR SINGAPORE HONG KONG TOKYO

© OXFORD UNIVERSITY PRESS 1971

PRINTED IN GREAT BRITAIN BY
W. & J. MACKAY & CO LTD CHATHAM, KENT

To those whom I knew as
colleagues and pupils
at
Sandhurst

ACKNOWLEDGEMENTS

No historian can hope to progress without the co-operation of archivists and librarians, and without their permission to quote from the materials in their charge. I am very thankful for these privileges to the Librarian, Dr. R. Bingle, Mr. A. Farrington and the staff of the India Office, London; to Peter Hayes, Boris Mollo and the staff of the National Army Museum, Camberley; to the Hon. David Erskine and the Librarian of the Royal United Services Institution, London; to Colonel R. Attoe, Lieutenant-Colonel E. N. Thursby and the Trustees of the Regimental Museum of the King's Shropshire Light Infantry, Shrewsbury; to the Librarian of the Royal Army Medical College, London; to Major R. St. G. G. Bartelot of the Royal Artillery Institution, Woolwich; to the Librarian of the University Library, Cambridge; to Commander Godfrey of the Public Records Office, London; and to Dr. S. V. Desika Char and the Director of Archives, National Archives of India, New Delhi.

It is a pleasure to record my gratitude to the following, who must share the credit for any merit the work may have, but who are in no way responsible for its weaknesses or for the views it expresses: Dr. R. J. Moore, whose guidance and encouragement sustained me during the long period of research and writing; William McIlwee, whose trenchant and unstinted comments made me aware of the considerable blemishes in the first draft; Professor Michael Howard, Dr. C. C. Davis and Professor K. Ballhatchet for their valuable suggestions; Delegates and staff of the Press in the University of Oxford for the sympathetic interest they have taken in the work, and for the confidence they have expressed in it by undertaking to publish; Mrs. Jean Lane, my patient typist; and my friends Akbar Khan and Mahendra Singh Chaudhuri of Delhi, interpreter and driver, in whose cheerful company I passed sultry April days trekking in the hills of Himachal Pradesh, looking for *feringi* graves and Gurkha forts.

London, October, 1969.

CONTENTS

LIST OF PLATES

LIST OF MAPS

ABBREVIATIONS

Mins. of Ev.	*Minutes of Evidence*
E.I.U.S.J.	*East India United Services Journal*
P.R.N.W.	*Papers Respecting the Nepaul War*
Sec. Cons.	Bengal Secret Consultations
Pol. Cons.	Bengal Political Consultations
Mil. Cons.	Bengal Military Consultations

Detailed descriptions of these and all other sources are in Appendix 3 and in the Bibliography at the end of the volume.

Statistics, and quotations from printed works, have been referred to their sources, and the politically important manuscript sources have been specified. Specialists wishing to trace the manuscript sources of a less general, military and biographical interest on which the text is based are invited to consult the typescript version deposited in the Senate House Library, University of London.

PART I

I

THE GURKHAS

THE highest mountain range in the world separates India from Tibet. In Sanskrit it is called *himalaya*, meaning 'region of snow'. Before man existed, it rose from the sea, lifting with itself rivers which originate in Tibet. These rivers still reach down to the sea; but their journey is much longer now, the ancient ocean having receded and exposed the alluvial plain of north India, or Hindustan. Earthquakes and landslides testify that the causes which raised the Himalayas continue in operation, moulding them into some cosmographic design whose completion man will never witness, and which will come about as though he had never been. But if the mountains prefigure a future of which man will not form a part, the foothills in their shadow have long formed a part of his past. Settlements have existed for uncounted generations in the valleys and on the slopes of the temperate zone below the unmelting snows. This is country where spruce and deodar forests grow two hundred feet tall, where natural colours have a prismatic purity, and where white peaks dominate the distance, filling half the horizon with preternatural silence, and the mind with unanswerable questions.

One of the largest and most densely populated of these valleys is that of Nepal. Its early history is obscured by an apocrypha of fable and romance. Buddhist legend avers—and this much geological evidence confirms—that the Valley was once a lake. The saint Manjusri, coming down from China, drained it dry by opening the southern rocks with a blow from his sword, and allowing the water to flow down to India as the Baghmati river. The earliest inhabitants were probably members of the Kirata tribe—a short, flatfaced people of Indo-Mongolian stock and Tibeto-Burman tongue,

The main disputed frontier areas are boxed

▨ Land approx. 5000 feet and over

⊞ ⧄ Territories administered by the East India Company

▤ East India Company protectorates

```
0      50     100    150   Miles
0   50  100  150  200  250  Kilometres
```

MAP 1. North India in 1814

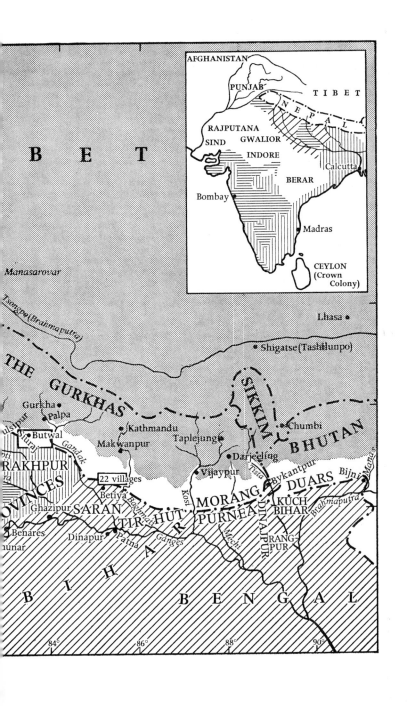

B E T

Manasarovar

Tsongpo (Brahmaputra)

Lhasa •

• Shigatse (Tashilunpo)

THE GURKHAS

Gurkha •
• Palpa
• Butwal
• Kathmandu
Makwanpur
Taplejung

SIKKIM

• Chumbi

BHUTAN

• Darjeeling

RAKHPUR
OVINCES
• Ghazipur
• Benares
unar

• Vijaypur

22 villages

Betiya

SARAN
TIR
HUT
Dinapur
Patna
Ganges

MORANG
PURNEA

Bykantpur

DINAJPUR

KUCH
BIHAR

RANG-
PUR

DUARS

Bijni

Brahmaputra

BIHAR

B E N G A L

84°   86°   88°   90°

Inset map

AFGHANISTAN

PUNJAB   T I B E T

N E P A L

RAJPUTANA   GWALIOR
SIND   INDORE   Calcutta

BERAR

Bombay

Madras

CEYLON
(Crown
Colony)

who came from Assam and north-east India. Several centuries before the Christian era, they were joined by the people who still
inhabit the Valley in considerable numbers, the Newars. The
language of the Newars, which is similar to that of the Kiratas, and
their features, which often even now betray Mongolian ancestry,
indicate that they were either a second north Indian group or a
tribe from Tibet. The Newars were a literate race, with an advanced
culture. Their industry and artistry have given the Valley its distinc-
tive architecture and sculpture, and their language has preserved
its folklore and early history. In the earliest stages, Buddhism was
probably the main religion of Nepal; but when a system of monarchy
replaced the old tribal republican form of government, the kings
were invariably Hindu, and modelled themselves on the monarchs
of the plains. Another north Indian people, the Licchavis, founded
the first recorded Hindu dynasty in Nepal; and Indo-European[1] or
not (they could have been Mongolian), they adopted titles used by
the Rajputs,[2] introduced the classical Hindu institution of *varna*
(the division of society into four immutable categories), and even
persecuted the Buddhists. The Kiratas, apparently displaced by
the Licchavis, moved into the hills east of the Valley, where their
descendants are still to be found. The Newars, however, submitted
passively to the rule of Hindu monarchs, and often became converted themselves. They are still divided into worshippers of the
Hindu deity Shiva (*Shivamargis*) and worshippers of the Buddha
(*Buddhamargis*). The Licchavis, who were in Nepal from the first
until the eighth century, built a powerful empire and extended their
dominion even beyond the Himalayas. Soon Nepal became the

[1] The word 'Aryan' was formerly used to designate the Sanskrit-speaking
tribe or tribes who, originating probably in eastern Europe, invaded India at the
dawn of its recorded history. It was devised by the distinguished orientalist Max
Müller, from the Sanskrit word *arya*, meaning 'noble', which the authors of the
early Sanskrit epics used to distinguish their own people from the darker indigenous inhabitants of north India. The term never was universally accepted
as an ethnological label, and since the Nazis propagated the notion that the
'Aryans' were a fair-haired, blue-eyed 'master race' (it is more likely that they
were, in fact, Mediterranean or 'Brown' people) it has been generally dropped.
It is retained only to describe the group of languages (Iranian, Sanskrit, and the
descendants of Sanskrit, all forming a branch of the larger Indo-European
family) associated with the people in question.
[2] Rajputs (literally, royal progeny) are a Hindu caste of the ksatriya or military
category—the second in the four *varna* of the brahminical system. The modern
Rajputs appear to be descended from the white Huns and Gujars who came to
India from central Asia in the sixth century.

client of a kingdom whose real centre was Tibet, but she exercised a strong cultural influence, passing on her own artistic idioms to Tibet and mediating the transfer thither of Buddhism from north India. In 704, Nepal broke away from Tibet, and a few decades later the Nepalese Licchavi dynasty came to an end, with the accession of a king called Amsu Varman, who, according to one chronicle at least, was not of royal blood but a noble (*thakur*) who had married into the royal family.

Almost nothing is known about the history of the first two and a half centuries of the Thakuri dynasty. We know only (from Petech's researches) that it had three lines, and that during some two hundred years the Valley was divided into two kingdoms, in one of which there was a relapse to the Mongolian institution of joint rule by a pair of monarchs. Unity was ephemerally regained at the end of the eleventh century under King Sankara Deva, who ruled from Patan; but the Valley reverted to anarchy when he died. In an interlude of darkness and confusion, for which native chronicles, concerned to purify the genealogies of later monarchs, are no source of enlightenment, the Thakuri dynasty faded into oblivion and the last of the 'Newar' dynasties, the Malla, took its place. The period was an unhappy one, with raids from north India, especially from the kingdom of Tirhut. Nanya Deva of that country made a predatory ascent into the Valley about 1100, and further excursions followed; but in 1324 it was as a refugee that Hari Sinha of Tirhut made his way there, fleeing the army of the Muslim Sultan of Delhi, who had invaded Bengal. Hari Sinha was a patron of Sanskrit letters and exercised a strong influence on the development of Hinduism in the Valley, but there is no record that he ever became its king. This was a tragic time in the history of Nepal. Hordes of Muslims shattered its solitude on two occasions at least in the middle years of the fourteenth century, and probably it is these iconoclastic visitations which account for the disappearance of all temples of older date than the fifteenth century.

From a background obscured by this chaos, a strong man, Jaya Sthithi Malla, emerged—deliverer and unifier of the Nepal Valley and one of the most notable rulers in its history. He sought to give legitimacy to his succession by marrying the daughter of Hari Sinha and then having the chroniclers record his father-in-law as a king, but was not content to justify his claim to power with spurious pedigrees alone. Nepalese society long bore the imprint of his sagacious administration. His system of weights and measures remained in use until recent times, and his legal codes are theoretically still valid. He made his kingdom a sanctuary for the laws and traditions of Hinduism. They were recorded and codified by pundits from India, and the valley of Nepal became the repository for a way of life menaced with extinction by the Muslims on the plains. Even the Buddhist society of Nepal, while tolerated, was carefully graded as a hierarchy of castes. The early Malla kings combined zealous Hinduism with an interest in local culture. Jaya Yaksha Malla, grandson of Jaya Sthithi, patronized native letters and raised Newari to the status of an official language. Unhappily, these halcyon days were the prelude to another long period of strife. The kingdom's precarious cohesion was lost when Jaya Yaksha, on his deathbed, divided his realm between his three sons, who soon fell to quarrelling and fighting among themselves. The Valley remained divided into the warring principalities of Bhatgaon, Patan, and Kathmandu until an adventurer from the west, Prithvi Narayan Shah of the little hill state of Gurkha, took advantage of the jealousies separating each from the others to establish his own authority over all and found the dynasty which still endures.

The Gurkhas are not a tribe or a caste, but a miniature nation of several tribes and castes. The only features which they all share are descent from the original subjects of Gurkha state and a dialect called Gurkhali or, nowadays, Nepali. The martial energy which enabled the Gurkhas to conquer the Nepal Valley and then forge a huge empire in the hills was the attribute of one group in their community—the Chetris. The word *chetri* is a vernacular distortion of the Sanskrit *ksatriya*, meaning warrior and designating the second of the four divisions of Hindu society; but in the Himalayan hills it has lost its generic quality and acquired special significance. The Chetris have the basic characteristic of a caste,[3] which is the smallest endogamous unit in Hindu society.

[3] *Caste* is a Portuguese word, denoting the *jat* of Hindu society—a group which is endogamous and commensal. The system of caste organization probably had economic origins, and it grew up independently of the classical brahministic division of society into *varna* (literally, colour), though an attempt was made to harmonize the two systems by classifying the castes as *brahmana* (priestly), *ksatriya* (warrior), *vaisaya* (peasant) and *sudra* (serf). The Chetris are an endogamous group. The only subdivisions are *thar* (clans), which are generally exogamous, and *gotra* (comprising descendants of one remote ancestor), which are strictly so. *Gotra* are subdivisions of *thar*, of which there are about three dozen, scattered widely through the Nepalese hills to Kashmir. Most traces of

Ethnologically, the Chetris are related to the Khas, or Khasias, of north-west India. The Khas migrated up into the Punjab hills and the central Himalayas early in their history. They appear to have been among the original Indo-European settlers in north-west India, and tradition links them with the five sons of Pandu (the Pandavas) who are featured in the Sanskrit epic *Mahabharata* (1000–500 B.C.) Some hill dynasties still claim descent from the Pandavas. There is undoubtedly a basis of truth to such assertions. One of the social institutions of the modern Khas is polyandry, which they almost certainly contracted as a result of early contacts with the aboriginal populations of north India, and a society with such an alien custom was clearly known to the authors of the poem, since all the sons of Pandu were married to the same wife. It is also a fact that by the time the *Law Book of Manu* was drawn up (200 B.C.–A.D. 200) the Khas had lost all high status. They were therein listed among the *vrishalas*, or outcastes, as a race of ksatriyas who had fallen by the wayside from seeing no brahmins. It is probable that they were ostracized because of their polyandry and other habits derived from aboriginal societies, which the brahmins now despised as perverse. A modern view is that the great war in the *Mahabharata* symbolizes the conflict between early Indo-European settlers of debased blood and unorthodox customs and later, purer-bred arrivals. It may well be that the Khas' movement northwards into the western and central Himalayas was part of a retreat of older settlers before the new waves of immigration, represented in the *Mahabharata* by the ultimate withdrawal of the Pandavas into the mountains. The certainty is that by the dawn of the Christian era the Khas had been banished to both the social and geographic periphery of the Hindu cosmos, and had dispersed throughout the Himalayan hills from Kashmir to Nepal. They adhered to the simpler, or Vedic, forms of religious code and ritual which were becoming obscured on the plains by alterations and refinements introduced by the brahmins.

At some time around the eleventh century, two groups of Khas migrated into western Tibet and established themselves as ruling cadres in Purang and Guge. Later, these dominions were united under a single family which adopted the popular title Malla (literally, wrestler). Their predatory raids proved very troublesome

the endogamous tribal castes which originally made up the Chetri group seem to have disappeared.

to the rulers of the Nepal Valley. This family's power reached its
zenith in the middle of the fourteenth century under King Prithvi
Malla, who ruled over an extensive empire. It included Guge,
Purang, and territories in the hills as far as the west of modern
Nepal. This dominion seems to have disintegrated after Prithvi
Malla, for no record of his successors has been found and raids
into the Nepal Valley ceased; but it is possible that the Mallas who
came into prominence in the Valley at this time were scions of the
western dynasty. The suggestion receives a measure of support
from the fact that it was in the time of the early Malla kings in the
Valley that a Khas dialect was introduced there. One was in official
use at the durbar of Kathmandu before the end of the seventeenth
century. The reasons for the demise of the empire in the west are
not ascertained; but newly discovered records and lapidary inscriptions mention both the advent of a new aristocracy from the
plains and the Rajput city of Chitor, which, after the heroic resistance much sung in Rajput minstrelsy, fell to the Muslims in 1303.
This leads to the supposition that the collapse of the Mallas was
caused by the advent of Rajput exiles from India, who carved
principalities for themselves out of the family's dominions. Many
subsequent hill rajas claimed descent from the Chitor Rajputs.

These fugitives found in the hills extensively dispersed settlements of Khas, ranging in size from minor principality to substantial empire and using variants of what had once been a distinct
Khas language. The Chetri caste was the result of miscegenation between the immigrants and the resident hill societies. Its
members were born of Khas mothers and spoke a Khas dialect, but
were recognized as ksatriyas and allowed to wear the sacred thread,
the emblem of the two highest *varna*, in deference to their Rajput
or brahmin paternity. Many Khas conceded the right of spiritual
jurisdiction to the brahmins who came with the Rajputs from the
plains, and in return were admitted to the Chetri caste and allowed
to wear the thread. In the area of Gurkha, to the north-west of the
Nepal Valley, there lived the Magars, a Mongolian people. They
reacted to the influx of Rajputs and brahmins in much the same
way as the Khas. Many were converted to Hinduism, and many of
their women gave birth to the children of the immigrants. Both
converts and illegitimate progeny were accepted into the new
caste; and so in this area it came to include Magar names (such as
Burathoki, Gharti, Thapa) as well as Khas, Rajput and brahmin

ones. At first the authentic Rajputs from the plains probably held aloof from this new hybrid caste; but given the situation where their own clans were often exogamous, where their choice of marriage partners was very circumscribed, and where common ksatriya status made intermarriage less reprehensible, we can readily accept that the Rajputs were soon assimilated by the Chetris. In this way the new caste became a crucible for all the ethnic elements of the hills—Magar, Khas, brahmin and Rajput. Chetris still vary considerably in appearance. Most have a pronounced Indo-European bias and tend to be small and slight. Others retain unmistakably Mongolian features, and are more robust and muscular. Linguistically, they are more akin to the speakers of the Khas dialects of the hills than the Hindi speakers of north India.[4]

---

[4] Older theories concerning the origin of the Chetris were based on the assumption that the term had no significance except as a vernacular distortion of *ksatriya*. Lévi thought that the Mongolian Magar tribesmen were the earliest inhabitants of the western hills, and that they were the first to come into contact with the exiles from Rajputana. Basing his conclusions on the pioneer investigations of Hodgson, he took the present Khas to be the product of miscegenation between the Rajput and brahmin exiles and native Magar women. The illegitimate progeny of these unions, while keeping the names of their fathers, formed a *new* caste called Khas. Since its inclusion in the *Laws of Manu*, the designation Khas had lost any identification with a specific tribal society, and was used as a general pejorative for the barbarous hill peoples of the north. The brahmins now revived the old name as a label for the new caste, which was allowed ksatriya status. Membership of the new group was increased by the admission of Magar proselytes, and so became a hybrid caste including brahmin, Rajput and Magar clan names. Ultimately, the authentic Rajputs merged with the new ksatriyas or Chetris, and all became members of a single tribal caste called Khas. This theory, which recognizes no distinction between Khas and Chetri and sees the Khas as a new creation, was founded on the erroneous assumption that Nepali, the language of the Khas and Chetris of the Nepal Valley, was in itself a recent language—a mere patois or dialect of Hindi. Lévi considered its existence to be an important indication of the recent infiltration of Hindi speakers into the hills. It was Professor R. L. Turner who first contended that Nepali had its closest affinity with the much earlier Indo-Aryan dialects of the north-west Punjab—especially Kumauni—with which it has experienced important sound changes not shared by dialects of the plains. He reckoned that, at the most, southern languages such as Hindi lent words to Nepali, thus giving it a superficial similarity to themselves. When Turner published these views, in the preface to his *Dictionary*, he had no knowledge of any written Nepali more than a century old, and his conclusions were based entirely on his examination of sound changes. Recently, Tucci's *Report* on his scientific expeditions to west Nepal revealed the existence of a royal donation dated 1376 and written partly in a dialect which sufficiently resembles the modern language of Nepal to be called 'old Nepali'. This confirms Turner's theory that Nepali is related to dialects which were in use in the western hills long before the first major incursion of Hindi speakers; in fact it confirms that it was closely related to the language of the group of Khas

At the beginning of the eighteenth century, the country between the valley of Nepal and Kumaun was fragmented into
forty-six lordships, grouped into two loose confederations. In the
basin of the Karnali[5] river system were the *Baisi*, or Twenty-Two
Rajas; and further east, in the Narayani[6] basin, which comprises
the seven branches of the Gandak, were the *Chaubisi*, or Twenty-
Four. All paid theoretical allegiance to the Mogul Emperor in
Delhi; but the arm of Imperial authority, never having proved long
enough to control the hill states effectively, was becoming even
more enfeebled as the life blood of the Mogul body politic drained
away, and the intractable hill lords were left to themselves. The
resulting turbulence favoured the ambitions of the Shah family of
Gurkha, a little state among the Twenty-Four. This family, like
most nobility in the hills, claimed descent from the Rajputs of
Chitor. They called themselves Thakur—a Rajput title—and considered themselves to be a cut above the Khas, whom they affected
to scorn. In fact, they were almost certainly Chetris—ethnic mon-
grels of the type we have been describing. These proud people
gradually enlarged and marshalled their resources; and in the
middle of the eighteenth century, under the leadership of Raja
Prithvi Narayan Shah, they set about conquering the Nepal
Valley, an ambition which it took nearly twenty-five years to
accomplish. Kathmandu fell to Prithvi Narayan in 1768, and Patan
and Bhatgaon the following year. These conquests marked the birth
of the Nepalese state as it is known today. It was a state conceived
and nurtured by a minor martial aristocracy of Chetris, who made
their particular caste the sole repository of political power. The
intriguing thing about the Chetri caste is that while it was in itself
a product of the brahmins' accommodating adjustment to the
pressures of local necessity, it soon ceased to practise the hospitality by the grace of which it had itself been born. Quite when is
not sure; but at some time it ceased receiving converts from the hill

---

whose corporate and cultural existence it was the main achievement of Tucci's
expeditions to reveal.

Nepali is but one dialect among a number of related tongues known generic-
ally as *Khas kura* (Khas speech) or *Parbatiya* (relating to the hills). Modern
Nepali is often referred to by either of these names, but this in effect involves
using generic terms for an individual dialect. A much more satisfying label for
the language is *Gurkhali*, because this refers the dialect to the Khas of a specific
area.

[5] Called the Gogra when it reaches India.   [6] Called the Gandak in India.

tribes into its fold, and Magars who had become Chetris began to distinguish themselves from those left outside the caste by the designation 'Chetri' after their name (e.g. Thapa-Chetri). The Gurungs, another Mongolian tribe domiciled north of Gurkha, who with the Magars formed the bulk of the Gurkha army, were excluded altogether from the new caste and denied the privilege of calling themselves ksatriyas even when professed Hindus. Khas who found themselves outside the caste when it became closed had to be content with an inferior status. Such were, apparently, the Khatris of Gurkha. The Newars were excluded without exception. Such exclusion was inconsistent with the usual pragmatism of the brahmins, whose practice in effect, if not in theory, was to draw up a hierarchy of castes designed to embrace all the Hindus of a community and then arrange such a distribution of those castes between the four *varna* as would describe its social and political organization. In Nepal, the brahminical system was not and is not a reflection of the Hindu community. Religiously orthodox groups of Gurungs, Magars, Newars and Khas, having been excluded from the Chetri caste despite the sanction which precedent would appear to give for their inclusion, have found no allowance made for their political or military qualifications in the national order of precedence. Their status was defined only in negative terms. They could not claim parity with the Chetris, and had no acknowledged right to wear the sacred thread. When we remember that this state of petrification favoured the hegemony of the Chetris, by making it impossible for these groups to acquire the social status which might justify their pretensions to power and influence, we have perhaps a clue at hand to help explain the characteristic anomaly of Nepalese society. It may well be that the development of the caste system was prevented from working itself out with its accustomed logic as a result of a determination on the part of the Chetris of Gurkha to maintain political control. It is at any rate indisputable that the legal system which they introduced rigorously perpetuated the existing hierarchy of castes and made further development impossible;[7] and it is equally certain that they made political power the perquisite of a narrow oligarchy of Chetri families.

[7] Hodgson, in 'On the Law and Legal Practice of Nepal', remarks on this, but ascribes it to a conscious desire, on the part of refugees from Muslim bigotry, to preserve the traditions of Hinduism undefiled. This would appear to be far too sophisticated an attitude to attribute to the unidealistic and untutored Gurkhas, who were quite ready to waive the prescriptions of ritual when policy demanded.

The Gurkhas were an uncouth people with few pretensions to culture or the arts of peace. As Hindus, they generally respected the shrines and temples of the Newars; but they evinced little inclination to imitate their industry or their sophisticated urban style of life. As the new capital the Gurkhas chose the relatively drab town of Kathmandu, in preference to the more opulent centres of Patan and Bhatgaon, and they showed reluctance to abandon their smallholdings and mud huts. Their interests were almost exclusively martial, and they idealized conquest and valour in battle. Prithvi Narayan paused only briefly to consolidate his position in the Valley before resuming his career of acquisition. He made a feint at the Twenty-Four Rajas, but his main interest at this stage was directed to the country of the Kiratas, in the basin of the Kosi river. The objective was Vijaypur, a town in the foothills across the Kosi in that portion of the lowland called the Morang. It was the eastern capital of a Rajput family whose three branches controlled a far-flung empire extending from the Kosi basin to Makwanpur, the territory just to the south of the Nepal Valley. Makwanpur was already in the Gurkha Raja's grasp, and his generals now attacked Vijaypur. The Morang had for some years been fermenting with civil war, its Raja having been murdered and the throne become the object of rival claims from his uncle and the Dewan, so it fell an easy prey. The Morang was overrun, the regicide Dewan ferreted out and killed, and the remains of the royal family expelled into India. The Gurkha Raja's next concern was the state of Sikkim, whose boundaries in those days stretched in the south-west to Baikantpur on the plains, and in the north-west to the Arun river in the hills. Sikkim was a colony of the Lepcha tribe, a Himalayan people who were unique in that they had acquired for rulers not Hindus from the plains but Buddhist princes from Tibet. The Sikkim Rajas also exercised a tenuous authority over the Limbu tribe on the eastern bank of the Arun river. In the middle 1770s the Gurkhas made preparations for an invasion of

Kirkpatrick recounts that the Nepalese army was authorized to consume chauri bullocks during its expedition into Tibet (1788–92) on the ground that these animals were not distinguished by the long dewlaps which were the generic mark of the sacred bull (p. 120). Furthermore, the Hinduism practised by Prithvi Narayan Shah and the Gurkhas seems to have been far from undefiled. It was a primitive, sacrificial religion, characterized by worship of the most baneful forms of the female aspect of the deity Shiva, and betraying the persisting influence of pagan fertility rites and Tantrism.

Sikkimese territory. A warning from Tibet, which considered
Sikkim a protégé, and the death of Prithvi Narayan Shah (1775)
temporarily upset the plan; but skirmishing along the Arun
frontier continued until the Tibetan government ransomed peace
by consenting to move the frontier further east, making the Kankai
river the boundary in the lowlands but leaving Sikkim with Ilam
and Taplejung in the hills. The Gurkhas had no intention of
honouring the treaty, and barely waited for it to be signed before
launching a two-pronged attack, driving into Sikkim by the two
passes of Taplejung and Ilam. But the Lepchas were a virile race,
of the same mountain stock as the soldiers in the Gurkhas' own
army. They held up the Gurkhas for nine years. Only in 1788 were
the Gurkhas able to renew their onslaught, defeating the prince in
an obstinate battle fought near his capital[8] and compelling him to
flee to Tibet, where he was provided with men to continue the
struggle. With additional reinforcements from the Raja of Bhutan,
he returned to retrieve his capital. He drove the Gurkhas out, but
then his Bhutanese troops became mutinous from want of pay, and
the Gurkhas were able to take refuge in the fort of Nagri, to the
south, where they awaited reinforcements. Soon they were strong
enough to reconquer all Sikkim west of the Tista and compel the
Raja, his infant son and his loyal Lepcha general to withdraw into
the hilly fastnesses east of that river. This defiant band ensconced
themselves in the town and fort of Gangtok, whence they were still
harassing the Gurkhas when the British went to war against Nepal
in 1814. By then the old Raja had died, and his nineteen-year-old
son, Chogyal Namgyal, was governing the truncated patrimony in
close association with troops and advisers from Tibet. West of the
Tista, the Lepchas continued refractory, and the Gurkhas found it
wise to humour their pretensions by allowing one of their own
leaders to continue as civil governor and collector at Nagri. This
was Yuk Namchu, a nephew of the loyal Lepcha general. His other
nephew, brother to Yuk Namchu, remained at Gangtok as *chagzod*,
(chief minister) to the Raja. A large civil and military station was
constructed at Dhankuta, north of the old provincial capital of
Vijaypur, and became the administrative centre of all Gurkha conquests in this part of the hills. The new masters wisely conciliated

---

[8] Popular Lepcha legend represents this as having been 'near Pemionchi'—
see Geoffrey Gorer, *Himalayan village. A Study of the Lepchas of Sikkim*, second
edition: London, 1967, p. 237.

their fierce and recalcitrant Kirata and Limbu subjects by being satisfied with token submission. The revenues were lightly assessed, and allowed to be collected by the tribal societies' own representatives.[9] The Gurkhas took pains to appease the brahmins hitherto attached to the Vijaypur royal family by confirming and even increasing their free grants of land.

But it was to the west of the Nepal Valley that the main thrust of Gurkha expansion was directed. At first it was a career of conquest not by the sword alone, but by an opportunist mixture of attack, alliance, strategem and marriage diplomacy. Force was used with discretion, care being taken to avoid precipitating antagonistic coalitions before the Gurkha hegemony was consolidated. It was essential not to provoke the Raja of Palpa, who enjoyed preeminence among the hill chiefs and was a favourite tenant of the Nawab of Oudh. A marriage match was arranged between the Palpa Raja's daughter and the regent of Nepal during the minority of Prithvi Narayan's grandson, and it was the subsequent connivance of the Palpa family which enabled the Gurkhas to impose their authority over all the Twenty-Two and Twenty-Four Rajas. By 1790, all the mountain rulers as far west as the Kali river were either enfeoffed by the Gurkhas or replaced by their agents. Palpa alone remained unannexed, but henceforth its independence was more apparent than real. The Raja, Prithvi Pala, was twice inveigled into coming to Kathmandu, and twice incarcerated; but for the moment his connection with the Nawab of Oudh preserved him from death.

Beyond the Kali river lay Kumaun. Once the prosperous kingdom of the Hindu Chand dynasty, it had been suffering from malignant anarchy since the rule of a feckless raja in the early eighteenth century. Nominating and controlling kings had become the privileges of the highest bidder, and two factions of *zemindars* (barons) had been bidding for years without either offering a price in blood and ruthlessness which the other was not prepared to match. As the contention dragged on, rich provinces in the lowlands had been lost to Oudh; a rash of castles and fortresses had spread across the surface of the land; trade and agriculture had languished; and the last legitimate Chands, helpless pawns, had been exterminated. The most prominent member of the Mara faction was Harak Deva Joshi, a restless, scheming supporter of the

---

[9] *Rais* in the case of the Kiratas; *subas* in that of the Limbus.

Chands who had turned kingmaker and sponsored two pretenders since the extinction of the royal family. In 1790 he was in exile on the plains. The Phartiyal faction, his mortal enemies, had seized power by playing his own trick and invoking the support of neighbouring Garhwal. Harak Deva Joshi now riposted by encouraging the Gurkhas to invade Kumaun. Dividing their force into two columns, they crossed the Kali and defeated Raja Mahendra Singh in Gangoli province in the north, and his uncle Lal Singh in Kali Kumaun province in the south. Both fled to the plains, and the victors occupied Almora, the capital, with no resistance from a populace weary after generations of anarchy. The Gurkhas hesitated to trust the wily Harak Deva Joshi too far, and planned to send him to Kathmandu, where he could do no mischief; but he fled west to Garhwal, his old refuge. Here he plotted as actively as ever and attempted to build an anti-Gurkha coalition. He hawked his cause around the courts of north India, with many crocodile tears and fluent stories of Gurkha atrocities, but found little active support until the British were preparing to invade the hills in 1814.

Once they had advanced beyond the Kali, the Gurkhas began to be perplexed by the problem of how to combine military occupation with an equitable colonial administration. In conformity to their usual practice, the land was divided and assigned in separate parcels to the officers and troops of the army; but the necessity of maintaining a large military establishment meant that the income from each portion was over-assessed, and the troops, who had no permanent interest in the welfare of the peasants and landholders, used brutal treatment and confiscated private property in order to realize the revenues. Even the wives and children of cultivators were seized and sold as slaves. The subsequent depopulation, with large numbers of farmers emigrating to India, alarmed the durbar at Kathmandu, which made efforts to improve the local administration and revise the land settlement. Brahma Shah, the member of the royal family who succeeded to the governorship of Almora in 1806, was congenial and just. Under his rule Kumaun became the object of special solicitude and favour. Orders were issued for the protection of private property, the enslavement of subjects was prohibited, rent-free grants of land were confirmed and a special influence was conceded to the brahmins and zemindars of the Phartiyal faction who had been in power when the Gurkhas arrived.

To promulgate injunctions was one thing; to have them obeyed, especially in areas outside the capital, another. The welfare of the peasantry would only be assured when troops and officers in the outlying districts were made fully accountable for their misconduct towards the civilian population. But instead of pausing now to attend to this and other pressing problems concerning internal government, the Gurkhas drove on still farther west, accumulating territories in a fever of aggrandizement. They were partly impelled by the sheer momentum of their own military advance; partly drawn by the political vacuum in the hills ahead; and partly stimulated by a revolution in Kathmandu which brought to power the imperialist Thapa party.

For twenty years, from the death of Prithvi Narayan Shah until the coming of age of his grandson in 1795, a Chetri family of noble extraction, called Panre, replaced the monarchy as the true source of authority within the state. It was Damodar Panre, Prime Minister during the regency, who carried the work of Prithvi Narayan to its logical conclusion, consolidating and extending the Gurkha empire without relinquishing due diplomatic discretion and political moderation. Rana Bahadur Shah came of age in 1795, but resigned the throne to his infant son four years later in deference to the wishes of his morganatic favourite queen. Soon after, this queen died, and Rana Bahadur was distracted to the point of insanity by grief. He began to perpetrate the most atrocious cruelties and profanities, and Damodar Panre, with the support of the brahmins, most of the durbar and all the vassals of the western hills, compelled him to withdraw to the holy city of Benares, on the plains of India, in the guise of a pilgrim. His youngest queen was left as regent. For the next few years, Damodar continued as Prime Minister, secure from the intrigues of the regent while he had the support of Brahma Shah, Rana Bahadur's illegitimate brother. This member of the royal family enjoyed the prestige and influence of an elder statesman. In a durbar whose members so often feature in the pages of history as monstrous allegories of perfidy, cruelty and greed, he was remarkable for his diffidence, sobriety and decorum. But a situation now evolved in which even all his goodwill was insufficient to save the Panres. Their inveterate rivals, the Thapas, were working for the return of Rana Bahadur. The doyen of the clan, Amar Thapa, had been imprisoned by Damodar Panre; but at Benares his young son, Bhim Sen Thapa, was pouring schemes into the unbalanced Rana Bahadur and ingratiating himself with the frustrated and jealous senior queen; while in the west his brother, Amar Singh Thapa,[10] was rapidly becoming prominent for his generalship. In 1803, the senior queen staged a *coup de théâtre*. She suddenly left her profligate husband and travelled up to Kathmandu alone, nonplussing the Prime Minister, but impressing the general populace by her courage and determination. She made herself regent, released Amar Thapa, and admitted him to the council of state. The following year Rana Bahadur followed her to Nepal. Prompted, no doubt, by Bhim Sen Thapa, who was at his elbow, he challenged the troops sent to oppose him as their true liege lord; and they, perhaps spontaneously, probably not, went over to him with enthusiastic protestations of loyalty. Damodar Panre was arrested and beheaded and Bhim Sen Thapa made Prime Minister. The melodramatic dénouement of this operatic episode in Nepalese palace politics came when Rana Bahadur was assassinated in the open durbar by one of his uncles. Bhim Sen Thapa retaliated to what he claimed was a Panre conspiracy by energetically purging the administration of the Panres and their coadjutors. Some fifty heads are said to have rolled in the Prime Minister's orgy of blood.

The main beneficiaries and probably the chief protagonists of this lurid interlude were the Thapas, a Chetri clan who had never quite lost the stigma of their mongrel origin. Chetris who prided themselves on their own purer Rajput extraction spurned the Thapas, and even treated them as a separate and inferior caste by refusing to eat with them. The Thapas had become embittered, and nursed secret pretensions. Their jealousy was directed in particular against the Panre family, whose control of all political appointments since the death of Prithvi Narayan had thwarted their ambitions. When their opportunity for self-assertion came, they exploited it with all the customary truculence of the newly emancipated. Bhim Sen Thapa, to be master of Nepal for the next thirty-five years,

[10] Both were called Amar Singh Thapa. The middle cognomen is omitted in the case of the one in Kathmandu in order to make distinction easier. Hyder Hearsey informed the government (*P.R.N.W.*, p. 47) that Amar Singh Thapa in the west was 'nephew' to Bhim Sen Thapa. This should probably read vice versa. In one letter in the English records (Sec. Cons., 27 Sept. 1815, no 43) Amar Singh Thapa in the west refers to Bhim Sen Thapa as his 'son'; but this is probably a translator's error, arising from the fact that in Nepali, as in other north Indian vernaculars, distinction is not always made between 'son' and 'brother's son'.

was only twenty-five when he became Prime Minister in 1804. He was tall and sinewy, with fine Rajput features whose constant animation betrayed great energy and a certain nervousness. His manner was in strange contrast to the vacant stare and mute incomprehension of the young *roi fainéant*, whose intellectual and physical development he purposely retarded by constant confinement and defective education. For the next 150 years, the Gurkha monarchy was to be no more than vestigial. While in Benares, Bhim Sen had carefully observed European manners and customs, especially those relating to military organization, and he subsequently attempted to introduce some of them into his own country; but he had acquired neither fondness for the English nor respect for their mode of political conduct. After his accession, Gurkha policy became suddenly more intransigent and rash. One of his first acts was to execute Prithvi Pala, the vain and selfish Raja of Palpa. Then his father, Amar Thapa, raised to the English rank of general, was sent with a large force to occupy all the Palpa estates. These were measures in marked contrast to the circumspection shown by the Panres in their dealings with this family. General Amar Thapa fixed his headquarters at Tansing and assumed the functions of governor of Palpa, which he discharged very pugnaciously. Most free grants of land were resumed and their brahmin possessors insulted. Brahma Shah, despite his sympathy for the Panres, did not perish in the purge of 1804. He was saved by his popularity and venerability; but soon after the palace revolution he was banished, on administrative business, to distant Kumaun. He went tormented by sorrow and worry. The Thapas he detested as low-born upstarts and their acquisition of power he lamented; but he knew that if his behaviour gave cause for the slightest suspicion, his family, kept in Kathmandu as hostages, would answer for it.

In Garhwal, and beyond to the Sutlaj river, the softly contoured hills of Kumaun give place to a more wild and angular topography, in which there are many precipices and chasms. There is no scattered distribution of small fertile valleys, as in Kumaun. The province's whole measure of open space is concentrated into one or two extensive tracts. In comparison with the barrenness of the rest of the country, the valley (*dun*) of Dehra seems extravagantly favoured. Varying from eight to ten miles in breadth, and nearly forty miles long, it is stretched between the Ganges and the Jumna in the first tier of hills and well watered by a filigree of rills and streams. In those days it was generously wooded with sal, sissu, pine, and all the familiar European trees. But tragedy was ever wont to attach to beautiful things, and for three generations this idyllic grove had been a source more of chagrin than of joy to the Rajas of Garhwal. The valley's riches, and its proximity to the plains, had combined to make it a favourite plundering ground for Sikh brigands from the Panjab and Rajput, Gujar and Afghan rulers from Rohilkhand. The Raja had been compelled to cede villages and whole sections of the territory as blackmail to various external princes and chieftains. In 1786 the Dun was actually annexed to the Rohilla kingdom of Saharanpur, and the Raja only regained it by a judicious marriage contract in 1800. The Gurkhas made preparations to march into this distracted kingdom as soon as they had subdued Kumaun; but their plans were interrupted by the outbreak of a war with Tibet and China on their northern frontier, and all available troops had to be withdrawn eastwards to deal with this danger. Meanwhile the Raja of Garhwal, in vain hope of reprieve, agreed to pay a tribute and keep a *vakil* at Kathmandu. He demonstrated his sincerity by refusing to compound Harak Deva Joshi's scheme for a coalition against the Gurkhas, but even with all his inoffensiveness could not deter misfortune. In 1801, the Dun was ravaged by Marathas from Saharanpur; in 1803, an earthquake devastated his capital, Srinagar; and later the same year the Gurkha army returned in increased numbers and crossed the Ganges into his territory. The Raja retreated to Dehra town, but the Gurkhas followed and defeated him. This slight and nervous young man showed courage in his hour of trial. He collected a mercenary force on the plains and returned to challenge the invaders in January 1804. It was a brave but futile gesture, and it cost him his life. His sons fled back to India and sought asylum in the territories of the East India Company.

The Gurkhas regarded the devastated condition of Garhwal and the barbarity of much of the population more as justifications for plunder than as incentives to constructive administration. The land revenues were grossly over-assessed, and the occupation troops left to squeeze from their assigned estates rents which bore no relation to their yield. Arrears increased, and there was armed resistance followed by brutal retaliation, depopulation and an increase in the trafficking of human slaves, used as a supplementary

currency. But the difficulties of colonial government, no matter
how urgent, were now insufficient to deter the Gurkhas from devis-
ing even more ambitious schemes of conquest. About this time,
Amar Singh Thapa, uncle to Bhim Sen, was raised to the rank of
Kaji, the highest for which those of non-royal birth were eligible.
It was this man's strong will which thenceforth dominated the
fortunes of his country in the west. Amar Singh Thapa, now nearly
sixty, had spent his life soldiering, but like most of his clan had
hitherto been allowed few hopes of high rank and influence. He
came suddenly into prominence after the Thapas' *coup d'état* in
1803, and immediately sought to add lustre to his reputation and
exalt his prince by pushing back the frontiers of the Gurkha empire
still farther, perhaps even to Kashmir. Had his judgement been
commensurate with his ambitions, he might well have gone far
towards accomplishing his aim. But his self-confidence overmatched
even his aspirations, and was ever leading him onwards when he
should have stayed to question and deliberate. Perhaps there was
some anxiety to make up for lost time in all this—the urgency of an
old man in a hurry; but there was also a strong trait of superstition
in his character, which caused him to place trust in religious por-
tents and prophecies but to be otherwise unamenable to counsel.
He was accompanied in these years by Shiva Dat Rai, the son of a
Bhotiya, or Tibetan, of oracular pretensions, whose predictions of
success and recounting of legends foretelling the victorious advent
of the Gurkhas seem to have determined the Kathmandu durbar to
carry the western campaign to the Sutlaj and beyond. The confidence which he derived from such sources enhanced Amar
Singh's courage as a soldier, but it made him more dreaded than
popular as a commander and blighted his judgement as a tactician
and a diplomat.

The country between the Jumna and the Sutlaj is not a particularly extensive area, when measured by the scale of distances
which characterizes the Indian sub-continent. It comprises some
five and a half thousand square miles, of which perhaps three
thousand are inhabitable. Yet at the beginning of the nineteenth
century this tract was divided into thirty states and principalities.
The inaccessibility of the territory, and the reluctance of the
Moguls to undertake the subjugation of the hills, had always combined to preserve it as a sanctuary for political refugees and ascetic
fakirs. Many Rajput princes had founded kingdoms here after the

great exodus from north India in the thirteenth and fourteenth centuries, and had remained undisturbed in their tumultuous feudal way of life ever since. Centuries of untended fever had caused a fortress to erupt on almost every rise in the country's broken surface. The original amorphous multiplicity had, by 1803, begun to crystallize into a recognizable political pattern. Four states had achieved power and growth at the expense of all the rest. They were Sirmur, adjoining Garhwal on the west; Hindur, partly on the plains and partly in the hills where the Sutlaj curves north to enter the mountains; Bilaspur above it, lying across the Sutlaj on its loop; and Basahar, straddling the river further up and separated from Bilaspur by the twelve tiny states which formed the group known as the Twelve Lordships (*Bara Thakuri*).[11] The remaining fourteen principalities were scattered in the basins of the Tons, Pabar and Giri rivers.[12] All these states had in theory owed tribute (*nazarana*) to the Emperor of Delhi, but the liability had never been much more than a licence for the strongest states to levy exactions on their weaker neighbours. Collected ostensibly on behalf of the Emperor, the tribute had seldom found its way into his treasury. The practice of accepting military service in lieu of pecuniary contribution was widespread, so the armies of these little states were often disproportionately large. But they were bedraggled and protean bodies. G. Forster, who passed through Bilaspur in 1783, described its army as 'about three hundred horse and eight thousand footmen, armed with matchlocks, swords, spears and clubs, huddled together on two sides of a hill in a state of deep confusion and filth'.

[11] Hindur was also known as Nalagarh; Bilaspur as Kahalur; Basahar as Kunawar. The capital of Sirmur was Nahan; of Hindur, Palasi; of Bilaspur, the town of the same name; and of Basahar, Rampur.

[12] An important source for the history of Gurkha westward expansion is the 'Memoir on the Hill States between the Tonse and the Sutleje' by Lt. R. Ross (Secret Consultations, 27 Sept. 1815, no. 41). The names of the Bara Thakuri as given by Ross and adopted in Walter Hamilton's *Gazetteer*, vol. ii, p. 612, are: Kionthal, Baghat, Baghal, Kothar, Kumaharasin, Bhajji, Mailog, Dhami, Kiari, Kunhiar, Mangal, Koti.

The other fourteen Ross lists as: Jubal, Kotgarh, Balsan, Kanatu, Karankulu, Detailu, Thioka, Pandur, Kiund, Utraj, Sarani, Sangri, Barauli, Darkoti.

Both J. B. Fraser (p. 52) and Hutchison and Vogel (vol. ii, p. 497) give different lists. Fraser lists eighteen instead of fourteen additional states, and his names have in many cases been distorted beyond recognition by the misreadings of his printer.

Hutchison and Vogel list the Twelve as: Kionthal, Baghat, Baghal, Kothar, Beja, Bajji, Mailog, Dhami, Jubal, Kunhiar, Mangal, Balsan.

The dynasties of Hindur and Bilaspur were cognate, and had for some centuries lived amicably side by side. Lately, however, Hindur had been ruled by a particularly energetic and ambitious raja, called Ram Saran Sen, who had been able to exploit the state of perpetual jealousy among the various royal houses to extend his own power at the expense of that of his cousin of Bilaspur, without precipitating a coalition against himself which was permanent enough to be dangerous. By usurping Bilaspur's suzerainty over the Twelve Lordships and annexing large areas of her cis-Sutlaj possessions, he had gone a long way towards mastering the whole tract of territory between the Jumna and the Sutlaj. Now he was meddling in the domestic politics of Sirmur, abetting a group of rebellious barons who destested their own Raja, Karman Prakash, as a bully, and despised him as an imbecile. Karman Prakash despaired of being able to retain his throne without outside help and implored Amar Singh Thapa to intervene on his behalf. Amar Singh sent a detachment of 700 men to quell the rebels, but it was encircled by a Hindur force at Jampta and forced to capitulate and withdraw. This was in May 1804. Meanwhile, in his picturesque little palace of frescoed stucco, slothful Maha Chand of Bilaspur was stirring indignantly. The combined encroachments of his kinsman, Ram Saran, and of Ram Saran's ally, the Raja of Kotoch across the river, had of late deprived him of the richest portions of his kingdom. Now, Amar Singh Thapa's talisman and religious mentor, Shiva Dat Rai, was a native of Bilaspur; and it seems that he used his powerful influence to arouse the Gurkha Kaji's interest in the plight of Maha Chand. Feeble and recreant though he was, it was this raja whom Amar Singh Thapa selected to be his special protégé. The Gurkha crossed the Jumna in person in October 1804, and entered the territory which a decade later was to be the stage of his crucial struggle against the British. He gave battle, defeated the Hindur troops at Ajmaigarh, and invested the forts of Ramgarh and Nalagarh. The garrisons were bribed to surrender, and Ram Saran Sen fled south to the fort of Palasi. Karman Prakash was restored to the throne of Sirmur as a Gurkha vassal, and Maha Chand was given nominal trust of all the territories he had recently lost to Hindur, including the Twelve Lordships. But it was Shiva Dat Rai who was made the real agent of Amar Singh in the new puppet state of Bilaspur. He now urged the Kaji to advance still farther and attack the Raja of Kotoch, who had robbed Bilaspur of her possessions on the west bank of the Sutlaj. Kotoch included the most renowned stronghold in the Himalayas —Kangra. Long after their authority had disappeared on the plains, the Moguls had preserved a garrison in Kangra. Its strength had become proverbial. The fort had been re-annexed to the patrimony of Kotoch in 1786, by vigorous young Sansar Chand, who aspired to the leadership of a revived confederation of hill states and who was even strong enough to cause perturbation among the Sikhs, now rising to pre-eminence on the Punjab plain. His durbar was brilliant, the resort of bards, adventurers and artists from all over Hindustan. Flushed by the prospect of the prestige which its conquest would confer, encouraged by his first easy victories, flattered by fresh prognostications of success and seduced by promises of alliance from the various trans-Sutlaj monarchs, Amar Singh Thapa had little heed for the weakness of his present position. He gave no thought to that perfidy of the hill rajas which alone had enabled him to march so easily across the Jumna; was barely concerned even by the Hindur troops who still occupied Chamba, Taragarh, Malaun and Surjagarh—strong forts within the territory freshly acquired by his army. Arrogant and self-assured, the Kaji overreached himself. In April 1806, he committed what he later admitted was a capital error, and crossed the Sutlaj with his main army, *en route* for Kangra. He carried Maha Chand with him, but had barely restored him to his old estates, when he learned that a thousand troops from Kangra had crossed the river in the opposite direction farther south, had joined Ram Saran Sen, and were attacking the Gurkha garrisons in Nalagarh and Ramgarh. The Kaji was forced to pause and send back a strong detachment to expel the intruders, but, impenitent, still disdained to ponder the wisdom of his ambition. The march against Kangra was resumed, and after a preliminary victory over Sansar Chand's troops at Barahati, the fort was reached in July. Attempts to take the place by storm miscarried, and Amar Singh was compelled to besiege.

For three long years the futile enterprise endured. Meanwhile the irrepressible Ram Saran Sen conspired and schemed and, with shrewder understanding and longer experience than his adversary of the chameleon hill rajas, was soon able to stir up an anti-Gurkha movement. It involved not only the Twelve Lordships, who began to withhold supplies from the Gurkha army before Kangra, but Ram Saran's own quondam victim, Karman Prakash of Sirmur, as well. Distracted by this treachery and dismayed at the sight of his army wasting away, Amar Singh was at length forced to consider the bitter expedient of a compromise. He sent a messenger to Sansar Chand; but the tall proud Rajput curled his lip and refused to treat with the agent of a Thapa. He demanded to treat with Rudra Vir Shah, brother of Brahma, whom alone he considered his equal in rank. Stung by this insult, Amar Singh dashed off a letter to Kathmandu, urging that Rudra Vir's treaty (which recognized Sansar Chand's right to Kangra in return for the payment of tribute) be not ratified. He insisted that the fort was on the point of surrender. Amar Singh never forgave the Shah brothers for this humiliation. He used his influence to have Hasti Dal Shah removed from the governorship of Garhwal, and to have Rudra Vir relieved of his command with the field army—though Brahma Shah remained beyond the reach of his vengeance in Kumaun. Amar Singh's petulance ruined his chances of withdrawing from Kangra with some semblance of dignity. Sansar Chand, who had already rejected one offer of aid from the leader of the Sikhs, Ranjit Singh, out of preference for the treaty of Rudra Vir Shah, now called on the Sikh again. He escaped from Kangra and made a treaty with Ranjit Singh—signed, it is said, in blood. He continued to humour the Gurkhas, hoping to embroil them with Ranjit Singh and keep the fort himself; and Amar Singh Thapa, unable to acknowledge, because of his pride, that he was being double-crossed, dallied with Sansar in the vague hope that he could either win over Ranjit Singh or take the fort in alliance against him. Ranjit Singh prevaricated until his time was ripe and then, in July 1809, put an end to all this clumsy intriguing by thrashing the Gurkha army, occupying Kangra, and making it perfectly clear that he intended to share it with no one. Grumbling and affecting to claim that he had been duped by the Sikh, Amar Singh Thapa led the remains of his army, decimated by famine and disease, in ungainly retreat across the Sutlaj, having undertaken never to pass that river again.

He vented his vexation by chastising the contumacious princelings who had plotted in his absence. The ungrateful Karman Prakash of Sirmur was peremptorily ejected, and several of the Twelve Lords were constrained to flee for their lives. Only now that he came to subdue it, perhaps, did Amar Singh realize how tenuous had been his hold over this wild and inaccessible region. His troops had to tackle the frustrating and arduous task of reducing numerous hill castles in remote principalities, of whose existence they had hitherto hardly been aware. The Thakur of Balsan proved especially refractory, and the Gurkhas suffered three repulses when trying to reduce his fort, Nagana. He joined with several of his neighbours and called on the Raja of Basahar for assistance. This raja obliged with 10,000 men. Amar Singh dealt with this new threat from the north in person. In May 1811 he marched from Subathu with a large force, finally took Nagana, and pushed on to the more hospitable and smiling landscape of the valley of the middle Sutlaj, where stood the Basahar capital, Rampur. The Kaji had chosen his time well. The durbar, confused after the recent death of the Raja and the accession of an infant to the throne, fled across the river on hearing of the Gurkhas' approach. After lengthy negotiation an agreement was concluded whereby the Raja was left in unmolested possession of his trans-Sutlaj territories in return for a tribute. The Basahar minister henceforth formed part of Amar Singh's growing and impressive retinue of retainers and clients. In cis-Sutlaj Basahar, the Gurkha administration again partook of the character of the country on which it was engrafted. While in Garhwal, whose population was untamed and defiant, the Gurkha rule was cruel and unmerciful, in Basahar, which lay astride the broad trading highway of the Sutlaj and whose denizens had derived culture and probity from a long tradition of commerce, it was considerably milder.

On the eve of the war with the British, the Gurkha empire was at its zenith. It stretched from the Tista river in the east to the Sutlaj in the west, a distance equivalent to that between the southern coast of England and the northern tip of Scotland; and its average breadth was not much less than that of Great Britain. In the space of half a century, the Gurkhas had unified, for the first time in history, a belt of territory which was the most beautiful, the most inaccessible and traditionally the most politically fragmented in Asia. There seems no reason to suppose that, had the war with the British not intervened, this empire would not have proved viable. Its great strength was the army by which it had been won and by which it was held, for no rival among the Himalayan states had a force more efficient and more loyal. Among the native princes of north India, only Ranjit Singh had a comparable army, but his energies and interests were centred more on Kashmir than on the Nepalese territories.

The regular army of Nepal was officered by Gurkha Chetris, but composed in the main of Mongolian hillmen—Magars and, to a lesser extent, Gurungs. These hill people, diminutive, thick-muscled and with oriental features and complexion, first showed their worth as fighting men in the army raised by the Gurkhas, and for this reason were thought by the British to be Gurkhas themselves.[13] They were ideal soldiers: immensely strong, loyal and tractable, and with a perfunctory religion which left them free of the restrictions which ritual normally imposed on Hindu soldiers. While orthodox Hindus always stripped and washed the whole body before eating, these hillmen made do with removing their headgear and washing faces and hands. They were cheerful, agreed to carry their own provisions, and were not fastidious about food. The peace establishment of the army was between six and eight and a half thousand, but by a system of rotation the full potential strength was about double this. It was exclusively an infantry force, and its organization had been copied from that of the East India Company's Bengal army. Initially, it was organized in companies; but when Bhim Sen Thapa returned from Benares he regrouped some troops into battalions, using the English title of captain for their commanding officers. This gave the Nepalese army much the same sort of organization which the Bengal army had had in the days of Clive. The involutions of British drill were mimicked from the beginning, and in Kathmandu the troops were paraded daily to English words of command, achieving such an efficiency in their exercises as would not have shamed the East India Company's own battalions. These routines were learned from British deserters who took service with the Gurkha Raja. In 1814 there were still two of these individuals in Nepal, called Byrnes and Bell. Byrnes was made a schoolmaster and taught the officers English, while Bell, a gunner, was made a colonel of artillery. They even seem to have given some musical instruction, for in 1816, at Makwanpur, Nepalese fifers entertained the astonished British troops with their own versions of *The Lass of Richmond Hill*, *The Soldier's Wife*, and half a dozen other English marching tunes. After the middle 1790s the dress of the regular soldiers was in

---

[13] The misconception still persists. The so-called Gurkha regiments in the British and Indian armies are composed not of Gurkhas but of the various tribes of the Nepalese hills whom it was the special policy of the Gurkhas to keep distinct from themselves.

quaint imitation of the Company's uniforms. There were red jackets with facings and white cross belts for the men, and fantastic outfits for the officers, concocted with little heed for the exact symbolism of British army dress. The rank of general was held by the Commander-in-Chief alone in the Nepalese army; yet the *suba* (provincial governor) killed by John Shipp in 1816 was dressed in the old-fashioned full uniform of an English general, frog lace and all. Prithvi Narayan Shah had himself distrusted Europeans and had been reluctant to employ them; but even he had been obliged to have recourse to Frenchmen to teach his artisans how to smelt ores and cast and bore cannon. Three Frenchmen were in charge of the Nepalese artillery until the middle 1790s, and kept very busy supervising the casting of guns, howitzers and mortars, and the manufacture of gunpowder. Byrnes and Bell also cast cannon in Kathmandu, and by the outbreak of the war with the British there must have been four or five hundred guns of all descriptions in Nepal. Even quite sophisticated artillery devices were adopted. The British discovered shrapnel shells and howitzers with tangent scales at Makwanpur in 1816. The Gurkhas did not only copy the Europeans. When the Chinese invaded Nepal in 1792, their army was provided with very light leather guns, which fired five or six rounds before bursting. Their antagonists promptly adopted the idea, and after the British had occupied Garhwal they found guns 'made of leather pretty thick, lined throughout with clay and an iron hoop rudely twisted round'.[14] They were so light that one man could easily carry two, used shot of about one pound, and could be fired three or four times before bursting. European muskets were imported from Calcutta by Prithvi Narayan Shah; but subsequently the Gurkhas set up their own manufactories, with the help of English deserters, and produced relatively efficient weapons. They were spoiled only by inaccurate balance and defective locks. The severest disadvantage suffered by Gurkha musketeers was the poor quality of their flints. These frequently snapped or missed fire, so it was essential to import flints from India to make the firearms work properly. With this, and the single other exception of saltpetre, the Nepalese territories provided all the raw materials essential to satisfy the Gurkha passion for military appurtenants: good-quality iron for muskets, swords and *khukuris* (short curved knives

[14] 'Extract of a Letter dated Srinagar', *Calcutta Monthly Journal*, vol. xxvii: October 1815, p. 366.

famous as the characteristic weapon of the hill tribes); copper and zinc for brass guns; lead for shot; and sulphur for gunpowder.

Having said so much, it must be emphasized that, for all its apparent sophistication, when actually in the field the Gurkha army neither acted like a European force nor owed its victories to European science. Of the regular army, perhaps half was organized in battalions, and these were kept in Palpa and in the Nepal Valley to provide for defence and furnish ceremonial *corps d'élite*. The remainder, still divided into independent companies, was dispersed throughout the wide length of the empire. It was very thinly spread, and recourse had to be made to irregular troops to thicken its texture. The greater part of the Gurkha field army consisted of local troops. In the west large numbers of the inhabitants of Kumaun and Garhwal were embodied as militia, officered by Gurkhas and supplied with muskets by the government, but with no uniform and with regular pay only when on foreign service. Otherwise they were paid a retaining fee in land. Of a force of between six and seven thousand men west of the Kali, between a half and two-thirds were locals.[15] In the eastern provinces, Kiratas and Limbus were enlisted. They received no pay, but were allowed to keep all they might obtain, specie excepted, by plunder. These tatterdemalion bands were very different from the trim English-style soldiers who manoeuvred with clockwork precision on the *Tundikhel*, the vast parade ground laid out in Kathmandu by Bhim Sen Thapa. Furthermore, the Gurkha officers, although they knew

[15] The most important sources of information about the Nepalese army are: B. H. Hodgson's 'Memorandum Relating to the Gurkha Army': Sec. Cons., 4 March 1825, no 16; Information submitted to the government by H. Hearsey and T. Rutherfurd (*P.R.N.W.*, pp. 27, 49, 55); Information from Capt. Richards (Pol. Cons., 20 Aug. 1813, no 34); Memoir by Capt. Raper: *P.R.N.W.*, pp. 145–6; Report on Hill Districts by Ochterlony: *Ludhiana Records*, pp. 399–400, 407; Information supplied by Capt. Hearsey to Capt. Richards: Pol. Cons., 23 July 1813, no. 34; Moorcroft, *Asiatic Researches*, xii, p. 513. Both Moorcroft and Hearsey were in agreement in estimating the proportion as one-third regulars, two-thirds locals. Ochterlony reversed the proportion. Hearsey estimated the whole army beyond the Kali at 6,000; Ochterlony estimated that beyond the Jumna alone at 7,000. Subsequent experience showed that Ochterlony's was an over-estimation—see below Ch. IX. A rough collation of available sources indicates that the strength and distribution of the *regular* army on the eve of the conflict was as follows:

War Strength of army—about 14,000.
Distributed between Kathmandu and Palpa (7,000), provinces east of the Kali (3,500), and provinces west of the Kali (3,500). Irregulars of equal strength west of the Kali would bring the total of troops there to 7,000.

English words of command, gasconaded in English uniforms and taught the rudiments of English discipline, had very little grasp of the fundamental principles of which all these were but the superficial expression. The daily parades in Kathmandu were little more than a decorative choreography, inspired by a love of ostentation and designed to give an air of martial circumstance to the capital. In the field, the strength of the army resided less in its collective discipline and in the training of its officers than in the powers of endurance and courage of its individual members, who were all natural guerrilla fighters. Tactics were elementary, and seldom involved more than the Gurkhas' favourite expedient of attacking simultaneously from two or three directions. Usually a volley of musket fire was sufficient to terrify the enemy into surrender or flight; but in cases of resistance they would surround their antagonist and starve him into submission. The Gurkhas were past masters in the art of stockade warfare. Within a few hours a force could be almost ineradicably ensconced behind a high *abatis* made of two parallel screens of wickered branches and filled between with stones, mud, sticks and any available rubbish. From these safe retreats they would harass the enemy with daring assaults, usually nocturnal. The scientific refinements, like the drill and the polish, were reserved for Kathmandu. Guns were so difficult to transport that their use was very limited. Apart from the light leather ordnance, the Gurkhas had only about three dozen small brass cannon in the west, and these had to be carried on slings or dragged along the gound. They roared impressively with their rough hand-beaten shot, but did little damage, because there was no means of aiming them. Carriages were very few, and often the guns were merely laid on the ground and fired by a trail. Far more important to the army than these cumbersome engines was its agility. There were no pack animals. All stores and supplies were carried by non-combatant camp servants. There were large numbers of these, for every soldier had his woman slave and his 'boy' (*keti*). Baggage was reduced to an absolute minimum. The troops had no tents, but slept under low makeshift shelters of blankets and sticks. An officer's camp equipage could be carried by one man, and the whole tentage of the commander required only six bearers. Supplies sufficient for three days only were normally carried. The army expected to provide itself from the country, and agents were stationed in all the principal towns and villages to buy and forward grain.

II

THE QUARREL WITH THE BRITISH

As the Gurkhas advanced westward, they were paced on their southern flank by the British, who were simultaneously pushing back the frontiers of their north-Indian empire. The eighteenth century was the age of the decline and fall of the Indian empire of the Mogul[1] Emperors of Delhi. Internal decadence enabled the Emperor's powerful provincial governors—such as the Nawabs of Bengal and Oudh in the north and the Nizam of the Deccan in the south—to assert their independence; while successive whirlwind raids by the monarchs of Persia and Afghanistan hastened the demise of Imperial authority without providing an alternative Muslim hegemony. The chief contenders for the Mogul legacy were the Hindus and the Europeans. The Hindu revival was probably inevitable. Hindu culture is essentially martial in spirit (Gandhi's interpretation of the ethic of non-violence to mean the prohibition of war being a modern departure), and the Mogul rulers, alien by virtue of their origin and their religion, had never been completely accepted by the subject races. The resurgent Hindus were the Sikhs, the Gurkhas and the Marathas. Their European rivals were the French and the British.

The Sikhs were a Jat sect—reformed Hindus, impatient at once of idolatry, caste and asceticism. After many vicissitudes, they wrested the Punjab and Sirhind from the Afghans, and dominated a turbulent medley of Turks, Pathans, Rajputs and Jats as a martial aristocracy. The Gurkhas seized the hills, with little opposition from anyone. The Marathas remained heirs to the rest, despite a resounding defeat at the hands of the Afghans at Panipat in 1761, but were cheated by the British of their inheritance. They were a wiry tribe of western India, which in the first decade of the eighteenth century became the agent of Imperial authority in the Deccan and south-west India. From Poona, the *Peshwas* (hereditary ministers)—the Maratha monarchy was otiose from an early stage

[1] Mogul = mongol; but the dynasty was in fact of central Asian Turkish origin, descended from Tamberlain the Great.

—directed imperialist expeditions which, by 1771, had made them masters of all central India, Rajputana, Malwa and Berar, and custodians of the Emperor himself. But the polity split into five independent portions. The states of Gwalior, Indore, Berar (or Nagpur), and Gujarat continued to acknowledge the titular suzerainty of the Peshwas of Poona, but the so-called 'Maratha confederacy' invariably disintegrated in times of crisis, and therein lay its rivals' greatest advantage.

The territorial power of the East India Company, a consortium of merchants trading under charter from the British Crown, germinated, like that of the Marathas, in southern India. Its first factories were at Surat and Bombay on the west, and at Madras on the east, or Coromandel, coast. But the Company's wars in the south, during the second half of the eighteenth century, were less against the Marathas than against the French, for even after Clive had captured the last French colonies (1761), a powerful Gallic influence persisted at Poona and at the independent Muslim court of Mysore. The wars fought by the English with Poona and Mysore between 1779 and 1799 were basically projections into Indian politics of the Anglo-French rivalry. The Company's real struggle against the Marathas took place in northern and central India.

It was self-defence and skilful opportunism, rather than premeditated ambition, that turned this group of British merchants into the rulers of an empire. The Company had trading posts in the area of Calcutta from the end of the seventeenth century, but with no territory and no army at first. Harassment from the Marathas in Berar and from capricious Nawabs of Bengal, plus greed for the reputedly immense treasure of the Nawabs, led Clive to form an army and claim a share of influence in the internal politics of Bengal. The share soon grew into a monopoly, and the Company began to control the Nawabs. It acquired tenant rights to certain territories, and in 1765 became a landed potentate in its own right when the Emperor made it *Dewan* (fiscal administrator in theory, farmer of revenues in fact) of the three provinces of Bengal, Bihar and Orissa. With these new responsibilities, the Company began to develop an administrative identity. The main emphasis during the next thirty years was on curbing the Company's own servants, whose orgy of extortion following the devolution of power in Bengal had brought the Company near to bankruptcy; but consolidation involved a certain extension of territorial power as well. In 1772, the fertile province of Kuch Bihar, wedged between the northern frontier of Bengal and Bhutan, was reincorporated into the territory of Bengal after a long independence. Its Raja appealed to the Company for help against the invading mountaineers of Bhutan, and Warren Hastings, Governor of Bengal at the time, was glad of this opportunity to annex the territory—though he firmly disclaimed 'remote projects of conquest', and stressed that his only aim was to complete the outline of the Company's dominions. A policy of self-defence, mixed with need for money, led Hastings to turn his attentions to the Muslim principality of Oudh, long effectively independent of Delhi, but now effete. To protect Bengal against the Afghans in Rohilkhand and the Marathas in Delhi, Oudh was made a buffer state and provided with a protective force, for which it was compelled to pay a subsidy.

The Marathas and the English remained in uneasy truce until the arrival of Lord Wellesley as Governor-General in 1798. Wellesley, brother of the Duke of Wellington, was a little man with an Olympian manner and panoramic vision. He viewed Indian politics in relation to those of Europe, and conceived an elaborate scheme of alliances with the native states designed to preclude the subversion of the Company's position in India by the French. The Nawab of Oudh was constrained to disband his own army, accept an increased subsidiary force, cede Rohilkhand and all territory between the Ganges and the Jumna in lieu of payment, employ no Europeans and leave the Company in control of his foreign policy. The weakest of the independent rulers, the Nizam of the Deccan, meekly submitted to similar terms; but Mysore, whose ruler Tipu Sultan flaunted his sympathy for the French in an attempt to preserve his independence, had to be coerced. It was Wellesley's attempt to bring the Marathas into this grand system of British hegemony which finally precipitated the long-pending clash between them and the Company. Poona and Gujarat agreed to accept troops, pay subsidies and forgo the employment of Europeans; but the other three states vigorously demurred at this betrayal of Maratha independence. Gwalior and Berar were at war with the Company from 1802 to 1804, but were then compelled to submit. Only Berar accepted a subsidiary force, but each received a British Resident and agreed not to employ Europeans. The blind Emperor, Shah Alam, was rescued from the clutches of Sindhia of Gwalior and set up as the mediatized King of Delhi, under the protection of a British Resident. All Maratha territory between the Jumna and the Ganges was annexed by the Company. It was combined with the estates in the same area ceded by Oudh in 1801, and made part of the Bengal Presidency under the designation 'Ceded and Conquered Provinces'.[2] Holkar of Indore then took up arms, and prolonged the contest until 1805, causing unexpected discomfort to the English commanders, Lake and Monson. Learning of this, the home authorities made known their displeasure in such a way that Wellesley was forced to resign. They had been uneasy about him for some time. He lorded it over his council, openly despised his employers, humiliated native princes and seemed to be loading the Company with debts and barren conquests. Thus, with his plans only half realized in the crucial area of central India, Wellesley was obliged to return home, and his successor, Lord Minto, was instructed to pursue a policy of retrenchment and neutrality. British protection was withdrawn from the states of Rajputana, and Indore and Gwalior, dangerous as wounded wasps, were left to conspire uncurbed. The territories of the Company and its clients had by this time assumed roughly the configuration of a huge question mark, following the northern and western outline of the subcontinent. The Ceded and Conquered Provinces, Oudh, and Bihar and Bengal formed the hook; Madras, the Carnatic, the Deccan and Mysore the thickened tail; and Ceylon (administered by the Crown) the stop. In the open-ended space of central India were the Marathas and the Rajputs.

In the years between Wellesley's resignation and the arrival of Lord Hastings as Governor-General in 1813, there were serious confrontations with the two remaining members of the trio of Hindu communities claiming the reversion of Mogul authority in northern India—the Sikhs and the Gurkhas. It seemed possible that the Company would find itself in conflict with one or both of these powers while Gwalior and Indore still remained sufficiently strong to seek revenge. This was the nightmare of a Hindu confederacy which alarmed Lord Hastings. The Sikh communities straddled the Sutlaj river, divided between the Punjab and the old Mogul province of Sirhind. Raja Ranjit Singh of Lahore had become the most powerful Sikh monarch, and he sought to extend his control to the Sikhs on the other side of the river. To prevent this, Minto was compelled to act against the letter of his instructions and

[2] Later called the North-West Provinces.

grant British protection to the Sirhind Sikhs, thus pushing further
west, to the left bank of the Sutlaj, the starting place of the hook in
the question mark of British territory. The Gurkha empire was
contiguous throughout its whole length to territories either
administered or protected by the Company. Before long, both the
Company and its hill neighbour found that with their new dominions they had inherited local disputes about borders.

There exists no greater contrast than that between the country
occupied by the Gurkhas, where the earth appears to have been
petrified in the full violence of some primeval fermentation, and
that in northern India then under the English Company's sway,
which is an immense plain, level as a lake and reminiscent of the
calm, luminous landscapes of Claude le Lorrain, with their groves
and deliquescent distances. From the Ganges eastwards these provinces were separated from the Himalayan foothills by a swampy
forest of sal, elephant grass and bamboo, where the air was dank,
close, and ceaselessly vibrating with the noises of mosquitoes,
cicadas and frogs. This fringe, called Tarai along most of the
Nepalese border, Morang in extreme south-east Nepal, and divided
into sections called *duars* on the frontier of Bhutan, is still the big
game hunter's paradise. At the time of which we are speaking, it
was intensely malarial throughout the summer and monsoon
months, from April to October—a place of dread, to be avoided at
all cost, save by the Tharus and other indigenous tribes, which
were immune to the infection. The mosquito's responsibility being
then unknown, the *awl* (malarial fever) was attributed to some
noxious miasma. According to the natives this emanated from the
mouths of large serpents who inhabited the northern mountains.
The European view was that it derived from putrefying vegetation
or stagnant water. Its effects were swift and horrifying: fever and
vomiting, followed in a few hours by raving madness and death.
The Company's northern territories, which stretched into this
inhospitable region, were bisected by the province of Oudh. West
of Oudh there were the Ceded and Conquered Provinces, of which
Rohilkhand and Saharanpur were the most northern; and east of
Oudh there were the districts of Gorakhpur, Saran, Tirhut,
Purnea and, in the extreme north-east of Bengal across the Tista
river, the district of Rangpur. These were the *moffussil*—the 'in-
terior' or 'up country' areas, as opposed to the Presidency capital,
Calcutta, which might be up to three months' journey away.

Europeans were few and far between. Besides the handful of magistrates, revenue collectors and military men, there were only those few who had managed to secure settlers' licences—essential for anyone who wished to live more than ten miles from Calcutta. They were mostly indigo planters, brutish and boisterous individuals, whose handsome villas with spacious verandas were becoming numerous in Gorakhpur, Tirhut and Purnea. European life centred around the civil stations. Each composed of district Judge,[3] Collector, Registrar, Surgeon and Postmaster, with a few army officers attached to guards and escorts, these were remote pockets of British society in country where the British had barely been heard of and where white faces still provoked consternation and amazement. There were no all-weather roads, so the military depôts— Dinapur, Ghazipur, Chunar, Cawnpore, Meerut—were built close to the river Ganges, which remained the principal highway. From these centres troops were distributed among the numerous outposts and frontier pickets.

The districts of Saran, Tirhut, Purnea and Rangpur formed part of the territories of which the fiscal administration was granted by the Emperor to the Company in 1765.[4] They were divided into the territorial assignments of various *zemindars*, who were, strictly speaking, hereditary rent collectors, but who by the terms of Lord Cornwallis's land settlement were recognized as proprietors. The rents for which they were liable to the Company were fixed in perpetuity. When the land settlement was made, the Company's officials were reluctant to concern themselves with defining the boundaries of the estate for which each zemindar contracted to pay the revenues. Interference in matters of this nature was held to be an infringement of the sacrosanct principle of privacy. This was not the province of revenue administrators, but of the civil courts, should zemindars feel disposed to make use of their services in cases of uncertainty. The result was, in the words of Sir George Campbell, that 'even the very first step towards the roughest settlement of modern days, the definition of boundaries, was not taken . . . There was a mere register of rent-paying estates, with the names of the proprietors, but no means of identifying the lands.' Quarrels concerning boundaries therefore inevitably arose. When two disputing zemindars were tenants of the same government, no

---

[3] Who also exercised the functions of magistrate at this time.
[4] Gorakhpur was ceded by the Nawab of Oudh in 1801.

grave issue was involved; but when one was a client of the Company and the other a tenant or agent of a neighbouring sovereign power, then a small domestic problem was transformed into an international border dispute. In the days of feckless Mogul rule, the zemindars in these districts had continuously disputed with the hill rajas about possession of the rich lowland border areas; and after the Company made them its clients and revenue contractors, its officers were soon faced with an avalanche of claims and complaints. Villages and tracts were reported to have been seized either by the Bhutanese or by the people of the Raja of Nepal. It was often impossible to make a satisfactory settlement. A collector or magistrate might be expected to form a judgement on the basis of quite preposterous evidence. The altercation between the Raja of Bhutan and the Company's zemindar of Baikantpur, whose mutual border meandered back and forth across the shifting Tista, was typical. When the Magistrate of Rangpur went to inspect the boundary of an estate belonging to Bhutan on the west bank of the river, he found that its distinguishing features were occasional streams, rivulets and ridges of earth. Elsewhere his only direction was the memory of his guide, who professed to recognize the frontier by the different colourings of the grass 'and other marks of the like nature which seemed to exist nowhere but in the fertility of the imagination'. The Raja of Kuch Bihar was in incessant dispute with the Bhutanese authorities concerning the villages in the area of their common frontier. In 1809, the Company set up a commission to examine the claims and counter-claims in question and even sent military assistance to its vassal when the inquiry indicated his complaints against Bhutan to be justified. Sometimes, encroachments were flagrant. The Bhutanese, for example, seized the estate of Bidyagong, in the extreme north-east of Rangpur, and asserted their right to nominate a successor when the adjacent zemindari of Bijni became vacant. But such remote and complex contests were more tiresome than important to the British officials. The Magistrate of Rangpur reported the Bidyagong affair, but the government decided than an annual rent of forty elephants was a loss too trivial to warrant giving offence to Bhutan. Bijni, way over on the Manas river, was the remotest ramification of the province of Bengal, and virtually nothing was known about the country and the nature of its connection with the Mogul empire. When the Bhutanese appointed their own candidate as zemindar in 1791, the

British authorities held a desultory inquiry, but forbore to press their own right, established by the investigation, to nominate a successor.

Company zemindars in areas farther west accused the Gurkhas of usurpation. Their complaints were numerous, elaborate, insistent, and often totally without foundation. They were bothersome to the collectors, busy with the administration of districts of vast extent; harassing to the magistrates, who had enormous backlogs of cases; and embarrassing to the government, which wished to avoid offending Nepal, and which, because its revenues had been settled on a permanent basis, was not the loser in cases of encroachment. At first there was no international problem. The Gurkhas showed themselves anxious to have these disputes settled peaceably, and the Company seemed prepared to make concessions at the expense of its own clamouring zemindars. In 1795 Cornwallis assured the Raja of Nepal that he was willing to define the long-uncertain border between the Morang and the district of Purnea in exact conformity with his representations; and writs and petitions from cheated zemindars of Tirhut were left to gather dust in the Collector's files. In the zone to the east of Oudh, the boundary between the Ceded and Conquered Provinces and the Gurkha colonies of Kumaun and Garhwal had been made so uncertain by the collusion and inefficiency of the Oudh officers who had preceded the British, and accurate records and surveys were so wanting, that the Company's servants were perplexed as to how to react when they saw the Gurkhas move into a fresh frontier area. Often, indeed, these incursions remained long unnoticed, for in the early years of British administration of these territories the Company's revenue assessments were necessarily tentative,[5] and its authority very tenuous. Rohilkhand had declined into a state of anarchy under the combined effects of Maratha invasions and maladministration by Oudh. Cultivators and farmers had relapsed into a state of instinctive resistance to all revenue collectors. Organized brigandage was rife, exacerbated by the continued existence of the small independent states of Rampur and Sirdhana, which were sanctuaries for fugitives from British justice. One of the first Company

---

[5] Wellesley proposed applying a permanent settlement on the Bengal pattern after a ten-year interval of shorter experimental assessments, but in the event it was a thirty-year settlement that was made. There were no zemindars of the Bengal type in these provinces, and the revenue contracts were made with the chiefs among proprietors of groups of villages.

collectors in Moradabad felt so insecure that he threw elegance to the winds and made an incongruous moat and mud rampart around his handsome cutchery. To the west, across the Ganges in the district of Saharanpur, almost every village was surrounded by a wall or ditch—testimonies to a long torment inflicted by Sikh raiders from across the Jumna. The large new military station of Meerut, outside the old town, had to be built on land reclaimed from the jungle; and crime was so rampant in the area that it was not unusual to stumble across the corpse of a murder victim even on the plain between the city and the cantonments. With so much else to distract them, it is scarcely surprising that the tiny number of British officials gave only perfunctory attention to the settlement of the northern regions, and only scant notice to the subsequent Nepalese incursions. Indeed, the marauding Mewati and Amir tribes had made alarums and excursions along the northern frontier so unexceptional, that such intrusions were often lost in the general confusion. Then again, British officers were scared by the climate of the Tarai and tended to avoid it, save for a few weeks in the healthy season, when they might hunt big game. It was quite by accident that the Magistrate of Bareilly noticed, in 1811, that the Gurkhas had built a fort in Kheri. This was a remote appendix of territory east of the Kali, wedged between Oudh and the hills. It had been assessed as part of the Ceded and Conquered Provinces, but its revenue had never actually been realized by the Company. The Magistrate was sure that the Gurkhas had not been in occupation of the tract two years previously, but, as he pointed out, no one could be sure that they were not entitled to it. 'Such is the undefined boundary between the two governments', he wrote, 'and our want of local information of the extent of our territories in the unexplored tract of country along the foot of the hills, that doubts may be entertained whether even the acquisitions of the Nepalese which are stated to appertain to the pergana of Kherigarh can be pronounced encroachment on our territories.'

Obviously, such a state of affairs could not be permitted to continue. The Directors of the Company wrote from London to censure the 'want of vigilance' or the 'defect in the system of management' which allowed boundaries to elude definition and anarchy to persist. 'It is unnecessary for us to insist upon the importance of having the limits of our dominions accurately defined', they pronounced, in February 1814. But the boundary question had already boiled to a crisis before the ship carrying this dispatch reached Calcutta. Long even before it was written, both the British and the Gurkha governments had changed their attitude towards the frontier problem. When the Thapas acceded to power, the Gurkha durbar became pugnacious and uncompromising. At the same time, the Company's government decided that its own laxity and complaisance in these matters had gone on long enough. The border must be clearly defined, once and for all, even at the risk of displeasing Kathmandu.

In one area, at least, defining the border was as simple as drawing a line on a map and then warning the Gurkhas that they would cross it at their peril. This could be done in the frontier regions adjacent to the recent Gurkha conquests in the western hills. Here the Gurkhas had had no time to establish themselves in the lowlands. As they held Kumaun and the territory beyond only by right of conquest, they had no *a priori* right to parts of these provinces which they did not actually occupy. Seizure of the hilly part of a raja's kingdom gave them no claim to the lowland portion if the raja had not formally resigned it and was able to defend it. Now the rajas expelled from the western hills were able to defend their lowland possessions, because the Company decided that it would support them in their determination to do so. It was made plain to the Gurkhas that they would invade these tracts below the hills only on pain of war with the British. Because the Gurkhas were not yet established below the hills, and because they had no treaty rights, it proved a simple and effective way of fixing boundaries. The Calcutta government, however, did not dispute the Gurkhas' claim to the mountain territories, and resisted considerable pressure to reinstate the rajas in the hills. Early in 1810, Amar Singh Thapa announced his intention of occupying certain villages on the plains of Sirhind on the justification that they belonged to Sirmur and Hindur, all of whose territories were now his by right of conquest. Colonel David Ochterlony, at Ludhiana, was Agent for the affairs of the Sirhind Sikhs brought under the protection of the Company by Minto in 1809. He had already been given clear instructions for such a contingency. He was to inform the Gurkha commander that all territories below the line of the foothills, whether previously attached to hill states or not, were now under the protection of the Company; but at the same time he was to make it clear that the Company had no interest whatever in the fate of territories within the mountains. But Ochterlony was spoiling for a fight. He urged that the Gurkhas be requested not only to give up their new possessions in the plains, but also to restore the Dehra and Kayarda Duns, in the first range of foothills, to the Garhwal and Sirmur royal families respectively. This, he claimed, would create a useful buffer region between the Gurkha and the British spheres of interest, besides enhancing the Company's prestige in the view of all the native states of Hindustan. He anticipated little resistance from the Gurkhas, whom he disdained as 'a body of ill-armed and undisciplined barbarians, who affect a wretched imitation of the dress, accoutrements, and constitution of a British native battalion and who might have been successfully resisted in such a country by less than a third of their numbers'.[6] Government patiently pointed out that it would be futile and discreditable to make such a demand, for it was unlikely that the Gurkhas would comply, and the expediency of compulsion was 'more than questionable'. In the event, Amar Singh did not act on his claim to the lowland villages, and the use of force even in the plains was unnecessary.

In the middle of 1813 there was a second frontier crisis. Amar Singh Thapa's men seized six villages which two of Ochterlony's Sikh protégés, Patiala and Hindur, affirmed belonged to their lowland possessions. Amar Singh claimed that they belonged to Sirmur and Kionthal, states in the hills which he had conquered and to all of whose estates he had right; and he asked for time to make reference to Kathmandu before relinquishing them. Ochterlony agreed to the delay—but only because the season was not yet fit for military operations. He was convinced, or affected to be convinced, that Amar Singh had no intention of abandoning the villages. Briskly, and with obvious enthusiasm, he set about making preparations for a punitive expedition, whose object was to be the expulsion of the Gurkhas from all the hill areas west of the Ganges. This brought him into contact with Captain Hyder Hearsey, a half-caste who had made his fortune by fighting as a mercenary with various native princes in the turbulent years before 1804 and by marrying a Muslim princess of Cambay. Hearsey had in his pocket his own plan for an invasion of the western hills. It had been concocted in consultation with Harak Deva Joshi, the quondam king-maker of Kumaun, and Hearsey had a special interest in its implementation, because in his other pocket he had a deed of right to

---

[6] *Ludhiana Records*, pp. 219–20.

Dehra Dun. He had bought this for a few thousand rupees in 1811, from the impoverished and exiled heir to the kingdom of Garhwal. Ochterlony proceeded on the assumption that the Governor-General, Lord Minto, would be of the opinion 'that the best way of enforcing the restitution of the disputed villages . . . would be to show our ability to do much more'; and his own 'firm persuasion' was 'that Amar Singh Thapa will compel us to dislodge his troops from below the hills'. But his assumption and his persuasion were wrong, and both his ambitions and Hearsey's hopes were for the moment to remain unsatisfied. 'It is . . . far from being the wish or intention of the Governor-General in Council to engage in any extended scheme of operations such as that contemplated [by you]. His Lordship . . . is, on the contrary, desirous of maintaining the existing relation of friendship with the Nepalese Government, and of effecting an adjustment of all disputed points by amicable negotiation, if practicable', wrote the Political Secretary. At the very most, and then only as a last resort, force might be used to eject them from the lowlands.[7] Meanwhile Amar Singh Thapa, confuting Ochterlony's confident assertion that he had been bluffing, did make reference to Kathmandu. The durbar made it plain that as far as it was concerned the issue was not to be settled according to whether the villages were or were not below the hills, but according to whether the Company or the Gurkhas had been in possession of them first. His government, in fact, was far more intransigent than the Kaji himself, who was embarrassed by these injunctions. He appealed to Ochterlony to spare his dignity. He had occupied the villages in the sincere belief that they belonged to the Gurkhas by right, and he could not now withdraw without losing face. Could not the Gurkhas and the Company share the contested territory? But Ochterlony was obdurate, and issued an ultimatum. Though peevish and insistent as to his right, the Kaji had no intention of risking a conflict with the Company, and he directed his officers to withdraw. Only when he actually inspected the disputed areas, several weeks later, did Ochterlony discover that two of the villages were decidedly in the hills.

Amar Singh Thapa had made a genuine concession because he was eager to try again to capture Kangra. He was convinced that the British were preparing to cross the Sutlaj and conquer the Punjab, and his idea was to use the occasion, with British acquiescence,

[7] *Ludhiana Records*, pp. 339–44.

to march once more against the fortress and avenge his previous humiliation. Ochterlony peremptorily disavowed such intentions; but once this Gurkha had formed his own interpretation of a situation, he was loath to change it. He continued to press for an alliance, persuaded of the self-evident correctness of his own assessment of British ambitions. Ochterlony, exasperated by this obstinacy, complained of Amar Singh's obtuseness and duplicity. But however offensive the idea might have seemed to the British, the Gurkha can hardly be blamed for assuming that they coveted the Punjab. Sansar Chand of Kangra drew the same conclusion. Indians who had been dazzled by the Company's meteoric rise could hardly be expected to associate it with reluctance for empire. Ochterlony's refusal to respond to Amar Singh's overtures made the Kaji feel humiliated, and his aversion to the British deepened; but he knew better than to goad them beyond a certain point. Almost in spite of himself, he sensed the profound unwisdom of a war with the East India Company, and the expression of his hostility was ever tempered by an instinctive respect for its power. Others of his race were not so circumspect, and in negotiations over disputed borders further east words and actions of uncontrolled impetuosity led to the collapse of negotiations and the declaration of war.

In the frontier areas in the zone east of Oudh it was much more difficult to define a boundary. It was too late now for the Company to draw an imaginary line along the base of the foothills and forbid the Gurkhas to cross it. With the consent of earlier governments and, in the case of Gorakhpur, with the connivance of the Nawab of Oudh's officers, they had become firmly established in the Tarai and Morang, effective inheritors of all lowland territories formerly ruled by the hill rajas they had displaced. These hill rajas, unlike those in the west, had not been able to protect their estates in the plains, because the Company had not felt disposed to assist them. The Gurkhas could therefore legitimately claim the estates as the fruits of conquest. Now if the British and Gurkha governments were to honour the limits of their respective dominions, it was essential to know exactly what lands and villages those lowland estates had comprised. Such knowledge was not easy to obtain, because in many cases the hill rajas were not the proprietors of their lowland tracts, but merely tenants in them of the Nawabs of Bengal and Oudh. In this area, then, resolving the problem was a great deal more difficult than drawing a line on a map. Here, the frontier had to be not created, but discovered: and this involved unpicking a complicated knot of precedents and rights.

Such a task demanded patience, good faith, and a compromising attitude of both sides. Until the fall of the Panres, the durbar of Kathmandu had reciprocated the Company's spirit of concession. The political trio pre-eminent in Nepal in the last decade of the eighteenth century had been anxious to remain on good terms with Calcutta. This group had consisted of Damodar Panre, the Prime Minister; Brahma Shah, who was a *chautarya* (royal hereditary counsellor); and Gajraj Misr, the *guru* (spiritual mentor) of the royal family. All three had fallen from power after 1803. Damodar Panre had been executed; Brahma Shah removed to Kumaun; and Gajraj Misr obliged to make a prolonged 'pilgrimage' to India. The new royal favourites, Prime Minister Bhim Sen Thapa, his father General Amar Thapa and the new guru, Raganath Pandit, considered themselves more as rivals than as vassals of the East India Company. Contacts were made with the various native states, Nepal's relationship with China was turned to special advantage and in exchanges with the British the old tone of cautious mistrust gave place to one of cavalier independence. When, in 1804, General Amar Thapa was sent to annex the territories of the Raja of Palpa, he did not stop at the hills. He sent officers down into the department in Gorakhpur called Butwal to collect the revenues, ignoring the fact that the Raja of Palpa had held this district as a tenant of the Nawab of Oudh, to whose rights in Gorakhpur the Company had now succeeded. The Gurkhas could argue from precedent, because they had been in possession of Siuraj, an adjacent department whose situation was similar, for sixteen years when the Nawab of Oudh ceded Gorakhpur to the Company. But, having discovered that Butwal was very fertile, the Governor-General was reluctant to lose the department, and he requested the Gurkhas to evacuate it immediately. He even offered to waive British rights to Siuraj as a compromise. But the Gurkhas were equally loath to abandon such a rich acquisition, and would go no further than offering to pay the Company a rent for it. This offer was refused; but the Company refrained from pressing its claim, and as year succeeded year Amar Thapa's men occupied more and more of the Butwal villages with impunity, taking British quiescence as tacit recognition of their right.

In 1811, one of the Company's permanently settled zemindars, the Raja of Betiya, in Saran district, took the law into his own hands and sent a body of armed men to seize some villages occupied by the Gurkhas. The Gurkhas claimed them as part of the inheritance of the conquered hill state of Makwanpur, but the Raja insisted that they were part of the estates for which he had contracted to pay rent to the Company. There was an affray, and a Nepalese *suba*, or civil governor, was killed. The Gurkha Raja, outraged, appealed to the Senior Judge at Patna, requesting him to punish the culprits. The Judge promised that impartial justice would be done. He passed the matter on to his subordinate, the Judge at Saran, who came to the conclusion that the *suba* had been as much to blame as the Betiya Raja. Accepting this verdict, the authorities in Calcutta decided not to chastise their zemindar; but in view of the fact that the Butwal issue was still unresolved, they proposed an Anglo-Nepalese commission to investigate the whole border question. The Gurkhas chafed at what they considered to be the Company's prevarication in favour of its own zemindars, but agreed to depute agents. For good measure they meanwhile seized more villages in Saran, making twenty-two in all.

The Company's chief commissioner was Major Paris Bradshaw, Head Assistant at the Lucknow Residency. He began by investigating and presenting the Company's claim to the Butwal and Siuraj tracts, while Mr. Young, the Saran Magistrate's Assistant, conducted preliminary inquiries in Saran. Paris Bradshaw was Irish, middle-aged, short, slight, dour and archaic. He still wore the old-fashioned hair powder and pigtail. His young brother-in-law, John Hearsey,[8] found him very much 'a gentleman of the old school . . . exceedingly prosaic'. His dispatches, with their enormous pleonastic sentences and stilted bureaucratic expressions, betray a rigid punctiliousness. Having no flair for persuasion, and an ill-disguised distaste for the wiles of oriental diplomacy, he was disliked by the Nepalese, who made several attempts to circumvent him. But it would have been impossible for anyone, even without Bradshaw's defects, to carry out Calcutta's instructions without incurring unpopularity. Bradshaw was instructed not only to demand the surrender of Butwal, but in addition to revive the lapsed British claim to Siuraj. He produced *sanads* and rent rolls to show that both belonged to the Company, but the Gurkhas were

[8] Later Major-General John Hearsey. He was Hyder Hearsey's half-brother.

unmoved. The Tarai territories were of vital importance in the economy of Nepal. Their revenues formed the only income from land which the Kathmandu exchequer received, because all other territory was allotted to the army in lieu of payment. Vainly, Krishna Pandit, a Gurkha commissioner who was well-disposed towards the British after residing in Calcutta as Nepalese *vakil*, suggested a compromise. If the Raja admitted British sovereignty in the lowlands, would the Company grant him on lease a tract along the foot of the hills? Calcutta took this as an implicit admission of British claims, and the Raja was sent an ultimatum by Minto. Either he gave up the lands, or they would be taken by force. Here the matter rested for a few months; the hot season of 1813 was at hand, and any military movements would have to be postponed until the autumn. Krishna Pandit fell from favour for his well-intentioned but apparently unwarranted initiative, and was recalled.

Bradshaw now proceeded to Saran, where Mr. Young had begun an inquiry concerning the twenty-two villages. His first act was to renew an initial condition laid down by the Calcutta government—namely, that these villages be surrendered to the Company pending any investigation concerning the question of right. The Gurkhas demurred, and were suspicious; but finally they consented, and the Company's officers occupied the hamlets and their fields. Major Bradshaw then announced that there would be no inquiry. Mr. Young's evidence was conclusive enough, and had already established the right of the Company to the lands.[9] There was no point in conducting another laborious investigation, because the Gurkhas, judging by their intransigence in Butwal, were bound to reject its findings in any case. Now this was a blunder. Bradshaw had given the Gurkha commissioners every assurance that a full investigation

---

[9] The Gurkhas claimed that the twenty-two villages were included in the *tappa* or sub-department of Rautahat, part of the Makwanpur estates which had been restored to the Nepalese in 1783 by Warren Hastings, after having been occupied by Captain Kinloch (see below, Ch. III). Bir Krishna Singh, Raja of Betiya, insisted that the villages were in fact in the tappa of Nanur, which had continued to form part of his own territories after the adjustments of 1783. Summing up the findings of Mr. Young's inquiry, the Magistrate of Saran later wrote: 'The whole of the evidence taken on both sides seems evidently to conclude in favour of [the Raja of Betiya] as some of the witnesses on the side of the Nepalese allow that he had had possession since [1765], whilst his own witnesses unanimously give evidence to his uninterrupted possession of upwards of forty years.' (Sec. Cons., 3 Feb. 1816, no. 21).

would be opened once they had surrendered the villages; and the Calcutta government, although it claimed that he had never been authorized to give such an impression, should have accepted the consequences of his mistake and allowed the inquiry to proceed. Furthermore, in asserting that the Gurkhas had rejected the findings of the Butwal investigation, the government was anticipating Kathmandu's reaction to that inquiry. The Gurkha commissioners had rejected nothing, but had merely asked for time to refer to the durbar, and the Raja's refusal to evacuate the contested territory was not in fact known at Calcutta until the end of 1813. The British were also inconsistent in their treatment of precedents. While willing to regard their own long-effective occupation of the twenty-two villages as 'sufficient ground, if there had been no other, for immediately resuming them', they refused to admit similar arguments in favour of the Gurkhas, who pleaded twenty-five years' possession of Siuraj. But then Gurkha tactics were equally dubious. The commissioners made a great show of indignation, and claimed that Bradshaw had deceived them, but at the same time betrayed their own insincerity by claiming that Young's inquiry had established their right to the villages; and when Bradshaw produced additional documents to reinforce the Company's claim, they refused to accept them on the ground that they had not been produced at Young's inquiry, whose findings they regarded as final.

Relations between Bradshaw and the Gurkha commissioners deteriorated to petty bickering. At the beginning of April 1814, the latter suddenly broke off negotiations and returned to Nepal. Bradshaw, in a plaintive tone of self-justification, expressed his cenviction that all their previous rudeness and intransigence had been designed to provoke him into some indiscretion which would make him appear responsible for what was in fact a predetermined cessation. It appears that the commissioners were summoned to Kathmandu to give their opinions in a debate which the Raja was holding to determine whether the Gurkhas should make a stand against the British. After the Raja's refusal to evacuate Butwal and Siuraj had been received in Calcutta in December 1813, a fresh demand, in the form of an ultimatum, had been sent. General Amar Thapa had no intention of yielding to such imperious representations. To humiliate the haughty British, by turning against them the model soldiers he had drilled and rehearsed with solicitude and pride, was the paramount ambition of this ailing but ferocious old war lord. At the end of March he summoned his energies for the journey to Kathmandu, and there used all his eloquence to urge resistance and disparage supine concession. Opinion was divided in the state. Bhim Sen Thapa was in favour of defiance; but Brahma Shah, his brother Hasti Dal and Amar Singh Thapa had, from the west, unanimously counselled restraint and concession. They feared that armed resistance to the British would engender full-scale war, and they knew the Gurkha state to be too weak to embark on military enterprises of that magnitude without risking annihilation. Urgently, they stressed the difference between the hill rajas and the East India Company: fighting the one was like hunting deer, but engaging in battle with the other would be like fighting tigers. The party of resistance, however, carried their case; and General Amar Thapa, now back in Palpa, was instructed to prepare the military defence of the territories under his command.[10] In reply to the Governor-General's protestation at the unceremonious interruption of negotiations with Bradshaw, the Raja retorted that Bradshaw had been rude and offensive, and that the Gurkhas had no intention of restituting lands to which Mr. Young's inquiry had established their incontrovertible right.

On 22 April 1814, the ultimatum for the formal surrender of Butwal and Siuraj having expired, the Magistrate of Gorakhpur ordered seventeen companies of native infantry to take possession. They met with no resistance, Amar Thapa's men retreating as they advanced. But the regular soldiers had to be withdrawn almost as soon as they had arrived, because of the malaria, and defence was entrusted to the personnel of a few *thanas* (police posts). On 29 May the Gurkha troops moved back into the now virtually un-protected territory, and attacked a *thana* in Butwal. Eighteen of the Company's policemen were killed and six wounded. The *daroga* (chief officer) was wounded, and surrendered. The Gurkha com-manding officer ordered him to be tied to a tree, and he was then shot dead with arrows. Two other police posts were attacked at the same time, and their occupants put to flight.

When the news of this atrocity reached Calcutta, early in June, the Governor-General and Council were in conclave on normal business. The council chamber in Fort William was not a place of

[10] The original account of this council of war is in Sec. Cons., 20 Oct. 1815, no. 54. It has been printed in several places, including Prinsep's *Political and Military Transactions*, vol. i, pp. 458–60.

harmony and relaxed co-operation. Suppressed animosity intensified the natural discomforts of the humid Bengal summer. The
Governor-General, the Marquis of Hastings,[11] was not popular
with his colleagues. The mode of his appointment and the nature
of his policies were both causes of resentment. Hastings, now in his
sixtieth year, was a soldier by education and experience. As Lord
Rawdon he had fought with distinction in the American War of
Independence and then in the Revolutionary Wars in the Low
Countries, where Wellington served under him. He was a typical
soldier—bluff and unsubtle, and never at his ease in Parliament. A
disciple neither of Fox nor of Pitt, he had lacked the personality
and the political skill necessary for forming a party independent of
both. It was his consistent loyalty to the Prince Regent that had
earned him the combined offices of Governor-General and Commander-in-Chief in India in 1812. The object of the dual appointment was to give Hastings a chance to recruit his personal finances,
crippled by extravagance and ostentatious largesse; but, however
financially remunerative, it cost him much in terms of popularity.
The friends of Sir George Nugent, the Commander-in-Chief, indignantly deprecated an untimely supersession whose only justification was the penury of the new Governor-General, and they had
used their influence to have a special post created for Nugent—that
of Commander of the Forces in Bengal.

Nugent, however, had sulked, and made up his mind to resign—
much to the annoyance of Hastings, who always fancied he could
soothe ruffled feelings. Nugent delayed his departure until December the following year, and meantime continued as Senior Member
of the Council. This meant that Hastings was now at odds with the
majority of his Council, which consisted of two other members
besides Nugent. Archibald Seton was a background figure, occasionally asserting himself in an attempt to preserve harmony but
more often overshadowed by Neil Benjamin Edmonstone, who was
openly sympathetic towards the erstwhile Commander-in-Chief.
But there were more fundamental points of difference between
Hastings and the self-assured Edmonstone than Nugent's supersession. Edmonstone was rigidly opposed to the style of policy
pursued by Wellesley, while Hastings was resolved to carry his
work to completion. The physical contrast between Wellesley and

[11] At this stage he was in fact still the Earl of Moira; but as he is better known
by his later title, it is probably in the interests of clarity to use it throughout.

Hastings was extreme: the one small but naturally imposing—animated, lean, and patrician-featured; the other large, combersome, and heavy-jowled—an avuncular figure who was too naïve not to seem pompous when he tried to be dignified. But they both had the same proconsular manner, love of display and superhuman energy and sense of dedication. Despite his early criticism of Wellesley, Hastings had lately found himself increasingly in sympathy with him, especially on the sensitive issue of Catholic emancipation, of which they were both in favour. It was Wellesley's grand scheme of Indian alliances, designed to obviate French subversion but left unfinished, which Hastings resolved not only to complete but to re-work into the instrument of British paramountcy in India. While Wellesley had striven to turn the native states into allies, Hastings was avowedly determined to turn them into vassals. In short, his policy was unashamedly imperialistic—a term often applied to Wellesley but perhaps better reserved for his successor. The East India Company was finally to claim the Mogul inheritance, by dropping the fiction of allegiance to the puppet Emperor in Delhi and assuming the tone and trappings of royalty itself.

It would be wrong, probably, to discount entirely love of imperialism for its own sake; but it does seem that Hastings's policy was motivated principally by a sincere fear that unless the British acted first, the native states would combine and drive the Company from India. Only paramountcy could pre-empt destruction. This way of thinking made it impossible for Hastings to treat the Nepalese encroachments as mere isolated border incidents. He interpreted them as the symptoms of a profounder and more insidious disturbance: the first stirrings of a concerted crusade among the Hindu states, whose apotheosis would be the expulsion of all Europeans from India. It was with a mixture of irritation and relief that he heard the Political Secretary read out the dispatch from Butwal, recounting the murder of the Company's police officer—irritation because he had never anticipated that his efforts to resolve the Nepalese problem by diplomacy could fail; relief, because he was beginning to suspect an alliance between the Gurkhas and the Marathas, and considered it wiser that the Gurkhas, obviously the better prepared, be defeated first, in isolation. But whatever Hastings's ulterior motives may have been, his colleagues and employers knew nothing of them, and would certainly never have condoned them if they had. In their view, the war was designed to end the anarchy attendant on the collapse of Mogul authority, which the Gurkhas were intent on exploiting to the detriment of the Company's revenues and of the security of its subjects and officers. It was, in other words, designed to turn the Company's *de jure* rights into a *de facto* authority. No one disputed the necessity of war, least of all Nugent, who assented almost mechanically to what he probably assumed would be one of what he had described as 'petty warfares on the frontiers of the British territories which rarely last more than one campaign, and which always end successfully'. The Court of Directors was fully reconciled to the use of force and as early as February 1814 sent a dispatch sanctioning 'a recourse to arms for the recovery and protection of the rights of the British Government'.

Military operations could not begin until the hot and rainy seasons had passed. The Governor-General took advantage of the interval not only to obtain information and make plans for the invasion, but also to require the Raja to disavow responsibility for the murder of the *daroga* and punish the culprits. He made it plain that if such atonement was not forthcoming, the two countries would be in a state of war. This was Hastings's last measure in the Nepalese crisis before his departure from Fort William on his tour of the upper provinces. He received the Raja's reply on 12 August, while at Patna. It evaded all mention of the fracas in Butwal, but made obscure references to the assassination of Nepalese police officers and accused Bradshaw of trespassing and violence. Its tone the Governor-General found 'evasive and even implying menace'.

It is difficult to estimate how far Hastings's suspicions of collusion between the durbar at Kathmandu and the Marathas was justified. There is no doubt that there were diplomatic exchanges; the Thapas had a relish for ambassadors and the appurtenances of empire, and stationed agents at many native courts. It was furthermore later revealed that the Peshwa of Poona had given secret encouragement to the Gurkhas with a vague and opportunist view to exploiting, somehow, any consequent diversion of British energies in the hills. But the existence of mature conspiracy is unlikely. No reference to aid expected from outside was made in the replies submitted by the state counsellors in the war debate in Kathmandu; and Amar Singh Thapa was so far from being confident of such support that he was aghast at the prospect of war.

Later, when the temerity of the durbar had brought him face to face with final defeat and ruin, he bitterly castigated the Raja for his folly at this juncture.

His main hopes of support were directed to the Sikhs and to China, though as the war went on he also wrote for assistance to Gwalior. His urgent concern, as soon as the affray in Butwal became known to him, was to avert, if possible, British military retaliation by opening a fresh correspondence with Ochterlony and, through him, with the Governor-General. He reiterated the Gurkha claim to the disputed lands, made excuses for the expulsion of the Company's *thanas* and repeated the offer to pay a rent for Butwal. The ambivalent tenor of his letters betokened a struggle between appeasement and defiance going on within him: the one prompted by his exasperation at the durbar's foolhardiness; the other by his pride and his obstinate loyalty to his prince, right or wrong. Unbending as far towards actual supplication as his independent spirit would allow, he invoked the precedent of sixty years' friendship between the two governments, and recalled his own concession in the case of the Sirhind lowlands in a plea for agreement. But, his fierce pride rejecting peace at the price of humiliation, he could not resist a note of challenge. Pointedly, he insinuated mention of Nepal's firm friendship with China, and warned all potential aggressors of the military might and iron resolve of his nation:

If . . . prompt injunctions are issued to the officers of the British Government who are stationed on the opposite frontier of the Palpa territory to desist from further sedition and contention, it will be proper and just, in as much as mutual litigations will cease. Otherwise, by the favour of God, the troops of the Gurkhas, resembling the waves of the ocean, whose chief employments are war and hostility, will make the necessary preparations to prevent the usurpation of any one place which has been in their possession for years past, and the flame of sedition will daily increase.[12]

To this communication the Governor-General did not see fit to reply, and Amar Singh's subsequent attempts to negotiate through Ochterlony were discouraged. He was asked to address himself to the Resident at Delhi; but the long-mooted deputation of an agent there never in fact came about. Once war had begun, the Kaji's tenders of negotiation became no more than subterfuge, designed

[12] *P.R.N.W.*, p. 70.

to distract the British and secure delays which he might turn to military advantage.

Nepal's main diplomatic expedient was to exploit her connections with China. As Chinese vassals, the Gurkhas were obliged to send a quinquennial embassy to Peking, and that sent in 1813 was much publicized. The Gurkha ambassador asked the Imperial authorities for military aid against the Sikkimese, who, he claimed, were proving contumacious, and this was apparently promised. It appears that about the same time the Chinese officials in Lhasa sent money, with a large escort, for the repair of a Buddhist temple in Kathmandu. The Gurkha government then propagated the idea that both the promise of military aid and the remittance of funds were gestures of support against the British. Bazaar gossip in Lhasa gave further currency to such notions, and it was in this distorted form that the intelligence reached the Company's officers in India. More likely to yield positive results in the way of military co-operation were the negotiations opened with Bhutan in September, 1814. The position of the Raja of Bhutan *vis-à-vis* the Company was similar to that of his Gurkha neighbour, for he too had his uncomposed border quarrels.

When the Governor-General announced his intention to make war, the immediate concern of the Kathmandu durbar was to gauge his sincerity, obtain intelligence of his preparations and delay their implementation. To this end, it pretended to be unaware that a state of hostility existed. An envoy was loaded with presents and sent down to Calcutta, ostensibly to submit the Gurkha Raja's formal congratulations to the new Governor-General on his accession and to resume negotiations concerning the frontier dispute. Bhim Sen Thapa instructed Parsa Ram Thapa, a *suba* on the frontier, to supply escort and bearers, and urged the agent to proceed speedily. 'Delay is improper. Whatever may pass in conversation, or whatever you may observe, hear and understand, do not write openly, but secretly and under disguise.'[13]

Bradshaw took advantage of the rainy months of July and August to occupy the twenty-two villages on the Saran frontier, whence the Gurkhas tried to dislodge him by poisoning the wells. At the end of August the first skirmish of the war took place, with the capture of a Gurkha *thana* called Kachurwa. It was therefore with some astonishment that Bradshaw learned of the arrival at Parsa

[13] *P.R.N.W.*, p. 371.

Ram's headquarters of a Gurkha *vakil* with gifts of gold, silks, trinkets and elephants for the Governor-General. On instructions from Headquarters he refused to allow him to proceed farther. No friendly missions could now be received; only agents with plenary powers to sue for peace. The *vakil*, called Chandra Sekhar Upadhyaya, was told that he was at liberty to return to Kathmandu. But Chandra Sekhar ignored the intimation, and tried surreptitiously to obtain a passport. He was unsuccessful, but still remained on the frontier, with the ostensible design of meeting the Governor-General, then touring the upper provinces, and the covert purpose of obtaining intelligence. The Gurkhas, after such a long sequence of unimplemented threats and confident of the strength of their natural defences, were probably still unconvinced that the Governor-General really intended to invade Nepal. It seems that, at the most, they expected him to seize the lands so long contested on the plains.

In Palpa, the arch-sponsor of Gurkha defiance prepared for war with the febrile enthusiasm of the moribund. Alone among men of military experience in the state, General Amar Thapa had been flagrantly averse to compromise. With his son, Bhim Sen Thapa, determination to resist derived more from youthful impulsiveness and vanity than from reflection and experience. But with the General himself it was reasoned conviction which urged him to canvass war. He had supreme confidence in his carefully nurtured Palpa battalions, which were fully equal to the most brilliant *corps d' élite* in Kathmandu. He coveted the influence and the prestige which would accrue to the Gurkhas in the eyes of every native power in India if they could but successfully resist the legendary might of the East India Company; and he remained assured that if the worst came to the worst the Gurkhas could always retire from the contest on their own terms, since they could never be defeated outright in the mountains. Then, at the end of October 1814, the old General died, having launched his country on the most strenuous contest in its history.

III

THE MATTER OF HIMALAYAN TRADE

ON 2 December 1814 the Governor-General was at Moradabad, on the plains near the border of Kumaun. A heavy
shower had just cleared the air, and looking northwards
Hastings could see the Himalayas quite clearly. He was moved by
the view, and wrote in his diary:

There was an odd sensation in contemplating a spot in the globe where
the foot of man never trod, nor was ever likely to be planted. This
immense barrier would seem sufficient to limit the concerns of India;
yet at this moment I am speculating on the trade which may be carried
on beyond it, should the present war with the Gurkhas leave us in
possession of Kumaun. From that province there are valleys between
the hills which afford a passage of not much difficulty, and greatly fre-
quented, into Tartary. The holding of Kumaun would give us the
exclusive purchase of the shawl wool, to be paid for in cutlery, broadcloth, and grain.[1]

The ambition to trade across the Himalayas, and thereby link
the British territories in India with the vast regions of Tibet and
China beyond, was not new and had, at its inception, been connected with the idea of a war against Nepal.

In 1767, when Prithvi Narayan Shah of Gurkha led his army
into the Valley of Nepal and set about destroying its three kingdoms, the Calcutta government decided that its own commercial
interests were sufficiently menaced to justify an attempt to contain
the Gurkhas by military intervention. Consequently, in June of
that year Captain Kinloch marched to the assistance of the Raja of
Kathmandu with a force of 2,400 men. The government's more
immediate reason for sanctioning this step was because it wanted
to preserve the local trade between north Bengal and contiguous
districts of Nepal—a trade which the Gurkha career of conquest
was upsetting; but wider ambitions were stirring even then. It was
not only reasoned that old patterns of trade would be preserved,
but speculated that new ones might be created. Why should not

[1] Bute, *Private Journal*, i, p. 246.

Nepal be used as a channel to Tibet? So the notion was born, conceived of need and ignorance: need for new sources of precious metals, to counterbalance the drain from India caused by the demands of the East India Company's establishments in China; ignorance of almost everything relating to Nepal and Tibet. The expedition was a failure, not to say a disaster, with only a third of the troops returning. The immediate enthusiasm for a conflict with Nepal diminished, and Kinloch was not permitted a second try. However, the attractive assumption that a trans-Himalayan trade was possible persisted, grew and flourised. The idea soon became the subject of discussion in India, and of inquiry in dispatches from London. Why should not the looms of Halifax provide woollens for the inhabitants of windswept Tibet and distant China? There was something epic in the conception. As the idea became familiar, so it seemed more natural; and soon it seemed so natural that the Company's statesmen in India began to wonder why the Himalayan passes were not thronged with merchants carrying up English broadcloth and metals into Tibet and returning with wool from the mountain goat, gold, musk and borax. It seemed ordained by the logic of commerce that mutual needs should be so satisfied. From the premise that a particular state of affairs naturally should exist, it is only a short step to the inference that such a state of affairs at one time did exist; so it comes as no surprise to find a famous enthusiast of the cause of trans-Himalayan trade, Brian Hodgson, later referring to 'that great commerce which naturally ought to, and formerly did subsist between the vast cis and trans-Himalayan regions'.[2] The idea that new trading connections might be created had become transformed into the argument that old ones should be revived. Because the Gurkhas were building their empire across the eastern Himalayas at the time when the thinking of the British was evolving in this fashion, it was inevitable that they should be held responsible for the obstruction which the British theory postulated. By the time Warren Hastings[3] became Governor of Bengal in 1772, the rationalization of the East India Company's commercial problem had been neatly completed. Formerly (according to the theory) the trade between Bengal and Tibet, via Nepal, had been very considerable. But with the wars and oppressions of

[2] *Selections from the Records of the Government of Bengal,* xxvii, p. 12.
[3] Not to be confused with the Marquis of Hastings, Governor-General at the time of the 1814–16 Nepal War.

the Gurkhas, the rhythm of interchange had been broken, merchants deterred, and the trade all but destroyed. This was the
interpretation which Warren Hastings adopted with eagerness, because the outflow of treasure from Bengal was unabated, and he was
something of a romantic where unknown horizons were concerned.
Armed with this well-rehearsed argument, and with some presents
of English produce to enhance its attractiveness in the eyes of the
Tibetans, an amiable Scotsman called George Bogle was sent to
Tibet in 1774, by way of Bhutan. His mission's object was to promote commercial intercourse between Bengal and Tibet by arranging for merchants from both places to meet regularly in Bhutan. He
was particularly instructed to acquire specimens of the goat which
provided the wool for the famous shawls of Kashmir, and of the
Himalayan yak, the fibres of whose tail were used in Europe to make
lace.

In a word, Warren Hastings's policy was to bypass the Gurkhas.
The idea of attacking them and forcing open a passage for trade
was still canvassed, but events occurring since the abortive Kinloch
expedition had offered the chance to try another route. The
Bhutanese had come down from their mountains and attacked
Kuch Bihar; and the molested Raja having solicited aid, Warren
Hastings, as we have seen, sent a force to help him, determining at
the same time to use the opportunity to acquire Kuch Bihar for the
Company. Captain Jones's men had a hard time of it, what with
malaria and the ferocious resistance of the Bhutanese; but by
April 1773 the enemy had been sufficiently alarmed to seek outside
help. Bhutan,[4] as a Buddhist country, had a close religious and
cultural affinity with Tibet, and ethnographically was at one with
that country. While the Deb Raja[5] dealt with mundane administration, the Dharma Raja concerned himself with religious affairs, and
held himself the spiritual vassal of the Dalai Lama of Tibet. It was
natural, therefore, that in her plight Bhutan should look to Tibet
for support. The most important pontiff in that country after the
Dalai Lama was the Panchen Lama, whose see was at Tashilunpo[6]
in southern Tibet. It was the Panchen Lama who now intervened,
by sending to the Governor at Calcutta a letter in which he sug-

---

[4] Correctly *Bhutant*, meaning the end of Tibet. *Bhot* is the Sanskrit name for
Tibet.

[5] *Deba* is a Tartar title, corresponding to governor, or viceroy.

[6] For this reason he was often referred to by English writers as the 'Teshoo'
Lama. Tashilunpo was also known as Shigatsé.

gested the expediency of clemency towards the truculent Bhutanese. With great diffidence he offered a few presents. These were most interesting. They included sheets of Russian gilt leather, talents of gold and silver, bulses of gold dust, bags of musk, Tibetan woollen cloth and Chinese silk. The gifts were conveyed in chests of professional workmanship, with dovetailed joints. Here were proofs of 'an extensive commerce, internal wealth, and an advanced knowledge of the arts of common life'.[7] The opening afforded by the Lama's address was not to be missed, and Bogle was sent to return the compliment and at the same time blaze a trail for merchants and traders. The opening of Bhutan would be the British riposte to the Gurkhas' closure of Nepal.

Thus, at first glance, it appears that the sentiments expressed by Lord Hastings at Moradabad in 1814 betoken the survival of a policy which was half a century old; they would seem to indicate that it was the continuing desire to open channels for commerce through the Himalayas which contributed to cause a second and much more serious war against the Gurkhas in 1814. An attractively simple theory—but dangerous: a sure enticement to error. There are flashes, which warn of dangerous rocks beneath the calm surface.

In the first place, events had come to pass in that half-century which made it quite unrealistic to suppose, in 1814, that a war with Nepal could facilitate access to Tibet. Even in Warren Hastings's time, indeed, it had been unrealistic to suppose so much. Had the Company's servants been less predisposed in favour of convenient assumptions, they would have sensed the futility of their aspirations. Warren Hastings implied that his scheme for a trans-Himalayan trade was in no way revolutionary. All that was involved was the removal, or the circumvention, of artificial obstructions which the Gurkhas had put in the way of the commerce which under normal conditions would circulate across the Himalayas, linking central Asia and Hindustan. But on closer inspection it seems that he had no grounds for such an assumption. The idea of a flourishing former trade through the eastern part of the Himalayas, at least, was probably chimerical.

There can have been little to suggest that Nepal, previous to the Gurkha conquest, had been a great and thriving entrepôt of trade between Bengal and Tibet. Some interchange had been carried on, of course. Since the mid-seventeenth century Patna, the biggest

---

[7] S. Turner, *Embassy*, pp. xii–xiii.

town in Bihar, and the most renowned for commerce, had attracted merchants who carried on a trade with Tibet through the passes of Nepal. There was always someone at Patna who would barter gold, borax, yaks' tails or musk from Tibet for coral, betelnut, nutmeg, cottons and woollens; but probably the volume of such trade never exceeded a feeble trickle. It was a peddling business in luxury goods, carried on mainly at the behest of the wealthy and the curious.

The severest discouragement to a direct intercourse between the high Tibetan plateau and the plains was the dramatic contrast in climate between the two regions. The mountain passes were open only in the months of summer, when the lowlands of India were either seared by heat or drowned by the solstitial monsoon. Nothing could then draw down the inhabitants of Tibet, who dreaded the climate of Hindustan at the best of times. If contact was to be made at all, they were therefore best met half-way, at a place where the climate was not too extreme for either party. The eastern area of the Himalayas was the least suitable for such a meeting. Because of the malaria, merely to walk in the Tarai during the hot and rainy seasons was death; so at the very time when the mountain passes into Tibet were open and busy, the southern belt of jungle was silent and deserted. There were no roads leading into Nepal, and the rivers, deceptively broad and slow near the plains, soon led travellers back to a pristine confusion of chasms, gorges and cataracts. No wide river valleys found natural highways here. When Francis Hamilton went to Nepal with the British embassy in 1802, he followed a route to Kathmandu which was reckoned to be one of the most practicable. Even so, the difficulties were formidable and in one defile eighteen miles long the winding Rapti river had to be forded no fewer than twenty-two times. Such topography was typical of the whole southern slope of the eastern Himalayan range, from Bhutan to Kumaun in the west. Roads were rare, and where they did exist, as in Kumaun, they were intended and were suitable only for pilgrims. The natives of Bengal, smothered in the caress of a sultry climate and enervated by the spontaneous fertility of their soil, were loath to endure the rigours of cold and danger in the mountains, and only a few intrepid speculators undertook the whole journey to Tibet themselves. Such were the Kashmirians and Armenians who had establishments at Patna. Their expeditions were fraught with alarming hazards, as well as with the great expense incurred by the unavoidable use of human carriers. The peripatetic *gossains* (Hindu friars) also found their way into Tibet by way of the Nepalese hills, and peddled in drugs, spices, dried fruits, precious stones, pearls, coral and perhaps a little cloth—'articles of great value and small bulk'.[8] Otherwise, the inconvenient coinciding of the seasons and the natural difficulties of the way meant that any trade between Bengal and Tibet had to be carried on by the agency of middle men, like the Newar entrepreneurs in Nepal and the hill peasants in Kumaun. In Kumaun, indeed, the trade had to pass through two agencies, the migratory peasants of the southern slopes acting as a medium between the fairs on the plains and the Bhotias, who inhabited the high hollows of the ghats, or passes, leading into Tibet. By ancient usage, only the Bhotias had the privilege of direct communication with traders from beyond the passes. Tobacco, glass beads, hardware, coarse local textiles and grain were loaded by the hill people on to short-legged goats and mountain sheep, who alone could manoeuvre the rugged pathways with confidence. Fine manufactures and expensive articles were brought up only when previously bespoke. From the Bhotias they received the usual trans-Himalayan products—borax, salt, musk, and various drugs and spices. Checks, obstructions and risks not only tended to restrict commerce to articles of smallest bulk and greatest value; they also raised Indian prices to a level which made them uncompetitive in the increasingly crowded luxury market of Tibet. Coral beads from Bengal had always been notoriously expensive in Tibet, and by the beginning of the nineteenth century were being undersold by imports from Russia. European commodities from Bengal suffered a similar fate; Russian traders could sell cloth from France, for example, at a rate below the cost of English woollens from India. Such were the consequences of goods from the plains having to pass through so many pairs of hands. Additional inhibitions of a political nature prevented the development of a trade in shawl wool across the eastern Himalayas. By a treaty dating from the end of the seventeenth century, the state of Ladakh, an erstwhile province of Tibet situated in the valley of the upper Indus and separating Tibet from Kashmir, was possessed of a strict monopoly in this commodity; and the Kashmirians in turn had the unique right of purchase from the Ladakh dealers. It was consequently very difficult for strangers to buy wool, or to obtain specimens of the shawl-wool goat.

[8] Markham, *Bogle and Manning*, p. 125.

Trade through the eastern Himalayas before the Gurkha conquests cannot, then, have been a 'great commerce'. The very fact that it came to a halt under the slight pressures imposed by the Gurkhas betokened a feeble circulation in these constricted arteries. A really healthy trade would have survived much more than that. It is true that Tibet had strong commercial ties with Kathmandu. She relied on the Kathmandu mint for her coinage; Nepalese artisans and traders settled in considerable numbers in Lhasa; and the route from the Valley to the passes into Tibet was well trodden by traders from the north. Similarly, the scope of the trade of north India extended to the Nepal lowlands, and a considerable interchange in timber, rice and other local produce was carried on between the Tarai, the Morang, and neighbouring districts in India. But it was as if these two points—the Kathmandu Valley and the Nepal lowlands—were the extremities of two separate commercial systems.

The British were looking at things from the wrong standpoint. Having familiarized themselves with the eastern sea approaches, built up Calcutta and come to know Bengal, they did not at first appreciate that the internal trade of north India was traditionally centred in the north-west, the natural emporium of Hindustan being where its political and cultural focus had always been—in the Punjab and Rajputana. The plains of the north-west were the meeting place for merchants who came by land from Tibet and Kandahar, or by sea to the ports of Gujarat. If we would know how India got her shawls, her salt, and the borax and musk of which Tibet was the richest source in the world, we should look towards the western Himalayas, where the valley of the river Sutlaj provided a broad natural highway directly linking the Punjab with the plateau of western Tibet. The small state of Basahar,[9] in the Punjab hills, had acquired great importance as a convenient halfway stage on the route from Ladakh and Tibet; and it was at Rampur, the capital of that state, that sellers from Kashmir, Ladakh and Yarkhand came down to meet the lowland traders and exchange the precious merchandise of central Asia for the wheat and manufactures of the plains. The inhabitants of Basahar betrayed by their politeness and probity a long tradition of commercial experience. In the words of an English traveller[10] of the second decade of the nineteenth century, they had become the 'commercial

[9] Known alternatively as Kunawar.
[10] James Baillie Fraser, *Journal of a Tour*, pp. 264, 489.

carriers between Hindustan and Tartary, as also between Tartary and Kashmir, frequenting the routes from Leh in Ladakh to Lhasa and Shigatsé and Nepal, on trading speculations'. It was by the Sutlaj route, no doubt, that Indian merchants travelled, when they went to the great annual fair at Gartok, capital of western Tibet, where every September traders from Ladakh, Kashmir, Tartary, Yarkhand, Tibet and China haggled, bartered and bargained, filling the streets with cacophony and colour. This was the area where the very best shawl wool was produced—a fact which, together with the monopoly enjoyed by Ladakh and Kashmir, made the western Himalayas the natural centre of the trade in this immensely profitable commodity. The Punjab hills between the Indus and the Sutlaj were laced with roads, pathways and river valleys—a plexus of ramifications from arteries of commerce which led to the Punjab in the south, to Attock and Peshawar in the west, to Kashmir and Ladakh in the north, and to Tibet in the east. Whenever the Patna merchants quarrelled with the Imperial customs officers at Gorakhpur, they would abandon the route through Nepal in favour of a journey far to the west, where they could meet merchants from all quarters at Kabul. The commerce pursued through Nepal by the Kashmirians at Patna was in any case but of ancillary importance: a digression from the main east–west orientation of their trade. The principal caravans plied the lateral valleys which run between the Himalayan ranges and link Ladakh and Kashmir with east Tibet, taking made-up shawls mostly, and bringing back raw wool and Tibetan produce. Certain subsidiary enterprises had inevitably germinated by the wayside. The Patna merchants were only minor agents, engaged principally in collecting otter skins for the China market from Dacca and the maritime provinces in the Ganges and Brahmaputra deltas.

So the anxiety of the British, in Warren Hastings's time, to vindicate the policy of promoting trade with Tibet through the eastern Himalayas caused them to invoke precedents which had no foundation in reality. That great commerce linking Tibet, Nepal and Bengal was a tempting mirage in the uncharted tracts of the past. The same anxiety was also creating what we might call the traditional view of the part played by the Gurkhas in this phase of Himalayan history, which attributes to their pugnacity a state of affairs really created by something else.

In the final analysis, the Gurkhas in Nepal and the British in north India were pursuing parallel policies with regard to Tibet. The ultimate aim of both was to foster their own commercial contacts with that country. Just as the British were convinced that the opening of the trans-Himalayan markets was vital to their commercial welfare, so the Gurkhas realized that the prosperity of Nepal depended on close economic ties with Tibet. The exchequer derived very little income from the land, because by the Gurkha system the greater part of the rent due to the crown was assigned as payment to the army. The state therefore relied all the more on the Tibetan trade for its money income. Not only was this a vehicle for taxation; it was also a source of direct profit, because returns were made largely in bullion which merchants were compelled to exchange for Nepalese currency at the mint in Kathmandu. The government secured a clear profit of some 8 per cent on these transactions. Further profits were derived from the privilege which Kathmandu had acquired of minting currency for circulation in Tibet. The Nepalese crafts of refining and working the precious metals depended for their sustenance on the custom and raw materials of Tibet, and many were the Nepalese residing in Lhasa as goldsmiths and silversmiths, plying their trade in dim-lit basement workshops beneath the Gurkha emblem of the sun and crescent moon.[11] Finally, the Gurkhas depended on Tibet for their salt, a vitally important commodity, which was not found in their own dominions.

It was therefore of great importance to the rulers of Nepal not only that Tibet be kept open for a free commercial interchange, but that what trade there was from the plains to Tibet be confined to the channels through Nepal. There was not sufficient to be shared, and far from obstructing such a commerce, the Gurkhas did their utmost to encourage it. The very beneficial treaty which had given Kathmandu the right to mint Tibet's currency had also closed the Sikkim route to the plains by levying heavy customs duties on goods going that way. It was with considerable concern that the Gurkha Raja heard of Mr. Bogle's expedition to Bhutan and Tashilunpo, for it was obvious that its object was to divert traffic from his own country. He straightway wrote a stern letter to all

[11] By 1816 the number stood between two and three thousand—see 'Notices Respecting Tibet': Sec. Cons., 16 March 1816, no. 48; E. Huc, *Souvenirs d'un Voyage*, ii, 262. Huc calls them *Péboun*, which, presumably, is the Tibetan designation for the Nepalese.

the chiefs of Tibet, including the erring Panchen Lama, requiring them to have nothing more to do with the *feringis* [Europeans], but to 'follow the ancient custom'. He desired marts for the sale of Bengal goods to be built on the northern borders of his own kingdom, indicating that he would offer no obstruction to 'the common articles of commerce'.[12] It is quite clear from his letter how seriously he viewed this attempt to side-step Nepal. He declared that he had no wish for war, but reminded the Tibetans that he was a Rajput, and well prepared. It is true that the Gurkhas' efforts to enhance their kingdom's importance as an entrepôt of trade were not all calculated to have the desired effect. The new rulers in Kathmandu had but primitive notions concerning the wealth of nations and, considering trade as a vehicle of taxation rather than as a means to national wealth in itself, tended to favour a system of trading monopoly which facilitated the levying and collection of imposts. The taxes were often high—but this was nothing new. Musk had been subject to a duty of 25 per cent at Gorakhpur for over a century. Compared with states such as Tibet and Bhutan, whose governments reserved all trade to themselves, Nepal under the Gurkhas appears in fact to have been relatively favourable to commerce. The intention to encourage foreign trade was certainly there, even if the monopoly system and inadequate judicial safeguards tended to hinder its full realization. If the Gurkha state was reluctant to welcome British merchants as residents, the Calcutta government had only itself to blame. By invading Nepal in 1767, when the Gurkha empire was in the impressionable stages of infancy, it had created an anti-European complex, which thenceforth always had the edge over the desire to receive European traders and residents. The Kinloch expedition caused an abrupt cessation of Raja Prithvi Narayan Shah's tolerant attitude towards the Capuchin missionaries in Nepal, and they went the way of the gossains—expelled in disgrace as foreign spies. Thereafter the Gurkha durbar could never overcome the fear that any encouragement to British merchants might open the way for the Company's army; but there is nothing to suggest that it was averse to facilitating trade by means of Nepalese agencies.

British attempts to open other routes to Tibet merely served to complement mistrust with apprehensions for Nepalese commercial interests. Bogle's mission was not an isolated instance, but was

[12] Markham, *Bogle and Manning*, p. 157.

followed by several more embassies, the last being Captain Samuel Turner's of 1783. Such perseverance gave cause to fear that the English would ultimately seize by force what they could not win by diplomacy, and it is not unlikely that a determination to forestall a similar move by the East India Company was partly responsible for the Gurkha decision to invade Tibet in 1788. It is a fact that in 1814 Amar Singh Thapa evinced such a way of thinking, by declaring that only by conquering Tibet once and for all could Nepal hope to put an end to British ambitions in that direction, for Tibet had ever been the true object of their cupidity. But Gurkha commercial interests in Tibet were not being threatened by the British alone. Developments in Tibet itself had long been working to frustrate the customary intercourse with Nepal—and these developments are important, because they confute both the idea of an earlier eighteenth-century Himalayan trade and the contention that the Gurkhas were the main impediment to the existence of such a trade after the middle of the century.

Access to Tibet from the south had never been easy. In addition to the natural obstacles of the journey up from the plains, there were the Tibetans' mistrust of aliens and pagans and their inveterate dread of smallpox to make entry difficult for the lowlander. Ever since the extinction of the Buddhist dynasties of north India by the Muslims, in the twelfth century, and the attempts by the pagans to penetrate even to Tibet itself, they had shunned intercourse with Hindustan. As contacts with India weakened, so Tibet's awareness of her cultural and religious identity with China grew, fostered by the conciliatory policy of successive Chinese dynasties towards the lama hierarchy. When the Manchu dynasty was established in 1655, an unwritten concordat was created between the new Emperor and the doyen of the reformed sect of Buddhists, the Dalai[13] Lama. This *rapprochement* enabled the reformed[14] Buddhists to complete their spiritual victory in Tibet, and facilitated the Emperor's political control of Mongolia. Henceforth Chinese Emperor and Dalai Lama existed on a relationship of symbiosis, each in large measure dependent on recognition by the other.

[13] Dalai, from the Tartar word *talé*, means ocean. It signifies the omniscience and unlimited wisdom of the Lama.

[14] The reformers were called the Yellow Sect, after the colour of their dress. The old Buddhists wore red vestments.

Seditious influences from Mongolia soon compelled the Emperor to exercise the temporal functions of defender of the faith, and in 1720 Imperial forces enthroned the Sixth Dalai Lama at Lhasa and excluded a pretender. In 1728, civil war in Tibet caused a second Chinese military expedition, and this time when the tide withdrew it left an alluvium in the form of two Chinese Residents (*Amban*) and a permanent garrison. The revolutionary activities of certain political groups still persisting, an Imperial force marched into Tibet a third time in 1750. The position of the Residents was consolidated, and the Dalai Lama and state council thenceforth had to consult them on all questions concerning temporal government. As the Chinese hegemony intensified, so Tibetan policy began to betray a Chinese outlook. For example, the notorious Manchu jealousy of Europeans was clearly behind the expulsion of the Capuchin missionaries from Lhasa in 1745.

It would seem that closer political control over Tibet was accompanied by an increase of Chinese influence in Tibet's commercial life. Tibet had always relied almost exclusively on China for the things she did not produce herself—a trading connection that had its origin in the regular tribute caravans from Lhasa to Peking, which would return laden with rich reward from the Emperor. Tibetans had also bartered their horses for Chinese tea, from very early times. Later, it was from China, rather than India, that they obtained even European goods; and by the end of the eighteenth century the greater proportion of Tibet's trade was carried on via the garrison town of Siling, on the borders of western China. Furthermore, the Tibetans themselves, although possessing a flair for barter, tended to trade on an *ad hoc* basis to serve personal needs, and were so lacking in the spirit of association that members of the same family would often pursue their commercial interests independently. Consequently organized trade came to be almost exclusively in the hands of Chinese merchants and retailers.

Chinese control of Tibet's economy and trade relations naturally followed the assumption of political power, since commerce was traditionally a prerogative of the government and no trade existed but by privilege or sufferance. This was why the Chinese presence was constantly invoked by the Tibetans as an obstacle to any closer commercial ties with outside countries. Bogle grumbled that this was a stumbling block which crossed him in every path. That fostering trade was not as simple as bypassing the Gurkhas was shown by the failure of the experimental fair at Rangpur, in northeast Bengal, which, in the 1790s, was established as a mart for the Tibetan trade. Both Bogle and Turner had been satisfied that the arrangements concluded with Tibet and Bhutan had removed all serious impediments, and that nothing remained to hinder the trade. But the merchants did not come. Despite the Company's abolition of all duties and its willingness to pay the expenses of the caravan, the spark of life was never there, and the fair soon languished into insignificance. Turner especially should have realized that such expectations were futile, for it had been made quite clear to him that similar attempts by the Russians had been thwarted by the jealous Chinese. So long was the Chinese shadow, that it was whispered in the bazaars of Nepal and Tibet that the Panchen Lama, who had died of smallpox while paying his respects to the Emperor in Peking in 1780, had in fact been deliberately disposed of because of his friendship for the English.

It was surely not entirely a coincidence that about the time of Bogle's mission the currency arrangement between Nepal and Tibet became disturbed. It appears that the authorities in Tibet suddenly insisted that the Tibetan coinage, which was debased with copper, should be considered as equal in value to the purer silver currency issued by the Kathmandu mint. The Gurkha government demanded that the debased coinage be recalled, as it was a source of disadvantage to its own merchants, or that, at least, a fair rate of exchange be established between the two currencies. Negotiations were protracted for nine or ten years, but the Tibetans would not yield. A period of crisis followed, when Nepalese coin was withdrawn altogether, and trade between the two countries suffered a great decline.[15] In addition, the Gurkhas were exasperated by the Tibetan habit of selling adulterated salt, and by their levying of excessive and arbitrary duties on Nepalese merchandise. That their complaints had been justified in the latter instance was fully confirmed later, when a member of the Tibetan council of state evinced his culpability by committing suicide to escape the effects of Imperial displeasure.

[15] Nepalese and Chinese sources agree on this interpretation: cf. Kirkpatrick, *Nepal*, pp. 339–40 with Li, *Tibet*, p. 244 n. 154. According to Bogle's information, and to that of Moorcroft's informant, it was the Nepalese coinage which had been debased. See Markham, op. cit., pp. 128–9; *P.R.N.W.*, p. 91.

The situation must have borne the appearance of an urgent crisis to the Gurkhas because, although their field army was fully occupied in the western hills, they decided to risk Chinese retribution and make a punitive expedition into Tibet. This was in 1788. The gamble was not so ill-advised as it might seem. Their attack was unexpected, and the principal of the three generals sent by the Emperor to advise the importunate Tibetans preferred not to press the issue to a trial of strength. Instead, he came to a secret understanding with the Gurkhas and sent a false report to the Emperor. The Nepalese were promised a yearly tribute from the monastic authorities. The bond was not honoured, and in 1791 the Gurkhas invaded again. The Chinese Resident withdrew the new infant Panchen Lama from Shigatsé, the treasurer of the Tashilunpo Monastery fled and the lamas, pleading divine injunction, refused to resist. While the Gurkha army pillaged the monastery, the Imperial reinforcements ordered from Szechwan dallied; the principal Chinese general drowned himself; and all Tibet was in commotion.

When the Emperor learned what had happened, he had the timorous Resident of Shigatsé shackled with a cangue, and sent his best Manchu general, Fou-kang-an, at the head of an immense expeditionary army to chastise the Gurkhas. Meanwhile, the Gurkha force, gorged with plunder, had withdrawn into Nepal, leaving detachments to guard the passes. During June 1792 the Chinese army expelled the last Gurkhas from Tibet and prepared to invade Nepal. The Kirong pass was negotiated by Fou-kang-an himself, while detachments on either flank diverted the enemy's attention. The Gurkhas were pursued to the banks of the river Tadi, only twenty miles from Kathmandu, where they turned and made a desperate stand. It is said that the Chinese general, in a fury, drove forward his men by turning his own guns on them from the rear, and overwhelmed his adversary with a human avalanche. The Gurkhas, dismayed by their failure to secure aid from the British, had no resource save submission. They surrendered their plunder and their prisoners, and agreed to send a regular tribute to Peking, as vassals of the Celestial Empire. The old economic dispensation was cancelled, and money struck in Kathmandu was thenceforth banned in Tibet, where a new mint with Chinese experts was set up. All foreign trade with Tibet was subjected to the strictest regulations, and Tibetans were allowed to trade with outsiders only under licence and by approved routes. The Chinese Residents were made the sole medium of communication with other countries, and measures were taken which subjected ingress by foreigners to close official control. The Gurkhas' attempt to frustrate the closure of Tibet by the Chinese had merely precipitated that event. The Gurkhas did not relinquish hopes of retrieving their old privilege of minting currency for Tibet, but the tone of their solicitations in 1814 was markedly different from their earlier pugnacious demands.

The Gurkhas had received the painful and unequivocal warning that Tibet was claimed territory; but the admonition was clearly intended for the British as well. The military successes of the Company in India had made it an object of apprehension and mistrust even in Bogle's day, and now its failure to afford assistance to Fou-kang-an when so requested did not go unnoticed at Peking. Unknown to the British, the Gurkhas had completed the vitiation of the Company's reputation by their practice of dressing their own soldiers in red uniforms. Misled by the costume of the Nepalese, the Chinese general reported to the Emperor that not only had the British refused to help, they had also sent troops to aid the enemy. Lord Macartney was on an embassy at the Court of Peking when the Emperor received this intelligence, and shortly after was given an audience of leave. A letter was written by the King of England to the Emperor in 1795, explaining that in fact the British had attacked the Gurkhas in the rear. This did not impress the Chinese, who apparently assumed it to mean that the Company had taken advantage of the situation to further their own plans for conquering Nepal. A close watch was kept on English activities in northern India from then on, and officers on the Tibetan frontier were ordered to admit no Europeans. The Chinese *Deba*, or viceroy, of Gartok who was responsible for allowing the expedition led by the English traveller Moorcroft to enter Tibet in 1812 was summoned to Lhasa in disgrace. Irritating though it was to the British, in the eyes of the Chinese both Europeans and Gurkhas were tarred with the same brush. Nor perhaps were they so unjustified in their refusal to differentiate. The Gurkhas were emulating the British in every way; not only in the discipline and dress of their army, but also, in this instance, in determining to preserve economic privileges by force of arms. The war fought against Tibet by the Gurkhas in 1788 had not a little similarity to the one fought by the British at the other end of the Chinese Empire in 1842.

While, therefore, in the 1770s it had seemed that a war against

Nepal could open access to Tibet, by 1814 it had become quite clear that it would be unrealistic to suppose that any form of military activity in the Himalayas could achieve that object. Events in the meantime had demonstrated that the principal artificial obstacle to trans-Himalayan trade was not the presence of the Gurkhas in Nepal, so much as the jealousy of the Chinese guardians of Tibet. The fact had been brought home with startling clarity to the British in Calcutta by 'the extraordinary spectacle of a numerous Chinese force occupying a position which probably afforded it a distant view of the valley of the Ganges and the richest of the East India Company's possessions'.[16] There were, moreover, no grounds for supposing that the Chinese would have been less hostile towards the British had the Gurkhas not aroused their resentment. The Manchus' suspicion of outsiders was inveterate, and it was obvious that Europeans were the last in favour of whom they would discriminate. In the final analysis, the consequences of the Gurkhas' efforts to open Tibet had served less to embarrass the British than to enlighten them as to the inevitable outcome of a similar policy on their own part.

As the British became more powerful in India, they became more knowledgeable; but sometimes knowledge came too late to be of positive use. Such was the case with facts about the shawl-wool trade, which came to light after British sway had been extended westwards to the Sutlaj river. Textiles were the oldest and most important of the industrial arts of India, and the artisans of Kashmir were second to none in skill and fame as weavers. The gossamer softness, the beauty and durability of the long decorated wraps produced by the looms of Kashmir were admired by emperors of India, sovereigns of Persia and, not least, by merchants of England—who were no bad judges when it came to something made of wool. In the eighteenth century the Persian word *shal*, corrupted to 'shawl', passed into the English language. It was known that the great secret of the shawls lay in their raw material, which was more a down than a wool, being protected by the exterior coarse hair of the animal. The shawl-wool goat was found only in Tibet, and early attempts to introduce it into India and Persia failed. As we have seen, Warren Hastings was particularly anxious that Bogle should bring back some specimens of the animal. In the event it was Turner who managed to send some emasculated

[16] Kirkpatrick, *Nepal*, p. vi.

goats to Calcutta, but the unfortunate creatures expired in the suffocating heat. The trade would obviously have to be tapped at its natural source; but full facts concerning the commerce were not available until 1812, when William Moorcroft went to western Tibet.

Moorcroft, Superintendent of the East India Company's Stud, was thinking how best to improve the strain of the indigenous cavalry horse of Hindustan. This had become necessary because political events (the consolidation of Ranjit Singh's power in the Punjab and the withdrawal, after 1806, of British protection from the petty states below the Punjab in Rajputana) had made it difficult to continue acquiring horses from west of the Indus, where, in Kabul especially, fine-blooded animals were bred. For some years the Company had been compelled to rely on horses from its own territories for its cavalry mounts, and these beasts were small, weak, and vicious. In 1812 Moorcroft, in company with Hyder Hearsey, made a journey into western Tibet, travelling through the Gurkha province of Garhwal, ostensibly in search of better horses for breeding purposes, but in reality also in quest of the shawl-wool goat. It was the beginning of a private crusade for Moorcroft, a solitary, restless man with wild ideas, whose lifelong ambition was to open to the British the trade and resources of trans-Himalayan Asia. During his journey of 1812 he learnt about the Kashmirian-Ladakh monopoly, the location of the best wool-growing areas, and the organization of the trade. He brought back more than fifty shawl-wool goats to Moradabad, with hopes of introducing the breed into Scotland or Wales and, even more of a triumph, succeeded in buying wool in markets which were the preserve of the Ladakhis. This, he decided, was the beginning of a new epoch in British trade. But it was not so. Moorcroft's revelations came too late to draw the interest of his employers to the western hills, because while they had been dallying with Nepal and Bhutan in the east, Ranjit Singh had been forging a Sikh empire in the Punjab which took the shawl-wool trade into its embrace. He had made his designs on Kashmir obvious, and had so far established his eligibility to participate in the trade that merchants from Amritsar were allowed to buy wool in Gartok. Roads had been built, leading direct from Ladakh to Amritsar, which were causing the decline of the old route along the Sutlaj valley through Rampur and drawing the bulk of the shawl-wool trade through Sikh territory.

It seemed obvious, then, in 1814, that any attempt by the British to capture a share of the shawl-wool trade would prove objectionable to Ranjit Singh; and the political situation at this time made it something of a priority to avoid offending the Sikhs. British statesmen were having to reconsider all old ideas on the subject of the defence of India. In the time of Warren Hastings they had felt secure, confined as they were to Bengal and the Deccan, bounded by the sea in front and the territories of the Moguls and Marathas behind. Since then, however, frontiers had been pushed back, and states under British protection were found as far west as the left bank of the Sutlaj. Sea power alone could no longer defend the Company's possessions from external aggression, and thought had to be devoted to the problem of protecting the land routes which debouched into north-west India. The Hindu Kush passes were like the wings of a vast theatre, through which the prominent actors in Indian history had made their entry onto the ancestral stage of the Punjab plain. Conciliating the power which had control of the Punjab was an essential first step to preventing the drama of another invasion. Napoleon Bonaparte, fascinated by India, had definite plans to make the attempt in alliance first with Russia, then with Persia; and it became the primary object of British diplomacy to thwart his designs by making treaties with Persia, Afghanistan, Baluchistan and the Sikhs. The Sikhs were a special object of British vigilance, because Moorcroft had discovered that Russian agents were active in Kashmir and helping to discipline Ranjit Singh's infantry.[17] This caught the attention of the Court of Directors, which asked to be regularly informed of developments across the Sutlaj.

So far, we have examined political developments in India and Tibet which by 1814 would seem to have compelled a drastic modification, not to say the reversal, of the Himalayan policy conceived by early Governors of Bengal. But politics are only one side of the coin. Being primarily a trading concern, the East India Company might have risked the impolitic to secure the economically beneficial. It is therefore important to demonstrate that, simultaneously with political developments, changes had occurred in the

[17] In his letter of 7 Sept. 1812 to the Political Secretary (Pol. Cons., 18 Dec. 1812, no. 29, paras. 30–2), Moorcroft expressed his conviction that France was using Russia's ambitions in Central Asia as a means of promoting her own plans to invade India; and that the oppressed and ineffectively defended Gurkha provinces in the western Himalayas would be the natural corridor for a Franco-Russian incursion.

economic interests and outlook of the Company, which made trans-Himalayan trade commercially unimportant.

The East India Company had originally been interested in trans-Himalayan trade for three reasons:

First, because the drain of treasure from India was a cause of great concern, and Tibet was known to be a rich source of precious metals.

Second, because Tibet and the trans-Himalayan countries promised a natural and unlimited market for English woollen cloth, whose appeal in the tropical and sub-tropical peninsula was obviously limited. It was held that foreign trade should justify itself by creating an increase in the national store of treasure, and the East India Company was regarded as being under a special obligation to meet its liabilities in India as far as possible by the sale of English staple produce, rather than by the exportation of specie. In 1708 the United Company of Merchants trading to the East Indies accepted the obligation to export goods to the value of £100,000 annually, in return for its monopoly of the East Indian trade. The first war with Nepal and the early attempts to open Tibet were products of the Company's mercantilist tradition—the tradition of opening new markets and fostering new demands for English staples by exercising the power of arms and taking the risks which the privilege of monopoly postulated. Such quasi-scientific, quasi-commercial expeditions as those undertaken by Bogle and Turner were expressions of a type of enterprise which traced its origins back to the time when the old Merchant Adventurers first weighed anchor. Warren Hastings expressed this attitude when he wrote:

. . . it is impossible to point out the precise advantages which either the opening of new channels of trade, or in obtaining redress of grievances, or in extending the privileges of the Company, may result from such an intercourse; like the navigation of unknown seas which we explored not for the attainment of any certain or prescribed object, but for the discovery of what they may contain. In so new and remote a search, we can only propose to adventure for possibilities. The attempt may be crowned with the most splendid and substantial success; or it may terminate in the mere gratification of useless curiosity.[18]

Third, and finally, because a trans-Himalayan commerce would provide access to the shawl-wool trade. Such a unique and profit-

[18] Quoted by Alistair Lamb, 'Tibet in Anglo-Chinese Relations, 1767–1842, Part 1'; *Journal of the Royal Asiatic Society*, parts 3 & 4: 1957, pp. 165–6.

able commodity would have attracted the attention of a trading government under any circumstances, but from the 1770s the East India Company had a special reason for being interested. It was finding it increasingly difficult to transfer funds from India to England. Large sums of money were required in London. After paying dividends on East India stock, the Court of Directors needed funds to cash bills of exchange drawn on it in the possession of creditors and servants who wished to remit their assets from India to England; to provide for the upkeep of the Company's various establishments at home; to pay retirement pensions to the Company's servants; and to buy the English goods sent out to India and China as exports. As profits from the China trade, which were realized in London, were insufficient to meet these requirements, it became necessary to remit to England part of the assets which the Company realized in India. The export of bullion from India was deprecated, and the usual mode of remittance, that of buying goods in India and selling them in England, was becoming unprofitable. The produce brought from India, which constituted the Company's annual investment, was mainly cotton piece goods, which the Company manufactured itself in its own factories. But from the 1770s, the growth of the English cotton industry was reducing the home market for Indian cotton goods, and as a vehicle of remittance the trade in piece goods was transferring money to London only inefficiently, and running at a loss as a purely commercial enterprise. It is not possible to ascertain the exact state of the import trade from India, because the liabilities incurred on account of the India and China trade were not kept separate in the Company's books; but even according to the Company's estimates the import trade from India occasionally indicated a deficit, and it is probable that in fact the immense profits of the China trade were disguising a more considerable loss on the Indian. What nobody could dispute was the fact that funds realized in London from all sources did not meet expenses, and that the English establishment was running at a heavy loss.[19] The Company had on several occasions had to apply

---

[19] *Mins. of Ev.*, 1813, p. 485. It was impossible to define with certainty the nature of the loss. In conformity to its mercantilist ethos the Company made up its accounts as a balance of resources between England and India, maintaining no separation between its trading and its political operations. Hence, the figures could only show with certainty that the balance of payments was in favour of India (ibid., pp. 485, 505). In order to decide whether trade was subsidizing territorial administration, as the Company claimed, or territorial revenues trade,

to the Treasury for loans. Under such circumstances, a new Indian article of investment which promised to be not only a vehicle of remittance but also a means to profit was bound to arouse a lot of interest. This explains in great measure the sustained interest in the shawl-wool trade and in plans to manufacture shawls for the English and European markets.

Here are three reasons, then, as they existed in the last decades of the eighteenth century, to explain the prevailing concern to extend the limit of British commercial interest across the Himalayas. In 1814, these reasons no longer existed.

By the outbreak of the Nepal War in 1814, the main channel by which treasure had been flowing out of India—the channel to China—had been blocked. Sending Indian bullion to China to pay for the Company's tea investment had latterly been an annual practice, dating from 1757. The procedure had been necessary because few English commodities could be sold profitably enough in China to make it possible to pay for tea with exports alone. The practice continued for some thirty years, before it was realized that the produce of India could be used to finance the China investment. Indian raw cotton found a ready market in China, and by exploiting the demand for this commodity the flow of bullion out of India was soon stopped. The other product of India which the Chinese needed was opium, and this they absorbed with insatiable voracity.[20] Its importation was illegal, but private 'country' merchants

as its critics maintained, it would have been necessary to regard Britain and British India as a single field of economic operation and recast accounts as a balance between trade and territorial administration. This is precisely what Parliament ordered the Company to do in 1813; and when the affairs of the Company were re-examined in 1832 the new method in its books made it clear that the profits of commerce not only covered the payment of dividends, but supplied up to 25 per cent of a territorial deficit (1832 *Report*, pp. 51–3, 60). But the enormous commercial profits derived entirely from the China trade, not the Indian (ibid., p. 73).

[20] Michael Greenberg, *British Trade and the Opening of China, 1800–42*, p. 9. The importation of opium into China gave so much alarm to the Chinese government, that a further Imperial Decree banning the drug was published in 1800. The Company had long since prohibited the traffic in its own ships (Morse, *Chronicles*, vol. ii, p. 327), but the volume imported from India by pirates did not abate (Greenberg, op. cit., p. 221), and this illegal traffic was all to the advantage of the Company. Most of the opium was paid for with bullion, and much of this found its way back to India and into the Calcutta Government's treasuries, since the Company retained the monopoly of the internal trade in opium from its own territories, and derived enormous revenue from the excise thereon (*Mins. of Ev.*, 1832, Sec. 2, pp. 35, 45).

—that is, those engaged in the local trade of the Indian Ocean and China Sea—did not scruple to carry on a pirate trade, and in a short time the exploitation of this black market swung the balance of the trade from China's advantage to India's. The opium being paid for largely in bullion, treasure was soon flowing from China to India— a trend which was well established before the end of the first decade of the nineteenth century. In 1814, the outflow from the Bengal exchequer had by no means ceased, and the Governor-General complained of the demands for bullion from England, Mauritius, Ceylon, Java and the embassy in Persia; but shortages were transitory and the problem was by no means so urgent as it had been in the 1770s. Treasure was no longer scarce in India. So much is shown by the fact that loans could easily be raised to provide the government with cash—in excess even of its needs.

Eagerness to open new markets for English woollens had languished by 1814. Economic thinking still placed importance on the prosperity of the old staple industry, it is true. British woollens enjoyed preferential tariffs in Indian ports until 1845, and the prohibition on the export of raw wool from England was not repealed until 1825. But the East India Company had made it quite clear that its share of the good work would continue only so long as it retained its monopoly and privileges. 'If the private traders under new regulations should interfere with the Company's regular trade . . . the Company must be obliged to reduce their exports of the raw materials of the country, and the woollens of the country, in some degree . . .', said the Company's Accountant-General in 1813, and his reasoning is evident. The successful promotion of the sale of English goods in India depended on a careful nurturing of the market, and this was made possible only by the instruments of monopoly and privilege. Yet faith in monopoly and privilege was increasingly sapped by the spreading popularity of a new gospel—that according to Adam Smith, who had little to say in favour of the East India Company. The Company was forced to make its first concessions in 1783, when it undertook to supply a certain amount of freight annually for private traders; and thereafter the clamour of private merchants, who wanted to export to India on their own terms and in their own ships, became loud and persistent. The question of the renewal of the Company's Charter, due to expire in 1813, engrossed the attention of Parliament for a period five years before the event, during which the Company's apologists fought an eloquent defence; but there was no disguising the fact that the whole system of restriction, monopoly and privilege was moribund, and it is no wonder that the old eagerness to open markets beyond the Himalayas declined *pari passu*. After 1813, when the Indian trade was finally made open to all private traders, to have invoked the principles of Warren Hastings—intellectual curiosity, moral obligation, adventure—would have seemed quaint and outmoded. The opening of the Indian market registered a change in outlook among the British concerned with affairs of India. The servants of the Company were becoming more involved in collecting revenues, guarding frontiers and dispensing justice than in trading; and the men who inherited the legacy of commerce knew no debt to the old traditions of exploration, pioneering and willingness to risk all for the tale of an eldorado beyond. They acted more as merchants, less as adventurers, exploiting already established markets, calculating maximum profit and minimum risk, and treating the whole idea of trans-Himalayan trade with increasing scepticism.

So the inspiration and the sense of obligation to open new markets in India was fading; but, let it be at once admitted, so too was the necessity. The fact is that British woollens had not been faring too badly in India, though one would never think so, to read the evidence of witnesses called before the House of Commons in 1813. One after another they asseverated that the Indian market for British goods was glutted; that Indians had neither the inclination nor the means to buy European goods; and that the warehouses were already overflowing with unsold imports from England. They spoke impressively, and from experience; but a brief glance at the figures reveals a different situation:

Date	Value of European goods imported into India.[21]	Value of European goods left unsold in Indian warehouses at the end of the year.[22]
1791–2	£206,791	£401,512
1808–9	£615,982	£1,181,718

[21] See *Appendix 5 to IIIrd Report, 1811* (this shows the invoice value of goods and stores imported); and *Appendix 35 to IVth Report, 1812* (invoice value of stores alone). By subtracting the latter figures from the former, the invoice value of goods alone is obtained. The prime cost, as given in the text, is obtained by dividing the result by 110 and then multiplying by 100.

[22] Reckoned as two-thirds of the whole, as given in *Appendix 2 to IIIrd*

This single comparison of two years discloses a state of affairs that was typical. The proportion of goods remaining unsold at the end of successive years stayed in almost constant relation to the amount of goods imported. This means that the Indian market for English woollens—which comprised the bulk of the imports—was steadily expanding. This is not surprising, because more and more sections of the Indian population were coming into the sphere of British influence, and more native princes seemed to be dressing their soldiers, after the British fashion, in red broadcloth. Probably the agency of private traders helped, between 1793 and 1813, to reduce the price of English goods and extend their sale, but their shipments consisted mostly of wine and beer. It was the Company which, even after its monopoly was withdrawn in 1813, continued to export by far the greater part of the English woollens which found their way to India, and these were sold for increasingly higher profits as mechanization reduced the prime cost. The Company finally stopped exporting English commodities in the 1820s, but only because it did not wish to continue realizing assets in India while it remained so difficult to transfer them to London, and because its ships were becoming too full of troops and stores to carry goods for sale as well. The situation was, then, that a new fashion in economic thought, and a spontaneous extension of the Indian market had changed the whole nature of England's trade with India in the period between George Bogle's mission to Tibet and Lord Hastings's reverie in December 1814. The profoundest change—the supersession of woollens by cotton goods as the staple British product—was yet to come; but still, enough had happened by 1814 to make the attitude of Warren Hastings outmoded, and his Himalayan policy irrelevant.

On the other hand, the export trade to China was a cause of grave concern. The Company still felt an obligation to push the sale of British staples in China, because Parliament continued to allow it an unmitigated monopoly of the trade with that country. But it was proving a vexatious duty. The Company seems to have experimented persistently and diligently with new varieties of woollens and metals, and the amount of English goods actually

---

Report, 1811 (where the prime cost is presumably stated). Goods and stores from Europe were not accounted for separately from those purchased in India. The estimate of two-thirds of the one to one-third of the other was that used by the Company's own accountants.

exported to Canton steadily increased. They were sold, too—but only at a considerable loss. In the books of the Company's factory at Canton, for the seventeen seasons from 1792 to 1809, the accounts of only three show a net profit, and the total deficit over the whole period amounted to close on a million sterling. Even then, the profits on tea were disguising losses incurred by selling British produce. Until 1810, the Company's agents at Canton had bartered their woollens for tea—this being the only way of inducing Chinese merchants to accept them. Such a way of dealing in effect increased the price of tea, because the Chinese naturally expected a favourable exchange when accepting goods which were so difficult to sell on the Chinese market. So a thousand pounds' worth of woollens bought much less tea than a thousand pounds in cash. By paying partly in goods, the Company was foregoing a portion of its profits on tea, and affording a subvention to British staples which did not show on the accounts, where the woollens sold were rated at their barter price, and not at their market money value.

By 1814, the port of Canton had become the focus of the East India Company's trading activities, and the economic priority of the day was to widen the Chinese market for British and Indian goods, and improve the conditions under which English merchants operated in China. English interests in the China trade were at this time of crucial importance. India's potentiality as a tea-growing country was unknown, and the United Kingdom relied exclusively on China for its supplies of what had become its national beverage. An approximate average of one and a half millions sterling was invested in tea every year, and the returns hovered around the two and a half million mark. These were astronomical sums at a time when the national revenue did not exceed about sixteen millions. Yet, to carry on a commerce of such magnitude, the agents of the East India Company were allowed access to only fourteen specially licensed Chinese merchants, and their sole establishment on Imperial territory was a modest factory at Canton, where they were suffered to reside only during the season of business. The buying and selling, the bartering and chaffering once finished, and the ships once laden and under weigh for England, the Supracargoes, as the Company's agents were called, were obliged to retire to the Portuguese island colony of Macao, where they carried on their affairs until the opening of the ensuing season. They were forced to trade under the most frustrating and vexatious conditions. The benefit of open market competition was precluded by associations of Chinese merchants, and the local officials denied the English all access to the machinery of legal redress, manipulating the commerce in a spirit of private interest and petty despotism. It was a rankling thought that the prohibition of opium had reduced the guarantee of security for an essential trade to the corruptibility of local mandarins. The problems of the British merchants trading to China were matters of national concern, requiring to be handled by royal ambassadors rather than emissaries from a mere trading corporation. Thus it was that Lords Macartney and Amherst journeyed to Peking, the first in 1792 and the second in 1816, to plead the case of British merchants before the Celestial Emperor by authority of credentials from the King. The war with Nepal, intruding upon this delicate and crucial process of ingratiation, was an inconvenience and an embarrassment. Sir George Staunton, one of the Supracargoes, affirmed in 1813 that the trade with China was on a precarious footing, and 'liable to be disturbed by provocations which might be considered of a slight nature'.[23] It was not forgotten that Nepal was now, in theory at least, a vassal of China, and it seemed that an attack on her might well qualify as such a provocation and jeopardize Britain's most vital commercial interests in the East. Lord Hastings took care that the Supracargoes were given full details concerning the causes of the war and the attitude of the Calcutta government, so that an equitable case might be presented to the Chinese authorities. Major Bradshaw, Political Agent with the main invading force, was instructed to inform any Chinese officers who might confront the army that the British objectives were entirely punitive and not acquisitive; and it was his reluctance to offend the Chinese which helped determine Lord Hastings not to annex Nepal after her defeat. Recognizing that the maintenance of peace and amity with Peking was of 'such vast consequence to the commercial interests of the Company and indeed of the United Kingdom', he was furthermore prepared to withdraw the British Residency established in Kathmandu, and even to give tacit acquiescence to an Imperial occupation of Nepal, if this would mollify the Chinese.[24] Lord Castlereagh, the Foreign Secretary, took pains to brief Lord Amherst on the British position *vis-à-vis* Nepal before the departure of the Ambassador for China, and enjoined

[23] *Minutes of Evidence, 1813*, p. 439.
[24] Sec. Cons., 14 Sept. 1816, no. 43.

'great circumspection and discretion' if the topic was raised.[25] The only way in which it was suggested the war might help improve British commerce was by opening a trans-Tibet access to Peking, whereby direct representation might be made to the Emperor and the Canton officials circumvented. This notion was proffered by the Supracargoes, but only after they had heard that plans for the invasion of Nepal had been made. There is no question of its having influenced the government's determination to go to war. The idea seems to have gained no currency in Calcutta, where there was so little reason to expect that Imperial officials in Tibet would be any less obstructive than those in Canton, that the possibility was subsequently never even put to the test.

So far we have shown that of the three reasons which induced the Calcutta government to adopt a Himalayan policy in Warren Hastings's day, two had been superseded by 1814. The flow of treasure had been reversed by the development of the China trade; and the need to extend the Indian market for British staples had been eclipsed by the urgent necessity of removing obstacles which were impeding the sale of British and Indian produce in China. The shift of interest away from India to China not only made it seem less important to breach that mighty wall of snow and ice which separated India from Tibet; it made it seem prejudicial to commercial interests to try to, because the risk of offending China was involved. The third reason why the East India Company became interested in Himalayan trade was, it will be remembered, because it offered the possibility of making available another Indian commodity—shawl wool—which the Company would be able to use as a vehicle for transferring funds from India to England profitably. The days of cotton piece goods as a means of remittance, numbered even in Warren Hastings' time, were virtually over in 1814. English cottons had captured the home market, and the re-export trade, having enjoyed a brief prosperity after the 1799 Warehouse Act,[26] when almost all the calicoes from India were re-exported, had been killed by the Berlin Decrees, by which Napoleon closed almost all Europe to goods from England. Even private traders, after giving a slight stimulus to the import trade from India, had lost interest, and it became difficult to remit funds to England by buying, in

[25] Morse, *Chronicles*, iii, p. 282.
[26] This exempted goods destined for re-export to Europe from all but a small warehouse duty.

India, bills of exchange on the London branches of private houses of agency. The investments of these houses, chiefly in indigo, silk and sugar, were simply not large enough to require substantial advances from the Company in India. The Company continued to import raw silk and indigo at a loss, solely because there was no other way (apart from exporting bullion) of transferring resources directly from India to England.[27] Under these circumstances, interest in the shawl-wool trade did persist: to gain a share of it, to establish shawl manufactories, and to send a new and exotic luxury for sale in England seemed just the treatment to galvanize a jaded commerce. In 1815 it was decided to build a factory at Kotgarh on the Sutlaj, designed to attract some of the trade which was traditionally confined to Ladakh and Kashmir—though without success, it appears, until the final subjugation of Kashmir by Ranjit Singh in 1819 sent a number of refugee weavers into British territory, and even then obtaining wool remained an almost insuperable problem. However, the remittance problem had also been transformed and diminished by commercial developments. True, it was still difficult enough to transmit funds *directly* from India to London; but since 1774 a way of remitting *indirectly* had been discovered. This involved selling the Indian investment in China, buying tea with the proceeds, and realizing the profit on tea in London, in the usual way. In other words, assets were remitted to England via the agency of Canton. Thus while the sale of Indian opium in China by private merchants brought great quantities of treasure into India, the sale there of Indian cotton by the Company provided an alternative solution to the problem which at first had aroused interest in the shawl-wool trade. After all its other factories had been closed, an establishment was kept in operation at Bombay by the Company for the provision of cotton wool for the China market. The sale of Indian cotton became so important as a means of buying tea, that, later, it even began to be feared lest any increase in the sale of English twist and piece goods at Canton should adversely affect this means of remitting funds from India.

So, for the third and final time we find that a problem which in 1774 had led people to regard trans-Himalayan trade as desirable led them in 1814 to be more concerned about the security of the

---

[27] *Mins. of Ev.*, 1832, Sec. 2, p. 126. Saltpetre was also imported, in conformity to the requirement of Parliament. Indian raw cotton, because of its coarseness, was not favoured in Britain (ibid., pp. 276–7).

East India Company's commerce with China. The trade routes
linking London with Canton were the spinal nerves of the body
economic, and upon their soundness depended its whole health.
Free access through all the high passes into Tibet would have been
less valued than was a passport to China and an audience vouch-
safed by the Son of Heaven. No journeys through the frozen wastes
of central Asia were as momentous as those to Peking in a palan-
quin, pertaining as the latter did to the fate of a commercial empire
and involving as they did the harshest of all privations—that of an
Englishman of his dignity. Whether or not Lord Amherst should
kotow to the Chinese Emperor was an issue of much more import
than whether William Moorcroft was dead or alive somewhere out
in Turkestan. Wherever men pondered the issues of the day—in
brown-panelled rooms in Leadenhall Street; behind classical white
porticos in Calcutta; and over madeira and cheroots in English
houses in Macao—on one point they were always agreed, namely,
that the China trade must not be jeopardized. The English were in
no position to bargain or blackmail, because the Chinese did not,
in their own view, depend at all on foreign trade, and they made it
clear that trading facilities were in the interest only of those to
whom they were granted. They were no acknowledgement of
Chinese need, only a token of Imperial magnanimity. No, the only
way to retain trading privileges was to avoid studiously all policy
which might give umbrage to the Imperial court; and to extend
those privileges required conciliation and cajolery.

By 1814, then, British Indian diplomacy was being dictated by
two priorities: first, the necessity of good relations with the Sikhs;
second, the indispensability of a benevolent Chinese court. A
Himalayan policy was incompatible with both, and if we glance
over British diplomacy in the quarter century before the Nepal War,
we can see how such a policy was abandoned as the political and
economic processes which we have been describing developed.

In 1792 the Gurkhas agreed to sign a commercial treaty with the
Company, probably in the expectation that they would in return
receive help against the Chinese, who were at that time hammering
at the walls of Kathmandu itself. However, the Governor-General
of the time, Lord Cornwallis, made it clear to the Nepal government that he could not endanger the Company's commercial interests by fighting the Chinese. The most he dared to do was to
insinuate a British agent as peacemaker. This was Captain William

Kirkpatrick, the first English official to visit Kathmandu. Peace was made before he arrived, but he went on just the same in order to spy out the land and to supervise the implementation of the commercial treaty. The commerce in question was the purely local one between the Nepalese lowlands and northern India; the treaty made no mention of Tibetan trade. A subsequent native agent, Abdul Qadir, sent to Kathmandu by Sir John Shore in 1795, gathered useful information about it and suggested the setting up of marts for Tibetans in the coldest parts of the Company's dominions. It was soon after this that the government took measures to encourage the resort of Tibetan merchants to Rangpur; but no further effort was made to carry out Abdul Qadir's proposal.

In 1800, after the palace revolution in Nepal, the Raja, Rana Bahadur, was obliged to have recourse to the age-old expedient of the *personae non gratae* of Indian politics—a pilgrimage to Benares, on the Ganges. Exiled ex-rajas were irresistible playthings to the new Governor-General, Lord Wellesley, who had a penchant for intrigue, and he sent off an agent, Captain Knox, to Benares. Wellesley's idea was to act as arbiter in the political quarrel in Nepal, and restore Rana Bahadur as a puppet of the Company. There was no hope of this being accomplished, because the quondam Raja had no intention of being manipulated by the British; but the interest shown by the Company in the fugitive at Benares had a useful effect on Damodar Panre's government in Kathmandu, which agreed to a new treaty and an exchange of Residents with Calcutta. It seemed that the Company had at last acquired a foothold in Nepal. But the whole affair smacks of opportunism, and was really no part of a consistent Himalayan policy. Although the Nepalese durbar signed the treaty from a fear that the British would forcibly reinstate Rana Bahadur if it refused, the Governor-General had no such intention; and he was particularly careful that all clauses which might offend the Chinese were deleted from the treaty. Captain Knox went to Nepal as the first British Resident in 1801, and was instructed to obtain the maximum amount of information while arousing the minimum amount of suspicion. The very comprehensiveness of his instructions betrays extempore and opportunist thinking. He was required to investigate the possibility of facilitating commerce with Tibet through Nepal; but the injunction was given no particular emphasis, and was rather lost among the detailed instructions designed to promote local trade, especially in timber, between the Nepalese Tarai and north India. As it happened, the embassy was rather a shambles. From fear of offending China, Knox was enjoined to use no threats and, helpless before the obstruction and the prevarication of the durbar after the sudden and dramatic return of the senior queen from Benares, was left no resource save that of withdrawing with some show of pique. Had the British been sincerely interested, they could have retaliated instead by setting up their own government in Nepal. The occasion had never been more propitious for the extension of British hegemony into the eastern Himalayas. The political confusion in Kathmandu was such that even prominent Gurkhas desired to become vassals of the Company, and at about the same time the Raja of Sikkim appealed to the British for aid in expelling the Gurkhas from his country. But the Calcutta government took no heed of these opportunities. Knox withdrew, the treaty was dissolved and Sikkim was left to its fate. Had China been offended, the advantages would just not have been worth the price.

Thereafter, the Company's government's main concern was to avoid all involvement in Himalayan projects and politics. Calcutta appears to have been somewhat nonplussed by the home authorities' approval of Thomas Manning's plan to voyage to Lhasa from India. Manning was an eccentric, who had learned Chinese at Canton. He seems to have had no motive apart from private curiosity. After a bizarre journey disguised as a Chinese he did in fact become the first Englishman to reach Lhasa and set eyes on the Dalai Lama; but it does not appear that he received any support or assistance from Calcutta. At about the same time, Ochterlony tried to persuade the government to take up the cause of the hill Rajas of Garhwal and Sirmur, who had been dispossessed by the Gurkhas— only, as we have seen, to find that Lord Minto was distinctly cool towards the idea. Similar circumspection characterized Minto's handling of the border disputes with the Nepalese in north Bengal, where he showed that his inclination was rather to appease than to stand firm. When Moorcroft, footsore but triumphant, returned from Tibet in 1812, he did not receive the official acclaim he expected. There had been an unfortunate brush with the Gurkha authorities on the return journey through Garhwal, and his party had been arrested and roughly handled. The Nepalese Raja professed himself offended by such an intrusion into his territory by men who were uninvited and in disguise. Minto was all the more irritated by Moorcroft's expedition because it had been undertaken without sanction from Calcutta. Moorcroft was reproved for his cavalier and clandestine conduct, and told that if official permission had been requested it would not have been granted, seeing that such an expedition was dangerous, offensive to Nepal and directed to objects which were outside the prescribed duties of Superintendent of the Stud.

It might at first seem that the annexation of Kumaun after the Nepal War confutes the argument advanced above. Lord Hastings's interest in the province was undoubtedly stimulated by the fact that it offered access to Tibet and the shawl-wool trade; but if we examine the circumstances under which the decision to annex was made, we shall see that the attractions of a trading connection with Tibet were not present in the minds of members of the government when they determined to go to war. Preparations were being made for a conflict from the middle of June 1814, the plan being to commence operations at the beginning of the ensuing cold season. The idea that the Gurkha territories west of the Kali river might, if captured, offer passages into Tibet, evolved from the extensive inquiries of the interim period. One of the government's informants was Hyder Hearsey, and in memoranda of his was mention of the Niti and Mana passes, which lead from Garhwal into Tibet. This caught the attention of government, and Hearsey was asked for further details. On 24 August he wrote supplying more information, and described Garhwal with its rich valley, Dehra Dun, as a potentially thriving entrepôt for trans-Himalayan trade. The Governor-General was now intrigued by the possibilities which the province offered, and he contemplated annexing Garhwal 'not so much with a view to revenue as for the security of commercial communications with the country where the shawl wool is produced'.[28] Soon, however, it became obvious that Kumaun offered even better access to Tibet than did Garhwal. Knowledge of Kumaun's rich natural resources had already determined Hastings to claim the province as part of the just prize of war, and as it was clear that Kumaun offered the better trade routes as well, it was no longer necessary to consider annexing Garhwal. Only Dehra Dun would probably be retained, for purely strategic reasons.

There was no question of the war with Nepal's being undertaken in order to secure the trade routes through the western Gurkha

[28] *P.R.N.W.*, p. 65.

provinces. As preparations for war evolved, information came to light, and it became apparent that the war could be given an additional justification by the acquisition of such trading advantages. It became obvious later that Hastings's interest in trans-Himalayan commerce was subordinate to his conception of strategic and political necessities, and it would be quite unconvincing to suggest that he inherited Warren Hastings's willingness to make war for the sake of that commerce. War once decided on, however, it would have been unnatural to forgo such incidental opportunities as promised to make it more worth the trouble and expense. By annexing Kumaun, several such opportunities were realized. Besides a corridor to Tibet, the province offered mineral and timber resources of great richness and a position of major strategic importance. The Sikhs had already shown an inclination to cross the Sutlaj on the plains, and it was arguable that they would not have resisted much longer similar temptations farther up, in the hills, where the Gurkhas had been proving troublesome to them. The Governor-General considered that, by establishing the Company's military presence in Kumaun, he had removed the threat of the Sikhs invading the cis-Sutlaj hills and 'taking in flank one of the most valuable and important positions of our northwest frontier line'. If he tended to expatiate more on the shawl wool theme, it was probably because he appreciated that reasons of commerce were still likely to appear more cogent to the London authorities, whose aversion to further annexations had to be borne in mind, and who viewed the war strictly as a means of preserving existing rights. But his real interests were not commercial. It is significant, for example, that at the outset of the war he told Major Bradshaw that a trade agreement with Nepal was to be considered as a dispensable part of the provisional peace treaty, and that at the end of the war he showed no enthusiasm at all for the commercial treaty with Sikkim, who now found herself freed from Gurkha domination. Sikkim was a natural gateway to Tibet, separated as she was from Bhutan on the east by the Chumbi Valley, a long finger of Tibetan territory which reaches over the Himalayan crest and points down to Bengal. Yet Captain Latter, in charge of negotiations with Sikkim, received no instructions concerning a commercial clause in the Company's pending treaty with that state until he announced that he had suggested to the Sikkim officers that they would derive advantage from a trade with north India—'[in order] that by the sale of mangeit,[29] beeswax, ivory and other articles the Raja might be furnished with funds for the payment of his troops'. The Governor-General's reaction to this modest design was very nonchalant. 'It might be proper,' Latter was informed, 'as it seems . . . to be expected, that an article should be inserted in the proposed arrangement, for encouraging a free commercial intercourse between the two states.' Then again, the following extract from a letter to Canton, dated June 1816, has a tone which contrasts strongly with the zeal of his letters to London:

The approximation of the British territories and of states subject to its [*sic*] [? protection][30] to the dominions of China, will probably lead to a more or less extended commercial intercourse with the provinces of the latter state near the Himala range. It will [? not be][30] in the [? nature of][30] our policy to endeavour to force this intercourse, but we shall of course feel disposed to give every fair encouragement to it.

Actions were in fact even more cautious than the most guarded words; and far from 'every fair encouragement', the Governor-General displayed a diffidence which must have caused sad disappointment to those who had hoped the war would promote trans-Himalayan trade. William Moorcroft could hardly wait for the fighting to end to exploit the openings provided by the acquisition of Kumaun. He was well acquainted with Ahmed Ali, one of the Kashmirian merchants at Patna, who offered his services as *gomastha* (agent) should government wish to test the possibilities of a commercial communication with Lhasa. Moorcroft was eager to send him on an experimental expedition there, by way of Kumaun and the Garhwal passes, ostensibly as a private merchant (to avoid suspicion), but in reality under the government's sponsorship. This idea was redolent of the experiment of 1795, when Abdul Qadir was sent to Kathmandu to test the market for British goods. But the government now, fearing lest the agent should exceed his powers and compromise its position, was not all at keen to repeat the device. Ahmed Ali was given permission to go, but only as a private individual. The government undertook to find suitable samples of British merchandise, but only on the understanding that their value should constitute a loan at 6 per cent, without

---

[29] Mangeit, or Munjeet, is Bengal madder, whose roots are used in dyeing.

[30] Words omitted in India Office transcript, Sec. Cons., 15 June 1816, no. 17. But the sense is clear.

liability on the agent's part for losses incurred. Ahmed Ali chose
not to accept these terms, and the project lapsed.

Hastings had not forgotten that any attempt actually to exploit
the advantages he had so warmly invoked could easily endanger
the success of the more fundamental policy of propitiating China
and Ranjit Singh. The Imperial authorities at Lhasa had been
manifestly perturbed by the British invasion of Nepal, and Hastings
had no intention of deepening their suspicions either by sending
agents to Lhasa, or by hastening to utilize the passes to Tibet in the
western hills. Hastings ignored Moorcroft's suggestion that Ahmed
Ali should use the route through Kumaun and recommended instead that he travel by way of Sikkim. Captain Webbe was even
required to suspend his surveying operations on the Kumaun
border because they had brought him into contact with the Chinese
officials of Tibet. Lieutenant Ross, in charge of relations with the
cis-Sutlaj hill states afforded British protection after the war,
suggested that the government should probe the possibilities of a
commercial connection with the Raja of Kulu, a small state across
the Sutlaj which straddled the main trade route from Ladakh to the
Punjab. He pointed out that the trade in shawls and shawl-wool
could be tapped in Kulu, and drawn off into the Company's
territory. But in the view of the Governor-General, the plan was
'liable to considerable objections . . . since it might be viewed by
Ranjit Singh as an attempt . . . to form a connection with the
countries lying on the other side of the Sutlaj and as justifying any
measure on his part to renew his intercourse with the Sikh chiefs on
this side . . .'

Perhaps no one was more dismayed by the transience of the
revived interest in trade through the Himalayas than William
Moorcroft. He brooded over lost opportunities, and resolved either
to vindicate his convictions or crucify himself in the attempt. In
1819 he set off through Kumaun on an expedition to Bokhara,
encumbered with British merchandise which he hoped to dispose
of in the trans-Himalayan countries, thereby fostering new markets
for British goods. The government reluctantly sanctioned the
scheme, because again its ostensible object was to procure horses
for the stud; but it refused Moorcroft official designation and a
letter of introduction to the King of Bokhara. Fears of offending
Ranjit Singh undoubtedly weighed heavy with the government.
According to Hyder Hearsey, who refused to accompany Moorcroft

on this occasion, it would have been more favourable had he agreed to adopt the route from Bombay, via Persia, as suggested by Hearsey himself—presumably because this would have avoided contact with the Sikhs. Certain it is, that by subsequently interfering in the affair of Ranjit Singh's claims to Ladakh, Moorcroft brought down upon himself the severest official castigation. His mission was a failure. He reached Bokhara—disowned by his government, despoiled by bandits, chagrined and exhausted—but never returned. His fate remains mysterious. Trebeck, his companion, who also failed to return, wrote announcing his death in Afghanistan, in September 1825; but the French missionary, Huc, when in Lhasa in the 1840s, obtained convincing evidence of Moorcroft's arrival in that city, disguised as a Kashmirian, in 1826, and of his sojourn there, incognito, for a period of twelve years. It is just possible that in his mortification he chose to commune in exile with the shades of Warren Hastings, George Bogle and Samuel Turner, rather than return to the humiliation and disgrace which, he had been convinced, would await him in India if his expedition failed.

British Himalayan policy in 1814 was therefore fashioned by two types of necessity: that created by local border problems, and that deriving from more basic economic and strategic issues; and the two, like the surface and the deeper currents in a river, had ceased to pull in the same direction. The Nepal War was an interesting exercise in the art of diplomatic navigation, because it was an enterprise favoured by superficial but opposed by deeper forces; coming about because of the one set of exigencies, but in spite of the other. It was made acceptable by the need to define and secure the northern boundary of the East India Company's possessions, and to vindicate the Company's *raison d'être* as a government by defending the subjects under its protection; but at the same time it was made unwise by the more fundamental requirement of amity with the Chinese and the Sikhs. It was in the profounder forces of necessity that a metamorphosis had been wrought since 1774, the date of the first British expedition in quest of Himalayan trade. Their direction had ceased to correspond with that of superficial expediency. They now created powerful reasons against fighting another war with Nepal, and made it much more difficult to prevent such a war from turning into a diplomatic disaster.

IV

THE BENGAL ARMY

THE East India Company had three native armies, one at each of the three Presidencies of Madras, Bombay and Bengal. Each had its own British officer corps, general staff and commander-in-chief; but all were ultimately subject to the head of the Bengal force, who was Commander-in-Chief for all British possessions east of the Cape of Good Hope. These armies were regarded by the Company, and even by many of its critics, as wonders of their time. The high standard of loyalty and discipline inculcated in such large bodies of Asians by a tiny group of British officers was an object of pride and an habitual theme of self-congratulation. But by the time of the Nepal War complacency had outlived its justification. Serious flaws had begun to endanger the structure behind the variegated and impressive façade.

In 1814, the Bengal army was the largest of the East India Company's three. Robert Clive had formed the nucleus of a standing force in 1757, when he embodied and drilled a few hundred sepoys[1] according to the European method, in order to protect the Company's trading posts on the Bengal seaboard. Since then, the Company had become a dewan in its own right in north India, with territorial revenues to collect, frontiers to defend, and powerful rivals to intimidate; and the original small band had grown into an army of some 68,000 men. One of the most notable facts about its development was that it had latterly involved a shrinkage not only in the proportion, but in the gross amount of Europeans. When Clive had reorganized the army in 1765, he balanced a battalion of European infantry against every seven of sepoys, and in 1786 Cornwallis, convinced that the European contingent was 'the foundation upon which all [the Company's] power and dominion in this country must in many possible cases stand or fall', insisted on increasing the proportion to one to every six, thereby bringing the total of the Company's European infantry to about 6,000 men. These six single-battalion regiments had been reduced to three in

---

[1] Native infantrymen. From the Persian word '*sipahi*'—a soldier.

1796, and later to two; and in 1814 only one of these was serving in Bengal. Meanwhile the twenty-four native infantry battalions of 1765 had risen to fifty-four. The European foot artillery had remained constant, at three battalions. The native cavalry had increased from two to eight regiments,[2] while the only mounted European corps in 1814 was the single regiment of horse artillery. In numerical terms, the regular Bengal army on the eve of the Nepal War amounted to roughly 68,250 men of all ranks, of which the corps composed of Europeans accounted for about 3,200. The European contingent was thus only one-twentieth the size of the native army.[3] In government circles at home this ratio was regarded as quite unacceptable—Castlereagh, when President of the Board of Control, had reckoned that even one-seventh was too low—and over the years since 1788 the relationship had been rectified by the presence of royal regiments in India.

Partly because of technical difficulties (its recruiting officers did not bear King's commissions, and it had no recourse to martial law), and partly because of negligence and a failure to offer sufficient incentive, the Company's European corps had always been incomplete in numbers and wretched in quality. Cornwallis had been so alarmed by its inadequacy that he had adopted the view that all European troops in India should be employed by the King. The Court of Directors, however, had opposed augmentation of the royal troops in its territories, first because it would increase the jealousy of their own officers, over whom all Crown officers of the same rank were given precedence; and then because King's men were so much more expensive than sepoys, in whose fidelity the Court always affected to have an unshakeable confidence. The consequence had been that in 1788 Henry Dundas, President of the Board of Control, instigated legislation which compelled the Court to accept and pay for, within a certain limit, such royal troops as the Board deemed essential for the security of the Indian possessions, at the same time obviating one of the Court's objections by having a local King's brevet granted to all Company officers. Thereafter, the number and significance of soldiers of the Crown in India had grown in steady proportion to the increase in the size of the native armies. In 1787 there had been only six King's regiments in the peninsula—roughly 5,500 officers and men. In

[2] Each of 3 squadrons or 6 troops. A troop had 80 horsemen.
[3] See Appendix 2.

1811 there were twenty regiments, or about 20,000 men, which was the greatest number for which the Company was liable to pay by the terms of the act of 1788.

That act leaving it no option concerning the employment of a certain proportion of British troops, it is not difficult to understand why the Company chose to fulfil its obligation by receiving Crown regiments rather than by increasing its own European corps (which it was now entitled to do to the extent of 12,000 men). It would have been enormously expensive to maintain such a large European contingent. The service life of British troops in India was rapidly terminated by death, debility or insanity. Dipsomania was so rife among them, that they had to be kept constantly sequestered for fear lest they terrify the population by their drunken rampaging. But confining them to cantonments where their barracks were dark and foetid, where clubs, libraries (for the very few who were literate) and organized recreations were unknown, and where bazaar women and drink were the only diversions, merely hastened their deterioration. Most European soldiers had native concubines, and were reckoned to be responsible for the alarming growth in the half-caste population; and it was very difficult to prevent their acquiring crude 'country' liquor, or arrack, in addition to their allotted daily half-pint of rum. 'Rack', which could be had for as little as a few pence the quart, was often made even more noxious by the admixture of drugs. Their degeneration was consequently appallingly swift. It was estimated that a European soldier in the Company's service was fit only for a pension or a place on the invalid establishment after ten years' service; and in the 1820s it was considered necessary to deny King's troops the option of remaining with the regiments in India once they had passed the age of thirty. Many did not even survive that long. The annual death rate among European troops during the first half of the nineteenth century maintained an average of about one in fourteen, as a result more of alcoholic poisoning, disease and suicide than of battle casualties. Even communal suicides were known. The annual casualty rate from all causes, including invaliding, discharging and desertion, reached an average of one in seven.[4] In 1815, of 1,116 corporals and privates in the Bengal European Regiment, 922,

[4] Figures in this section are from Sir J. Ranald Martin's *Sanitary History*, and from the Bengal Annual Military Statement 1814–15, in the National Archives of India.

or 83 per cent, had served less than 7 years. In the foot artillery the proportion was 63 per cent, and in the horse artillery 47 per cent. The advantage of using King's troops under such circumstances is obvious. They were regularly replenished and relieved by fresh consignments from home, and the Company was spared the cost of recruiting and training a constant supply of replacements. This saving undoubtedly more than covered the extra expense created by the higher pay of royal troops.

Consequently, there were in 1814 two cavalry and six infantry regiments of the King's army in Bengal alone—a total of some 7,000 officers and men. Their presence increased the size of the European force in this Presidency to just over one-sixth that of the native; and it meant that that European nucleus with which the final responsibility for the safety of the Indian empire was believed to rest, and which was expected to provide a standard of loyalty and bravery for the natives to emulate, had ceased to be a part of the Company's own army.

While this increase in the size of the King's army in India had done much to mitigate the problem of expense, it had also, as the Directors of the Company had foretold, done much to aggravate the jealousy of their own officers. In Bengal and Madras in 1786 there had been about thirteen officers and men in the Company's pay for every one in the King's; but by the end of the first decade of the next century the ratio was only eight to one. As their numbers and significance had augmented, so too had the self-importance and snobbery of the officers of the Crown. The Company's officers had been made increasingly aware of the panache, the mystique, the prestige attaching to the King's army, and left in no doubt that the military service of a mere trading corporation was decidedly inferior. Furthermore, King's officers still enjoyed advantages and privileges which they did not share: such as senior rank at an earlier age, the highest positions, and honourable distinctions and decorations. Company officers were often commanded by King's men ten or fifteen years their junior, because the pace of promotion in their own service was so slow. They were now at last eligible (since 1813) for the rank of lieutenant-general; but there was no precedent to suggest that this would afford them access to principal staff positions and commands-in-chief at the various Presidencies, all of which had hitherto been the preserve of King's officers. Decorations from the Crown were extremely rare. Sir John

Malcolm, of the Bombay establishment, who had been made Knight of the military Order of the Bath early in 1814, was the only Company officer ever to have received the accolade. Brooding on their grievances, the Company's men had come to envisage themselves as the victims of a cruel prejudice, like 'a kind of Roman Catholic, and subjected to disqualification without having undergone the ceremony of conversion'.[5] Many were of the opinion that the Company's armies should be transferred to the Crown; but the contrary argument—namely, that the Court of Directors could not function as a controlling body if it was deprived of the power of appointment and dismissal—had so far carried the greater weight, and the policy had never got beyond the stage of discussion. So the situation persisted, in Bengal as in the other Presidencies, where the military assignment was shared between two distinct officer corps, divided by tensions which, like the force repelling identical magnetic poles, imposed contact only intensified.

Dissension among the officers was only one of the weaknesses resulting from the type of expansion which the Bengal army had been undergoing. Another arose from the fact that the rate of expansion had failed to keep pace with the accumulation of Company territory. Until the early 1780s the growth of the Bengal army had been progressive; but by then a fundamental change was being imposed on the Company's attitude towards its Indian possessions. In Pitt's India Act of 1784, a clause whose preamble affirmed that it was 'repugnant to the wish, honour and policy of this nation' to 'pursue schemes of conquest and extension of dominion in India' had removed the freedom of the Company's agents in India to make war arbitrarily. This legislation postulated a fully grown empire in a state of rest, a conception radically different from the notion—that the British territories in India were trading establishments in search of security—which had hitherto underlain policies of aggrandizement. A diminution of the Bengal army, and a redefinition of its purpose, had not unnaturally followed this transformation of outlook. Its normal function no longer being conceived as offensive warfare, but defence and internal security, extensive reductions had been made in the army in 1786 and a military peace establishment instituted. Further increases had been implemented subsequently, in response to the threat or the outbreak of war. There were enlargements on the occasion of the Mysore War in

[5] *Mins. of Ev.*, 1813, p. 173.

1790, and during the period 1797–1805, which saw the second Mysore War in southern India, the threat of invasion from Kabul and the Maratha War in Hindustan; but the army had not been maintained on a war footing once the crises had passed, and decreases had been made in 1796 and 1806. On the latter occasion, as well as reductions in the size of the regular force, the disbandment of various *ad hoc* bodies of irregular horse and foot, formed to relieve the regulars of internal duties, had been ordered. Each reduction being less than the amount of the previous augmentation, even the peace establishment had continued to maintain an overall expansion; but in the years before the Nepal War it had become obvious that this establishment was both unsuited in nature and inadequate in numbers for the functions it was expected to perform.

The reduction of nearly all the irregular levies in 1806 meant that the comparatively small regular army had recently been required to sustain the burden of such tedious and unprofessional duties as guarding jails, escorting stores, treasure and prisoners, supervising convict working parties and occupying police outposts. The infantry had had to be broken up into small detachments and dispersed over the whole area of the Bengal Presidency, which had been greatly enlarged in 1806 by the acquisition of extensive territories from the Marathas in Bundelkhand. Most of the men had been kept constantly on duty without regular reliefs or intervals of rest, and had besides been so thinly spread that whole districts in the north, contiguous to Nepal, had been devoid of regular troops. The cavalry was absurdly inadequate for the demands which had come to be imposed on it. Deterred by the relatively enormous expense of this arm—the monthly upkeep of a trooper's horse alone cost three times the amount of a sepoy's wages—the Company maintained in all Bengal but 6,000 regular cavalrymen, King's dragoons included. Yet there were now 2,500 miles of frontier to defend, of which vast stretches in the south were exposed to the depredations of Pindari chiefs who counted their horsemen in tens of thousands.

Sir George Nugent, Hastings's predecessor as Commander-in-Chief, had warned the Calcutta government that a serious deterioration in the discipline and morale of the army was being caused by such a severe overtaxation of its patience and resources. He wrote of 'the relaxed habits and occasional irregularities of detached parties, which from the great want of troops cannot be regularly relieved and [which] are therefore kept from under the eyes of their officers much longer than is for many reasons desirable'; and he complained that field exercises had become impossible:

Of the benefit of acting and manoeuvring in bodies this army is altogether deprived by its limited establishment being incessantly employed in internal duties, leaving no troops disposable for the purpose of forming a large permanent cantonment or an occasional camp, and by the scattered description of the forces over the surface of a vast territory . . . and yet the constant or at least frequent assemblage of troops in considerable divisions, or, on the lowest scale, to the extent of a brigade or two, is deemed indispensable to the proper organization of any regular army intended for the defence of great continental dominions.

The sepoys, finding it increasingly difficult to obtain the leaves of absence on which they depended for the settlement of their domestic and legal concerns, had been applying for discharges and, when unsuccessful, deserting in alarming numbers. 'Battalions thus became incomplete [and] a constant succession of expensive recruiting and of drills for recruits takes place to supply the loss . . . of formed soldiers, many even of the oldest and best of whom are known to seek their discharges or desert.' Nugent had expressed the opinion that the army needed to be increased by eight squadrons of cavalry (1,280 men) and three regiments of infantry (nearly 5,000 men).

By 1814 certain of the mistakes of 1806 had been rectified, and supplementary irregular corps were again in existence. They totalled some 14,500 men, and comprised a few bodies of quasi-military police, such as the Delhi Najibs, the Calcutta Militia and the half-dozen Provincial Battalions—all with only a European commander and adjutant; the Ramgarh Local Battalion, instituted by Nugent on an experimental basis, with a European officer to each company, to help defend the northern border; and two corps of irregular cavalry, constituted after the native manner, with the men supplying their own horses, uniforms and accoutrements in return for a monthly lump sum, and commanded by two of the officers who had come over from the Maratha service on the outbreak of the war in 1803 and who had since been entertained as pensioners by the Calcutta government. One was the renowned and dashing half-caste, James Skinner, and the other was an Englishman, William Gardner.[6] But there were still too few of

[6] See Appendix 2.

these bodies for them to be efficient. In April 1814 the commanding officer of the Patna Provincial Battalion wrote to the Patna Magistrate that he had had only between sixteen and twenty men (out of nearly a thousand) present in the lines during a period of five months, and that it had consequently been impossible for him to relieve the outposts in that period. Skinner's Horse was celebrated for its virtuosity as an ensemble; but in February 1815 Gardner told the Adjutant-General that it had been impossible for him to train his men even in the rudiments of collective discipline: 'They have been dispersed in parties of seldom more than 5 troopers, and such has been, from the first formation of the corps [in 1809], the pressure of duty, that as soon as a recruit was enlisted he was detached on command, by which many have scarce seen a drill or parade.'

As a result, when the horsemen were finally required to work together as a group to defend part of the northern border during the Nepal War, they proved restive and even mutinous and created more havoc than they averted.

To provide for the present emergency, the regular army had been put onto a war footing. Each company of sepoys had been increased from eighty to ninety privates, and the grenadier companies of battalions not actually in the field had been withdrawn and embodied into seven grenadier battalions, preparatory to being replaced by recruits.[7] By these means it was expected that some 9,500 extra men would eventually be available. Furthermore, the magistrates of frontier districts had been authorized to raise temporary levies of *barkandaj* (militiamen) to perform internal guard and police duties while the war was in progress. Hastings, however, was determined to use the occasion to increase the Bengal army's permanent establishment. He proposed the creation of three new infantry regiments; but the essence of his plan was the augmentation of the irregular part of the force, so that the regular army could be relieved altogether of interior duties and refurbished as a professional instrument. He demanded three more local battalions, nine additional provincial battalions, two new corps of irregular horse, and the expansion of Skinner's Horse from 1,000 to 3,000 men. His proposals became the issue of a strenuous controversy, and while the fighting went on in the mountains, a bitter

[7] An old-fashioned practice, now discontinued in the royal army.

dispute raged between the Governor-General's itinerant Headquarters and the Vice-President's circle in Calcutta. Because
Nugent had urged their necessity before Hastings's arrival, Edmonstone was prepared to accept the three additional regiments of
infantry; but he vigorously jibbed at the policy of permanently increasing the irregulars, and insisted that the proposed corps should
be treated as temporary expedients only. He argued that it was
essential to maintain regular troops in the interior; but his real
objections stemmed from a far more fundamental antipathy.
Hastings, under the influence of Wellesley's disciples, such as John
Adam and Charles Metcalfe, justified his military policy by invoking the indispensability of British paramountcy in India, or the
maintenance of a military establishment sufficient to defeat all
possible combinations of potential enemies. Military expansion was
essential to ensure the preservation of what had already been won.
It was an important tenet of this school of thought that paramountcy would in large measure pay for itself by creating a state of
stability in which existing revenue assets could be more completely
realized; but its adherents did not hesitate to draw the inference
that territories and revenues should, if necessary, be expanded in
order to provide for the predetermined level of military strength.
Advocates of paramountcy therefore rejected the premise that the
British Indian empire was normally in a state of rest—a premise
which Edmonstone conceived as hallowed and which he made it
his mission to defend. He questioned the practicability of a combination of all potential enemies, and argued that it was not only
unnecessary but gravely impolitic to fix a scale of military strength
in order to provide for what was at present a purely theoretical contingency. Such martial demonstration, suggesting eagerness to
expand territorial sway, was the one thing which would cause the
native rivals of the British to band together. Military augmentations would therefore precipitate the very danger they were
designed to obviate. The Nepal War once finished, he saw no
reason to apprehend subsequent altercations with any of the native
states, provided the Company made it clear that it had no acquisitive ambitions. Security could be guaranteed only by a state of rest,
so the regulator of military strength should be the actual extent of
dominion and the existing level of income.[8]

[8] Sec. Cons., 21 March 1815, nos. 1, 17; 4 July, no. 1, 30 Aug., no. 36.
Metcalfe's views are in Kaye, *Life*, i, pp. 400–5, 445–6; *Selections*, pp. 78–9, 146.

But Hastings refused to give way, and after the war he rescinded only those increases which he had intended should be temporary. His points of difference with Edmonstone were submitted to the Court of Directors.

While the process of expansion had been accentuating the internal weaknesses without alleviating the external pressures which were vitiating the Bengal army's efficiency, other measures, designed to rationalize the army's organization, had begun to be applied. Their success was so far at best dubious or incomplete; and in one important respect their effect had been far more deleterious than beneficial—largely because of the jealous and parsimonious way in which they had been conceded by the Court of Directors. By the period of the Nepal War the old-style and the new-style Bengal armies were rather like the two worlds which Matthew Arnold described himself as moving between—the one dead, and the other powerless to be born.

The condition was well exemplified by the state of the commissariat. Until the beginning of the nineteenth century, the army had been clothed, fed, and transported by private contractors—generally civilians. The system had long proved inadequate and unthrifty. Contractors had invariably furnished inferior materials, and they had frequently failed to meet their obligations. The shortcomings of the system had become especially manifest in the state of the ordnance cattle and their drivers. Contractors would buy the cheapest bullocks, and then confide them to native sub-contractors whose chief concern was to increase their own profits. Consequently, whenever it had been necessary to send a battering train of heavy artillery with an army in the field, the cattle had been found so emaciated and weak as to be incapable of keeping pace with the infantry. The drivers found by the contractors had been wretchedly underpaid and troublesome. They had ill-treated the animals and continually deserted. Delay and frustration from these causes had been so apparent in 1809, when a force was ordered to the west to deter Ranjit Singh from crossing the Sutlaj, that Hewitt, the Commander-in-Chief of the day, had become convinced that essential provisions and services must henceforth be supplied by a department of the army itself. A commissariat had therefore been instituted in December 1809, and given charge of the victualling of all European troops; the purveyance of boats; the provision and feeding of ordnance cattle, and of elephants and camels for camp equipage and stores; the supply and upkeep of horses for the cavalry and horse artillery; and the maintenance of carriage cattle and hackeries for the soldiers' personal effects. At about the same time attendants for the ordnance cattle had been subjected to military discipline, arrangements being made to have them provided partly by the commissariat and partly by a regular corps of ordnance drivers.

So far, the new arrangements had given much cause for satisfaction. Considerable savings had been realized in each department of the commissariat, compared with the cost of similar services from contractors, and on the occasions of punitive expeditions against the fortresses of Kalanjar and Rewa, in Bundelkhand, the ordnance bullocks had been so much improved that the heavy guns, with their carriages and tumbrils of ammunition, had kept pace with the infantry 'on the longest marches, over the worst roads, and in the hottest weather'. Resort to the temporary expedient of hiring cattle and carriage had not been necessary. Impressed, Nugent had expressed the opinion that 'no single improvement ever introduced into the Indian armies was of greater importance to their efficiency or more conducive to the general interests of the state than the Commissariat'.

Hastings shared this view. In his estimation the Bengal commissariat had a considerable advantage over even that at home, because its Commissary-General was not a civilian, but a military man, familiar, through personal experience, with the nature of the demands he was called on to satisfy. By 1815 several assignments had been added to his province, including the provision of tents and camp equipage; the purveyance of hospital and medical supplies; and the hiring and paying of bearers to carry the doolies for the sick and wounded, drivers for the hackeries, and the various coolies and carriers needed for the paraphernalia of the European and native soldiery.

But in its hours of trial the commissariat did not fulfil all the hopes it had inspired. Its resources bore little relation to the size of the army it was meant to serve. While it was capable of discharging its functions in times of peace and desultory warfare, it was unable to supply the needs of large divisions preparing for active service. The native soldiers were almost always left to provide their own carts and bullocks, and public establishments of coolies and porters were insufficient even for the provisions and ammunition for campaigns such as those in Nepal, where the difficult ground precluded the use of cattle. Furthermore, the commissariat did not assume even nominal responsibility for the transportation of the baggage of native and European officers. They were required to apply directly to the magistrates for their coolies and hackeries, and were expected to maintain enough bullocks and camels to enable them to move instantly at all times. Few of them did. One major-general of the Bengal army admitted, before the Select Committee of the House of Commons in 1832, that, although an officer was supposed to keep baggage animals, 'you never press[ed] him to have them unless he actually requir[ed] them' because they were easily hired. Even then, another officer affirmed that the Company's were better prepared than King's officers, 'who tend[ed] not to keep up carriage, which [was] a most expensive article, and rel[ied] on having time to muster animals when orders to march arriv[ed]'. The upshot was that when orders to march did arrive, no one was ready and there was the utmost confusion while officers, men and commissariat all competed and bargained for animals, coolies and carts. It was reckoned that, even under normal conditions, detachments of the Bengal army required three weeks to put themselves into motion, and the delay was correspondingly longer when the service, as that in Nepal, demanded carriage of an unusual description.

It cannot be denied that part of the blame for the army's dinosaurian ponderousness attached to the Bengal officers' own reluctance to rationalize their habits. They continued to expect to live as luxuriously in the field as in cantonments, with china, plate, table linen, condiments and wine. One major in the Meerut division of the Nepal force required four camels for his spare liquor alone, 'viz: 10 dozen [bottles] of Madeira; as much beer; 6 dozen of port; all the old claret without breaching the new chest that there may be; 2 dozen of brandy; 1½ of cherry brandy; and half a dozen of French liqueurs'. Continuing his letter of instructions to his wife, he added: 'a few bottles of sauces, mustard, etc., etc., would also be acceptable. These wants strike me more freshly as I had last night a party of 14 who drank 22 bottles out of my small stock of one liquor or another.'[9] This now seems preposterous; but in fact there was a genuine need for enormous quantities of drink, because methods of purifying water were uncertain and drinking wine and beer was the only sure way of avoiding cholera. Generally

[9] John Ludlow to his wife, 25 Oct. 1814.

speaking, extravagance was only half the problem. There were special
requirements, which the commissariat was incapable of accommodating.

The other main source of supply for the army was the clothing
agency—another department which owed its inception to the cause
of rationalization, but which was already finding its growth stunted
and its efficiency impaired partly by the dead weight of habit and
partly by the inveterate parsimony of the Directors. The old mode
of clothing the army had been to issue contracts to civilian entrepreneurs, who had been paid from the off-reckoning fund. This
fund was formed by the stoppages which were made from each
soldier's pay. The amount remaining after the contractors' accounts
had been settled would be shared among the staff and regimental
officers, in amounts varying according to their rank. That the
system had led to abuses is readily understandable. The officers
had been interested in keeping the cost of contracts as low as
possible; and the contractors in their turn had made up the uniforms
as cheaply as they could in order to increase their margin of profit.
The result had been that when the soldiers received their coats they
fitted abominably and were cut so sparingly that they would not
meet across the chest and belly and ended considerably short of
the wrist in the sleeves. Contractors had often failed to deliver, and
instead of the annual new jerkin to which he had been entitled, the
soldier had had to make do with one every two or three years. The
situation had become particularly deplorable after 1801, when a
committee sat at Fort William to devise ways of reducing the price
of clothing. Thereafter, entrepreneurs had still remained so anxious
to secure contracts and finger the advances that they took them at
quite unrealistic rates. Some had defaulted and absconded; others
had been ruined. Compensation, made available to the troops when
they failed to receive the clothing due to them, had been paid out
on six occasions between 1801 and 1808. Finally, in 1809, the contract system had been abolished and the army's own clothing
agencies set up. There had originally been three, administered by a
principal Agent and two Deputies, who had each received a fixed
salary. But removing the contracts had solved only half the problem. The old method of financing still persisting, the Agents had
soon found themselves at loggerheads with the colonels concerning
the distribution of the off-reckoning fund. Rather than abolish the
whole invidious system whereby the same fund, provided by the

troops, was required both to furnish an important emolument of the officers and to pay for the army's uniforms, long-term efficiency had been sacrificed as usual on the altar of immediate economy. Compensation for the loss of off-reckonings, in the form of increased pay, being unthinkable, the new system had been modified in order to preserve the old form of perquisite. In 1811, one of the agencies had been abolished,[10] and for the salary attached to the two remaining ones a share of the off-reckoning fund had been substituted, obviously with a view to dissuading the Agents from being too generous when providing for the manufacture of uniforms. Officers' off-reckonings had consequently not been affected by the operation of the agency system, and the uniforms of the men had been but marginally improved, the agency coat having about a sixth more cloth than the contract one. So the Bengal army remained shoddily dressed. However dashing they might have appeared to the casual glance, closer scrutiny would have shown the sepoys to be cramped into ill-fitting coats and tight shorts, which restricted movement so much that it was actually impossible to sit, or stoop to pick anything from the ground, without unbuttoning somewhere. In 1816 Hastings decided that long pantaloons, instead of the customary shorts, must, for the sake both of the comfort and of the smartness of the troops in the cold weather, be made a permanent part of the Bengal uniform; but in order to preserve the off-reckoning surplus the arrangement had to be made whereby they were issued not in addition to the jackets, but in lieu of them every other year. Still in the interest of those who shared the residue of the off-reckoning fund, all articles of dress were made in three sizes only and fitted to the men as best they could be by regimental tailors. In the King's regiments, on the other hand, every garment was virtually re-made to suit the individual to whom it was issued. The cheap and shabby turn-out of the Company's Bengal troops was commonly admitted to be the consequence of having the business of clothing administered by those who shared the profits.

Inferior workmanship extended to more vital things than uniforms. Although the Court of Directors would not allow muskets to be made in India, on the ground that neither the timber nor the workmanship was equal to that of Europe, the small arms which it consigned from home could not be compared to those

[10] The two remaining were at Fategarh and Fort William.

supplied to the King's army. General Horsford, of the Bengal Artillery, recalled that the locks of the muskets were badly sprung, making the triggers stiff, the aim unsure and the hammers difficult to re-cock. He considered the finish of the wood and iron work inferior. The bayonets he had found too short, with points so thickened (for strength and long life) that they would not pierce the quilted jerkins often worn by Indian enemies. Muskets frequently arrived from Europe with flawed barrels and split stocks, and swords with temper so soft that they snapped on trial. A special committee had been appointed to look into the state of the Company's weapons in 1809, but it seems to have contented itself with a perfunctory comparison of the King's and Company's arms in use with the Presidency guard at Fort William. Even so cursory an investigation had confirmed that the locks of the Company's muskets were 'rather inferior', but the committee had attributed this to the age of the pieces, finding that those in more recent assignments did not exhibit the same deficiency. They had reported favourably on the general state of the Company's small arms, leading the Commander-in-Chief to conclude that 'the arms supplied for the Honourable Company's service appear[ed] to have been much improved of late years, and to be now nearly, if not quite, as good as those supplied for H.M. troops.' The state of the weapons received in a consignment from England in 1811 had soon confuted his optimism. The Secretary to the Military Board had reported that numbers of these muskets had injured locks, broken sights and damaged ramrods. Many of the bayonets were cracked and broken in their weakest parts. The Board had found it impossible to attribute all the damage to the rigours of the journey, because there was no indication that the arms had been inadequately packed; but only guardedly had it dared to hint at 'bad workmanship' and to suggest that the arms were 'indifferent and liable to injury in a most essential part'. It had recalled that the Directors did not take kindly to having bad arms returned and were extremely sensitive to 'animadversions on the conduct of tradesmen under their immediate directions'. When giving evidence before the House of Commons in 1832, the Company's Inspector of Military Stores insisted that there was nothing whatever wrong with the muskets provided by Birmingham tradesmen for consignment to India. Such was not the opinion, however, of other witnesses, one of whom (Captain Macon, in the Bengal army since 1806) roundly declared them to be the worst he had ever seen. In truth, the situation probably was that most of the Bengal army was using weapons of indifferent quality made worse by age and shoddy maintenance. In infantry corps, repair of arms was at the discretion of commanding officers, who were supplied with monthly sums for the purpose. As they were allowed to keep any surplus, it is not really open to question that repair work, when authorized, was often carried out with a stricter regard for economy than for efficiency.

In the case of ordnance, the Directors' parsimony had combined with laxity in the upper ranks of the army itself to allow a deterioration in effectiveness. Of late, the standard of discipline and technology in the armies of the native princes had risen. European advisers—usually French or English deserters and adventurers—had become an indispensable part of the military establishment of every ruler with some pretension to importance. The Maratha, Sikh and Gurkha princes had formed forces drilled and armed in close imitation of the English model, and the Company's invincibility could no longer be taken for granted. If its armies were to retain their margin of superiority, they needed to raise their own criteria of efficiency; and this was something which they had failed to do. There was, in the Bengal army especially, a prevailing attitude of swaggering self-confidence. The language of the camp knew no reservations, no misgivings regarding the certainty of swift and easy victory. Anyone who voiced a doubt, who counselled caution, was jeered and called a 'croaker'. This disposition was especially manifest in the reluctance to make full use of guns, and in the dislike which military men had of being reminded that the English cannon had become proverbial in India. Despite the mystique which attached to artillery in the minds of all native soldiers, they preferred to attribute their victories to discipline, valour and the innate excellence of the British character. Nevertheless, this disparagement was undoubtedly also due in some measure to the fact that artillery was so cumbersome. Bengal's establishment of horse artillery was much too small. In 1815 it consisted of one regiment whose total strength was 312 and the light field pieces or 'gallopers' which were attached in pairs to each cavalry regiment. The foot artillery had to rely on teams of bullocks, which, although the commissariat had improved their quality, still remained slow and inflexible. They made even light field guns more a hindrance than an aid in the heat of battle, when swift and complex manoeuvring was required. Elephants, which were also used for the draught of heavy ordnance, were timid and unreliable under fire. They were terrified by the report of small arms, and liable to become unmanageable on difficult or uneven ground. The poor construction of the gun carriages further complicated the use of artillery. They were of solid teak and sissoo, and had to be made heavier than the gun itself to withstand the repeated shock of recoil. This meant that even a light field piece, a six-pounder, complete with carriage and with ammunition in the limber boxes, weighed about a ton. The design of the carriages, especially those in use with the six-pounders, and of the ammunition tumbrils was bad. Nugent had complained that those in use with the horse artillery endangered the drivers and distressed the horses. Designs do not appear to have been based on standard patterns. When giving evidence in 1832, one Bengal artillery officer asserted that two guns might be moving side by side in the field without the spare parts of one carriage being able to supply the other. It was often quite impossible to replace wheels and axle trees in cases of accident. Until Hastings instituted a transport train, shortly after the Nepal War, native mortar carriages had to be hired for the occasion whenever an expedition was planned. These constantly failed under the weight of the pieces, and made them more an impediment than an asset. This circumstance, together with the government's reluctance to make the outlay for expensive shells and platforms, had meant that mortars, which should have been an essential part of any siege train, had seldom been present in sufficient numbers to provide more than a widely spaced, and therefore ineffective, fire of shells.

Scientific knowledge in general, as well as guns in particular, was under-exploited in the Bengal army, because its practitioners laboured under disadvantages deriving from the Directors' stinginess. The engineers were the only officers (besides the artillerists) who were in any sense technical specialists. These officers were, in the first place, overworked. There were only thirty-one of them in the Bengal army at the time of the Nepal War, their number having slightly more than doubled since 1764, while the size of the army itself had more than tripled. One of Hastings's first recommendations on his arrival in India had been that the number of engineers must be increased. The second disadvantage was related to the first. Because the corps was so small, the contingent of high-ranking officers was minute, and most engineers were only subalterns or captains.[11] It was very rarely indeed that even the chief engineer with a division on service was a field officer. All those with the Nepal divisions were captains. This was a grave handicap in a service where (as we shall see) commanding officers were invariably old men who, because seniority alone was the qualification for promotion, placed more value on length of service than on expertise and who, because their arrogance had generally increased with their senility, felt it intolerably degrading to consult and be guided by officers considerably junior to themselves.

Over-confidence, a shameful inadequacy of artillery and an impatient disregard for professional guidance had already, by the time of the outbreak of the Nepal War, contributed to cause several costly military failures. The most spectacular had been at Bharatpur, a Jat settlement surrounded by some eight miles of mountainous mud wall, about 100 miles south of Delhi. In 1805 Lord Lake, the Commander-in-Chief, had interrupted his campaign against the Maratha chieftain Holkar in order to attempt to capture this place, because its raja had renounced his allegiance to the British and declared himself an ally of the enemy. Both Lake's force and his ordnance had been absurdly insufficient for the task. He had had less than 8,000 men; and while his heavy artillery had been sufficient to make a breach, his supplementary field pieces and mortars had been far too few to match the artillery which the enemy had been able to bring to bear in their own defence. Yet the premise which underlay the theory of siege warfare was that a greater force of artillery can be amassed on the perimeter of the larger than that of the smaller of two concentric circles. It follows that besiegers can take advantage of their position on segments of the larger circle to destroy the guns of the defenders on the perimeter of the smaller, and thereby enable the processes of breaching and storming to proceed unopposed. Lake had disdained to seek the advice of his engineers, the chief of whom was only a lieutenant. As Lake was no engineer himself, the results had been catastrophic. He would not delay to enable the nature of the difficulties to be ascertained, and the technical operations of the siege had been marred by haste and a disregard for even the most elementary rules of procedure.

[11] In 1815 the Corps of Engineers consisted of 1 colonel commanding, 2 lieutenant-colonels, 2 majors, 9 captains, 8 lieutenants, 8 ensigns, and 2 cadets: Bengal Annual Military Statement, f.155.

The wall had been opened three times in different places; but every time, instead of being the final object attained prior to the storm, the breach had been the primary achievement; and, as the mortars and field pieces, firing grape and shells, had been too few and too distant to prevent its being repaired during hours of darkness, pending the completion of other essential measures, on each occasion troops had been sent to the assault before even the most basic preparations and reconnaissance had been carried out. Four attempts had been made to storm the place, and all of them had failed because of these deplorable omissions. Plans to carry Bharatpur by a *coup de main* had finally had to be abandoned, and the rebel raja forced into submission by a blockade. The wages of impatience, arrogance, and rashness had been heavy: 2,500 men wounded, nearly 450 killed, and a severely impaired military reputation.

In so far as the Bengal army had taken the field at all during the period between the end of the Maratha and the beginning of the Nepal War, it had been employed in desultory siege warfare against the strongholds of various recusant zemindars in Bundelkhand, a wild and beautiful tract on the southern bank of the Jumna river, retained as part of the Bengal Presidency after the peace of 1806. Most of these feudal fortresses had been stormed successfully; but on three occasions, at Badekh, Komona, and Kalanjar, the mortifying experience of the failures at Bharatpur had been echoed. Each repulse had been on too small a scale to cause great disquiet; and as each had been followed by the surrender of the besieged, on all three occasions the reassuring conclusion had been drawn that the assaults had not so much failed as had a delayed effect. Taken together, however, they constituted an ominous indication that the mode of conducting sieges had been making freakish not defeat, but victory. On each occasion, as at Bharatpur, there had been a proneness to pin hopes less on guns than on men; an eagerness to hurl forward troops to accomplish what the engineers had scarcely prepared for. Kalanjar was a fort on the summit of a massive rock, and in order to gain the breach, the storming party had found themselves required to scale first a perpendicular rock face about twenty feet high and then thirty feet of broken wall. Ladders had been used to climb the rock, but as the men clung to the wall, where ladders could not be placed, fumbling for crevices and projections to gain a footing, they had been flicked off like insects by boulders and shot from above. Only one or two had reached the breach. The survivors had bitterly declared, what should have been obvious at the start, that such a fort could never be taken; and a later observer, himself a military man,[12] was astonished that it had ever been possible for any of them to climb as far as the breach. 'To us', he wrote, 'who journeyed for amusement up its stupendous sides, the ascent was most difficult and by the time we had gained the summit we were exhausted.' The King's 53rd Regiment, now a part of the Nepal force, had provided the storming party and had had 14 men killed and 128 wounded in this rash enterprise.

But perhaps the most baneful consequences of cut-price rationalization were the corrosion of morale and the sense of grievance among the European officers. In response to the changing climate of opinion, these officers had been given new standards of respectability to observe. The principle of Parliamentary control over the Company, expressed by the Acts of 1774 and 1784, the impeachment and trial of Warren Hastings for oppression and the appointment of Cornwallis as Governor-General with a brief to end corruption in 1786, had signalled a new solicitude for regularity, purity and efficiency in the government of the Indian possessions. The day of the buccaneer and freebooter was over. The change was caused partly by a growing humanitarian concern for the welfare of the people of India, and partly by anxiety on the part of East India stockholders and the Ministry lest undisciplined Company servants should destroy the goose which laid the golden eggs. The early years of the Company had been the classic age of venality and moral laxity, and its military and civil servants alike had enjoyed power without responsibility. Remuneration had been provided more by a dubious process known as 'shaking the pagoda tree' than by prescribed salaries and allowances. Commanding officers had been minor despots, dressing and administering their regiments much as they pleased and working in close collaboration with their native officers, with whom they shared the irregular perquisites of power. But the new pressures had wrought changes, designed to improve the tone and decrease the independence of the Company's servants. Officer recruitment had been regularized, and the old-style 'country' cadets, who used to come out to India in some civil guise and wheedle their way to a commission after their arrival, had become extinct. It was now essential for candidates to secure their commissions from the Directors in London, and cadetships in the

[12] John Shipp (p. 245).

Company's service had come to be regarded as a respectable provision for younger sons. Regiments had been numbered, uniforms standardized and regulations drafted to cover almost every aspect of military administration. A series of measures culminating in the major reorganization of 1796 had been implemented with a view to defining the position of the officers and making them the servants instead of virtually the masters of the army. Salaries and allowances had been prescribed to take the place of illicit gains—such as those secured by faking payrolls—and old-style emoluments such as the bazaar duty.[13] Furlough arrangements had been introduced in order to strengthen their ties with home and discourage the notion of settlement in India, and pensions provided that they might be freed from the necessity of making private fortunes. To protect officers from abuses of patronage, it had been decreed that promotion was to be strictly by seniority: up to the rank of major in the regiments, and thereafter in a single line. To prevent invidious supersessions, the practice of buying and selling commissions, which prevailed in the King's army, had been forbidden. Much more emphasis had lately been placed on seniority in the promotion of native officers,[14] especially in the commissioned ranks.

Although the European officers had themselves been among the most strenuous advocates of such measures as seniority promotion, paid leave and retirement pensions, it had not been long before they felt that they had made a bad bargain in surrendering their old advantages in exchange. Niggardliness in London had precluded the successful operation of the new regulations from the outset. The scale of pay and allowances had been pitched too low for the minimum rates to have any realistic relation to the costs actually incurred by young officers. In Bengal, where caste-consciousness was strong, Europeans could not avoid comparatively heavy domestic expenses, because each servant's caste closely limited his function and large establishments were unavoidable. The cost of military equipment was very high and almost always beyond the means of newly-commissioned officers. Most subalterns were consequently forced to borrow money—at rates of interest of up to 24 per cent if from native usurers—and remained burdened with

[13] A duty levied on liquor, tobacco, and drugs, which had been a perquisite of commanding officers.

[14] Native ranks were: naik (corporal); havildar (sergeant); jemadar (3rd commissioned rank); subadar (2nd commissioned rank); and (after 1814) subadar-major (1st commissioned rank).

debt until well into their careers. It was very rarely that an officer
was able to save money before he attained the rank of major; so
although they were now allowed three years' furlough after ten
years' service, most officers found that it was not until they had
been in the army for thirty years that they could muster the
enormous sum required for the passage home. It is a fact that
an officer was comparatively fortunate if he could contemplate
taking his leave after a period of service which was supposed to
qualify him for a pension. An officer was permitted to retire on the
basic pay of his rank after twenty-two years' actual service; but
promotion was so slow that he could expect to be only a captain at
the most after that time, and certainly in no position to think of
retiring. The Court's parsimony was throwing out of gear the
whole mechanism of seniority promotion, which could work
effectively only if officers had sufficient inducement to retire on
reaching a suitable age. But retirement was something which few
Indian officers, however high their positions, could afford to consider. Aged general and senior field officers clung to service, often
long after they had ceased to be fit for command, blocking the
channels of promotion to those waiting in the lower ranks. Although
twenty-five years (including three years' furlough) was considered
to be the maximum period of effective service, most officers served
double that time before they reached the rank of major-general. The
general stagnation raised the age and depressed the quality even of
lieutenant-colonels and majors to an appalling degree. When
Nugent inspected the Bengal army in 1812, he had found two
infantry lieutenant-colonels who were demonstrably senile, and
had had to remove them to the invalid establishment. No fewer
than fifteen lieutenant-colonels and majors had appeared 'altogether incapable, from age and increasing infirmity, of performing
the duties expected of them', but these he had forborne to remove
both from fear of increasing the expense of the invalid establishment, and from reluctance to offend the old officers, 'whom an
indulgent but pernicious usage [had] hitherto suffered to remain
unnoticed in the effective ranks of the army'. Death and subsidized
retirement were virtually the only modes of egress from the army.[15]
The latter was possible because the prohibition on the sale of
commissions was not rigorously enforced. It was the custom for the

---

[15] There was no system of retirement on half-pay, as in the King's army, to
relieve congestion.

junior officers of a regiment to subscribe sums of money to time-expired senior officers to induce them to retire. But the method could relieve a corps of one or two officers every year at the most, and did little to accelerate promotion. When it was decided, in 1816, to grant the brevet rank of captain to lieutenants of fifteen or more years' standing, no less than fifty-nine subalterns qualified for the award, of whom fifty-two had served sixteen years or more. One had been in the army for nineteen years. It must still have taken them several years to qualify for the pay and allowances of their new rank, because on an average it took twenty-three years to proceed from the rank of cornet or ensign to that of captain; eight years from captain to major; six years from major to lieutenant-colonel; and a further twelve years to full colonel. Until 1808 cadets had been commissioned at the age of fifteen, so in 1814 most of the Bengal army's general officers were in their middle sixties—and this in a climate which Sir Henry Lawrence asserted made Europeans 'old men at forty'.

Small wonder that the enthusiasm of most young officers soon gave way to apathy and despair. It was not long before they realized that they had as good as sold themselves into bondage. For the vast majority, a career in the Company's military service meant exile for life. Out of every 100 who went to India, about forty actually survived twenty-two years' service, but only six ever returned home to enjoy their pensions.[16] It was an exile made all the more insupportable by the refusal of the new public opinion to sanction anodyne for its harshest privations. As confidence in the superiority of western culture and technology grew, reinforced by the Evangelicals' denunciation of Hinduism as a force of darkness and turpitude, so intolerance of the Englishman who tried to reconcile himself to expatriation by seeking a new identity in an Indian way of life mounted. Lady Nugent had not been able to disguise her disapproval when she met the two young Assistants at the Delhi Residency, Fraser and Edward Gardner (brother of William), because neither shaved (whiskers were an exclusively Indian habit at that time) and both were vegetarian. Such eccentricities were increasingly rare in the army, and where they did persist were the objects of censure or derision. There was on the Bengal establishment in 1814 a major-general called Charles Stuart, who was known as 'Hindu Stuart' because of the enthusiasm with which he studied the languages, manners and customs of north India. An anonymous contemporary in the King's army, who published his impressions of a tour of India[17] in the early 1820s, was revolted by such habits, and he stigmatized Stuart in no uncertain terms: 'He is not treated as a madman, but would not, perhaps, be misplaced if he had his idols, fakirs, bedas, and shasters in some corner of Bedlam, removed from its more rational and unfortunate inmates.'

Every obstacle was put in the way of officers' strengthening their ties with India. They were not allowed to buy land, and marriage with Indian women was a fact of life whose existence was simply not acknowledged. Military, like civil servants who did seek consolation in such liaisons (and they were in the majority in these days before the advent of the English '*memsahib*') had to endure the unhappiness of seeing their wives and children the victims of a cruel proscription. Native women were ostracized by European society; and the position of Anglo-Indians, or half-castes, was miserable in the extreme. They were barred from Company employment and denied most forms of legal and social recognition.

The Court of Directors, ever seeking ways to economize, had little sympathy for pleas of hardship. It impatiently brushed aside the argument that it was impossible for a subaltern to avoid incurring debt, affecting to believe that this was a false generalization based on the extravagance and improvidence of a few. Already, by the time of the Nepal War, it had drawn up a revised scale of allowances, which would reduce officers at certain stations to half batta (allowance) and abolish most of the perquisites remaining to commanding officers. Not for the first time, the Bengal officers embarked on a long and acrimonious wrangle with their employers, contesting every clause of the new plan in language of unmeasured contumacy. They had reacted in the same way to the regulations promulgated in 1796, so perturbing the Governor-General of the time, Sir John Shore, that he had modified the plan in accordance with their protests. In a pique, the Court had dismissed him; but

[17] *Sketches of India, Written by an Officer for Fireside Travellers at Home*, 225. Stuart is not named, but there is no doubt that he is the officer referred to—cf. his entry in Hodson's *List*, part 4. Kincaid, in *British Social Life in India*, p. 118, notes that during Wellesley's incumbency 'it was no longer fashionable in Government House circles to profess an interest in Persian poetry or Hindu metaphysics.' See also Spear, *The Nabobs*, pp. 137–43.

had nevertheless been forced to accept his alterations. Encouraged by the success of their recalcitrance, officers had treated the new regulations with contemptuous disregard. Studied defiance and organized protest were becoming part of the way of life of the Bengal officer; and, as one witness remarked before the House of Commons in 1832, 'where officers of an army meet, form committees, appoint delegates, subscribe funds, talk of "rights infringed", "compacts broken", "bad faith" of their rulers . . . it is idle to talk of military subordination.' The exasperation of the officers of the Madras army had already simmered to the point of mutiny when, in 1809, they had felt that they were being petulantly victimized by the civil authorities for objecting to various measures of military retrenchment; and it is possible that a similar trauma would now have convulsed the Bengal army, had the latest plan for reductions not been published at a time when the officers' energies were absorbed by the struggle against Nepal, and had Hastings not postponed its implementation and submitted it to an officers' committee for consideration. But on this occasion the effect of resistance was more to delay than to modify the scheme, which the Court was obviously determined not to be browbeaten into abandoning, and its final application in 1828 was to be the signal for a fresh outburst of virulent indignation.

Acerbity and insubordination often gave way to lethargic indifference when the prospect of active service arose. Joseph O'Halloran was a talented and popular officer in the infantry, and he had completed thirty-four years' service by 1814. Yet he was still a major, and only twentieth in the line of succession to a lieutenant-colonelcy. It was difficult for him to feel much enthusiasm for the pending campaign. He wrote to a friend: 'I expect, in a few days, the command of a battalion . . . to join the expedition against Nepal—a point about which I am perfectly indifferent, for my zeal has subsided into sullen apathy, from the disappointment of my hopes'.[18] Others turned to drink, to gambling, to beating up the Indians and to insulting and fighting each other. Plunged as they were, without any training, into the strange and claustrophobic military stations of India at the age of seventeen, sixteen or even fifteen, and allowed power and freedom when they

[18] Quoted by Mr. Hume during a debate at East India House—*Asiatic Journal*, vol. i, 1816, p. 70. O'Halloran is not named, but he is the only officer who fits Hume's description.

most needed discipline and guidance, it is not surprising that many officers throughout their lives showed signs of arrested psychological development. Some never outgrew the adolescent's association of virility with depravity, and gambled, drank or duelled their way to disgrace and death. In an existence with long periods empty of duty or distraction, the most trivial incidents were inflated into dramas and the slightest irritation was fostered into factitious rage. Animosities were deliberately cultivated and exaggerated to leaven the dead weight of ennui and fill out the vacant hours. Almost all officers, even the most cautious and best-tempered, received challenges to duels at some time in their careers, which it was better for them to quit the army than refuse. Many sudden deaths were ascribed to cholera which in fact had less natural causes.

Most competent officers found a refuge from regimental life, and a means of adding to their pay, in extra-regimental appointments; and the corps were being drained of their best talent by the growth of the general staff, by the increase in the number of local and provincial battalions and by the practice of employing military men in political capacities. Nugent claimed that an establishment which assigned the same number of officers (forty-five) to an infantry regiment of two battalions as was allowed to a single-battalion regiment in the King's army was even in theory too low. He reckoned that every infantry company and cavalry troop should have a captain at its head, as in Europe; instead of which the ratio in the Bengal army was only three captains to a cavalry regiment of six troops, and four to an infantry battalion of ten companies. Even this low complement was never full. It was not unusual for more than half of a regiment's lieutenants and captains to be absent on local leave, extra-regimental duty or sick pay, at the same time.[19] The reorganization of 1796 had fixed the proportion of just over two European commissioned officers to every hundred men in the native infantry regiments. It was calculated that during the Nepal War the ratio stood in practice at one to a hundred.[20] This attenuation was all the more pernicious because the officers who were left

[19] Nugent's Report of 20 June 1813: Sec. Cons., 6 Aug. 1813, no. 4, para. 74; Badenach, op. cit., pp. 9–10; Nugent to Torrens, 26 Sept. 1813: Nugent MSS, f. 174. An essential defect in the system was that officers absent on leave or extra-regimental appointments remained on the paper strength of their regiments.
[20] *Military Sketches of the Goorkha War*, p. xi.

in the regiments were generally the least able, the most inex-
perienced and the most discontented.

It was becoming very unusual for officers to take personal interest in the welfare of the native soldiers, and most had great
difficulty in communicating with them even on parade. None was
required, and few bothered, to have knowledge of the native
languages. The Adjutant of a regiment was supposed to act as
interpreter, but even he was not required, at this stage, to undergo
an examination to test his linguistic capability. He generally knew
enough Urdu to read orders and translate commands; but as his
pronunciation was often bad, and as Urdu was an unfamiliar dialect
to the Hindi-speaking sepoys, he was hardly a medium by which
the officers could know their men or the men their officers. The
regiment was in fact ceasing to have any real significance as a cadre.
The junior Europeans were frustrated, indifferent, prefectorial and
incomplete in numbers; while the seniors were mere birds of
passage, who happened to alight in a regiment only because it
offered the vacant rank to which they were entitled. Under these
conditions even regimental officers' messes were impracticable.

The essence of the tragedy of the Bengal army is that this
deterioration in the quality of its regimental officers happened at a
time when other processes were affecting the discipline of the native
ranks and making it imperative to improve that quality. While the
administration of the army was being rationalized, the attitude of
the mass of the native soldiery was being altered by contrary influences. Evidence suggests that the sepoys were becoming more
sensitive about the precepts and tenets of their castes, and less
amenable to even the basic requirements of a European military
system.

The Company had always preferred to recruit for the Bengal
army from among the brahmins and ksatriyas, the highest of the
four groups into which the multiplicity of castes in Hindu society
is divided; and in particular from among the brahmins and ksatriyas
of Bihar and Oudh. Bihar was a province of the Company, and
Oudh a protectorate; and in enlisting high-caste Hindus whose
families comprised the majority of landowners in these territories,
the Company was pursuing the ideal of a 'yeoman' army whose
members would have a personal interest in the preservation of the
government they served. The high-caste Hindu from these provinces also had the advantages of an imposing physique, a keen

sense of honour, and a sober and tractable disposition. By 1814 they constituted a large majority of the Bengal sepoys. Muslims were extremely few in infantry regiments, but tended to predominate in the artillery and cavalry. As a result of the recruiting techniques of commanding officers, infantry companies were even more homogeneous than the larger divisions. Battalions were usually raised at once in a single area, and when additions were required for the component companies,[21] the sepoys' relatives present at headquarters were generally enlisted. Otherwise, when he wanted a few men, a company commander would tell the sepoys about to go home on furlough to bring back their relations. In May 1814 Lieutenant Thomas Thackeray, commanding a company of the 2nd Battalion, 26th Native Infantry, had written an interesting letter to his brother, describing both the consequences and the purpose of this type of recruitment:

I am at great pains to fill up the vacancies which occur in my company by brothers of the best sepoys, and seldom entertain a recruit who is not in some way related to a man already in the company. I have succeeded so well that I have now four full brothers of one family, three of another, and out of ninety men I have not twenty who are not connected, either by consanguity or marriage, with some of their comrades. Men naturally become attached to the service in which they have so many ties.[22]

The infantry company was therefore developing a double identity: on the one hand it was acquiring new significance as part of an institutionalized army (for the forces tended to be distributed in companies rather than in battalions); and on the other, it was developing into something of an institution in itself. The gravity of the situation lay in the fact that the two identities were the results of virtually contradictory processes. The self-perpetuating groups which the infantry companies were becoming were far from being moulded by the rationalization which was being applied to the army as a whole. They were defined by caste regulations and a system of social precedence which had nothing whatever in common with such military concepts as rational distribution of labour and hierarchy determined by rank. A moral dilemma was coming to

---

[21] There were 10 companies in a battalion.
[22] J. T. Pryme and A. Bayne, *Memorials of the Thackeray Family*, p. 488. Cf. *Mins. of Ev.*, 1832, Sec. 5, p. 23.

dominate the native soldier's existence. Military duty and ethical obligation were incompatible and competing for his loyalty. The one demanded compliance with the exigencies of the service and deference to its system of rank; the other forbad travel by sea and the performance of manual labour, and required lower-caste native officers to bow in submission to brahmin privates. All the while this type of recruitment was preferred, the predicament was bound to exist, because the sepoys became more self-conscious about their standards of conformity as their companies developed into coteries of their own neighbours and relatives. The crucial problem was how to prevent the Hindu, irrational, personality of the infantry corps from subverting their rational, military one. It was a case of schizophrenia which only two therapies could cure: one was tightening the attachment of the sepoys to their European officers; and the other making battalions and companies more heterogeneous by recruiting from among a wider selection of tribes and religious groups.

Rationalization was by its very nature making it increasingly difficult for the first cure to operate. It deprived commanding officers of their old instruments of influence. From princely dispensers of patronage and favour, objects of veneration and propitiation, they had been reduced to mere overseers, enforcers of written regulations. Until 1805, a commanding officer had been permitted to address civil judges on behalf of his men, and this enabled the latter to circumvent the cumbersome formalities of the legal machinery and secure swift attention for their suits. The privilege had been abolished in 1804 for sepoys residing in the Company's own territories, and those hailing from Oudh were to lose it in 1815. The channels of justice were so cluttered, and so jealously guarded by venal native acolytes, that now that sepoys had to pursue their claims in the normal way even the most indulgent furlough was insufficient to complete a process. With this dispensation had been removed not only a principal reason for sepoys' deference towards their commanding officers, but one of the fundamental attractions of service with the Company. Landowners large and small had made it a policy to have one son at least in the army precisely in order to enjoy this benefit; and it had undoubtedly been a greater incentive to enlistment than a monthly wage of seven rupees (about 14*s.*) which had been fixed in 1779 and not thereafter significantly altered despite the steady rise in the cost of living,[23] and a pension which, though available after fifteen years' service, was not adequate to live on until thirty or forty had been completed.[24] This change in the status of commanding officers had been bound to produce an introspective tendency among the body of sepoys: a relapse into the more instinctive and less materially inspired sense of attachment to their social and religious leaders. To arrest this process those very qualities were needed in the generality of regimental officers which the parsimony of the Court was making impossible. If regimental duties had been made the most instead of the least rewarding aspect of service with the Company; if the best instead of the worst officers had stayed to lead and be in daily contact with the men, the situation might have been retrieved. The conduct of the British Indian armies, more perhaps than that of any others in modern history, was a reflection of the quality of their regimental officers. The Hindu soldier, though proud, was most content to manifest his pride in steadfast loyalty to the officer who had won his respect and affection. When serving under such men, sepoys of the Bengal army could be devoted, brave and eager to a degree incompatible with caste conformity. That their behaviour varied according to the quality of their officers is demonstrated by the very unpredictability of their reactions when required to embark for foreign service. On several occasions they had been prevailed upon to undergo sea journeys—to Madras in 1758 and 1768; to Sumatra in 1789 and 1791—which, as well as being nauseating physical experiences, were officially *tabu* for Hindus of caste. At other times, certain groups had refused. Between 1782 and 1784, four regiments had had to be disbanded for unsoldierlike conduct when required to embark for Madras; the army had been purged of another battalion for a similar reason in 1795; and in 1824 a regiment mutinied when required to embark for service in Burma. It is significant that the court of inquiry set up to probe the last affair censured the lieutenant-colonel commanding. 'He had not the art of gaining esteem, but seemed to have an unhappy factious disposition. On parade he managed ill, got angry, and harassed the men by continually doing the same thing, and by keeping the corps out

[23] Barat, *Bengal Infantry*, p. 304.
[24] *Mins. of Ev.*, 1832, Sec. 5, p. 178. The sepoy's 7 rupees, which included full allowance and from which a deduction was made for the off-reckoning fund, was higher than the wage received by the peasantry, but lower than that received by many natives employed as servants by Europeans—ibid., p. 41.

unusually long in hot weather.'[25] The regiments now needed qualities of leadership which were far in advance of those which the average regimental officer could provide. They needed men sympathetic and imaginative enough to manipulate simultaneously the two forms of organization—Hinduism on the one hand, European military embodiment on the other—which the army paradoxically represented; who had sufficient skill and knowledge to cause them to mesh and work together as a single entity. Very few officers ever evinced such understanding, mainly because they lacked even basic knowledge about the men with whom they were dealing. It is not that it was omitted to impress officers that they should respect the 'prejudices' of the natives. On the contrary, the injunction was reiterated with tireless insistence. It seems to have found its way into every order, every dispatch, every commentary, in one form or another. Apparently, what nobody realized was that in order to respect prejudices it is necessary to know exactly what they are. Cadets were given no formal instruction whatever in the history, culture, or religions, and only the most cursory in the languages, of India, before being posted to their regiments. The subjects with which they were expected to have some acquaintance were mathematics, science, classics, topographical drawing, chemistry, swordsmanship, and French. Hindustani (Urdu) was on the curriculum at Addiscombe,[26] but instruction was woefully inadequate, and it was almost unknown for a cadet to be able to express himself intelligibly to his servants on arrival. The experiment had been briefly tried of giving cadets language training on their arrival in India. A college had existed for the purpose at Baraset, just outside Calcutta, for seven years.[27] But the place had been in a state of continuous riot, and had had to be closed for lack of order and discipline. So ensigns and cornets were now again sent straight to their regiments, with the vague hope that they would somehow acquire essential knowledge on the job. Yet even when with his regiment, there was little in the duties of an officer which made familiarity with the habits and language of the sepoys either

[25] Quoted by Barat, op. cit., p. 217. Dr. Barat also makes the significant observation that when 6 more regiments mutinied, the colonel commanding was in no case present with his corps.

[26] A military Seminary founded by the Company in 1803. The majority of cadets 'educated themselves' and then applied for certificates of proficiency from professors at the Woolwich Academy.

[27] 1801–11, with a break during the Maratha War.

imperative or convenient. Courts-martial for sepoys were composed of native commissioned officers, and the main body of Europeans took no part in the trials, which must have been one of the best sources of instruction about the lives, habits and language of the men. It was easy for the regimental officer to continue to make the same mistakes, to go through his career without accumulating enough knowledge and experience to provide him with criteria for his own conduct. Those officers who did, from natural curiosity or concern, acquire such knowledge, soon found the opportunity to take their skills to staff or political appointments. In most cases, the very fact of an officer's having remained long with his regiment was an indication of his deficiency in the sort of aptitude which that regiment most needed. Sir John Kaye, in his history of the mutiny of 1857, wrote of regimental officers as 'men who could scarcely call for a glass of water in the language of the country, or define the difference between a Hindu and a [Muslim].' They were frustrated, bored and bewildered, and often added unpopularity to their incompetence by affecting to despise the Hindu 'prejudices' which in reality they did not understand.

The regimental officer had been the talisman of his sepoys, the receptacle of their loyalty and their link with authority. His eclipse had left a gap which not only insulated them from the object of their allegiance, but also encouraged private fantasy, speculation and fear. The sepoys had no sense of devotion to the Company itself, whose nature was too abstract and foreign for them to grasp (though they had at one time endowed it with the personality of an old woman), and their fidelity, in their new isolation, depended increasingly on the satisfaction of their superstitions, on the favourable augury of success and on cabalistic assurances of the continuing benevolence of fortune (*iqbal*). The native commissioned officers were not in a position to compensate for the deterioration in the number and quality of European regimental officers. They are curiously shadowy figures in the history of the Indian armies before 1857. The senior ones were liable to be commanded by the most callow subaltern, and it was never even made clear that they had authority over the two European sergeants attached to each native battalion. As current opinion was that all Indians were corrupt, their opportunities for important independent command had almost vanished; and they found themselves unqualified for staff positions which, in an increasingly institutionalized army, demanded high standards of literacy. Some European officers scorned them as clumsy and uneducated, and it appears that far less courtesy was now shown them than had been the case in the old days. If they were no longer received into officer society, neither were they accepted by the sepoys as being truly in the interests of the men and, consequently, in any crisis in the relationship between officers and soldiers they merely stood aside, and had little part.

The most serious indication that the medium of communication between authority and the ranks was collapsing had occurred not in Bengal, but in Madras. Here, in 1806, attempts to introduce innovations in dress and discipline (all in the cause of rationalization) had engendered a panic of fear and resistance. The new Commander-in-Chief, Sir John Cradock, had ordered that whiskers were to be trimmed in a uniform manner; that a leather cap was to be substituted for the turban; that caste marks were not to be worn on parade; that sepoys on guard duty should even answer the calls of nature in a military fashion, by waiting until enough men were in the same condition and then being marched down in a party—and so on. The policy had been silly and unnecessary, but hardly exceptional in a military context. In some regiments the new regulations had been enforced without trouble, but in the garrison at Vellore they had led to open mutiny. More than anything else, the rebellion had been a symptom of the crass incompetence of officers at regimental level, and it was afterwards suggested that had they been able to communicate with the men in their own language, the innovations would have caused no trouble. Without the necessary assurances from their officers, the sepoys had been bewildered and alarmed by regulations whose purpose they did not understand, a prey to agitators who disseminated the idea that they were part of some sinister plan to enforce mass conversion to Christianity; and the officers, at first unable to communicate and then themselves unable to understand, had succumbed in their turn to exaggerated apprehension and vicious reprisal.

The dangers inherent in the practice of restricting recruitment to the high-caste Hindus of Bihar and Oudh were not appreciated until it was too late to make changes. It appears that with the decline in the influence and capability of commanding officers, control over recruitment passed out of their hands. When, several years after the Nepal War, the experiment was tried of mixing other groups (chiefly Sikhs) into the infantry regiments, the Oudh and Bihar men refused to accept them, and bullied them out of the army. Bishop Heber mentions the case of a naik who was removed from the army by the government because he had become a Christian. There seems to be good ground for suggesting that the almost pathological fear of offending native 'prejudices' which prevailed in high quarters after the Vellore mutiny combined with the general ignorance among regimental officers of the exact nature of those prejudices to undermine the whole reality of European authority. More than one commentator of the first half of the nineteenth century insinuated that the superficial amenability of the Hindu sepoy was disguising the fact that control not only over recruitment, but also over a much wider aspect of the army's functioning, had ceased to be vested in its nominal masters; and it was complained that many indulgences were allowed the sepoys on the justification of caste precept which in reality had no such sanction. 'We should respect their casts', declared one critic[28] in 1821, 'but not descend with them to the indulgence of mere childishness—of things not meant or demanded by their faith, but assumed and imposed on our weakness and mistaken liberality.' 'The assumptions of vanity and laziness are too extensively admitted in the Bengal army', wrote another,[29] the following year. When giving evidence before the House of Commons in 1832, Captain Macon claimed that 'the most trifling alteration in dress [was] frequently made an excuse for discontent, and [that] this [was] artfully worked on by the natives of caste, such as the brahmins or priests'. Even Sir Henry Lawrence admitted that the ordinary sepoy was 'pampered and petted'.

By trying to treat the rationalization of the Bengal army as the justification for immediate economies instead of the means to long-term ones, the Court of Directors had brought that army into what can only be described as a state of arrested transformation. Rationalization had been allowed in principle and had even begun to be applied, but had then found itself stalemated by parsimony. The financial means and the local initiative necessary to bring it to completion were being denied. In 1814 the tragic paradox which was the gravest result of such myopic policy was already apparent.

[28] 'Carnaticus', *Asiatic Journal*, vol. xi, no. 65: May 1821.
[29] Author of *Military Sketches of the Goorkha War* (p. 53).

The quality of regimental officers was becoming seriously impaired by the grudging manner in which rationalization was being applied; yet it was only by means of superior officers at this level that the process itself could hope to be successful. Regimental officers were the only agency which could give meaning, in the eyes of the sepoys, to the injunctions of anonymous authority: they were the nerves essential to interpret the European mind of the army to its Asiatic body.

V

PREPARING FOR WAR

HASTINGS'S strategy for the invasion of Nepal shows him to have been abreast of the most recent developments in military thought. He appears to have had a certain knowledge of the ideas of Bourcet, the advocate of calculated dispersion in mountain war, and of Guibert, whose panacea was mobility[1]—a knowledge he could have acquired either by academic study or by following the campaigns of Napoleon, the theorists' most famous pupil.

He had to take account of the limited time available to an army based on the plains. Troops could not cross the Tarai until late October, and would have to be back in India by the beginning of the following April. After that time, malaria raged in the lowland jungles and marshes, cutting communications. Because time was so limited, both a conventional assault on the enemy capital and a Napoleonic-style attack on the enemy field army (leaving the capital to succumb more easily or even spontaneously later) were out of the question. Hastings reckoned that their mobility, and the ruggedness of their country, would enable the Gurkhas to avoid that decisive battle on which a single concentrated attack must rely for its success. Instead, therefore, of choosing between the enemy capital and the enemy field army, and leaving time to do the rest, he decided to divide his resources and launch independent but simultaneous attacks against them both. He was confident that the country could in this way be subjugated during a single campaign. The strategy of division would, besides preventing the enemy from prolonging resistance, considerably simplify the manipulation of the offensive force. It was known that valleys in the mountains were generally barren and often so constricted that it was impossible to dress a line of a thousand men. By dividing the army, problems of logistics would be minimized and increased rapidity of advance assured.

Extending the principle of diffusion even further, Hastings determined that each of his objectives—the army under Amar Singh

---

[1] See Liddell Hart, *The Ghost of Napoleon*, Chapter Two, *passim*.

Thapa, and that in Kathmandu—must be attacked not by a single force, but by two co-operating columns. This would prevent the two areas of operation from merging, by pinning down and keeping separate the two victims. He reasoned that if the advance on Amar Singh Thapa was supplemented by a column on its right, which could occupy the Dehra and Kayarda Duns and block the ghats across the Ganges and the Jumna, the field army would be prevented both from retreating towards the capital and from receiving reinforcements from it; while, if the main column advancing on Kathmandu was supported by a thrust on its left, this would bar the way to and from the west, making it impossible for the army in the capital to withdraw into the impenetrable hills of the Gurkha region or to receive assistance from the field army or Palpa.

Hastings selected the river Kali as the line dividing the eastern from the western theatre of war. In the eastern theatre, two columns were to march into the hills. The principal column of 6,500 men was to be commanded by Major-General Bennet Marley. His base and rendezvous was to be Dinapur, and his assignment the capture of the hill fort of Makwanpur, just south of the capital, and of Kathmandu itself. On Marley's left, a much smaller force, comprising somewhat less than 4,000 men, was to advance under Major-General John Sulivan Wood from Gorakhpur and occupy the disputed frontier lands in Siuraj and Butwal. The immediate aim of this force was to create a diversion in favour of the Kathmandu column, but if circumstances permitted it was to proceed to the capture of General Amar Thapa's headquarters at Tansen, the occupation of the town of Palpa, and the severing of the lines of communication between Kathmandu and the west.

In the western theatre, two forces were to converge on Amar Singh Thapa. The right-hand column, under Major-General Rollo Gillespie, consisting of about 4,500 regulars, was to move from Saharanpur into Dehra Dun and Kayarda Dun, occupy these valleys and the ghats on the Ganges and Jumna, and then veer left to support the activities of the second or left-hand column. This was to be under the command of Ochterlony, now promoted Major-General. He was given 6,000 men, and required to push forward from Rupar on the Sutlaj against the main army of Amar Singh Thapa. Once the two columns had coalesced, Gillespie was to assume the over-all command.[2]

---

[2] Hastings's own summary of his plan is in *P.R.N.W.*, pp. 702–3.

That, basically, was the plan. Again following a Napoleonic precedent, Hastings labelled his four columns 'divisions'. Each was organized as a brigade and a reserve and each had supporting artillery. Hastings had it in mind to throw forward yet a third column into the western theatre, to the east of the other two, against Kumaun, but intended to wait until the enemy was fully occupied in other quarters. In the meantime, however, a corps of *najibs* (irregulars) was to be raised in Rohilkhand in preparation for the projected operation. Gurkha recruiting agents had already been active among the fierce Muslim Pathan tribesmen of north Rohilkhand, and Hastings judged that enlisting them for the British effort would have the additional recommendation of denying the enemy the benefit of their services. Who better qualified to raise and command the force than Hyder Hearsey? Moorcroft had brought him to the notice of government as an informant of local knowledge and military experience; and Hearsey, overjoyed at the possibilities offered by a war with Nepal for the realization of his secret claim to Dehra Dun, had eagerly solicited a part in the projected conflict with the Gurkhas. Early in November he was instructed to raise a corps of 1,500 *najibs* in Rohilkhand. The Governor-General's remaining concern was to provide for the defence of the frontier of Purnea and Rangpur, bordering the far eastern provinces of Nepal. This task was entrusted to the new Rangpur Local Battalion, with a few companies of regulars, under the command of Captain Barré Latter. His headquarters were at Titalia, on the flat watery lowlands directly south from Darjeeling.

To make assurance double sure, Hastings fixed the strength of each principal column at twice the amount which his advisors estimated as necessary, and thereby mustered a force of 21,000 men to oppose an enemy whose strength he correctly estimated as 16,000

Careful collation of available assessments gives these approximate figures. A comparison of the figures given by Hastings in *P.R.N.W.*, pp. 703, 708, 712, and 715 with the details concerning the composition of each force given in ibid., pp. 195, 196, 197, and 433, shows that his figures are roughly correct only for Ochterlony's column. In the case of Gillespie's force the figure 2,343 for native infantry must be a misprint for 3,243, and no allowance is made for the regiment of native cavalry and the detachment of King's cavalry. The assessment on p. 715 for Marley's force (7,989) is too high. The Return for 23 Dec. 1814 gives the total combatant force as 6,686 (pp. 518–19). The figure for Wood's column on p. 712 is an overestimation. The *Calcutta Monthly Journal*, vol. xxv, Dec. 1814, p. 381, computes the force at 3,700. This seems much more likely. By March 1815 some 35,000 regulars and 13,000 irregulars were involved in the war.

at the most. He took care to include a good proportion of European troops in the invading columns. It was a common conviction that sepoys were most confident when they had a European example to emulate, and such encouragement was obviously going to be all the more necessary in the unknown country of the hills, which super-stitious dread and religious awe made them reluctant to enter, and where there would be no room for cavalry support or the familiar and reassuring textbook dispositions of infantry. Generals Marley, John Wood and Gillespie each had a battalion of King's infantry with his force, besides European artillery. Ochterlony did not have any European infantry, doubtless because his force was to be joined by Gillespie's at an early stage. Ordnance was provided on a generous scale, and Hastings advised his generals not to hesitate to make use of it. But he was convinced that mobility would be their most useful attribute, and he personally designed a howitzer carriage which could be dismantled and carried in separate por-tions. A similar pattern was adopted for the carriages of light cannon.

Special clothing was ordered to be issued to the troops at govern-ment expense. The customary thigh-length shorts of the sepoys were demonstrably unsuited to the cold weather and rough country of the hills, so both clothing Agents were instructed to make large quantities of cloth pantaloons. The orders were not placed until the middle of August, but somehow the second Agent, at Calcutta, was able to produce 7,000 pairs of pantaloons and an equal number of flannel *banyans* (waistcoats) by the beginning of October. This was sufficient to supply Marley's column, but John Wood was still waiting for his complement to be made up at the beginning of December. The provision of the two eastern columns proceeded even more slowly. The first Agent, at Fategarh, had in store cloth sufficient only for 4,000 pairs of pantaloons, and he had to apply to Calcutta for replenishment. He was still waiting in the middle of October. His pantaloons were apparently intended for Gillespie's column, but they could not have been ready in time to accompany the force. They were probably sent after it. Short ankle boots, with hobnails, and special caps were also prepared.

Persuaded that the army could not hope to feed itself from the country, Hastings ordered the formation of frontier depots, each with provisions for six months. Grain was plentiful at that time of year, and by prudent management was bought cheap. Each maga-

zine on the frontier was made sufficiently small to avoid creating a
local rise in price, and then supplemented by the formation of four
similar depots at regular intervals in its rear. On the withdrawal of
grain from the frontier, its stock could be made good by a requisition on the depot behind, which in its turn could be replenished
from the third, and so on. To carry provisions into the hills, mules,
tanyans (mountain ponies), elephants and camels could be used,
but the traditional bullocks would ultimately have to be replaced by
human porters, who cost half as much again to hire, and were only
perhaps a third as efficient. For this reason, every effort was made
to prune the convoys of superfluities. Forty Europeans were
assigned to each tent, instead of the normal sixteen, and no tents
at all were issued to the sepoys. In all the columns save the main
Kathmandu one, the system was adopted whereby the normal
foreign-service ration of the sepoys, which was over ample, was to
be halved in amount but offered free, and whereby provisions for
fifteen days, instead of a month, were to be carried. For easier
transportation, the Europeans' salted beef and spirits were put up
in small kegs, better adapted to human carriage. Throughout the
five months preceding the commencement of operations, dispatches
flew by express to and from the itinerant Headquarters of the
Governor-General, plans were drafted, troops were mustered at
their respective rendezvous, information was sifted, supplies were
gathered. Hastings surveyed the bustle and was well pleased:

I cannot conceal my having formed the highest expectation of a brilliant
and rapid termination of the war. The several divisions were, in numerical strength, fully equal to any opposition which the resources of the
enemy could subject them to encounter, and were, I may venture to say,
on a footing of efficiency in every branch of equipment unknown in
former wars. In the important article of supplies, for which it appeared
probable that the troops would be obliged to depend on our own depots
with little assistance from the country, the most able arrangements were
made by the Commissariat, and every article of necessary consumption
provided on a scale of utmost amplitude.[3]

On one issue only did he still have misgivings. The defences of
the whole Bengal Presidency were going to be dangerously weakened
by the withdrawal of troops who were scarcely sufficient for the
task of defence even when present in full strength in times of peace.

[3] *P.R.N.W.*, pp. 722–3

The war in the hills would naturally be followed with close interest by the Marathas and Ranjit Singh, and the merest hint of British embarrassment might precipitate irresistible attacks on the Company's denuded frontiers. This risk made it doubly essential that the hill campaigns be over as swiftly and as brilliantly as possible.

Remaining doubts about the adequacy of his invading columns to secure their communications and garrison captured forts were removed by a plan which, Hastings was confident, would bring hordes of supernumaries flocking to the British standard. All his informants assured him that, if he promised them liberation from the Gurkhas and the restoration of their ancient rulers, the subjugated hill peoples would be eager to provide active support for the invasion. Under this impression, he determined to court the allegiance of all available hill chiefs.

Although the plan had its origins in military considerations, it could not have been better calculated to solve the Governor-General's dilemma concerning the disposal of the territories which he expected to conquer in the hills. Their restitution to the Gurkhas would be out of the question if that troublesome race was to be prevented from recommencing its aggressions; yet on the other hand 'the annexation of the conquered country to the possessions of the Honorable Company [appeared] to be entirely inexpedient in every point of view in which the Governor-General [had] been able to consider the question'. Reinstating the exiled hill chiefs was obviously the answer, and it was decided to apply this policy to all the Gurkha territories except the Nepal Valley, the province of Kumaun and the Tarai lowland. The first the Gurkhas were to be allowed to retain; the last two Hastings resolved the Company should annex, as reparation for the war.

The man most obviously qualified to raise local rebellion was the indefatigable Harak Deva Joshi. Now nearly seventy, he was led at last out of obscurity into the light of official notice by Hyder Hearsey, who described him as 'the Earl of Warwick of [Garhwal and Kumaun] . . . a perfect instrument whose name the Gurkhas dread'. Hearsey claimed that he had 6,000 men at his command in Kumaun and a great influence over many of the exiled hill rajas. Hastings hoped that Harak Deva would be able to organize a force to seize the passes on the Jumna above Dehra Dun, thereby thwarting any plans which Amar Singh Thapa might contemplate for retreat to the east by the rugged routes of the north. Though fully aware of the government's intention to keep Kumaun, Harak Deva agreed to exert all his influence in favour of the British invasion. It was feared lest the head of the Phartiyal faction of Kumaun, Harak Deva's old rival Lal Singh, now at Kashipur, should sabotage the Company's plans, especially since the Gurkhas in Kumaun had taken pains to conciliate the Phartiyals; but in the event he gave no cause for apprehension, and seems to have abandoned politics for a life of piety and religious contemplation. Once plans to annex Garhwal had been abandoned in favour of the decision to keep Kumaun, the heir to Garhwal (Sudra Sen Shah), now in exile at Farakabad, was invited to join the British force in Dehra Dun 'to add his personal encouragement to the popular effort against the Gurkhas'. He was assured that his exertions would be rewarded by his restoration, and a proclamation was issued to his erstwhile subjects promising emancipation from Gurkha oppression.

Krishna Singh was a scion of the Sirmur royal family, and had been a leader of the revolt against the imbecile Raja Karman Prakash. Hyder Hearsey's private scheme for the invasion of the western hills, the notes for which were submitted confidentially to government by Moorcroft, assigned him a role as a partisan. Ochterlony was also acquainted with him, and suggested that if he was given money to purchase arms and pay his men he might raise a considerable body of auxiliaries—1,000, perhaps, or even 4,000. The proposition was readily agreed to, and the Resident at Delhi was instructed to advance funds to Krishna Singh for this purpose. The political settlement of Garhwal was to involve the perpetual exclusion of Karman Prakash, and the installation of his young son on the *gaddi* with Krishna Singh as regent. Ochterlony was confident that Ram Saran Sen of Hindur, now a Company protégé in the lowland remains of his once-extensive kingdom, would provide two or three hundred armed supernumeraries and a greater unarmed force to clear roads, carry supplies and act as guides, if promised a patent of restoration. The pledge was sanctioned, and a proclamation was addressed to all the other hill chiefs of this region, offering reinstatement under British guarantee in return for aid against the Gurkhas. Ochterlony further hoped that Raja Sansar Chand of Kotoch would volunteer to co-operate with the British. Sansar Chand had a considerable body of infantry trained and commanded by a wild and bibulous deserter from one of the King's Irish cavalry regiments, called O'Brien, who was known to Ochterlony and who now professed to be anxious to help the Company. Ochterlony was sure that Sansar Chand would be eager to avenge the loss of Kangra, indirectly the fault of Amar Singh Thapa, by allowing O'Brien to cross the Sutlaj and attack the Gurkhas simultaneously with the British. The government was enthusiastic at the prospect, seeing that Sansar Chand would be in a position to prevent Amar Singh's retreat westwards across the Sutlaj. But on no account was he to be encouraged to utilize the British invasion as a screen for the recovery of Kangra—a move which would offend Ranjit Singh and possibly furnish him with an excuse to enter the conflict on the side of the Gurkhas.

In the eastern theatre, General John Wood was instructed to invite the co-operation of the Raja of Tulsipur, whose old hill estate of Dang was now under Gurkha sway, and supplied with the draft of a proclamation encouraging rebellion among the inhabitants of the lands previously ruled by the Twenty-Two and Twenty-Four Rajas. The heir to the Palpa dominions was to be approached and encouraged to muster and arm as many followers as he could. Bradshaw was to urge the Raja of Ramnagarh to assert himself for the recovery of his ancient possession of Tanhu in the hills. But the most sanguine expectations of all were held of the heir to the Makwanpur dominions. In its heyday, the Makwanpur empire had stretched to the border of Sikkim and included the Kirata settlements of the Kosi basin, but it had then suffered tripartite division among members of the royal family. The prince of Makwanpur was the sole survivor of this family, and heir to the whole of its dominions. The government assumed that Makwanpur subjects now in the Gurkha army would 'readily flock to the standard of their ancient princes'; and Captain Latter, in command on the frontier east of the Kosi, was instructed to embody all the Kiratas who it was anticipated would rush to aid the cause of their legitimate chief and the Company. The Magistrate of Rangpur was requested to attempt to communicate with the Raja of Sikkim, still defying the Gurkhas from Gangtok.

Hastings had great confidence in his strategic and political schemes, and could not conceive the possibility of prolonged resistance from the Gurkhas. He devised a peace treaty which was designed to leave them 'a substantive power—however reduced in dignity, character, and resources'. The terms which Bradshaw, as

Political Agent, was to offer were: submission, due atonement for the outrage in Butwal and surrender of the officers responsible, relinquishment of all claim to the disputed lands, indemnity for the expenses of the war, recognition of all engagements made by the Company with the hill chiefs and the abandonment of all rights in lands captured by the British. In the first days of the war, Bradshaw was approached by the two surviving nephews of Damodar Panre, who were living as exiles in India. They hoped to secure the Company's support for an attempted revolution in Nepal; but this much Hastings refused to countenance. The overthrow of the present Kathmandu government would be a project fit for consideration only in the event of protracted resistance—'an extremity' he told the Court of Directors, 'which I did not contemplate'.[4]

Few people expected a serious war. 'Private advices, on the authority of which considerable reliance is placed, hold out reason to hope that the war will be speedily brought to a satisfactory and bloodless conclusion, by the entire submission of the Raja of Nepal to all the stipulations demanded of him', the *Calcutta Monthly Journal* assured its readers in November 1814. Such was certainly the tenor of opinion at Headquarters. Hastings even envisaged the possibility of a submission so hasty as to 'prevent the actual commencement of hostilities'.[5] His confidence caused him to be almost casual when selecting his commanding officers. He put each 'division' under the officer already commanding in the district where it was to be assembled, and forbore to lead one of the columns himself—thereby yielding to a wish to be fair towards his generals and to 'a natural repugnance to appear as if I were seeking petty opportunities for distinguishing myself'.[6]

The source of the Governor-General's optimism was his conviction that 'the difficulties of mountain warfare were greater on the defensive side than on that of a well-conducted offensive operation'[7]—and this, as Napoleon could have told him, and as the war was to demonstrate, was a major misconception.

---

[4] *P.R.N.W.*, pp. 257–8, 721.   [5] Ibid., p. 134.
[6] Aspinall, *Letters of George IV*, ii, p. 14.   [7] *Summary of Operations*, p. 132.

PART II

VI

FIASCO IN GARHWAL

AFTER the termination of their so-called military road, which
led from Kathmandu to Srinagar in Garhwal, the Gurkhas'
route to the west was known to pass through three main
points, all fortified. From Srinagar, the route went to a ghat on the
Song river, which flows across Dehra Dun and joins the Ganges in
the south-west corner. This point was protected by the fortress of
Kalanga. From Kalanga, the route struck west across Dehra Dun
to the Jumna. On this there were serveral fords and ghats, but all
were dominated by the important position of Kalsi, situated in the
angle formed by the confluence of the Tons and the Jumna. Beyond
the Jumna, in Sirmur, the route lay through Kayarda Dun and past
the town of Nahan at its western extremity. From there it continued
to the Sutlaj, through hidden alpine byways. Before joining
Ochterlony, Gillespie was to sever this line of communication.
First, Dehra Dun, Kalanga and the Jumna passes were to be
occupied; then he was to cross the Jumna into Sirmur, and capture
Nahan.

Robert Rollo Gillespie, of H.M. 25th Dragoons, was the most con-
troversial military officer in India. A diminutive, truculent and con-
ceited Irish aristocrat, he was the cynosure of circles where duelling,
drinking and sadistic sport were prescribed conduct and where his
lust for fame could masquerade as a sense of honour. During a wild
and scandalous youth, he had on several occasions fallen foul of the
law. The story of his altercation with eight nocturnal desperadoes,
who broke into his quarters in San Domingo to murder him, in
which he fought them off single-handed and killed six, had carried
his name into all the drawing-rooms of London. But it was as the
Hero of Vellore that Gillespie was best known. In July 1806, within

fifteen minutes of news of the mutiny at nearby Vellore reaching Arcot, where he was in command, Gillespie had roused a squadron of his regiment, saddled, mounted and set off to the rescue at a furious pace, while the rest were limbering the guns and preparing to follow. The gate of Vellore fort being in the hands of the mutineers, he had entered by climbing a rope let down the wall by the European survivors, then rallied the remnants of the garrison and kept the enemy at bay until the guns arrived from Arcot and blew open the gates, admitting the relieving force.

In October 1814, however, this dazzling reputation was in danger. Disgrace and humiliation were threatening Gillespie.

The trouble had begun with the decision to expel the Dutch from Java in 1811. Gillespie had played his usual conspicuous part in the operations, and had then been appointed commander of the British occupation force. He had soon quarrelled violently with the civilian Lieutenant-Governor, Stamford Raffles, whose measures of military retrenchment he opposed and whom he despised on personal grounds as a churlish upstart. Fretting to be free, he had pestered the Commander-in-Chief, Nugent, with requests for a transfer. Finally, another officer had been found to take his place in Java and Gillespie was given command of the Second Division, Field Army, in Bengal. In the euphoria of release, he had made effusive demonstrations of reconciliation with Raffles, and the two had parted in October 1813 apparently on the best of terms.

Now on board the *Troubridge*, bound for Calcutta, had been Mrs. Blagrave, who hated Raffles. She was the wife of an acting secretary to the Java government, whom Raffles had dismissed for dishonesty, incapability and insubordination. Blagrave's appointment in Java had in any case only been temporary; but instead of proceeding to Amboina, for where he was professedly bound, he had challenged Raffles's power to dismiss him without reference to the supreme government, and gone to Calcutta to seek redress. The fact that he was in considerable debt no doubt increased the grudge that he and his wife bore against Raffles. What had happened on the *Troubridge* can only be surmised; but it seems that Mrs. Blagrave had got the ear of Gillespie and by a judicious use of backstairs gossip and tearful accusation (and, perhaps, amorous favours) had revived all his old detestation of Raffles. On arriving at Calcutta he had consulted Blagrave and then submitted a formal indictment of Raffles's administration, concentrating on the matter of the sale of

MAP 2. Illustrating the operations in Garhwal and Sirmur in 1814

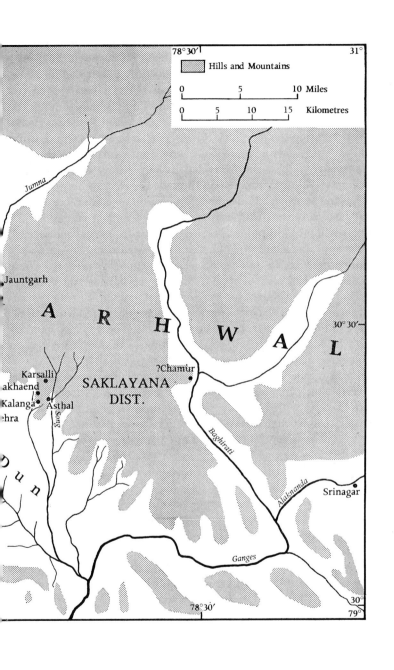

government lands in Java and the Lieutenant-Governor's participation as a private purchaser. Raffles had easily refuted the charge
of venality, and had made Gillespie look a fool for good measure.
He had pointed out that Gillespie had been in Java during the
whole episode, had known of it, yet had said nothing. Among the
minor heads of indictment, Gillespie had accused Raffles of exces-
sively debasing the new Java coinage; yet the records showed that
Raffles had in fact advocated a nearer approximation to the Calcutta rupee, only to be overruled by members of his Council—
including Gillespie. Raffles had then made counter-charges, which
purported to expose Gillespie as a slave-driver and a lecher. The
first charge related to the impressment of unpaid labour for the
construction of Gillespie's private house at Chipanas; the second,
to the appearance one night, at the orphan school in Samarang, of a
man employed by Gillespie, who demanded a virgin. These
accusations had shocked the Calcutta government, and Hastings
had admonished Raffles for tasteless recrimination. But Raffles was
angry, and instead of withdrawing the charges had added another.
Apparently, on a further occasion, Gillespie had actually sent soldiers to seize a slave girl from the house of Mr. Sluyster, in
Batavia.

By now, the whole sordid affair was an embarrassment to the
government, which was anxious to silence Raffles. 'After all, what
is to be done with Gillespie? There is no competent tribunal here
to take cognizance of his conduct as a military man', said the
Government Financial Secretary to Charles Assey, who had gone
to Calcutta on Raffles's behalf. Assey, reporting this to his chief,
wrote: 'If we are to judge from the secretaries of the sentiments of
the Governor-General himself, it is the question of disgrace on the
Major-General which forms a great obstacle in the judgement of
the present case; it is satisfactory however, to recollect that if such
should be the inclination in Bengal, there is an ulterior tribunal . . .'

On the eve of his departure for Nepal, Gillespie was probably
not completely sane. The head wounds he had received at Cornelis
may well have unbalanced a mind already unsettled by megalomania
and alcohol. Even before their first quarrel, Raffles had remarked
on his strange starts and wild freakish behaviour; and Lady Nugent,
who had 'long and many conversations with him' after his arrival
in Bengal, was convinced that 'his mind was certainly sadly disturbed.' 'I could not but see', she wrote in her Journal, 'that

natural impetuosity and his extraordinary vanity and love of fame had led him into false ideas and errors that would embitter his future life.' Then, on top of all this, had come Raffles's accusations, threatening him with ignominy that he had not the moral courage to face and filling his sick brain with a craving for the fresh glory that was its only certain antidote.

The troops moving up from Meerut were delayed by the usual lack of baggage animals, and it was not until late on 19 October that Gillespie's division was assembled on the sultry plains north of Saharanpur. It consisted of about 4,400 fighting men, 900 of them Europeans. Besides the King's 53rd Regiment of Foot[1] (1st Battalion), the latter consisted of a troop of the 8th, or Royal Irish, Dragoons, and a detachment of horse artillery. The native complement comprised about 3,000 sepoys, 138 pioneers, some 200 gun lascars[2] and ordnance drivers, a regiment of native cavalry and a *risala* (troop) of Skinner's Horse. Cavalry was provided for use on the level spaces of Dehra Dun, where it was hoped it might confound the Nepalis, who were unaccustomed to contending with this arm. Non-combatant public servants swelled the force to some 10,000; and then there were about 5,000 camp followers and officers' private servants. In response to strong recommendations, officers had reduced their baggage to what they considered to be a minimum; but this was obviously not going to involve any spartan self-denial. Major John Ludlow, commanding a battalion of native infantry, still needed six camels even before he had packed his supply of spare liquor.

Gillespie was not satisfied that his force was adequate—especially since Hastings's plan required the establishment of numerous detached posts. The Governor-General agreed to provide another battalion of native infantry, but this could not be expected to join the division until Dehra Dun had been occupied. Gillespie sensed that Hastings was perhaps underestimating the difficulties in prospect, and privately he even admitted presages of disaster —an uncharacteristic sentiment. While waiting for his force to congregate, he was restless and irritable, and he began to put his

---

[1] Later the King's Shropshire Light Infantry.
[2] Each company of European artillery (composing several details, one to each gun) had native gun lascars attached. Their function was to man the drag ropes, guard and serve out the ammunition, and carry the match. They were not supposed, for political reasons, to serve the gun itself.

instructions into operation even before all the troops had arrived at Saharanpur.

There were two principal passes into Dehra Dun through the Siwaliks, as the foothills in this area are called: the Timli pass in the west, and the Mohan pass in the east. On the morning of 19 October Lieutenant-Colonel Carpenter, already at Saharanpur with his battalion of native infantry, was sent with his sepoys and three pieces of light artillery to force the Timli pass and secure the Jumna. At daybreak the following morning a detachment of about 1,000 men, including two companies of the King's 53rd and the native cavalry, was sent under Colonel Sebright Mawby of the 53rd to march into the Dun via the Mohan pass and seize the fortress of Kalanga. Hastings had suggested that the Kalanga column be sent without artillery; but Gillespie, more wary, decided to send the two cavalry 'gallopers' (six-pounders) with Mawby. He obviously expected the passes to be heavily defended, because on the 21st the remainder of the 53rd was ordered off to the village of Jaundra, below the hills and equidistant from both passes, so that it could support either detachment in case of need. As it happened, the Timli pass, at least, was not guarded at all. Carpenter cleared it on the morning of the 20th, moved up the Jumna posting pickets at the main ghats, and reached Kalsi unopposed, the Nepali garrison having withdrawn to the fort of Birat, further north.

As Carpenter entered Dehra Dun, Mawby left Saharanpur. He made his way through fine flat country where the rice crop was ripe, until within view of the jumbled crags and humps of the Siwaliks. The detachment camped for the night at the ruined town of Khiri, on a marshy riverside, then on 21 October made a four-mile march to the hills through a sparse jungle of stunted trees and grasses, disturbing game of every description. The Mohan[3] pass was in fact the route of a river bed—now almost dry, and very stony. The main force halted below the hills while Captain Fast, on his own offer, pushed forward with two companies of sepoys to secure the top of the pass. It was not unguarded. The Nepalis had strongly stockaded the crest, but Fast was easily able to scatter the few defenders. At midnight he sent down word that he had got possession of the top.

The rest of the detachment began to move up an hour before

---

[3] Sometimes called the Khiri pass, after the town at its foot.

daylight. The pass was only three and a half miles long, but so entangled in trees and cacti that the troops had to march on the river bed itself. This was not only painful, but also dangerous, because the stones and boulders had no hold in the sand, and rolled underfoot. The cavalry were compelled to dismount, and the guns had to be dragged up by men. It was eleven o'clock before the ascent was completed. Two hours later, Mawby's force marched into the little town of Dehra, situated in a wilderness of high grass with groves of sal and sissu, and abounding with tigers, elephants, peacocks and every other variety of game.

Once camp was pitched, the Colonel and his staff rode about five miles to the north-east to reconnoitre Kalanga fort, but by the time they approached the hill on which it was situated the light was failing and it proved impossible to form a useful impression of the position. About midnight, a letter was sent to the castellan, Bal Bahadur Singh, demanding the surrender of the fort. Tradition recounts that he tore it up, observing that it was not his custom to deal with correspondence at such unseasonable hours. Early on the 23rd Mawby and his officers, this time with an escort of light infantry and cavalry, went again to reconnoitre. Their examination of the ground was very cursory, because Mawby was fearful of being cut off by prowling enemy detachments. He nevertheless felt he had seen enough of the position to plan a full-scale attack, to take place the following morning. That night, Carpenter arrived in Dehra, thus increasing Mawby's force to 1,300 infantry, 300 cavalry, and 5 light guns.

Kalanga fort, also called Nalapani, was on the highest point of one of the low spurs which jut southwards into the Dun from its northern rim of mountains. On its western side, the Kalanga spur plunges almost vertically for 1,000 feet to the valley floor. The eastern flank slopes away more gently until, about a mile from the summit, it suddenly drops 600 feet to the Song river. The most accessible approach is the southern, which is still marked by a stony road from Dehra. This climbs steadily, but not too steeply, for about three miles, before reaching the so-called table land. This is a narrow strip of fairly level ground 200 feet below the summit, and separated from it by the deep furrow of a watercourse (the Nalapani) which comes down from the north and then turns west in its descent to the valley. The summit itself is thus in the form of a knoll naturally moated on two sides. Its slopes formed a glacis for the fort, which perched on its highest point. The spur was then, as now, thickly planted with birch and poplar, save in the vicinity of the fort, where it was clear like a tonsure. The fort was irregular in shape, following contours of the ground. Its outer defences, no more than twelve feet high, consisted of a double palisade filled with stones, surmounting a mud rampart. This glorified stockade was reckoned to harbour some 600 people, of whom not more than half could have been in any sense soldiers.

At half-past four on the morning of 24 October, Mawby advanced his infantry and guns to the foot of the southern aspect of the spur and sent the cavalry round to the village of Rajpur, north of the fort, to intercept the enemy if they should attempt flight. At dawn, the infantry climbed to the table land without opposition—save for the harmless fire of a few small cannon from the fort. A fatigue party of the 53rd then went down for the two six-pounders, and dragged them up within an hour. The guns were opened on the fort soon after, and continued their fire for several hours; but by eleven o'clock they had not made any impression on its defences. Mawby decided that they must be got nearer, and had one pushed up the table land along the road leading to the fort. But it was then discovered that, at the end of the table land, the road turned sharply left, dipping severely to cross the watercourse. This obstacle, and the fact that enemy outposts were dispersed over the whole distance, induced him to abandon the operation. His artillery was obviously too light to make a breach, and he considered the place too strong to be attacked without preliminary cannonade. The force therefore returned to camp that same afternoon. Mawby's decision was in perfect consonance with Hastings's instructions, which strictly enjoined that Kalanga was not to be assaulted without heavy artillery should reconnaissance show its use to be expedient.

When he heard of the safe arrival of Carpenter and Mawby in the Dun, Gillespie was relieved, and imagined the most tricky part of the first stage of his operations to be over. He wrote to Ochterlony, making him a provisional promise of collateral aid in Sirmur about 1 November, and ordered the dragoons and three light companies of sepoys to march from Saharanpur to a position on the east bank of the Jumna, near the foot of the Timli pass, where they would be ready to cross the river. He then took a small escort and briskly followed Carpenter up the Timli pass into Dehra Dun to inspect Kalsi, Birat and the Jumna ghats. It was on 25 October, while engaged in this examination, that he received Mawby's report of the unsuccessful attempt against Kalanga. He had not reckoned on having to give his own attentions in that direction, and was vexed at having his plans interrupted by what he thought was Mawby's timidity. But Kalanga was a stumbling block and would have to be removed—removed quickly, too, if he was to keep his promise to Ochterlony. On the 25th he sent word to Mawby that he would join him at Dehra the next day, and ordered those parts of his army still on the plains to march without delay into the Dun.

For the dragoons and light infantry on the Jumna, and for the corps at Saharanpur, the journey to Dehra Dun was relatively easy and quick. The former were already at the foot of the Timli pass, and the latter had only to follow the main route from Saharanpur to the Mohan pass—well trodden by now. But for the eight companies of the 53rd at Jaundra the march was much more difficult. They had to move eastwards to reach the Mohan pass and, as the nullas draining down from the foothills flow in a southerly direction, the route lay across the numerous watercourses, instead of parallel to them. The road was, furthermore, bad and very tortuous. The force broke ground at 5 a.m. on 28 October, and trudged about twenty miles in the course of the day, crossing no fewer than five running streams. It was hot, and the column straggled badly, the luggage and sick taking all night to reach the camping ground at Khiri. Here the tents had to be pitched on low marshy ground beside a nulla, where water oozed out of the soil in the footprints of the camels. The troops lay in the damp all night and the baggage became soaked. Gillespie, not aware of these difficulties, sent a liverish note to Lieutenant-Colonel Buckland on the 29th, requiring him to make haste. Camp was struck at one o'clock, but before the march was many hours old many men had collapsed by the roadside. Not more than four or five miles had been covered by dusk and that night camp had to be pitched in the pass itself, on the stony river bed where there was no level ground and no place to drive a tent pin. It was nearly noon the next day before the sick and all the stragglers had come up. Because of the heat and the exhaustion of the troops, it was ordered that the march be halted until moonrise; but the officers caused chaos by trying to send on their baggage and private servants in advance. The public bearers and camp followers drifted after them, pursued by swearing soldiers. As the sides of the ravine converged to form the narrow summit of the pass, the camels and their attendants were forced together into a suffocating mass. Many animals fell, blocking the road, and the din was stunning. It was dark before the baggage was out of the pass, and ten o'clock before all the men had followed. When the force was finally in some sort of muster order, the march to Dehra was resumed. The distance was about ten miles.

Bruised and tired out, they reached Dehra at midnight, only to find it deserted. Fresh tent marks were visible in the moonlight; but there was no sign of the army and by some oversight no guide had been left to indicate where it had gone. The men had to wait for three hours while the acting Quartermaster probed around gingerly for signs of the vanished army. Finally he found the new ground, which was three or four miles to the north-east, at the base of Kalanga hill. Wearily, the men trekked forward again and finally stumbled into camp just as the clocks were striking four. Only the native cavalry were there to explain what was happening, because operations against Kalanga had already begun and all the infantry had taken up positions round the fort. A few hours later, when the dawn was breaking, the sound of gunfire echoed around the valley; and soon after, just as the men were thinking that they could get some rest at last, an urgent order arrived from General Gillespie. Three companies of the 53rd were to march to the table land immediately.

Gillespie had joined Mawby on the morning of the 26th, in no sweet temper. Early on the 27th he went out to examine the fort and spent an exhausting day reconnoitring. He appreciated the strength of the position, but did not doubt his ability to take it.

Here I am [he wrote breezily to Major-General Grant Keir] with as stiff and strong a position as ever I saw, garrisoned by men who are fighting *pro aris et focis* in my front and who have decidedly formed the resolution to dispute the fort as long as a man is alive. The fort stands on the summit of an almost inaccessible mountain, and covered with an impenetrable jungle, the only approaches commanded, and stiffly stockaded. It will be a tough job to take it; but by the 1st proximo I think I shall have it, *sub auspice Deo*![4]

He chose an advanced position for the camp, nearer the foot of the hill, and ordered the preparation of fascines, gabions and scaling ladders. By 29 October the dragoons and light infantry from Timli

[4] Printed in the *Memoir*, p. 219.

and the infantry from Saharanpur had reached Dehra with the rest of the artillery; but there was still no sign of the remaining companies of the 53rd. Gillespie, determined to have the fort by 1 November, made plans to act without them. The available force was divided into four columns and a reserve, which were to attack Kalanga simultaneously from all accessible quarters—the north, the east and the south. After a preliminary bombardment, Captain John Fast was to close in from the village of Lakhaend, on the north-west flank of the spur; Major Kelly from the village of Karsalli, on the crest of the spur about two miles north of the fort; and Captain John Campbell from the hamlet of Asthal, on the eastern ridge near the brink of the Song river ravine. The main force with the scaling ladders, under Carpenter, and the reserve under Major Ludlow were to attack from the table land. At daybreak on 30 October the Major-General ordered camp to be moved to the advanced position, preparatory to a commencement of operations the same afternoon.

At three o'clock, Carpenter's column made for the table land. The Nepalis opened a fire from the fort, but it was ill-directed and erratic, and did little damage. Ludlow then followed with the reserve, and after him came the pioneers and the guns. As the guns were all comparatively light—there were two brass twelve-pounders, two six-pounders and a couple each of small mortars and howitzers —they were taken from their carriages and strapped to the backs of elephants. The strength and perseverance of these animals were titanic. They disliked steep or uneven ground; yet they now mounted the pathway to Kalanga carrying loads of six and even twelve hundredweight. By working all through the night, the pioneers had the guns in battery by daybreak, facing the southern defences of the fort across the watercourse.

At about midnight, while these preparations were going forward, Gillespie at last received news of the approach of the 53rd and, before retiring to his tent, he left orders that they were to remain in the camp for its protection. In the early hours of the morning of the 31st, the first stages of his plan were carried out. Kelly left camp for Karsalli at two o'clock, and Fast and Campbell moved to their respective rallying points an hour later. Each had synchronized his watch with the Major-General's and all had been carefully briefed. A signal was to be fired exactly two hours before the assault, the purpose of this interval being to give each officer time to correct his distance from the fort—for it was anticipated that the guides might be unreliable. The signal was to be the discharge of five guns preceded by a silence of five minutes; and Gillespie, expecting a breach to be ready by noon, gave his officers to understand that they should listen for the signal at about ten o'clock. In his field orders he laid great stress on the importance of simultaneity in the various attacks, of compactness in the columns, of judicious use of bayonets and, above all, of composure: 'Let emulation actuate all; but corrected by steadiness and coolness—no breakings of ranks or running for who is to be foremost in the contest—each column must be a mutual support—and every soldier actuated by the principle of cool and deliberate valour will always have the advantage over wild and precipitate courage.'[5] Never can a man's example have belied his precepts so blatantly as Gillespie's was to do, that day.

He rose at five o'clock, and at the first glimmer of day rode up to the table land. At sunrise the guns exploded into action. After they had been open for an hour and a half it had again become obvious that field artillery could do little damage at so great a distance. Shot after shot either fell short, or flew over the fort; and the few that landed on target had too little impact to damage. Gillespie fidgeted and fumed and decided that he must put an end to all this futile fumbling by another spectacular escalade. Was he not the acknowledged past master of the art of daring assault? By eight o'clock, dudgeon and vanity had destroyed all self-control and he ordered the signal for the attack to be given.[6] His officers were aghast, and besought him to delay until the appointed time, urging that a breach could yet be made in the four hours remaining. But the Major-General irascibly waved aside such counsel, and the prescribed discharges had to be made: three at intervals of a minute, and then two in rapid sequence. This was Gillespie's first blunder. The officers with the supporting columns, thinking that they did not need to pay special attention to the pattern of gun fire for another two hours, did not recognize the signal.[7]

[5] Printed in the *Memoir*, p. 224.
[6] The *Memoir* says seven o'clock, but this agrees with no other account. It is obviously calculated from the time of the assault, and is based on the assumption that no culpability attached to Gillespie.
[7] Mawby's dispatch (*P.R.N.W.*, p. 439) says that they did not hear the signal —but this can hardly mean that the guns were inaudible to them. The sound of ordnance travelled so well in the hills that when this division was before Nahan,

Just before nine o'clock, a party of Nepalis, which had moved out of the fort during the night to a position on the eastern end of the table land in order to harass the parties working at the batteries, moved up with the obvious intention of taking the guns in flank. In great excitement, Gillespie ordered a howitzer to be turned on them. A dose of grapeshot checked the party; and when charged by a group of sepoys at bayonet point, they dispersed and began to retreat. To Gillespie, already devoured by feverish impatience, the retreat of this party was an irresistible cue for action. He commanded Carpenter and Ludlow to pursue and enter the fort on its tail. This was his second, and inexcusable, error. Only one hour had elapsed since the signal; and even though it might have been argued that the time of the signal itself had been fixed only approximately and was liable to variation according to circumstances, the lapse of two hours between the signal and the storm was the essential ingredient in the plan of operations. But this did not deter Gillespie, who fancied he could change the plan even at this late hour. He sent urgent missives to the officers in charge of the supporting columns, commanding them to attack immediately. But that very contingency which the two-hour lapse had been designed to compensate had materialized, and their guides had led the supporting columns astray. Gillespie's orders, though sent in duplicate by different routes, never reached their destinations. It was at this stage that the Major-General sent down for three companies from those of the 53rd which had just arrived in camp. Here was another capricious order which, conflicting with a previous one, failed to have the desired effect. Instructions having been left that these companies of the 53rd were to remain in the camp for its protection, dispositions had been made accordingly. The arrival of fresh orders found the regiment quite unprepared, as well as jaded, and the officer designated to lead the detachment to the table land, Captain Wheeler Coultman, could not be found. Three companies were hastily put under arms and paraded, but for about half an hour the utmost confusion prevailed and no move was made. Part of the summit of Kalanga spur being visible from the camp, the troops were actually the spectators of an action in which they were supposed to be taking part.

---

the guns of Ochterlony's column, some 30 miles away, were audible to it. The *Memoir* says that Kelly and Fast did not hear—but this hardly explains Campbell's failure to arrive.

Once begun, that action unfolded swiftly to a half-ludicrous, half-tragic, climax. Carpenter's force consisted of about 600 men, including the two companies of the 53rd which had arrived in the Dun with Mawby and 50 dismounted Royal Irish Dragoons. It was supported by Ludlow's, originally 900 strong, but now reduced to 136 sepoys and 50 dragoons as a result of successive detachments made during the night. The dragoons were put at the front of the combined column of attack, and it soon became obvious that this was a grave mistake. They had splendid *brio* as they sprinted down the table land, veered sharply left to cross the watercourse and surged up the eastern glacis of the fort in pursuit of the retreating Nepalis; but it was a pace which the infantry, encumbered with knapsacks and muskets, and the pioneers, labouring under the scaling ladders, could not equal. When between sixty and eighty yards from the fort, the dragoons reached some huts protected by a semicircular stockade. They chased the enemy from this position; but now that they were almost up with their prey they found themselves much too far in advance and entirely unsupported. Nepali soldiers were swarming over the walls of the fort to support their comrades. *Khukuris* unsheathed, they engaged the oncoming dragoons in a fierce hand-to-hand struggle, thrusting within the point of the sabres and parrying every swipe before it could be completed with shields borne on the left arm. These they wielded with dazzling dexterity. 'There was no end to the damn pot lid', recalled one dragoon later, 'no getting over, nor under, nor round about it. It was like bad luck—everywhere!'[8] Within a few minutes, fifty-eight dragoons were lying wounded and four dead. The onslaught had been checked, and the Nepalis clambered back into the fort, ready to resist the next wave of assailants with shot, arrows and stones.

The pioneers and the infantry battled their way grimly through this cascade of missiles. Lieutenant Ellis of the engineers sprang ahead, to encourage the pioneers, but was shot dead while placing the first ladder against the wall. The pioneers wavered and then fell back in disorder to the huts, abandoning the ladders as they retreated. The infantry, headed by the two companies of the 53rd, advanced, but were soon forced to retreat and take cover behind the stockade. At about this time the huts caught fire. The scaling

---

[8] Letter signed 'Parry': *E.I.U.S.J.*, vol. viii, April 1836, pp. 274–6.

ladders were destroyed in the blaze and all means of entering the fort lost.

Hearing of this check, Gillespie became frantic. Notwithstanding that there was no breach in the defences, that none of the supporting columns had made its appearance and that the three companies of the 53rd ordered up from the camp an hour ago still had not arrived, he refused to give up the assault. The idea of failure made him giddy with rage. He dashed off a note to Carpenter, exhorting him to keep his post to the last extremity for he intended coming up to command operations himself, and sent another furious summons to camp for the dithering three companies of the 53rd. Meanwhile all fire was ceased.

It was now about ten o'clock. In the dim forest around the fort, the officers heading the supporting columns, after having led their men all through the night and morning by widely circuitous and almost impenetrable pathways at the behest of treacherous guides, called a halt, took out their watches and listened. For half an hour no firing was heard from the batteries; and when it recommenced there was only a confused cacophony of sound. Artillery, musketry and some unidentifiable explosion could be heard, but nothing recognizable as the anticipated signal. Concluding that Gillespie was not yet ready to forewarn them of the assault, they adjusted their positions and waited patiently.

At half-past ten, Wheeler Coultman and the three companies of the 53rd at last arrived on the table land with two horse artillery six-pounders, drawn up by the men. Gillespie harangued them for their delay. He swore loudly that he would take the fort or be killed in the attempt, and ordered them forward with the guns. The troops, who hated Gillespie for his vicious strictness in matters of drill and dress, advanced morosely, pulling the guns by the drag ropes. They went down the table land to the point where the road turned left to cross the watercourse, then down one side of the channel and up the other to the eastern glacis of the fort, where the two assaulting columns were still sheltering behind the stockade from a heavy fire. Here Gillespie and his staff came up, and there was a hasty council of war. One of the dragoons of Ludlow's detachment had discovered, in a north-western wall, a gateway to the fort, in which was set a wicket. He offered to guide the General to the spot. Gillespie eagerly consented and, accompanied now by Ludlow, the three companies pressed on, leaving one of the guns at the stockade to cover the advance. They had to pick their way among the dead and wounded strewing the ground; but the huts were still burning and the smoke provided a screen for the movement. Turning right close under the walls of the fort, the party proceeded round to its north-western side. There, sure enough, was the wicket; but Bal Bahadur, expecting an attempt to force it, had left it open and constructed barricades of stones and logs in the gap. Across this formidable obstacle appeared the nozzle of a cannon.

Lieutenant Kennedy of the horse artillery ran on ahead to select a position for the six-pounder, which he managed to bring within thirty or forty yards of the wicket. One or two rounds were fired and they apparently crippled the enemy gun. Gillespie ordered Ludlow to lead the 53rd to the assault. As they advanced there was a flash in the wicket, and a discharge of grapeshot killed seven men and wounded many more, showering the air with blood and lumps of flesh. The troops recoiled. Ludlow tried to rally them, while Gillespie sat transfixed by rage, watching them grope and flounder helplessly under an avalanche of shot, arrows, darts and stones, fired and hurled furiously from the defences by children and women as well as men. Ludlow himself was struck by a stone on the thigh. Then, seizing their opportunity, the Nepalis again clambered out of the fort, rushed up to the six-pounder and, with great aplomb, silenced it by cutting the only sponge staff in two.

Gillespie, finally roused from his paroxysm, ordered a retreat, and violently abused the troops for having failed. He seemed liable to order them to go back, but Ludlow remonstrated, insisting that it would be senseless to attack again in front. He suggested that the gun might instead be taken in flank, by moving a column obliquely to it. Gillespie's reaction was not coherent, but Ludlow saw that he 'seemed to approve'. The two companies of the 53rd which had formed part of Carpenter's column had by now arrived from the stockade, and Gillespie ordered Ludlow to lead them down the right flank of the gun while he formed a second detachment to send in from the left. The Major mustered his men; but they had already seen too much of the punishment inflicted on their comrades, had already been too long exposed themselves and loathed Rollo Gillespie too intensely to act with any confidence. Ludlow saw that no sooner had they moved than they edged farther to their right, into the shelter of a depression in the ground. Rather than interrupt the advance, he tried to accommodate the deviation by inclining with them, but the men ducked into the depression and started sniping. When Ludlow neared the wicket, he had only four soldiers with him. He turned and pleaded with the others, crying out that if only eight men more would come on he would enter the fort; but he was ignored. 'I addressed a sergeant, which was the only person of authority I found in advance,' he recalled, 'but he turned a deaf ear to all I could say.' He was convinced that this attempt could have been successful, because the vigour of the defenders' resistance now seemed to be slackening. The men of the 53rd stubbornly spurned their opportunity. They had determined to destroy their hated general—even, if necessary, at the price of destroying themselves.

Their dogged restiveness sent Gillespie berserk. He had cheated danger so often, that he had come to regard his life as charmed. There was no instinctive check to the impulse of rage and despair. Screaming and waving his sword, he dashed forward into the torrent of fire. A musket ball struck him in the chest and brought him sprawling to the ground. He died before he could utter another word. Lieutenant O'Hara, Ludlow's adjutant, fell almost at the same time and Captain Byers, Gillespie's aide-de-camp, was wounded in the leg. Both these officers had rushed after the Major-General—though whether to support him or restrain him is not clear.

It was just before 11.15. A short distance away, in the forest to the rear, Captain John Campbell was at the village of Asthall, still waiting for the signal gun. For some time he had heard confused firing, but, remembering Gillespie's emphatic injunctions, dared not move in anticipation of his cue. He grew increasingly uneasy, however, as the sounds of commotion continued and the signal still was not fired. Finally, fearing that there had been some mistake, he decided to advance. He arrived on the scene of action just as Ludlow was giving the order to retire and, if a few minutes too late to be of any use to Gillespie, was at least able to cover the retreat and bring down the gun, which was in danger of being lost.

The command now devolved on Mawby, who immediately withdrew the army from the hill, resolved to relinquish all plans for a further attack until he had heavy battering ordnance. Bal Bahadur permitted the dead and wounded to be brought down from the hill; but many of the corpses had already been stripped of their clothing and were horribly mutilated. When the reckoning was complete, it appeared that of the European officers, 5 had been killed and 18 wounded; of the men and native officers, 30 killed and 210 wounded.

Gillespie's body was preserved in spirits, and at four o'clock on the morning of 1 November a small cortège bore it down to Meerut. On 6 November it was interred with full military honours and minute guns, one for each year of his life, thundered out at Calcutta. But he was not lamented. The officers of the 53rd were frankly glad that he had gone. 'It is the general opinion here', wrote Henry Sherwood, Paymaster to the regiment, 'that Gillespie's death has saved the army . . . As long as he had lived, the Europeans would have remained unresisting to be killed.' In Meerut, the ladies giggled at his funeral, so tickling was the idea of his having been laid in spirits—'a pickle when alive, and a preserve when dead!'

When Hastings heard of the disaster, his immediate reaction was to blame Gillespie. Even while making suitable decent acknowledgement of Gillespie's merits, he could not disguise a surge of irritation at the thought of 'the discredit to our arms and the baneful influence which this reverse must have upon the future operations' —especially as it had apparently been caused by the very impetuosity against which he had so earnestly cautioned the Major-General. On 10 November he wrote to Lord Bathurst:

The good fortune which had attended him in former desperate enterprises induced him to believe, I fear, that the storm of the fortress of Kalanga might be achieved by the same daring valour and readiness of resource whereby he had on other occasions triumphed over obstacles apparently insuperable.

The assault, in which he was killed at the foot of the rampart, involved, as I conceived, no possibility of success; otherwise the courage of the soldiers would have carried the plan notwithstanding the determined resistance of the garrison.[9]

Such was the obvious interpretation of the evidence available to Hastings at this stage—that is, his own knowledge of Gillespie's character and the official dispatch submitted by Mawby. Information in the dispatch was incomplete, because Mawby had not been a witness of the final assault, Gillespie having ordered him to remain on the table land to receive yet another two companies of the 53rd summoned from camp. In subsequent weeks, Hastings received private accounts of the day's events. His principal informants

[9] Quoted in Robert H. Murray, *History of the 8th King's Royal Irish Hussars*, vol. i, p. 371.

were Captain John Sparks Byers, of the Royal Artillery, who had been Gillespie's A.D.C., and John Ludlow. Byers had seen the perfidy of the 53rd, and was never likely to forget it. Mawby unsuspectingly referred the Governor-General to him for further information, and Byers was soon on his way from Saharanpur (where he had gone to recuperate from his leg wound) to Headquarters, at Lucknow. John Ludlow was an intimate of George Fagan, the Adjutant-General, and through Fagan he made known at Headquarters his own version of events. When Hastings had heard these reports, his assessment changed and his high opinion of the 53rd became transformed into disgust. Henceforth that regiment and its commanding officer, Colonel Mawby, were, as far as he was concerned, on trial. Should they fail or falter again, he could not be expected to be indulgent.

Sebright Mawby was a graduate of the Royal Irish Regiment of Foot; handsome, courteous, brave and experienced. He had served with the 53rd since 1804, when he had been appointed Lieutenant-Colonel in that regiment, and had commanded the first battalion during all its ten years' service in India. That the men esteemed him well enough to follow him even on the most daunting service had been proved by their outstanding behaviour at the storm of Kalanjar in 1812. Mrs. Sherwood, an astute judge of character, always wrote of the Colonel and his wife in terms of respect and affection. But the misbehaviour of his regiment at Kalanga naturally reflected on him and his fellow officers, earning them the contempt of Company officers like Ludlow, in whose view the King's regiment had cravenly betrayed Gillespie.

Mawby withdrew the camp to a position about a mile and a half in advance of Dehra. He considered that Gillespie's ground, wild and jungly, gave the enemy too many opportunities for ambuscades and night attacks. He also felt compelled to abandon attempts to straiten the fort, because his force had been reduced by over 1,000 men as a result of casualties and the detachment of troops to reinforce the garrison at Kalsi. Furthermore, that assistance from the local populace on which Hastings had taught his officers to reckon had in the event proved unforthcoming. Dehra Dun itself was virtually deserted—Ludlow affirmed he had never seen a country so devoid of population—and all the efforts of William Fraser, the Political Agent, to arouse the zemindars of the northern regions of Garhwal had proved abortive. Deprived of their arms and cowed by the threat of Gurkha reprisals, the inhabitants had chosen to await the result of the operations at Kalanga before committing themselves to the British cause. The ensuing fiasco had obviously done nothing to banish their diffidence, and Nepali foraging parties could still roam the northern areas without harassment. Fraser had had the idea of compensating for the lack of spontaneous local support by organizing a corps of partisans, including 'people employed as guides, deserters from the enemy, and mountaineers volunteering their services'. But recruitment was slow, and by the end of November not enough men had been collected even to police the Dun and collect its revenues.

For three weeks there was consequently little activity, but, despite a certain boredom, spirits in camp remained high. No one doubted that the campaign in the Dun would be brought to a swift and decisive conclusion once the battering guns had arrived, and meanwhile the army basked in the lingering warmth of a mild autumn. The salt provisions failed; but this was more a blessing than otherwise, for the slaughter of cattle was authorized and the Europeans enjoyed the rare luxury of fresh meat. There were besides game, fruit and nuts in plenty.

The battering train arrived on 24 November. There were four eighteen-pounders and two eight-inch mortars. With them came the extra battalion of native infantry which Hastings had promised Gillespie, two more companies of light infantry and the remainder of Carpenter's battalion (the 1st/17th Native Infantry), which had been left at Meerut for its protection. Mawby now put into operation his plan for a third assault on the fort of Kalanga.

Early on 25 November he deployed troops round the fort to prevent the escape of the garrison. Ludlow was sent with a force to the table land, Major Baldock to the watercourse on his right, Captain Bucke to Lakhaend and Captain Coultman to Asthal village. The tents in the camp were left standing in order to confuse the enemy. The guns in the fort fired on Ludlow's detachment as it ascended to the table land, but again did little damage. This time, the main column ignored the main road and pushed round the skirt of the spur, in the direction of the Song river, to mount its south-eastern flank. The way was longer and much more difficult than the road, but entirely out of sight of the fort. The column then proceeded along the eastern ridge and encamped under Kalanga village, about a mile north-east of the fort on a level some 500 feet below it. Here its rear was protected by the majestic ravine of the Song. Captain Carmichael Smyth, the engineer sent to replace the wounded Ensign Blane, had, after a careful reconnaissance, wisely decided to abandon the table land as a position for the batteries. By approaching from the north-east, the guns could be pushed much nearer the fort, for the watercourse was only about 200 yards distant from the eastern walls. If he could but get the guns from the new camp to the watercourse—a distance of nearly a mile, all uphill—the old difficulties concerning aim and impact would be eliminated. The eastern approaches of the fort were cleared by a small advance guard composed of men of the 53rd under Captain Parker. By four in the afternoon, they had moved to within 250 yards of the north-eastern aspect of the fort, where, throughout the night of the 25th, Carmichael Smyth supervised the construction of batteries. The heavy howitzers and two twelve-pounders were placed in position during the night, and by seven the next morning the four eighteen-pounders had been dragged up. The batteries opened fire at noon. Even at this range, many shells missed the small enclosure of the fort, and not until one o'clock on the 27th, after nearly six tons of eighteen-pound shot had been discharged, was the breach reported ready. Mawby examined the gap in the defences through his glass. It looked wide, and the slope up to it was gentle. He had no doubt that the moment to storm had come.

Major Ingleby of the 53rd was to command the storming party. The grenadiers of the 53rd were to lead, followed first by a battalion company of the same regiment and then by the grenadier companies of the native battalions. All were instructed to move with muskets unloaded and to carry the breach with the bayonet. Equal divisions of the light company of the 53rd were to move up on both sides of the column and slightly in advance, with their pieces loaded. Their task was to cover the advance of the storming party and pick off defenders in the breach or on the walls.

Ingleby did not get far. He was wounded early in the action and forced to withdraw. Captain Parker took his place at the head of the 53rd grenadiers. Once they had crossed the watercourse, the ascent of 200 yards or so up the eastern glacis was easy, and within a few minutes Parker and his men were below the great gash in the fort's outer wall. They clambered over the debris as far as the breach, and then halted in consternation and horror. The breach was cut high in the parapet of the fort's defences, and by scooping out the rampart behind the enemy had made a drop of about five feet. The surface of the pitted rampart was thickly planted with sharpened stakes. Behind these was another sharp drop, for the body of the fort was sunk like a gravel pit into the rock, where Nepalis crouched with spears and muskets, ready to repel all intruders. It seemed that if anyone leapt down, he was bound to impale himself and then be shot like a stuck pig. In their brief moment of hesitation, all the grenadiers who had mounted the breach were either killed or wounded, and Parker drew back to warn the others. Lieutenant Harrington was just behind him and, not realizing why he faltered, savagely elbowed Parker aside, determined to save the impulse of the charge. Parker caught him by the sash.

'It's useless! We can't get in.'

'I must go!' Harrington tugged himself free. But he was too late. The rest of the storming party, seeing the unexplained disconcertment of the European grenadiers, had slowed their advance and hung back. The momentum was lost. Harrington, in a defiant effort to reanimate the men, drew his sword and clambered onto the breach. He in his turn stopped short, when he saw why the grenadiers had faltered. Turning, he ran along the whole width of the breach looking for a point of entry and then, facing the men, was seen to raise his hands in a gesture of hopelessness. A second later he was shot in the back.

Scores of defenders now strafed the glacis with bullets, stones and arrows, but the Europeans kept formation and did not turn. In contravention of their instructions they loaded their muskets and began returning the fire. The sepoys, who dreaded arrows even more than musket balls, which at least were invisible, readily followed their example. All movement ceased, and the operation degenerated into a sniping contest. There was little cover on the glacis, and casualties were heavy. Dejection and apathy took a hold on all the troops. One keen young subaltern of the 53rd, still not aware of what was causing the stoppage, called out eagerly to his men: 'Go on, my boys, go on!' 'Go on yourself, and we will follow you', came the surly rejoinder. The superstitious Muslims attached dark significance to a third failure; and one group of native grenadiers, those of the 1st/6th Native Infantry, had their morale badly shaken by the loss of their favourite officer. Captain John Campbell, a stalwart of six foot three, the most popular officer in the regiment, was shot by an arrow as he stood on the glacis after surviving the storm. Long after, one of his sepoys[10] still remembered how the surgeon said that on account of its broad point the arrow could not be removed; how, in his agony, Campbell wrenched it out himself from a frothing wound; how they carried him down; and how the whole battalion became steeped in sorrow. 'I never expected to see my Captain Saheb recover. He was so loved by the men of his own company and in the regiment was such a great favourite, that his absence was hard to bear. The regiment had lost its champion. [Campbell] Saheb was sent to England.' Campbell in fact died. 'How deeply do I deplore his loss', sighed Ludlow, his commanding officer. 'Ending sure, the poor fellow preserved his wonted good-humoured smile to the last and uttered fine kind thanks to the friends he was parting from. Alas! Poor Campbell . . .'

Mawby, not realizing that the reluctance of the troops was caused by something more than the determined resistance of the defenders, ordered Lieutenant-Colonel Buckland to take the remaining companies of the 53rd to reinforce the storming party. He gave strict orders that they were to ascend to the breach without firing a shot. Because of the hail of missiles, only a few of the fresh detachment managed to mount the breach and return, and they too pronounced the descent to be impracticable. Just before three o'clock, Buckland sent a message to Mawby to say that if a twelve-pounder and a howitzer could be brought nearer the breach, something might be done. Presumably his intention was to clear the breach of defenders and make it lower, so that the men could get on to the rampart behind. In great haste, two pieces were taken out of the battery and conducted across the watercourse and up to the glacis by Lieutenant Luxford of the horse artillery. The howitzer was brought to the foot of the breach itself, but before it could even be fired Luxford had been fatally wounded and eleven of his men felled. By now, the nature of the difficulties had been explained to the Colonel, who was mortified to think that he had kept the troops futilely exposed for close on two hours. He immediately ordered a retreat, regretting only that he had not done so earlier. He had no complaint to make concerning the conduct of

---

[10] 'Sita Ram', in *From Sepoy to Subadar*, pp. 19–20. The way in which its account tallies with those of other sources seems to reinforce this work's claim to authenticity. It renders the captain's name as Burrumpeel, which is probably a printer's misreading for Kurrumpeel—a phonetic rendering of Campbell. Sita Ram's corps can thus be identified as the Grenadier Company of the 1st/6th N.I. This battalion became the 3rd N.I. in 1824.

the army. On the contrary, he warmly praised 'the great gallantry of men who were exposed till 3 o'clock to a most galling fire of musketry and matchlocks . . . showers of stones, spears and arrows'.

It was now felt that the only recourse left was to continue the batteries open until the whole eastern face of the fort had been razed. Seven hundred rounds of eighteen-pound shot had been expended, and only 500 remained. To husband the supply, the bombardment was continued at a slower rhythm. Meanwhile, the losses were counted. Four officers had been killed and seven wounded. Of the men and native officers, 36 were dead and 431 wounded. This made a total of 478 casualties, of which almost half had been sustained by the 53rd. Losses for both attacks amounted to nearly 750, which was appalling, because the total number of enemy did not exceed 600. Thirteen bodies were retrieved on the morning of 28 November with Bal Bahadur's permission. They had again been barbarically mutilated. Harrington's had both legs torn from the trunk.

The guns thumped on, and by nightfall on the 29th had done so much damage that there was nothing left for them to aim at. They were therefore silenced at last, preparatory to being moved in front of a fresh target further to the left.

At about two o'clock in the morning, there was a sudden clatter of musket fire as Captain Bucke, guarding the wells on the southern glacis, was attacked by a party of the garrison which had crept out desperate for water. Bucke's men returned the fire and drove them back into the fort. All was silent for about half an hour; then, at about three o'clock, another, larger party streamed out of the breach and down the southern glacis. This time they were obviously intent on escaping, under cover of the jungly water course. A large number were killed, wounded, and captured, and only a small group of about 70 got away. Major Kelly, commanding in the trenches before the battery, listened for sounds of movement in the fort; but nothing stirred. He ordered forward a force of grenadiers, who advanced cautiously, for it was a known ruse of the Gurkhas to inveigle their victims into a position by inducing them to think it abandoned. But an impatient drummer boy ran forward to the breach ahead of all the others. He peered into the dark interior, then turned round crying that the fort was empty (*khala hai! khala hai!*). The men began shouting and cheering, and the drums beat out the grenadiers' march. Kelly then entered the fort and took possession. It was four o'clock on the morning of 30 November.

The inside was still dark, but the sickening stench and the terrible moaning forewarned the victors of the scale of their destruction and the price of the garrison's defiance. Lights were brought, and they gazed in horror on a miniature Golgotha. They had to enter carefully, for fear of treading on the dead and dying. Henry Sherwood was one of the first to visit the fort, and he was overcome with nausea and compassion:

The fort was very small, and the whole place covered with bodies. On my right in a small redoubt were two small brass guns; one of them in a space not above ten feet long and six feet broad, and there lay seven bodies across each other. In going from one enclosure to another (for the place seemed all small enclosures) the same kind of objects appeared. Within the body of the fort we heard groans and cries of 'Pani! Pani!' ('Water! Water!') and on descending, never was anything so shocking. The fort itself was trenched across in every direction, and these trenches were about two feet deep; in them the unhappy people had endeavoured to find shelter. There were 86 dead bodies lying in this small place. The wounded were in a most wretched state. Those who could in any way move had attempted to get out: but others were calling for water, and our officers were assisting, as well as they could, by pouring water out to them. Some of the poor creatures had lain there for three days with their limbs broken. I shall never forget one young woman with a broken leg, lying among the dead. She was partly covered or entangled among dead bodies, and as she could not move, she held her mouth open for water so anxiously that there is no describing it. We could not get near her, but Heathcote poured water at her mouth from a distance, which she received. There was another woman, herself unhurt, but she had a wounded baby at her breast. She seemed dreadfully distressed, but the child was taking its food, and did not seem to mind it. There was a soldier-like looking Gurkha also lying on a bed in the fort. His wound had been in his head, and had taken away his senses. He was making figures in the bloody dust with his fingers. The most affecting sight was two little girls, one about four years old, the other about one. Their father and mother had both been killed. They were both taken care of, but the elder screaming very much, fearing she should be separated from the younger.

When I again visited the fort, it was partially cleared. 97 dead bodies had been burnt, but this was only a part, for all around the fort you might see the marks of imperfect burials. The ground was rocky, and it was difficult to dig into it, so that I could still count 30 bodies lying only half buried, in many cases having a leg or an arm above the ground.

This day I saw the horrors of war; and indeed, horrible it is.[11]

He reckoned that Kalanga could never have been captured. 'I do not see how it is possible to take such places, if properly defended; for although you knock down the wall, yet the body of the fort being sunk within the rock is not to be destroyed; and of the shells very few entered the fort, although it seems to be the fashion to say otherwise.' John Ludlow disagreed. 'Thank God', he wrote, 'the place is ours on almost easy terms; for after seeing the interior . . . I'm persuaded that our army, or rather the eastern part of it, never would have taken it—though I declare to God that I saw no obstacles which ought to have deterred brave men from getting in.'

The informant of the *Calcutta Monthly Journal* reported that 'the physical obstacles at the breach were found on examination to be less formidable than had been supposed.' There is no doubt as to which opinion weighed most with Hastings. In his view Kalanga was 'a place certainly of no great strength or extent, destitute of a ditch, laid open by a breach up which a carriage might have been driven, and defended by a garrison whose only means of resistance consisted in their personal gallantry'. He blamed Mawby and the 53rd for the failure.

His judgement was inferred from two premises. The first was that the failure of the second attempt was caused not, as thought at first, by the temerity of Gillespie, but by the delinquency of the 53rd Regiment. In this, it must be admitted, there was a substance of truth. The second premise was that the breach had been practicable on 27 November; and from the two he deduced that the participation of the 53rd was the common cause linking both failures. But the second assumption was not sound. It was based on the information of private advisers, of whom Ludlow was undoubtedly one, and it must be remembered that no one except the officers and men of the 53rd had been in a position to examine the breach *at the time of the storm*. All subsequent inspections, including Ludlow's, had taken place three days later, under circumstances quite different from those experienced by the assaulting party and when the breach had been considerably enlarged by a

---

[11] An amalgam of the account in the MS. journal and that contained in a letter to his wife, printed in Kelly, *Life of Mrs. Sherwood*, pp. 465–7.

further 500 rounds of eighteen-pound shot. All things considered, it seems reasonable to assume that on 27 November entry into the fort had been as impracticable as those who looked into the breach maintained. But the Governor-General was not feeling reasonable. A letter which he wrote to the Prince Regent's Private Secretary in January 1815 makes it quite clear how his assessment of the 53rd's behaviour in the second assault had changed; and how his new knowledge of that event, taken in conjunction with reports concerning the state of the breach on 27 November, made him ignore the probability that the presence of the 53rd at both failures was no more than circumstantial.

. . . part of the troops who have behaved remarkably ill [in the second attempt] [he wrote] vindicated their shyness by expatiating on the unexampled courage shown by the enemy—as if there were any peculiar degree of valour in the continuing on the top of a high rampart when the assailant has not the possibility of getting at you. This opinion of the enemy became so current, that when the [third] assault took place, or rather was ordered, there was no getting the soldiers to follow their officers to a breach up which a coach might have been driven.[12]

Reports in this vein wrecked Mawby's reputation in the Horse Guards.

I am sorry to hear so bad an account of the 53rd [wrote Sir Henry Torrens, Private Secretary to the Duke of York,[13] in a letter to Hastings later the same year]. The Duke was very partial to this corps—and he is convinced that their misconduct is entirely owing to the apathy and worthlessness, as an officer, of Colonel Mawby. It will not be easy to prevent this officer from experiencing the ill-effects of your report, tho' you so kindly endeavour to qualify it.

Hastings prided himself on his chivalry, and his indignation against the 53rd was so much the greater because he had inadvertently blamed the dead and defenceless Gillespie for the failure of 31 October. To redeem his injustice, he now began to emphasize Gillespie's positive qualities. 'Had he survived', he told the Prince Regent's Secretary, 'he would have prevented his division from duping itself into fear.' He announced his intention of erecting a cenotaph in memory of the Major-General, and his attitude towards Raffles, whose charges against Gillespie he had been investigating,

---

[12] Printed in Aspinall, *Letters of George IV*, ii, p. 14.
[13] Commander-in-Chief of the British Army.

became virulently hostile. It was discovered that Raffles, before making his charges against Gillespie, had actually received a report from the Resident at Samarang which apparently cleared the Major-General of one of the charges of abduction, at least. This incensed Hastings, who told Raffles: 'You appear to have given currency to a gross charge against a meritorious and highly esteemed officer when, as far as appears, you had the means of refutation in your power.'[14] He demanded an explanation.

But it was not only from a concern to rectify an unfair traducement that Hastings defended the dead Major-General. He had reasons of state, too. At the time of his death Gillespie had become a patriotic symbol. In recognition of his exploits in Java he had, in January 1815, been gazetted Knight Commander of the Bath; and when the news of his death reached England it became the occasion of various poetic tributes in the Byronic style, of a vote in Parliament for a monument in St. Paul's, and of a panegyrical Memoir dedicated to the Prince Regent as 'the history of a soldier whose VALOUR could only be surpassed by his LOYALTY, and who closed his career of labour and glory by devoting himself at the moment of perilous extremity as an example to inspirit his troops'. Hastings must have been acutely aware that if Gillespie's reputation was posthumously sullied the Prince Regent would be ridiculed, the *état-major* both in India and at home made an object of derision and the dignity of the British administration in India compromised.

Raffles was difficult to hold at bay. He refused to withdraw his accusations, pointing out that the report of the Resident at Samarang related only to the first charge of abduction and was in any case not conclusive. On the matter of the second charge, he did no more than refer the Governor-General to the records of the Bench of Magistrates for confirmation of the fact that a slave girl had been forcibly removed from Mr. Sluyster's house and transferred to Gillespie's. Hastings refused to admit that Raffles's explanations were satisfactory; but as both he and the Calcutta Council had publicly acknowledged that Gillespie's indictment of Raffles had been totally unjustified, the latter had no further personal motive for pressing a case against his dead antagonist and was content to forget the whole unsavoury business. If the stain on his private character had not exactly been removed, Hastings was now sure that

[14] Quoted by Eric Wakeham in *The Bravest Soldier*, p. 239.

Gillespie's professional reputation could be preserved. Probably it was with the intention of rendering this service, as well as of castigating the 53rd for their having sabotaged his own precious strategy, that he took the rash step of announcing that a court of inquiry would be set up to examine the causes of the failures at Kalanga. Despite the general terms of its commission, it became commonly known that the object of this court was to investigate the conduct of Colonel Mawby and the 53rd. No official censure could be pronounced until the court's findings were known; but Hastings disguised his own sentiments so ill, and conducted the whole affair in such a way, that innuendo and gossip had achieved the destruction of the reputation of the 53rd even before the court had convened. Gillespie, meanwhile, became exalted as a hero. 'The gallant Gillespie would, I am sure, have carried everything, had he not been deserted by a set of cowardly wretches', wrote Charles Metcalfe in June, 1815, expressing a sentiment which had become widespread.[15]

The officers of the regiment, recalling its sacrifices at the siege of Kalanjar in 1812, the vainglorious selfishness of the man its reputation was being sacrificed to vindicate and the heavy losses and adverse circumstances attending the third assault on Kalanga; and experiencing the undissembled hostility of a Governor-General who was flagrantly prejudging an issue he had instituted a court to investigate, not unnaturally became embittered and resentful. Knowing that however well they might acquit themselves in subsequent operations they would still in the end be subjected to a degrading scrutiny, their enthusiasm for the present service gave place to apathy and inhibition. For the débâcle which followed from this collapse of morale, Hastings had only his own persecution of the regiment to blame.

For some days before the evacuation of Kalanga, a body of about 300 Nepalis had been seen moving about the hills on the other side of the Song river. This was assumed to be a reinforcement sent to the fort from Nahan. Mawby's concern after the flight of Bal Bahadur was to prevent his joining this party, and at half-past two on 1 December Ludlow set off with a party of about 450 sepoys to intercept him. They arrived back in camp at nine o'clock the next morning, dusty, tired and with lacerated feet; but triumphant. They carried two captured stands of colours, with which Mawby

---

[15] Printed in Kaye, *Life of Metcalfe*, i, p. 409.

was 'mightily pleased'. After crossing the gorge of the Baldi river and clambering up a shrunken track with deep chasm on either side, they had descried the enemy camp fires by night, when the land was transfigured by moonlight. A short sharp raid with bayonets by a courageous vanguard of three officers and 100 men had been sufficient to disperse the combined force of Nepalis, and Ludlow estimated that about sixty must have been killed. His own casualties were no more than four seriously wounded.

This little victory, the work of the native troops and their officers alone, coming so soon after the humiliating setbacks at Kalanga, served to strengthen Hastings's conviction that the King's troops had so far set a harmful rather than a salutary example to the sepoys. Mawby was instructed to offer the Commander-in-Chief's thanks to the officers involved and to make a gratuity of 100 rupees to Guru Singh, Ludlow's intrepid spy.

Although considerably weakened, the Nepali band was still at large in the hills north-east of Dehra Dun, and the zemindars in contact with Fraser soon made it known that it had retreated through Saklayana district, plundering as it went, and taken post in the strong fort of Chamur, situated on the west bank of the Baghirati river. Here it was joined by another group, this time from Srinagar, which swelled its number to 400. Fraser urged that if the inhabitants of interior Garhwal were to be encouraged to assist the British, this enemy eyrie would have to be captured, for it overawed all the eastern section of the province. Hastings, however, was anxious for the main force to push westwards into Sirmur and reduce Nahan, now that the essential part of its work in Dehra Dun had been accomplished. The occupation of Kalanga had been followed by the enemy's evacuation of Birat, the strong fort just to the north of Carpenter's position at Kalsi, and this had completed the British domination of the central section of the line of communication between the eastern and western sections of the Gurkha empire. Letters subsequently intercepted at Birat revealed that the operation had been completed none too soon. Ranjor Singh Thapa, commanding at Nahan, was expecting a reinforcement of two or three hundred men from the east by way of Srinagar, which was an important magazine for the manufacture and deposit of military stores. The garrison of Birat had, unfortunately, also escaped into the hills, and it was expected that it too would make its way to Chamur. But Hastings felt that the reduction of this place could safely be left to Carpenter, appointed to command the Dun occupation force. He was to be assisted by all the irregulars that Fraser could spare, and the Political Agent was authorized to increase the levy of these auxiliaries as far as he thought expedient. Mawby was now ordered to take the main army to Nahan—but not by way of the Kayarda Valley. It was thought that this route would prove too obstructed, and he was directed to use the road along the foot of the hills instead. One of his last tasks in the Dun was to supervise the destruction of Kalanga fort. True to his instructions, Mawby had every vestige of the place erased, and scarcely a stone now remains on the hilltop as a monument to the bones that are buried there.

The army, which had moved back to its old camping ground near Dehra on 3 December, now began to make preparations for a move. On the 6th, the heavy guns and field artillery left camp; but before the rest of the force could follow, the dry autumnal warmth gave place to cold persistent rain, which fell as snow on the nearest range of hills. For two days Mawby delayed his departure, hoping for better conditions; but by the 9th there was still no sign of an improvement and, instructions from Headquarters being so peremptory, he decided he could wait no longer. The troops marched at seven that morning, up to their knees in mud as they passed through Dehra. Labouring under the weight of sodden tents, the camels slipped and slid uncontrollably. Progress was slow and uncomfortable, and the army did not enter the Timli pass until 11 December. A whole day was occupied in manoeuvring the pass itself, which was thirteen miles long. Happily, the road had been repaired for the preceding artillery, and by one o'clock the main part of the force had at last quitted the territory of Garhwal and arrived in Company territory once more, at Fyzabad, on the plains.

Here junction was made with the artillery train, and the whole force (save the horse artillery and two of the eighteen-pounders, sent back to Delhi) trailed ponderously down the eastern bank of the Jumna, looking for somewhere to ford the river, which had been swollen by the recent heavy rain. It was not until 13 December that a ferrying place was discovered, about four miles above Chilkana. But there were only six boats, and to bring the whole army and ordnance across in these took four days. Crossing the commissariat and bazaar was a labour of Hercules. The camels were terrified of the boats and violently refused to enter them, hooting, grunting and shedding their loads into the river. In the turmoil, many were either killed or lamed. Later, a place shallow enough to ford was found a few miles up river, and the majority were taken across there.

Once the Jumna had been cleared, the army began its march along the skirt of the foothills, through the lush, well-cultivated country of the protected Sikhs. On the morning of 17 December, when the weather was suddenly bright and clear, officers caught their breath as they had their first glimpse of their next objective— Nahan, the capital of Sirmur. It was a cluster of miniature white cupolas, towers and minarets, shining among the clouds on the grey hills to the north like something from an Arabian romance.

On 18 December, after the arrival of Major Kelly's battalion from Dehra Dun, the army struck northward from the town of Sedaura, and after about ten miles began to ascend the hills into Sirmur. Climbing first in the defile of the Markanda river, and then branching to the right up the course of a subsidiary nulla, the force came to the village called Mojamand, which was about six miles south from Nahan. The river-bed made a bad road: very stony, and littered with large rocks and boulders. It was nightfall on the 19th before all the guns had been brought up to the camp.

At seven o'clock that same evening a guard of honour was drawn up to greet Major-General Gabriel Martindell, of the Company's service, appointed successor to Robert Gillespie.

VII

STAGNATION IN SIRMUR

MARTINDELL's was a very different character from Gillespie's. He was courteous, gentle, unaffected, and so withdrawn in his social habits that he seldom visited or entertained. In his younger days he had shown vigour and perseverance, if not much imagination, and the battalion of native infantry which he had raised and commanded as a major had been generally recognized as one of the best in the service. Appointed to command in turbulent Bundelkhand in 1804, he had done useful work of pacification and earned the 'approbation and applause' of the Governor-General.

But by 1815 the effects of forty years in the Indian climate, of which the last four or five had been soured by failure and the loss of the confidence of his superiors, had begun to show. His ardour had become dampened; his self-assurance sapped. His siege of Kalanjar of 1812, although counted a success, had nevertheless involved the repulse of the storming party with severe loss; and it seems that from this time the ageing officer had begun to lose all taste for responsibility and to become a prey to vacillation and excessive caution. In 1813 he had been ordered to advance with a force of over 6,000 men into Rewa, a principality in east Bundelkhand whose Raja was refusing to honour the terms of his alliance with the Calcutta government. The Political Agent in Bundelkhand having sent an ultimatum to the Raja, Martindell had been instructed not to delay his march and his operations against the fortress for anything less than the arrival of the Raja or his deputies in his camp, for the season was advanced and the rains imminent. Martindell had reached Panna, his rendezvous, on 8 April; but instead of advancing forthwith, as ordered, had dithered there in a state of nervous consternation because his spies had brought reports, which were obviously false, that the Pindaris were intending to create a diversion by invading the Company's territory in another quarter. He had then been sent the 'most urgent and positive orders of the Commander-in-Chief to proceed . . .

without any reference to external circumstances which were . . . beyond the sphere of his cognizance'. Yet still he had dallied, now waiting for an artillery train from Ajaigarh—'although he was in possession of the Commander-in-Chief's unqualified opinion that his march ought not to be delayed on that account'. On 23 April he had moved at last, 'having . . . remained inactive at Panna during the period of a fortnight at the most critical season of the year, and when the delay of a single day might have hazarded the success of the expedition'. To crown this display of ineptitude, Martindell had waited in advance of the fortress of Rewa for the arrival of the Raja or his agents and the junction of reinforcements from Mirzapur, ignoring strict instructions to chastise some of the Raja's particularly contumacious zemindars; and had then nego-tiated and concluded, entirely without authority, a treaty with the Raja. This had caused considerable embarrassment. The whole business of negotiation had had to be reopened and the military operations against the zemindars held over until the following season. Official approval and thanks had been publicly withheld from Martindell on this occasion, and he had been permitted to relinquish command of the Rewa force.

In March 1814, at the age of fifty-five, he had resigned his command in Bundelkhand and withdrawn to Cawnpore.

Hastings's reasons for withdrawing Martindell from his semi-retirement to command the army in Sirmur were hardly flattering.

The selection of Major-General Martindell for the command [he told the Secret Committee of the Court of Directors], was founded on the general character which he had acquired in a long course of service; the hope that the occurrences attending his command at Rewa in the year 1813 would have stimulated him to exert himself in regaining the ground he had lost in the public estimation on that occasion; and, more than all, the difficulty of finding any other unemployed officer of rank suffi-cient to exercise so large a command.[1]

But there was little reason to hope that Martindell would prove able to seize this opportunity to repair his dilapidated reputation. His disgrace had made him self-doubting and subservient, and his command in Sirmur could only have succeeded had he been surrounded by purposeful subordinates. Instead of that, the officers of H.M. 53rd, whom he knew well and on whose advice

[1] *P.R.N.W.*, p. 737.

he was therefore most inclined to rely, were discouraged and diffi-
dent. As a result of their double failure at Kalanga and the
Governor-General's vendetta, they shrank from all projects which
seemed to involve the slightest risk of another repulse. Company
officers like John Ludlow, on the other hand, quickly grew
impatient of policies which they considered to be supine and timid.
They fretted for a more dynamic leadership. Subjection to two
contradictory influences made Martindell hopelessly uncertain and
bewildered, and he found it more and more difficult to make
decisions.

Having commanded in Bundelkhand for a considerable time, the
Major-General was as accustomed as any officer in India to mountain warfare; but the scene of his present operations surpassed
in difficulty anything even in his experience. Nahan nestles
compactly on a plateau, which rises some 3,000 feet above the level
of the lowlands, and which is shielded to the north by a massive
ridge of hills. The Markanda hugs its north-western skirts, taking
a route down through the hills and across the mottled plains that
is visible for miles when winter rains have purged the air. There
are occasional groves of pine, shisham and wild fruit trees on the
surrounding slopes, but the vegetation is mostly scrub and flower-
ing thorn, spread sparsely, so that the light ochres and lunar
textures of the ground show through. The eastern part of Nahan,
round the citadel, is walled, and then seemed immensely strong.
The camp site of the British army was six or seven miles to the
south, and separated from the town by the valley of a tributary of
the Markanda. The road ascending from this nulla to the town was
about five miles long. It was a mere track scratched on to the
surface of the rock, all sharp angles and hairpin bends, and so
narrow and steep that it seemed impassable for any animal. It was,
furthermore, defended at almost every turn by a stone redoubt in
the shape of a star. Hastings, appreciating that the army must be
dispirited after the repulses at Kalanga, had advised Martindell to
blockade the place, rather than risk an assault; but such a recommendation, in view of the inaccessibility of Nahan, seemed superfluous. A storm must have been suicide.

Martindell made up his mind to move the camp to a spur
farther to the north-east, which was only about four miles from
Nahan ridge, and ordered Ludlow to occupy the position with a
small force. Soon after Ludlow had left, intelligence was received

that Ranjor Singh Thapa had abandoned the town and retired to the fort of Jaithak in its rear. This seemed too good to be true, but Ludlow was instructed to probe his way forward to test the truth of the report. The journey was an exhausting half-day's work, and some of the camels fell and were dashed to pieces; but not a shot was fired in resistance as the troops walked into the neat and narrow streets of Nahan. By one o'clock, the British flag was flying over the citadel.

Henry Sherwood marvelled that the enemy had ever allowed the advance to reach the town, which seemed as though it might have been defended for ever. 'The Gurkhas at one moment defend themselves well, not only with bravery but with judgement; and at another, neglect the commonest means of defence', he wrote. But then he had not yet seen Jaithak.

Artillery might conceivably have been brought to bear on Nahan; but to bring it to bear on Jaithak, whither Ranjor Singh had now retired on the advice of his father, Amar Singh Thapa, was apparently a physical impossibility. This stone fort was rectangular, with bastions at each corner, and tiny. It measured only about twelve yards by eight. Clinging like a swallow's nest to a pinnacle, it seemed invulnerable. To bombard it, guns would first have to be brought up to Nahan—which seemed hardly practicable, for a start—then somehow directed at a target which was not only three miles distant as the crow flies, but some 1,600 feet higher again.

It stands altogether detached [wrote Henry Sherwood, in despair], and is of so great a declivity that we have no idea how we are top roceed . . . It is doubtful whether, with all our exertions, we shall ever be able to make a road for the guns and mortars even to Nahan . . . Even if this is done, can they proceed farther? And even if they do, can they find a spot to throw shells from (for a mortar cannot throw at above 45 degrees elevation)? . . . As for the great guns, they appear out of the question.

He thought that the only hope lay in a scheme of protracted investment, because the fort was reputedly short of water. 'However,' he added, 'take it ever so easy, even without the loss of a man, I think it one of the most ill-judged, ill-conducted enterprises ever heard of.' His feelings seem to have been shared by most of the other officers of the 53rd.

If he had decided to act in the spirit of their assessment and tried to starve Jaithak into surrender, Martindell would have been acting in full harmony with Hastings's instructions. But he reckoned that his force was too small, his maps too inaccurate, and the approaches to the fort obviously too many and too dispersed, for a blockade to be effective. He became sure, in fact, that the position of Jaithak made it better suited to bombardment. It perched at the angle of two rising mountainous ridges, which converge to form an arrow-head pointing towards Nahan. It obviously could not be bombarded from Nahan; but it could conceivably be bombarded from one or both of these ridges. True, the guns would have to be brought to the ridges; but after his experiences at Kalanjar, Martindell was no novice in the art of moving heavy ordnance to seemingly impossible places, and dogged perseverance was one of his old qualities which he still retained. He therefore resolved to brave the misgivings of Mawby and the officers of the 53rd and opt for bombardment. Hastings was quite happy to defer to this decision. It was first necessary to bring the guns to Nahan, so the pioneers and fatigue parties were set working to widen the road which led up from the artillery park, at the foot of Nahan hill. Knowing this would be a protracted operation, Martindell decided to establish a position on each of the ridges in the meantime.

During the night of 26 December, two columns were formed for this purpose, the intention being to seize the two ridges simultaneously, each force causing a diversion in favour of the other. Ludlow, with about 800 men, was to take the left, and Major William Richards,[2] with about 500, the right ridge. Acting in concert, these forces would, it was reckoned, outnumber the Nepalis, who were estimated to be about 1,000 strong. Each column had a couple of six-pounders and two small howitzers, carried on elephants; and it was reckoned that both should reach their positions before daylight. Richards, having farther to go, set off at about a quarter to eleven that night. Ludlow moved at one o'clock the next morning, and engaged the enemy first.

The enemy's main water supplies were derived from wells on these ridges, so they were heavily guarded. They lent themselves well to defence because they were both dominated by the pinnacle of Jaithak. Their crests were, furthermore, jagged, and almost every peak along them was crowned with a picket or a stockade.

Ludlow's destination was a peak about a mile from the fort on

2 Later General Sir William Richards.

the left ridge. The distance from Nahan was some six miles, 'but equal to twenty from the ruggedness of the road'. Dawn was already breaking when he began to climb up the side of the ridge; and the column, hampered by the ponderous elephants, had become widely scattered. When about two miles from the point at which they were aiming, the front half of the column, which comprised the grena-diers of the 53rd and some companies of native light infantry, passed under the enemy's first position on the crest, which was a stockade. They had now lost the cover of darkness and were within range. The Nepalis in the stockade shot at them, but Ludlow commanded his advance guard to reserve its fire—unless warmly engaged—until it reached the crest. The force passed under two more posts,[3] each of which opened fire, but the men, well covered by the uneven ground, pressed on obediently and did not stop to retaliate.

By eight o'clock, the advance was within 200 yards of the summit. The fourth and principal enemy post was just ahead—strong, and generously garrisoned. Ludlow was still under good cover, and he called a halt to enable the column to consolidate. While he was still waiting for his own battalion, the 1st/6th Native Infantry, which was toiling a long way behind, a guide brought word that consider-able enemy reinforcements were on their way down from the fort. Ludlow now had about 400 men at hand and, after a rapid assess-ment of the alternatives open to him, he decided to try to take the unreinforced post with the men he had, instead of waiting to attack it with his whole force, which would give the enemy reinforcement time to come up. He gave the order, and the European grenadiers and native infantry charged with fixed bayonets up the remaining section of the ascent, scattering the enemy from the post. John Ludlow was an energetic and impulsive officer. In taking this position on the crest, he had done what he had been ordered to do; but his men were eager and the Nepalis in disarray, and in such a situation it would have taken more than the letter of his instructions to restrain him. He urged his men to give chase, so that once they had reached the crest they did not stop, but turned sharply right to push their adversaries back up the ridge. The next peak in the direction of the fort was topped by the ruined village of Jampta, where the enemy had their third post. The grenadiers of the 53rd

[3] Circular depressions in the ground still mark the sites of these stockades, but the ridge is now considerably more wooded than it was then.

reached it first, and the Nepalis, still unformed and unsteady, fell back to their second position to make their stand. Down went the grenadiers again, and up to the second post, a picket. Here the struggle was savage; but the Nepalis, still winded and dazed, were finally forced to retreat yet again, to their first post, which was the stockade. Behind that lay the cantonments of the fort itself. It was now about half-past eight. Faces gleaming with sweat, buoyant with triumph, tendons taut and trembling, the grenadiers and their officers turned eagerly to Ludlow for the word to charge the stockade. This time, the commander hesitated. His better judgement warned him that it was strong and already reinforced; that his own force was small; and, his rear being so far behind, that he was without support. But he was too grateful for the valour of his men, and too excited by their success, to be resolute and stern, as they surrounded him, clamouring, beseeching and reproaching. 'Why, sir, there ain't more than eight or ten men in the stockade, and bye and bye there'll be as many hundred!' Instead of positively ordering his men to halt, as he later admitted he should have, Ludlow could only implore them to spare themselves. 'You have already done more than I expected. Why not take breath awhile, and wait for the others and the guns? Let them come up, and then we'll see what can be done.'

Even as he was speaking, two or three of the grenadiers roared out *huzza!* and part of the light infantry leapt forward. Ludlow could still have stopped them, but he succumbed to the fever which forces winning gamblers to go on when it is obvious that they should stop. He consented to the charge, trying to convince his better self that, since even a positive command could not then have restrained the men, this was the only way of sparing them the stigma of disobedience.

It was a lapse that he lived to regret bitterly. The men rushed ahead. The Nepalis, strengthened by reinforcements from the fort and steadied by a few minutes' respite, allowed them to come close. Then they sallied out on either side of the stockade and charged them, with *khukuris* drawn, from both sides and from the front simultaneously. Ludlow's party reeled away—not down the crest of the ridge the way they had come, but sideways, over the flank of the ridge. The Nepalis followed noisily, forcing them to stumble, slip and slide down the precipitous mountainside. Ludlow managed to rally them for a few minutes farther down; but ammunition was low and it was impossible to keep up a consistent fire. The enemy, increasing in numbers all the time, poured over the crest like spilt liquid, and Ludlow had no option but to retreat again.

In this, his moment of greatest need, he was forsaken by his own corps, which formed the rearguard of his column. When the van-guard was repulsed, the sepoys of the 1st/6th Native Infantry had come as far as Jampta; but then, instead of moving forward to support the grenadiers and light companies, which, because their communications were entire, they were well able to do, they became so terrified by the sight of events in front that they refused to form and began to back away. Officers shouted and swore, struggling to make themselves heard above a rising babble of fear: but all their efforts to impose order were made vain by the crucial defect in the military system which this crisis exposed. Casualties at Kalanga had so depleted the battalion's small complement of European officers that only three were on duty, and this was simply not enough to allay the panic of 400 men. The military machine could not accommodate Ludlow's human error of allowing the column to become too extended. The men of the 1st/6th, instead of advancing to succour comrades who were fighting for their lives, took to their heels and fled.

Ludlow, on the side of the ridge, worked desperately to hold a position. Twice more he rallied the men; but twice he had to yield his ground. On the last occasion, his musketry spluttered into silence. There were no more cartridges and, as he still received no support from the 1st/6th, he had no choice but to order an un-covered retreat. It became a rout. Breaking formation entirely, the men partly ran, partly fell and partly jumped down the rocky slopes, crashing through the tussocks and wildly clutching at branches to control their descent. So precipitate was their flight, that the remains of the detachment were back in camp by ten o'clock. The casualties amounted to 151, of whom about a dozen, including one officer, Lieutenant Munt, were killed. Ludlow him-self reached Nahan unhurt, save for a sprained ankle, but he burned with shame. 'I should have thought it a friendly ball that had brought me to the ground', he wrote to his wife. He blamed his own unmastered greed for triumph for the repulse at the final stockade; but for the fiasco into which it had needlessly developed he blamed the lack of European officers and the reluctance of his own 'raggamuffin set of a corps' to meet *khukuri* with bayonet.

Hastings was disturbed by such grave misconduct on the part of native troops, especially since he had been in the habit of indirectly reprehending the King's men by paying the sepoys marked compliments and praises. Nevertheless, his inclination was still to treat this behaviour as altogether exceptional—'a circumstance almost unheard of in the Bengal army'—and he forbore, in view of 'the peculiar circumstances of the public service . . . and of [Martindell's] detachment in particular', to inflict condign punishment. All he ordered was that the European officers who had been commanding the corps should report any instances of cowardice on the part of the native officers which they had noticed, and that all so accused should be immediately dismissed. He feared the effects of stronger punishment on native troops already subjected to the unusual stresses of mountain war—and not without reason. Even his mild censure and the few courts martial which followed it seriously undermined the morale of the 1st/6th, and in subsequent weeks the corps lost over 100 men by desertion. Hastings, as Commander-in-Chief, could not avoid officially expressing his regret that the column had not moved more slowly and that Ludlow had not been able to restrain the men in advance; but George Fagan, the Adjutant-General, privately assured Ludlow that his personal reputation had not suffered:

I read extracts and parts of your letter where descriptive of the scene and of your own feelings to Lord [Hastings], who has been pleased to allow me to tell you privately 'that it has not in the slightest degree impaired his good opinion of you; and that the misbehaviour of troops, whether proceeding in one case from blind and precipitate rashness, or in the other from backwardness, often ruins the best conceived hopes of success and renders every effort of their leader vain'. Do not then suffer yourself to be depressed, my dear friend; you have already established sufficient claims to public favour and approbation and to the confidence of your superiors, and you will continue to increase them.

Poor 53rd! Nothing they could do was right. At Kalanga it had been their shirking and now it was their 'blind and precipitate rashness' that was responsible for failure. Officers of the 53rd deeply resented this last judgement, and it long remained an issue of controversy in Indian military circles. Critics of the native army attributed it to a blind prejudice in favour of the sepoys and their officers among servants of the East India Company.[4] This was not

4 See *Asiatic Journal*, vol. xi: London, May 1821, p. 432.

its real cause, however. Ludlow was partly responsible, because he admitted his own error with the sort of manly frankness which was especially calculated to put Hastings into a forgiving mood, and at the same time implied that he had risked his own reputation in order to spare that of the men; but there is no doubt that, more than anything else, it was the deep grudge he had borne the 53rd ever since the incidents at Kalanga that influenced Hastings's attitude.

While Ludlow dealt with the left, William Richards marched north-east towards the right-hand ridge. When he left Nahan, at a quarter to eleven on the night of 26 December, there was not enough ammunition in camp for his column to be supplied with spare cartridges, so the men left with only those they had in pouch. A sergeant's party was left to bring on the extra rounds when they had arrived from the park. This party followed with the spare cartridges in the early hours of the morning, but by some negligence was not provided with a guide. In the darkness it lost its way, and the sergeant had to leave the ammunition with the coolies in a convenient village while he went back to Nahan for help. He returned to the village just before dawn, only to find that Nepali prowlers had bagged the ammunition. 60,000 cartridges had been lost.

Richards's march was sixteen miles. The stony pathway plunged and mounted, and was never more than wide enough for single files. He was always having to call a halt, to enable the rear and the ordnance elephants to come up. The last two and a half miles were unremitting steep ascent, and it was not until eight o'clock in the morning of the 27th that the advance guard reached the crest of the ridge. Fortunately, the point where it ascended, a peak about two and a half miles from the fort, was not defended. As there was water close by, Richards halted for two hours, to allow the stragglers to come up and to take some rest. Then he advanced along a narrow footpath on the northern side of the ridge, taking possession of successive peaks, and finally reached a pinnacle which was only about 1,000 yards from Jaithak. He was greeted by musket and gun fire from the fort; but this did little damage, and by noon he was firmly established in this position, which was called Peacock Hill.

Near one o'clock, the Gurkha drums beat to arms, and a considerable force assembled and paraded under the walls of the fort. Richards could tell from their number, which was about 1,500, and from the silence in the direction where Ludlow was supposed to have ascended, that something had happened to upset the plan for concerted action. He thought that Ludlow must have been recalled for some reason—which meant that his own 500 men had the undivided enemy force to deal with. Soon after, the Nepalis moved down from the fort and began an attack with guns and musketry. Their fire was directed against Richards's advanced post, which was on the slope before the summit he occupied; but its position was so well protected that casualties were trifling.

Towards four o'clock, however, when the spare ammunition still had not arrived and when there was still no sign of activity on Ludlow's ridge, Richards's anxiety began to mount. He wrote a note for Martindell describing his situation, and had two sepoys disguise themselves and take it to Nahan. Meanwhile, finding that the British fire was slackening, the Nepalis became bolder and made several attempts to storm points in his position. Deciding he must concentrate his resources, Richards called up a party which he had posted to guard the well in a hollow some 300 yards below his left, and to husband the remaining ammunition, gave strict orders that all fire be reserved until the last possible minute. It was a notorious weakness of the sepoys that they could seldom be made to do this. They would always squander their cartridges by firing before they could have accurate aim. But on this occasion the instruction was scrupulously obeyed, and the men eked out their precious cartridges with stones.

Soon the light began to fail, and the enemy edged nearer. Again and again bands of them tore up to the breastwork which the pioneers had built in front of the advanced post and tried to force their way in; but each time they were repulsed. The European officers spared no effort to inspirit the men. Even the surgeon, Darby, took a musket, slung a cartridge box over his shoulder and made good use of both whenever he could snatch a few minutes from medical duties. Lieutenant Thomas Thackeray, commanding the light company of the 2/26th Native Infantry, still could not use his right arm, which had been wounded at Kalanga; but he made Richards promise that he might deal with the enemy if they charged again. He was an uncle of the future novelist, William Makepeace, who was at that time a small pale boy of four living in Calcutta. Soldiering was a vocation which claimed the passionate and exclusive devotion of this twenty-five-year-old subaltern, and his ambition to realize its best ideals in his own conduct burned with brilliant and destructive intensity. He had already crammed a decade of campaigning into his short life, crossing swords with the Marathas and the rebellious rajas of Bundelkhand. His men revered him as a paragon, and all immediately volunteered to repel the next attack. When the Nepalis assaulted again, for the eighth or ninth time, Thackeray and his company careered lustily at them and swept them back down the hill.

By half-past seven it was quite dark, and the enemy muskets spurted luminous tongues. Ammunition was almost spent, but Richards remained confident. His situation was strong and his losses no more than about twenty killed and wounded, and he reasoned that by now a reinforcement must surely be at hand. Then, almost simultaneously, he received two messages from Martindell. They were both to the same effect, and he could hardly believe that he had read them right. The General had sent no ammunition and no reinforcement; only curt and peremptory orders that he was to return to camp at once.

At half-past nine that morning, when he received news of Ludlow's defeat, Martindell immediately wrote to Richards, ordering him to return to camp. Now that it would not have the benefit of a diversion on the left ridge, he feared that, if it was allowed to continue, the column would be destroyed. By another oversight, the guide and intelligence staff had failed to make arrangements for messengers to be posted along the route of the column, so these instructions never arrived. This was soon apparent to all officers in camp, because Peacock Hill was fully visible from Nahan and Richards's movements could be closely followed through telescopes. There was no way of signalling, because no code of flags had been arranged. Martindell therefore sent another, very urgent note.

Then, soon after noon, two things happened, which completely changed the whole tactical situation. First, news arrived that Richards's spare ammunition had been lost; and then the engagement on Peacock Hill began. The spectators in Nahan were sickened by their powerlessness to avert what seemed certain tragedy. But soon a buzz of excitement broke the agonized silence. They realized that Richards was holding his position. There was perhaps still time to send fresh ammunition from camp. Soon it was obvious not only that he could be saved, but also that he could be given the means of securing a victory. Eagerly, a young subaltern called Robert Stevenson volunteered to take a couple of companies with spare cartridges to Peacock Hill. But events had moved too fast for the General. Incredibly, he declined the offer, and merely continued to send Richards orders to retreat.

Martindell's reflexes were so paralysed and his imagination was so impoverished, that he was completely incapable of grasping the significance of the developments on Peacock Hill. Having begun with the assumption that Richards could succeed only if Ludlow succeeded, his mind remained prisoner to that idea and simply refused to register the visible evidence, which plainly indicated that Richards could succeed in spite of Ludlow's failure, provided he was sent reinforcements and ammunition without delay. It never occurred to him that the failure of the operation on the left ridge only made it the more essential to exploit the success on the right, and that by continuing to send orders to retreat instead of men and cartridges he would not only ruin a splendid opportunity but probably bring about a disaster. With egregious stupidity, he took no heed of the likelihood of one of his missives arriving after dark and compelling a party of exhausted men without ammunition to retreat blindly, by hair's-breadth mountain pathways, with an enemy three times their number in pursuit.

It is axiomatic that in all tactical withdrawals the most dangerous role is that of the covering party. For them, success in a gamble against overpowering odds is only the prelude to even greater jeopardy, because their acutest peril comes only after they have held the enemy at bay for the benefit of the main party, when they have to withdraw themselves. Richards was now faced with the invidious task of selecting a corps to fulfil this suicidal function. He chose Thackeray's company, because they still had most of their ammunition unused, this having been kept in reserve for any accident. It is said that Thackeray ignored the pleas of some of his men, who urged him to make his way back to camp and leave them to do the job alone. He and William Wilson, the twenty-two-year-old Ensign of his regiment, were devoted friends. They had made wills in favour of each other to symbolize their attachment. Inspired by Thackeray's determination, Wilson insisted on staying too. They were joined by Ensign Stalkert of the 1st/13th Native Infantry, and by William Turner, Ensign of the 1st/27th. Stalkert and Turner were supported by a good proportion of sepoys from their own companies, but all told there were scarcely 200 men to resist 1,500. Thackeray formed two squares on heights commanding the escape route. He and Wilson remained with the one in advance, while Turner commanded the one to the rear. The men fixed their bayonets and performed prodigies of valour in an effort to stem the enemy advance until the main force was clear. Behind them, there was a frenzied stampede as the narrow pathway down from Peacock Hill became choked with men. Mercifully, the night was fine and the way lit by a brilliant, brittle disc of moon.

The covering party managed to keep the Nepalis at bay for half an hour, but then Thackeray's group was forced to retreat, in a desperate bid to escape encirclement. Soon half of them had been shot down, and the rest were surrounded. As they made a dash and tried to cut their way free, Thackeray was hit in the chest by a bullet, and collapsed. Realizing that he was finished, he told Wilson to take command; but Wilson himself was soon felled by a musket ball which shattered his thigh. The Nepalis swarmed everywhere. Men not killed were captured, and only seven of Thackeray's company escaped. The command now devolved on Turner, who, realizing that there was nothing more he could do, shouted to his men to disperse. They fled in every direction, running and stumbling to the limit of their strength into the night.

The first men of the main column limped into Nahan at one o'clock the next morning, giddy from hunger and fatigue; but the remnants of the covering party straggled in for days afterwards. One group had fled northwards, to the Giri Ganga river, where they were found by friendly villagers, who fed them and guided them back to camp. Another forty were taken prisoner. Despite the threat of death, they refused to enter the enemy service and were finally released on parole the following day. Ranjor Singh sent in the wounded, a courtesy unknown in India; but many of the bodies recovered had been mutilated. Wilson had been helped away by Turner but, weak from loss of blood, had been unable to go far. Turner had gone on alone to find help. He had soon been accosted by a small party of Nepalis, and threw himself down a precipice and crawled into a cave to escape capture. Thereafter he had wandered lost and hungry in the jungle for two days. At last he was found by an old peasant woman, who fed him and had her son lead him back to Nahan. Turner never forgot her kindness, and had a pension settled on her for life. He gave some indication concerning Wilson's whereabouts, but the Ensign was not found alive. Thackeray's body was not recovered for several days. All the officers of the camp, including the Major-General, were at his funeral, and none could hide his emotion. The surviving sepoys of his company defied the strictest rules of caste to bury him with their own hands. Moved as he had seldom been in all his long military career, Hastings issued a special Order in honour of Thackeray, 'whose heroic spirit and personal example animated his little band to as daring an effort of zeal and courage as ever distinguished any portion of the Bengal Native Infantry, and, His Excellency may say, any description of troops whatever'.

The total of Richards's casualties was 306—well over half his force. Of these, eighty-one, including three officers (Thackeray, Wilson and Stalkert), were killed. Hastings was amazed by Martindell's behaviour. 'The Commander-in-Chief concludes', ran a sarcastic letter from the Adjutant-General, 'that some insuperable objection must have intervened to prevent your supporting either column, or taking measures to cover its retreat, after you were apprised of the failure of Major Ludlow's attack'. It was later learnt that, had Richards persevered, the enemy would have abandoned Jaithak early the next morning.

This double calamity was all the more vexing because it made it essential to strengthen the Sirmur division. By virtually denuding the stations of Hansi and Rewari and by detaching a battalion from his own escort, Hastings was able to muster a reinforcement of twenty-one companies of infantry, or nearly 2,000 men. But casualties, desertions, sickness and the detachment of troops for the occupation of Dehra Dun had reduced the original strength of the force by over a half, and even after the arrival of eleven companies of his reinforcement Martindell had only 2,700 effective men at his disposal. True, he also had Fraser's irregulars, but he placed little faith in them. Nervous and downcast after the disaster of 27 December, he complained that his force was too small for its assignment. Jaithak was, he knew, expecting reinforcements, because Bal Bahadur Singh had left Chamur and gone to a new stronghold at Jauntgarh, on the east bank of the Jumna behind Dehra Dun, whence Major Baldock, with a party of troops from Dahra, had failed to dislodge him. It could only be a matter of time before he reached Jaithak. Dispatches in this querulous vein elicited no sympathy from Headquarters.

Hitherto [observed the Adjutant-General acidly] it has not been the habit of Company officers to calculate whether they have a numerical superiority to the enemy. The introduction of a principle so novel and so infallibly destructive to our Empire can never be admitted by the Commander-in-Chief. But his Lordship directs me to say, that were this species of computation allowed, he apprehends it could not apply in your case, as he believes your numbers to be considerably beyond those of Ranjor and Bal Bahadur Singh united. When you represent the advantages of Ranjor Singh's position, His Lordship thinks it escapes you that a situation which presents peculiar difficulties of approach must be one to which the means of egress and communication are equally embarrassing when the skill of an antagonist is deployed in availing itself of these obstacles.

I am instructed to say that it is the province of the Commander-in-Chief to weigh the possibility of the enemy's receiving reinforcements. To you, His Lordship looks for the vigorous employment of such force as the ability of the state affords the means of furnishing to you. Did you feel the nature of your command too embarrassing to you, which His Lordship would be deeply loath to imagine, it would be incumbent on you to express it; for in holding it . . . you are pledged to your country to aim with your utmost energy at the fulfilment of its objects.

Martindell was quite crushed by this rebuke, and he offered his resignation. The offer reached Headquarters within a fortnight; but no reply was sent for another two weeks, and it was not until the end of March that Martindell knew of the Commander-in-Chief's decision regarding it. The sense of uncertainty under which he worked in the meantime hardly helped to make his leadership more assured.

In the first weeks of the New Year the weather turned very cold, and there were some stormy nights. The army's misery was worsened by inertia, because all activity now ceased, pending the arrival of reinforcements and the transportation of the heavy guns to Nahan. The road from the park to the plateau was pronounced ready on 31 December, but experience proved otherwise. After prolonged efforts to get the guns up this pathway the attempt had to be abandoned as hopeless, because there were too many turnings to give scope for even pull. A new, straighter road had to be started on another part of the rock, and was not expected to be ready until the end of February. Meanwhile, the Nepalis strengthened their defences by constructing another stockade on the left ridge.

While Martindell awaited his reinforcements and his guns, he had all the approaches to Jaithak reconnoitred, only to find them apparently impassable for artillery. This confirmed him in his resolution to suspend all operations until the heavy guns had arrived at Nahan—though quite how he expected this to alter his predicament it is difficult to understand, if all roads from there to the heights were reckoned impracticable. He can hardly have contemplated bombardment from Nahan, over three miles' distance, when at Kalanga it had failed over 800 yards. As Ludlow saw it, he had become so obsessed with silly fears concerning the safety of his guns that he was incapable of thinking of anything else until he had them in the town, and all his attentions had become engrossed by the progress of the road. Probably he found a welcome means of escape from the real problems of command, without, however, abandoning all semblance of involvement, by busying himself with preparations for the removal of the artillery park. Ludlow confessed he had no idea what the Major-General's ultimate plans were, and 'positively had the fidgits' as he waited for evidence of some tactical purpose to emerge from his dithering.

There is but one road now by which we can get up decently [he wrote to his wife on January 30th] and from this we may be cut off, or, what is worse, perhaps obliged to attempt it with great loss, if we give the enemy more time to defend it . . . I know you must have been in expectation of something decisive having taken place 'ere this, whereas we are less prepared to set about it than we were on the 29th of last month, the day on which I would have followed up the first attempt before any additional defences were made. In my humble opinion, these great delays are the causes of all our failures; they not only betray the poverty of our resources, and give the enemy time to strengthen theirs; but they moreover damp the spirit of our troops from the very inaction incident to them.

William Fraser, the Political Agent, was even more exasperated by Martindell's procrastination. Never were two characters less compatible. Fraser, a young laird of Inverness, was garrulous, opinionated and highly extrovert. He was destined to die at an assassin's hand, as unconventionally as he had lived. Although he had chosen to make his career in the Company's civil service, temperamentally he belonged to its army. An intimate friend of James Skinner, he loved to pose as a military expert, and modelled himself on the old-style 'Hindu' officers, more common in the days of Clive than now, who wore whiskers in imitation of their sepoys, abjured pork and beef, and hunted big-game on foot. Irresistibly attracted to any affray, he had accompanied Gillespie to the assault of Kalanga on 31 October and received a serious arrow wound in the neck. Metcalfe, whose Assistant he was at the Delhi Residency, found him ungovernable and full of wild ideas; but the younger and more zestful Company officers, Ludlow and Frederick Young especially, readily accepted him, for there was usually a substratum of sound reasoning to his outspoken views. His imagination and vitality would have operated as healthy antidotes to Martindell's diffidence had not the General been unresponsive to all advice save that of the officers of the 53rd, and had Fraser's own manner not been so much less persuasive than outrageous.

Finding the inhabitants of northern Sirmur (of the provinces of Jubal and Jaunsar especially) to be more spirited and seditious than those of Garhwal, Fraser planned a partisan army for the interior, with himself as commandant. Krishna Singh, now in camp, whom he found 'a remarkable character for activity and bravery', he proposed should be his assistant; but after the disasters of 27 December Headquarters cancelled both this project and all plans for the detachment of regular troops into the interior. Martindell was nevertheless instructed to provide whatever irregulars he could spare to support the rebels, and to encourage them to harass foraging parties from Jaithak.

The irregular force, the brainchild of Fraser and commanded by his close friend, Lieutenant Frederick Young, was by now over 4,000 strong. But less than half were *paharis* (hill men). The failure of the local inhabitants to come forward in larger numbers was, in Fraser's opinion, a clear indication that the British had done more harm than good to their cause by advertising their policy of restoration. As far as he could see, the presence of the son of the dispossessed Raja of Sirmur in the British camp, with several of the royal family's civil officers, was, far from encouraging local resistance to the Gurkhas, tending to confirm the people in their present allegiance. This was especially so in the case of the inhabitants of Jubal, among whom enthusiasm for the Company's war was tempered by the fear that in the event of its victory they would be made subjects of the Sirmur house—a prospect they dreaded even more than domination by the Gurkhas. Even in Sirmur proper Ranjor Singh Thapa was far more popular than the old royal family. The upshot had been that recourse had to be made to lowlanders of various descriptions—Sikhs, Pathans and Mewatis mostly—to swell the numbers of the irregular contingent. It was therefore a tatterdemalion band, hastily raised, hardly trained, racially and religiously heterogeneous, and, what is more, issued with ancient matchlock muskets, loaded cumbrously with separate shot and powder, instead of modern flintlocks and cartridges. Martindell can hardly be blamed for having had little confidence in them.

Nevertheless, it was a band of these irregulars which broke the long tedium of inactivity and set the army in motion again, by means of a minor but notable success against the enemy. Some 375 were posted on an eminence called Boneta, about nine miles west of Nahan, to help intercept Nepali foraging parties. At daybreak on 31 January, they were attacked by about 250 of Ranjor Singh's choice warriors. They acquitted themselves splendidly, not only repulsing the enemy, but also killing twenty-three and wounding many. Ludlow waited restlessly for Martindell to react to this opportunity; but the General pondered and dithered, and it seemed that it must be lost. On 1 February, however, the irregulars actually moved forward to the western end of the ridge and occupied, unaided, a prominent height called Nauni, which was about three miles from the fort. Reassured by this unexpected performance, Martindell finally made up his mind to venture another attempt to occupy the left ridge. At eight o'clock the same night he sent Lieutenant-Colonel Kelly to Nauni with 1,200 men. Two small mountain guns, transported by bearers, were sent after him—but no field ordnance, because the road was reckoned impracticable for elephants. It was a gruelling march; only between eight and ten miles in length, but of full eighteen hours' duration. At about eleven o'clock on the following morning, all the troops remaining in camp were turned out and paraded under arms on the northeastern point of the Nahan plateau, in order to draw the enemy's attentions from Kelly. The feint was successful, for the Nepalis hurriedly made a stockade in the supposed path of this force and Kelly joined the irregulars on Nauni unopposed. 'This move I heartily rejoice at, for I was afraid our general was asleep and would have given time to the enemy to prevent our getting up at all', Ludlow told his wife with a sigh of relief; 'I think, my dear girl, there is every chance of our getting possession of Jaithak within ten days.'

But fortune never smiled on Martindell. No sooner had the movement been completed than a change in the weather threatened to thwart his hesitant initiative and drive him back even deeper into his limbo of despondency and disappointment. The wind rose, the sky darkened, the temperature dropped, and it began to rain. It rained continuously for three days and nights. It was heavy, glacial rain, driven by raging winds. Tents were dragged down; notepaper became so damp that the ink would not dry; the light was so bad that at three o'clock in the afternoon it was impossible to write or read without a candle; and all the time, everywhere, was the sound of running water.

On bleak Nauni hill the sufferings of the sepoys were pitiful. Kelly had marched in haste, without tents or spare provisions, and it proved impossible to send these up to him while the vile weather lasted. His men huddled abjectly under makeshift shelters, which they formed by throwing their blankets over bars supported by crossed sticks at either end, like roasting spits; but the *kamals* were made of coarse wool and absorbed the wet like blotting paper. There was little fuel for cooking, and even the few scraps of timber that were found proved too damp to ignite. By the third day twenty sepoys and twelve bearers had died of exposure and scores were seriously ill.

Martindell grieved, and wrung his hands. He would probably have abandoned the position altogether had he not received a note from Major Baldock on 5 February, which said that Bal Bahadur, whom Baldock had been trailing, had eluded him altogether and crossed the Tons river—the last major obstacle in his progress to Jaithak. This meant that a reinforcement of between five and six hundred men was about to reach the fort. The weather cleared for a few hours on the same day, and John Ludlow, with his own battalion, a six-pounder and two mountain guns, was sent to relieve Kelly. Kelly's drenched and shivering detachment arrived back in camp that night, thirty of the men on stretchers.

At about eight that night, after Ludlow had reached his destination, the deluge began again.

I have not got your daily despatch to me, [he wrote to his wife on 7 February] nor could I well expect it in such weather as we have had, it never having ceased for a moment to rain ever since we have been up here. It has been very trying for the troops, especially those who have been exposed to it without any covering at all [probably the irregulars]. Thank God today we have had a few hours of dry weather, and as the sun is peeping out I trust it will favour us with its genial influence, for never did poor fellows want it more. Many of the servants as well as sepoys have fallen sacrifice to the inclemency of the weather, and I had just now a report of one of my poor bearers, a Bangywalla, having died coming up. With regard to myself, I never was better, although I have been without a bed and have not changed my clothes these three days. This is not weather that severely injures the constitution of Europeans, but natives cannot stand such cold. I'm told that it snowed here for an hour last night, but as it lay not on the ground 'till morning I did not witness it.

I feel much more contented up here than I was below . . . I have the honour to maintain a post here with 400 men which has been previously held by 1,200. It is a very strong one indeed, and provided the elements do but favor us would be impregnable to any force the Gurkhas would send against us. We have, besides my own force, 1,100 irregulars which will prove of merit and [? — illegible] in case of attack. But the enemy know the strength of our position too well and have too much dread of our guns to make any such attempt. They are withal full 3 miles distant from us with a large dale between us and them.

On the 8th, the rain turned first to hail and then to snow, which soon lay three inches thick on the tents and in drifts of three feet on the ground. At Nahan, the Europeans were in their element, pelting each other with snowballs; but the natives, who had never seen snow before, were flabbergasted and miserable. Nor were the lowland sheep and cattle of the commissariat any happier. 'The cattle are dying and lying in all directions', wrote Sherwood; '800 sheep are reported dead belonging to our regiment.' On Nauni hill the snow was even deeper, and Ludlow's force became completely cut off. Supplies and reinforcements could not be sent to it for five days.

Since 4 o'clock yesterday [he told his wife on the 9th] we have had neither snow nor rain, but an exceeding hard frost; and the snow is now on the trodden roads so many cakes of solid ice. The stupendous hills around all covered with snow present to Europeans a grand and congenial sight—but not so to the natives. Fuel as you may suppose is exceedingly scarce, and it is here so especially, there being no other tree but the fir, which is not particularly numerous . . . There is this advantage in fir, that it burns readily green, from the quantitity of turpentine which is in it. I am greatly in hopes from the clear appearance of the weather, and [it] being withal new moon today, that all bad weather is at an end. Most sincerely do I trust so on account of the troops, who have suffered every privation, and I must say with unexampled constancy.

Finally, the sun came, and the sound of trickling water was
heard again. On 10 February the road was considered passable, and
a reinforcement of 450 sepoys, with another three six-pounders,
was sent to Ludlow under Captain Watson. The paths, however,
were still very slushy, and two elephants slipped over precipices and
were killed. 'The road is difficult beyond measure; everyone [is]
wishing that Lord [Hastings] would look at it' wrote Sherwood
feelingly. After the junction of the reinforcement the spirits of the
troops at Nauni were high, and his men told Ludlow that if he
would lead the way to Jaithak, they would follow.

But there was little likelihood of his doing that. Martindell had
no intention of allowing Ludlow to burn his fingers twice. Now
that he had, almost in spite of himself, got artillery on to one of the
ridges, the bombardment of Jaithak again seemed feasible and his
decision to reduce the fort by this means appeared justified after all.
From now on, Martindell clung to the notion of bombardment with
a desperate faith and refused to be distracted by any incidental
opportunities for other forms of tactics. He simply ignored the fact
that, to be successful, bombardment needed to be combined with a
blockade; that unless the enemy were prevented from escaping, the
guns might merely drive them to another hill to the rear, where it
would perhaps be impossible to attack them.

The Nepali defences on the left ridge were now increased to two
stockades, and the Major-General had to obliterate these before he
could move his guns up the ridge and bombard the fort. On 12
February, all the light infantry companies were sent up to Nauni
with two heavy mortars, and Ludlow was instructed to advance
about 1,100 yards to an eminence called Black Hill, which, it was
judged, would be a good position for a battery. Irregulars under
Frederick Young were left to guard Nauni. But before the bombardment of the stockades could begin, two things happened. Bal
Bahadur finally entered Jaithak, and Ranjor Singh's men occupied
Peacock Hill, the important position on the right ridge which
Richards had been ordered to abandon on 28 December.

Bal Bahadur reached the fort that same evening, 12 February.
'He ought to have been prevented long ago', grumbled Ludlow,
who witnessed the entry from Black Hill. Estimates of the strength
of this reinforcement varied. Pessimists of the 53rd, like Sherwood,
reckoned that the force was 700; while Fraser, less alarmist,
realized that the number could not exceed 400 at the most. When

Headquarters demanded to know why Bal Bahadur had not been intercepted, Martindell blamed Major Baldock.

It is a fact that he derived little collateral co-operation from the force in Dehra Dun. As far back as December, Lieutenant-Colonel Carpenter, left in charge there, had been told to give priority to an attack on Chamur, where Bal Bahadur was then lodged. But Carpenter's force was so small—only just over 200 strong—that he had felt compelled to wait for reinforcements before beginning operations. In the meantime Bal Bahadur had moved west to Jauntgarh and here, in early January, had successfully resisted the efforts of 400 regulars and 600 irregulars under Major Baldock to dislodge him. Soon afterwards he had moved on again, still westwards, towards Jaithak. He had been harassed by some local partisans of Jaunsar district on his way to the Tons river; but Baldock's force, hampered by deep snow and the ruggedness of the country, had been too far behind to afford any support, so the elusive Gurkha had crossed the river with little trouble. Troops from the Dun did not attack Jauntgarh again until 11 March, when the remaining garrison of about 300 withdrew eastwards across the Baghirati river. Chamur was not attacked by a British force until 20 March, when its occupants too retreated across the Baghirati. Both the expelled groups made their way to Srinagar in east Garhwal, now become the new enemy rallying point.

Now that the fort had had its garrison increased, mastery of Peacock Hill, which commanded the wells on the right ridge, was of crucial importance to Ranjor Singh Thapa, and he sent men to fortify the peak. 'It ought to have been taken possession of by us long ago', seethed Ludlow; 'I wish in Heaven the General would show a little more activity and not give the enemy time to add to his defences.' He wanted to open his mortars to distract the Nepalis' attention from their stockade-building, to which proposal Martindell reacted by announcing that he was coming up to Black Hill to examine the position for himself.

His visit was made on 14 February, when, in consultation with Mawby, now his *alter ego*, he fixed on a spot at the foot of Black Hill, about 300 feet below Ludlow's present position and some thousand yards distant from the nearest Nepali stockade, as the site for the batteries. The emplacements were duly constructed that night, but Ludlow received no orders to put the guns in. The Major-General had been suddenly distracted by a report that 500

Nepalis from Amar Singh Thapa were on their way towards Jaithak. Trembling for the safety of his artillery park, he suspended all operations on the left ridge and even recalled a reinforcement which had just been sent there. Ludlow described news of this recall as 'the most discouraging information based on the strangest reasoning [he] ever heard of', because the route of the Nepalis was supposed to lead them directly by his own position, while the Major-General had a force at least four times their estimated number in Nahan. No confirmation being received of the report, two six-pounders were carried down to the batteries on the 16th. Fire was opened on the 18th, when the two mortars were also in position; but by then Martindell, advised by Mawby and Captain Battine, the artillery officer, had decided that the distance of the batteries from the stockades was too great for light ordnance to have any effect and that the eighteen-pounders would have to be brought up.

At this stage, the battering guns were not even as far as Nahan, and it was only on the 19th that the road on which the pioneers had been labouring for three weeks was pronounced ready. It took 200 men two days to get both guns up, so the operation, an object of general wonder and interest, was not completed until the evening of 20 February. Work on continuing the road to Black Hill was started on the 18th.

Meanwhile, the reinforcement from Amar Singh Thapa was again reported to be approaching and Frederick Young, with Krishna Singh and 2,000 irregulars, was sent from Nauni to intercept it. They left Nauni on the morning of 19 February and struck due north, making for the Sain range of mountains, stretching horizontally behind Jaithak, where Young expected to encounter the enemy party. After a march of forty-eight hours, he finally caught up with his prey at nightfall on the 20th, at a place called Chanalgarh, 15 miles from Jaithak and overhanging a deep chasm through which the Jelal river tumbled in noisy cataracts. He scribbled a hasty note to Ludlow: 'I am at length up with the enemy, but he has got such a post I really know not what to do. His force does not consist at present of more than 500 fighting men and a number of followers. We have upwards of 2,000. Is it not a shame? But I fear if I was to order an assault the men would not go on—at least so Krishna Singh says. I am really so tired I cannot keep my eyes open, so excuse this short epistle. We had the Devil's own march . . .'

Krishna Singh had in fact lost his nerve, and far from being of assistance to Young was nearly the cause of his destruction. The irregulars held the enemy party in check during the night, but on the morning of the 21st the Nepalis made a sudden effort to break the blockade. They fired a few volleys and then drew their *khukuris*, to try to cut their way free. Suddenly the rumour flew around the ranks of Young's force that a reinforcement of 2,000 enemy troops from Jaithak was at hand. The notion was absurd. Jaithak was fully fifteen miles away, and there were not that many troops in the place; but it wrought panic among the irregulars, who threw down their arms and fled. They were hotly pursued. Many fell to their death over precipices; others were either slaughtered or mutilated by the Nepali knives. 180 were killed and 273 wounded, and nearly 1,500 deserted either there and then or subsequently. Krishna Singh attempted to extenuate the flight by claiming that the enemy had numbered between 1,200 and 1,400; and there was little reason to doubt that he had been the author of the pernicious rumour concerning reinforcements.

This unfortunate affair widened beyond repair the rift between Fraser and Martindell. Fraser refused to abandon the irregulars, and arrogantly reaffirmed his faith in them. He laid most of the blame for the catastrophe on Krishna Singh, 'who', he claimed, 'from incorrect information or personal apprehension fabricated and used a mischievous falsehood'. Young said that such a heterogeneous and inadequately trained band should never have been employed without a seasoning of regulars to inspire and support them, but Fraser disagreed. He even disputed the superiority of the Nepalis' flintlocks over the irregulars' old matchlocks. Martindell, on the other hand, was vexed and mortified to think that he had ever been led to trust the irregulars. 'I can no longer place any dependence on the few troops of this description who remain,' he wrote firmly, refusing to listen to Fraser and discriminate in favour of the mountain soldiers at least. The Political Agent went off in a huff, and conducted his own inquiry into this affair. He submitted a questionnaire to Young, and then, having embellished Young's replies with his own comments, sent the document to Headquarters without bothering even to inform the Major-General.

At the end of February, Fraser heard that the elders of Jubal province were at last stirring and needed arms and men. He suggested that a force of irregulars be sent, proposing to accompany them himself; and Martindell, glad to be rid of him, agreed. Departure was delayed for some time by the demoralized and refractory state of the irregulars. New levies were no sooner added than droves more deserted, reducing the mean strength of the corps to about 1,400, and detachments showed themselves timid and unsteady in face of even the most trivial hazards. When Fraser finally left camp, with 450 men on 15 March, Martindell heaved a sigh of relief. But his respite was short. Hastings was growing very disturbed at his fecklessness, and began to bombard him with unpleasant missives. On 11 February, the Adjutant-General wrote:

The Commander-in-Chief . . . [expresses] . . . his anxiety that Colonel Ochterlony should derive the aid of a more active cooperation from the force under your command, and His Excellency trusts you will speedily endeavour to afford it to him after the First Battalion, the 15th Native Infantry shall have arrived.

On 25 February he wrote:

His Excellency cannot but view with increasing anxiety the appearance of continued inactivity in your proceedings. The reinforcements which have been sent to your division at such an inconvenience to the public service, and the large addition which has been made through the zeal and activity of Mr. Fraser to the irregular force . . . amounting, His Excellency understands, to about 3,684 men, have authorised the expectation of results commensurate to so great a preponderance of strength.

And on 1 March:

The Commander-in-Chief observes that your last is dated from Nahan, and not being aware of any advantages which that place affords as a headquarters while operations are going on . . . requests to be informed of the reasons which induce your remaining so long at that place. As a position it appears to His Excellency to engross an undue share of solicitude, as well as a much larger portion of your force than circumstances seem to warrant or require.

The advanced state of the season; the little expectation your despatches hold out of any speedy commencement of active operations, notwithstanding the large force at your disposal, cannot but fill the mind of the Commander-in-Chief with unusual anxiety for the public interests so deeply involved in the success of the army under your command. In the absence, therefore, of all positive and specific information as to your present plans and intentions, I am directed by the Commander-in-Chief to request you will state fully and explicitly what you propose to do towards the accomplishment of the service which has been specially entrusted to your direction.

Wearily, Martindell strove to impress on his unfeeling chief the nature of the difficulties and deficiencies with which he was having to contend—poor, even useless intelligence; terrain difficult beyond the conception of those who did not actually see it; and, worst of all, lack of men. He insisted that he must guard Nahan, because it was his magazine, depot, treasury and link with the plains, and he claimed that he had no troops to spare for the occupation of the heights north-east of Jaithak, which was essential if the place was to be blockaded until it could be bombarded. The badness of his intelligence and the obstructions of the ground cannot be disputed; but it was absurd to plead insufficiency of troops. By this time he had at his disposal some 6,000 regulars alone, while Ranjor, with all his reinforcements, could not have had more than 2,000 men of all descriptions. The principle behind his operations was, he repeated, bombardment; but by now he was so nervous that as his plans matured, his confidence in them drained away. Calculations of success began to change into prefigurations of failure and he became inhibited by false premonitions. 'The ground along the whole ridge is very unfavourable, being so narrow as not to admit a company to form abreast', he observed in his dispatch of 1 March, 'and the point on which Jaithak is built is of such steep ascent that in the event of a breach being effected the result of an assault will be very doubtful.'

It was his misfortune that he was surrounded by King's officers who, instead of providing opinions against which he could measure his own and find them false, shared his lack of confidence and so gave a semblance of corroboration to misgivings which were in fact quite unjustified. On 6 March he again asked to be allowed to resign his command if the explanations he had provided proved unsatisfactory. Hastings made it plain that they did prove so; but he forbore to dismiss Martindell 'because', the Adjutant-General explained coldly, 'there would be no explaining the procedure so that it should not carry with it, to the conception of the public, an unqualified condemnation of your conduct'. Dissatisfied as the Commander-in-Chief was, he intended his admonitions more as a private stimulant than as a formal verdict. But the plain truth was that Hastings had no option but to bear with Martindell, because there was no officer of sufficient rank available to succeed him.

The progress of the road from Nahan to Black Hill was be-devilled by vacillation. It was begun along a route designed to utilize part of the course of the Markanda river, but on 23 February some bearers and camp followers were cut off and plundered in the ravine between Nahan and Jaithak by a party of Nepalis using the watercourse as shelter. This mishap persuaded Martindell that the route was too hazardous, so it was abandoned for another, more to the west. After two days this was found to be even more exposed to enemy raids. Work was therefore resumed on the first road, much to Ludlow's exasperation. 'I like not this chopping and changing in a commander. It bespeaks so much indecision—a quality which I expected not to find in General M, tho' I now perceive he has it in an impardonable degree. In truth his whole command has been a comedy of errors throughout—or perhaps a tragicomedy you may term it.' The next day, the 27th, two engineers went down to examine the road and were promptly fired on by a lurking party of Nepali snipers. They consequently reported the road to be far too dangerous, and yet another was begun, this time about midway between the two abandoned ones. For some days work continued uninterrupted, but officers of the 53rd were still uneasy, maintain-ing that the road passed too closely under the enemy stockades on the crest of the ridge for comfort. As always, the Major-General finally came round to their way of thinking, and on 2 March he ordered the engineers to turn the road to the left 'to save the troops [from] being unnecessarily exposed'. So the pioneers and fatigue parties laboured on, always expecting some fresh, capricious change of plan, and now sweltering in warm weather. Spring in the north Indian hills is the nearest thing to paradise that sinful man can know, and in the exiled Briton the wild apple blossom, the awakened bees, the returning cuckoos and the aromatic breezes evoke a poignant, bitter-sweet nostalgia. But for the Britons campaigning in 1815, these things all had an ominous significance. They were warnings that the season was waning fast: advanced harbingers of the monsoon, during which all operations would have to be abandoned.

While the road for the eighteen-pounders was being made, the Nepalis constructed yet a third stockade on the left ridge, in advance of the second and just their side of the ruined village of Jampta. The distance was still too great for the British ordnance to hinder them, and the arrival of the battering guns was awaited on Black Hill with mounting impatience. John Ludlow found an escape from the boredom of inactivity by continuing to unburden himself in letters to his beloved and devoted wife at Meerut, to whom he described how the road finally approached completion.

> Camp, Black Hill, 7th March.
> I am happy to say that the General is now working most seriously and with effect on the road for the 18 pounders. They have not as yet got to the next rocky part, but hopes are entertained that if it cannot be cut through . . . the road may be so brought over the summit of the hill that an 18 pounder may eventually be got over it. If this even can be managed, a month instead of two would then finish the work—nay, if he increases the working party with Europeans, which he yesterday did, it may be got through perhaps quicker . . . But under any circumstance, the delays are most impolitic, [as] evidenced by the enemy throwing up their today's stockade. It will cost more lives to drive them from this than we could have lost in bringing up the guns by a road more direct.

> Camp, Black Hill, 8th March, 1815
> I am happy to say, my Love, that a hint from Head Qurs has made our General exert himself a little, and he has further 3 days past put upwards of 500 men as a working party on his favorite road. By dint of exploring and perseverence they will manage I hope to get the guns over the pinnacle of a rocky hill which it would have been in vain for them [to attempt] by the regular footpath. There may be some danger in bringing the guns over after the road is made, owing to the narrowness of the ridge; but of the practicability of this I shall be better able to tell you tomorrow, as Smith, the Chief Engineer, is gone down to look at it, and I shall have his report tonight about it. Stevenson seems to think it may be finished in ten days . . . That will be quite a relief to us, for when these fine guns are up matters will go on famously—provided only that our commander takes advantage of circumstances and does not permit the enemy to retreat to other ranges of hills further back, which they have already contemplated and will do if not hindered.

> Camp, Black Hill, March 11th.
> The road is very nearly finished: but there are yet two places in it so steep and rugged that the artillery officer, Captain Battine, thinks the guns cannot be brought over them without some alteration. This possibly may occasion a few additional days' delay. I suspect the General will be wishing bye and bye that he had commenced on the road more direct, for that would have been finished many days ago, and the guns,

by reason of its gradual ascent, very easily got up. But the working party getting through the road [as] they have done, have performed wonders.

> Camp, Black Hill, Sunday, March 11th.
> Our road for the guns is again subject to some alterations, and it will depend on the General whether this alteration shall take a fortnight or two days' additional work. The General, without seeing the road, has ordered it to be turned—i.e., taken round the rugged part; whereas the engineers have recommended it to be scalped—i.e., the pinnacle to be taken off. The latter will require two days to execute, so that in 6 days altogether it might possibly be finished.

The engineers apparently prevailed this time, because the road was pronounced ready on 13 March. It was five miles long, with many high humps and low dips after it quitted the Markanda valley and zigzagged across the craggy skirt of the left ridge. Many parts were little more than spaces cleared of vegetation and loose stones, where hollows in the ground had been filled up and smoothed; elsewhere it was a footpath widened by cutting back the bank and artificially raising the outer edge. Its ascent up the flank of the ridge, following the straightest of possible routes, appeared from a distance almost perpendicular and dizzily precipitous. In one place it followed the narrow spine of a rocky spur which jutted out from the ridge like a natural buttress, with an immense cavity on either side. 'It may reasonably be doubted', wrote James Baillie Fraser, brother of the Political Agent, who arrived in camp on 14 March, 'if ever till this period it had been contemplated to drag guns of such heavy metal up precipices so high and rugged, and over so many of them.'

The eighteen-pounders were moved from Nahan at daybreak on 14 March, 200 soldiers of the 53rd and a party of gun lascars allotted to each gun. Martindell was in agonies of apprehension for their safety. The whole army was put under arms and Colonel Kelly sent with a battalion of sepoys and two six-pounders to cover the road—'and for what? Because, forsooth, our General was fearful the Gurkhas would come and run away with them!' snorted Ludlow. In truth, the General need not have imposed such an additional strain on the army. The Nepalis were far too engrossed by the spectacle to interrupt it. Hundreds came out of the fort and watched the operation, as if mesmerized into a state of horrified fascination. First the guns were let down the northern face of

PLATES

PLATE I

b. Tomb of Sir R. R. Gillespie, Meerut

a. Tomb of William Wilson, Thomas Thackeray, Lt. Munt and Ensign Stalkert, Nahan

PLATE II

a. Sir Jasper Nicholls

b. Sir Robert Rollo Gillespie

c. The Marquis of Hastings

d. William Fraser

PLATE III

a. Bengal Sepoy

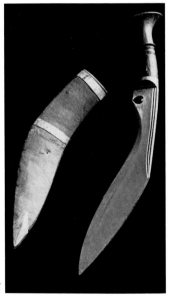

b. A Nepalese *Khukuri*

PLATE IV

Kalanga Hill, from the south east. The depression to the right is the ravine of the Nolengani

PLATE V

Jaithak pinnacle, from just below Nahan

PLATE VI

Jaithak pinnacle, with the ruins of the fort, from the west

Nahan Hill, each held back by its team of Europeans, and guided by lascars with levers on either side. They were then moved along the course of the Markanda, the easiest stretch of the route, and brought to the road proper, which branched away towards the ridge. Progress was painfully slow, and the guns were brought only half-way on the first day. During the 15th the army was again kept under arms while the operation was completed. James Baillie Fraser watched from a distance as the first gun moved up to the crest of the spur:

Main strength was necessary to drag it up the straight road which, viewed at a distance, seemed perpendicular; and the men in detail, with the ropes and guns attached, appeared right up and down on its face. On the edge of steep precipices, again, more caution was necessary; for then, had the huge engine swerved the least to one side, it must have tumbled down to the gulf below, whence it could never have been recovered, and probably many lives must have been lost with it. Several times I trembled as I saw it verge towards the edge and the ground crumble beneath it; but it moved on majestically, following the mass of men that drew it . . . and on the morning of the next day the two heavy guns were placed in battery.[5]

They opened fire on the morning of 17 March, aimed at the nearest stockade, and continued open for two days. On the evening of the 18th the stockade was still standing and a deserter reported that the total of the enemy's casualties did not exceed half a dozen. Bombardment was again being beset by the problem of aim. The stockade emerged only some five feet above the ground, and any hits on so small a target at 800 yards were due more to luck than to science. But the artillerists persevered, and by the next evening some effect was at last visible. The stockade itself appeared to be in ruins, and his more vigorous officers advised Martindell to assault. The Major-General refused, insisting that the trenches, which extended from each side of the stockade over the flanks of the ridge, were still too strongly defended. Instead, he ordered the construction of another battery for the eighteen-pounders at a point about 350 yards from the nearest stockade and to the right of Jampta village. A special path had to be cleared along the ridge for this purpose, and the first gun could not be moved up until daylight on the 20th. By the evening the stockade was a pile of smoking debris;

[5] *Journal of a Tour*, p. 88.

but there were still Nepalis in the trenches and the gun parties were now within range of their musketry. Twenty-two casualties had already been sustained, and the Company officers urged Martindell to waste no more time and storm the position immediately. Again he refused. Instead, he ceased all fire for the night in order to make a road for yet another battery—this time for the six-pounders, in advance and to the left of Jampta, at a point which was only 200 yards from the remains of the stockade. In the morning he was quite surprised to discover that the enemy had repaired their defences during the lull in the bombardment. They had re-erected a breastwork at the back of the demolished stockade, and dug a new trench behind that—thereby turning their old rear into a new front. Ludlow had warned Martindell of the likelihood of their doing precisely this, and was sick with exasperation to find his prediction fulfilled. 'I have more and more reason to be disappointed at the faults and blunders caused by insupportable procrastination . . . I suppose the General will not allow another night to pass without molesting them. If he does there is no saying what may be the consequence, for nothing is so dispiriting to troops as to let a favourable moment pass by without taking advantage of it.'

But that night, 21 March, there was still no attack, much to the disgust of the men, who wanted to repay the enemy in kind for the discomforts of trench duty. The positions at the advanced batteries were so exposed that, with all their shot and shell, the British were unable to inflict more casualties than they suffered.

The next afternoon, a few irregulars who had been sent to act as sharpshooters took advantage of a slackening in the enemy fire to creep up the glacis of the stockade almost to one of the flanking trenches. Spontaneously aided by a few sepoys who were at hand, they plunged in among the enemy and soon seemed on the point of gaining the trench and turning the position. James Baillie Fraser was convinced that they could even have captured the stockade. But when their action was pointed out to the Major-General, he was shocked by their rashness and immediately had them called down.

Martindell's disastrous circumspection was less an expression of personal timidity than a result of the counsel of officers of the 53rd, who persistently eschewed assault as too risky. Mawby was Martindell's *éminence grise*: always at his elbow and completely dominating his meek and submissive personality. 'Unluckily', wrote Ludlow, whose own advice was constantly ignored, there are advisers at our fountainhead who ruin everything in the way of enterprise and who, I firmly think, expect the enemy will surrender at discretion without our attacking them.' We have only to note that Captain Chepmell, Mawby's Major of Brigade, described the eagerness of the sharpshooters as 'foolish' to confirm the identity of these advisers. Prevented by influences of this nature from escaping the trammels of self-doubt, humbled by successive bastinados from Headquarters; and bemused by the problems of warfare in such inaccessible country, the unhappy Major-General lapsed into a state of complete mental deference to the King's officers. Four days later, after three precious months and untold quantities of stores and ammunition had been spent in preparation for the exercise, he made the extraordinary decision that he would not, after all, attempt to take Jaithak by assault. He suddenly decided that 'the hill on which the fort [was] situated [was] not to be carried by assault if defended'. Weak and tired, he surrendered at last to the pressures of more powerful personalities. 'I did not deem it necessary', he told the Adjutant-General, 'to call for the opinions of the senior engineer and artillery officers . . . especially when I adverted to their periods of service compared with my own *and those of other officers under my command*' (author's italics). The allusion speaks for itself. He now announced that he had decided to reduce the fort by blockade, and invoked Ochterlony's example in a pathetic attempt to reconcile the Governor-General to his change of plan. Hastings was incredulous, and at a loss to understand why the grounds for this decision had not been obvious from the start. Angrily, he accused the Major-General of having squandered months of time and labour as well as huge quantities of valuable stores and ammunition.

Martindell's first move in his new scheme of operations was to send William Richards back to the right-hand ridge, whence he had been so prematurely withdrawn on 27 December. With 1,100 sepoys, about 600 irregulars under Frederick Young and Krishna Singh, and two small mortars, he left camp on the morning of 31 March. This time his operation was completely successful. With a small advance guard and his own battalion, he drove a Nepali force 1,000 strong from Panjal peak, slightly south of Peacock Hill. His casualties were only eight killed and fifty-one wounded, and the whole operation was a clear vindication of the worth of the native troops, even in mountain warfare, when properly handled.

It is indeed a success which ought to inspire you with a just confidence in the officers and in the troops under your command [the Adjutant-General told Martindell]. The Commander-in-Chief trusts you will have availed yourself of the obvious advantage afforded to you by this defeat and discomfiture of so large a part of the force opposed to you. The consequent division of the remainder of it will have presented to you a most favourable opportunity for restricting the enemy's movements and really establishing that close blockade on which you have placed your dependence for the reduction of the fortress. His Excellency will await with considerable impatience the accounts of your further proceedings, as your views must undoubtedly have become more distinct and defined through the important success of that division, on which you would not have calculated when you intimated the outline of your plan.

His Excellency will also hope to hear that you have seen cause before this to reduce the force you have hitherto kept in inactivity at Nahan. In the position of the division of your command relatively to that of the enemy, His Excellency conceives no apprehensions could be entertained for the security of the town of Nahan were it left to the protection of a corps far short of that which is now allotted to its defence.

Hastings should by now have known better than to expect so much of Martindell. Having switched his attentions to the tactics of blockade, Martindell pursued them with somnambulistic inflexibility and had absolutely no heed for contingent advantages if they seemed to require tactics of assault. The evening of 2 April was the ideal time for an attack on the stockades of the left ridge, since it was known that the pick of the Nepali troops had been withdrawn to support the force attacked by Richards; but no move was made—either then, or in the days and weeks succeeding. 'If the Genl. would take the stockades to the west, I could then close in on this side, and we might do something', cried Richards. 'We must have patience, I see; but even that is almost exhausted. I know mine is, although I believe I have as great a stock as most people.' The Major-General ceased to react in any professional sense to the events going on around him. He moved through each day in a semi-comatose state, making a few motions of command, but in reality avoiding all decisions and doing nothing more than mechanically forbidding any measure which involved the slightest risk. John Ludlow made himself very unpopular by repeatedly advocating more assertive measures, and Martindell always tried to edge away when he went to make reports.

I went to him only two days ago [wrote Ludlow to his wife on 12 April] and told him I observed 50 to 60 men with a chief descending from the most southern stockade to interrupt some working parties of ours half-way between this and Nahan, who came shooting up and destroying the company. I asked him if I should detach a company or two from my post, which was nearest, to endeavour to cut them off from the fort, which might easily have been done, as the Gurkhas had got quite down into the nulla and were much nearer this than the fort is. The old gentleman began to shy about, asking continually where they were, and I as frequently pointed out several of them. He at last told me there would be no use in sending after them, and he should direct Kelly [in charge at Nahan] in future not to risk his working parties so near. Fraser also reported the same evening that a party of 150 Gurkhas had gone out to the north-west to forage and that they would not return until the following night: but this was by him taken as little notice of as my report. Major Ingleby of the 53rd I hear last night proposed to reconnoitre the trenches of the stockade as he believed there were few men in them. The General thanked him for his zeal, but would not risk valuable lives. I hope he gets many of these hints, if only to convince him of the general sentiment which prevails in this army. I confess my military ardour is beginning very much to evaporate; and whose could not when matters are so ill-conducted? If we do stay out the rains, which please God we may not yet, all of us so doomed will have no one to thank for it but the man who commands us.

The army on Black Hill groaned under the tedium of an unbroken routine of trench duty at the batteries interspersed by listless periods of relief in camp. The guns continued a desultory cannonade against the stockade, and by the end of the second week in April over 3,000 rounds of ammunition of one kind or another had been expended. Reliable sources represented the enemy force as 200 at the most in the nearest defences and 300 in the post behind. These 500 were the only troops they had on the southern side of the fort. Martindell had, with his irregulars, upwards of 9,000 men lying idle before it. One day a Nepali deserter came into Ludlow's post at the batteries, bringing with him as a propitiatory offering five British six-pound cannon balls. He explained that Ranjor Singh Thapa now had an immense store of these. The atmosphere in camp grew very strained. William Fraser, recalled from Jubal by the resumption of operations against Jaithak, was no longer on speaking terms with the Major-General and treated him with undisguised contempt. On 4 April (false) reports were circulating that Bal Bahadur Singh had been severely wounded in Richards's action, so Fraser sent a note to Jaithak under a white flag, offering medical aid. Ludlow, who was then commanding in the trenches, saw that the messenger, whom he thought sent by the Major-General, had been received by the enemy and that they had stopped firing. He therefore ordered the British guns to cease until the exchange had been completed. Martindell, whom Fraser had not troubled to consult or even inform of the measure he had taken, was surprised when the batteries were suddenly silenced without his orders, and he asked for an explanation. Yet such was the man's torpidity and so complete his loss of self-respect, that he did not even complain at what was, after all, an inexcusable impertinence on the part of the Political Agent. Only one section of the officers professed to believe in some inscrutable wisdom behind the commander's behaviour, and that was the group which surrounded Mawby. 'If we are to go by appearances we are not one step nearer taking the fort than we were a month ago,' wrote Henry Sherwood to his wife at the end of April, 'but I believe the General knows what he is about.' The entry in his journal for 25 April reads thus: 'We are building small redoubts on the top of Black Hill and Nauni as protection to our rear. The younger men laugh at the precaution and give them ridiculous names; however, it is but prudent to be secure, for the enemy may have 6,000 men while we have not 2,000 in any one [section of the] army.'

Such an estimate of the enemy's force was demonstrably fatuous. Even at its greatest extent the garrison of Jaithak could not have exceeded 2,000 fighting men, and how many of those could have been trained soldiers is a matter for conjecture. After the beginning of April Ranjor's force was furthermore dwindling all the time, because deserters came into the British camp every day. Yet wildly exaggerated conceptions of the enemy's strength continued to cripple enterprise not only before Jaithak, but in Dehra Dun as well. On 1 April the Major-General received a dispatch from Lieutenant-Colonel Carpenter, who complained that there were not enough troops in Garhwal to garrison the four main captured fortresses (Kalsi, Birat, Chamur, and Jauntgarh) as well as to guard all the ghats on the Ganges and Baghirati rivers. Lieutenant Menteith, commanding at Chamur, had reported that a force of 600 Nepalis from Srinagar was prowling on the eastern bank of the Baghirati, and had complained that it was quite impossible for his 250 irregulars to guard all the ghats over a thirty-mile stretch of river. Martindell immediately wanted to send extra irregulars to Carpenter, and he requested Fraser to increase the levy. For Fraser, this was the last straw. He diagnosed the request as a symptom of the appalling credulity, ineptitude and lack of imagination which had bedevilled the campaign from its inception. He took his pen to reply to Martindell, and drove it at a furious pace. He poured scorn on the absurd estimates of the enemy's strength current among British officers, who had allowed themselves to be duped by 'arrays of rusticks, ploughmen, carriers, camp followers, women, boys, and old men'.

Menteith's supposed 600 from Srinagar, he disdainfully demonstrated, must be more like 215, or 300 at the most; and with indisputable cogency he argued that had that officer but thought, or been allowed, to organize his force as a single mobile unit instead of dispersing it into small fixed parties, it could have moved swiftly to any place where the Nepalis threatened to cross the river and would have been more than adequate to stop them. He attacked the supine tendency to attribute physical as well as numerical superiority to the enemy:

On the point [of] . . . the physical and moral superiority the Gurkhas are said to possess over our troops I shall say little, and I could wish that the general impression in their favour was less prevalent. But supposing that it does exist, is superiority in equipment, in discipline, in members to be quite overlooked? Will no species of superiority be admitted in our favour? Will not the boldness of the enemy increase in proportion as we fail in confidence, enterprise and success, and their assurance and energy grow up as diffidence and indecision mark the steps of our troops?

Hastings was entirely on Fraser's side, and considered his views 'just and luminous'; but he nevertheless felt that, in deference to the declared opinion of the commander of the division, the levy of irregulars should be increased. Martindell wanted 7,000, but Fraser subsequently reported that it was proving difficult to bring the levy, which stood at just over 6,000, to this amount. To make good the deficiency, he wanted to arm and embody the Nepali deserters, of whom there were now nearly 500 in camp, derived partly from Jaithak and partly from Chaupal, a fort in Jubal which had been forced to surrender. They had provided willing and invaluable instruction to the engineers in the art of making stockades. 'I am of opinion that they will be found trustworthy and faithful, and always a hardworking and serviceable body' wrote Fraser. Martindell opposed the idea; but Headquarters supported Fraser, and so one of the British Gurkha regiments was born.

Soon after, Fraser and his brother quitted the camp and went to Jubal again, taking another motley body of irregulars to reinforce those already there. The main object of the expedition was to incite the inhabitants to attack the various Nepali garrisons scattered between Jaithak and the scene of Ochterlony's operations; but as it happened, the timely defection of the Basahar Raja, which led to the defeat and dispersal of the enemy army of the interior under Kirti Rana, made its services unnecessary. The Frasers were nevertheless not disposed to return to camp. Leaving a part of their force to occupy Chaupal, they embarked on a tour of the cis-Sutlaj Himalayan states which was quite a voyage of discovery. James Baillie described the journey in a book which earned him the admiration of Sir Walter Scott. His brother's conduct in the campaign was later rewarded, at his own request, by the grant of the brevet rank of Major in the cavalry corps of his friend, James Skinner.

Meanwhile, Martindell made cautious and feeble efforts to straiten Jaithak. On 12 April he sent Captain Wilson and a battalion of sepoys to occupy a peak about a mile to the left of Black Hill and almost immediately behind the fort. From here, a clear view was had of the rear of the nearest stockade, which had been built into the back of the one destroyed.

They have erected strong sheds made of large timbers to keep them from the shells [wrote Ludlow after a visit to Wilson's post] and have others lower again, nigh the stockade, which look more like dog kennels than anything else. In [the] rear of and about their trenches each man seems to have a hole or cave, like bears' and wild beasts' to retire into from the effects of the shells. Their number, however, is truly contemptible, and very few of them are real Gurkhas.[6] Indeed, the deserters say there that there are not more than 20 Gurkhas in the first stockade and trenches.

---

[6] The men whom the British knew as 'real Gurkhas' are described by J. B. Fraser as having 'broad Chinese or Tartar-like physiognomy . . . small eyes, flat nose, and meagre whiskers . . . stout square make, and sturdy limbs'— from which it is obvious that they were not Gurkhas at all, but Mongolian hill-

A few days later, Wilson moved round still farther and another force was sent to occupy the hill he vacated, so that Jaithak was completely surrounded. But by now Ranjor Singh had the measure of the man against whom he was pitted and had little difficulty in breaking his blockade whenever he wished. If he wanted to send out a party to forage for grain, he would circulate a report through the British spies in his camp that he intended to attack one of the British positions. Alarmed, Martindell would then immediately put all his men under arms and order them to the defence of their posts, thus leaving the Nepali party free to roam abroad. The only retort to this stratagem which he could devise was the destruction of all the grain, now fully ripened, within a ten to fifteen mile radius of Jaithak—a cruel and odious measure, which can hardly have helped to popularize the British cause among the local farmers and peasants. It was clear from the large number of deserters who came into the British camp each day after the last weeks of April that the measures to starve the garrison were beginning to have some effect; but at Headquarters they despaired of ever seeing the fort completely succumb under the Major-General's palsied grip.[7] He was sent another reprimand, and with it a solemn warning:

It appears to the Commander-in-Chief that the posts you have established are at much too great a distance from the place you mean to invest, as well as too few in number; and that you do not detach parties sufficiently often to endeavour to intercept the supplies which it must be obvious the enemy has it in his power to receive from the country—particularly by night.

The very advanced state of the season; the glorious successes which have attended the British arms under Major-General Ochterlony in Hindur and under Colonel Nicolls in Kumaun, contrasted with the little apparent advancement of public interests in your quarter render the state of our operations before Jaithak highly detrimental to the interests of the state, a source of continued anxiety to the Commander-in-Chief, and, His excellency fears, of discredit to our military character.

---

men—Magars and Gurungs. Real Gurkhas were similar in appearance to the native Khas of Sirmur, with whom Fraser mistakenly contrasted them.

[7] On 12 April Ludlow wrote to his wife: 'You are right in supposing me no favorite at headquarters here, tho' I have given no reason for displeasure, excepting, it might be, in a way which I thought it was my duty to deliver my opinions and to recommend while I held the command on these heights somewhat more activity. In these suggestions I have entirely met the concurrence of the Hd. Qur. folks, which to me is quite sufficient.'

You spontaneously . . . took upon yourself the formidable responsibility of abstaining from attack upon the positions which your instructions directed you to attempt reducing. By that act you pledge[d] yourself to effect the surrender of Jaithak through starving the garrison. You ought to be apprised that should Ranjor Singh now come to a convention for the evacuation of the fort and country (a measure not attributable to your operations but to our conquest of Kumaun) a rigid enquiry will not the less be made into the measures taken by you for the prosecution of that plan which you had engaged should prove effectual; and were it to appear that those steps which could alone make a blockade successful had been omitted, the consequences would be very distressing.

Barely a week later, in a dispatch dated 17 May, came the dismissal which was now too late to be a *coup de grâce*. Ochterlony's operations to the west being almost at an end, he was instructed to proceed, as soon as Amar Singh Thapa capitulated, to assume the command at Nahan. Martindell was informed that he might proceed to Sahanranpur, Moradabad or Bareilly, as best might suit himself, to await further instructions. He was in fact spared the ignominy of actual supersession. Before the arrangement could become operative, the war in Sirmur had come to an end. On 21 May, when violent winds and hail announced the advent of the rainy season, Ranjor Singh Thapa, deserted by all his best soldiers and convinced, after receiving news of the Gurkha collapse both to the west and to the east, of the futility of further resistance, formally surrendered. The campaign had lasted slightly more than five months.

Henry Sherwood went to examine the enemy defences, and was 'astonished at the weakness of the works'. He nevertheless added that the natural strength of the position was 'very great . . . almost insurmountable'. The Field-Engineer, Captain Carmichael Smyth, whose opinion regarding the practicability of bombardment and assault Martindell had declined to seek, had other views. After inspecting the fort and the defences before it, he gave it as his judgement that the very confined terreplain of the fort 'precluded the possibility of protracted defence after our guns were once placed in a situation to bear upon the walls'. The only obstacles to their gaining such a position had been the stockades on the left ridge, 'which had they been attempted, must unquestionably have been in our possession in the course of twelve hours'. In his view, therefore, 'no difficulty or obstacle whatever existed to the possession of the whole of the enemy's position which might not have been very readily and easily surmounted.' Such was the conclusion dictated by technical data. In fact, the fort could never have resisted at all. It was full of loose ammunition and gunpowder, and a single shell would have blown it sky-high.

The subsequent fate of Gabriel Martindell forms a most eloquent indictment of the military system of which he was a product. Despite his demonstrable mental exhaustion and lack of self-confidence, he was neither induced to retire nor even removed to the invalid establishment. On the contrary, he continued to hold posts of high responsibility—the charge of a column in the Pindari war in 1818 and the command of the First Division, Bengal Field Army from 1820. He died a lieutenant-general, still on the active list, in 1831, aged seventy-six. The inquiry into his conduct of the siege of Jaithak which Hastings had threatened does not seem to have taken place. The reason for this may lie in the fact that the Major-General was in 1815 included among those Company officers who were made Knight Commanders of the Bath.[8] Hastings was probably apprehensive lest publicly disgracing Sir Gabriel should compromise the dignity of the Prince Regent. Perhaps he realized too that the delinquency of a single senior officer could only be, in the final analysis, but a symptom of fundamental defects—defects which were sapping the whole military system of the East India Company and which even he must despair of rectifying by superficial measures of chastisement.

The misconduct of a King's officer, however, was a different matter, and Sebright Mawby was not spared the deserts of his regiment's malefaction. The 53rd left Nahan early in June and proceeded to Fort William in Calcutta, where it was joined by some officers from its second battalion. The new arrivals, who had been on service in Spain, jeered their comrades for their failure to take the paltry hill fort of Kalanga, mocking and deriding 'Indian' troops and old soldiers. The atmosphere of the mess became highly charged. There were violent arguments, and two duels even took place. Untold damage was done merely by the prospect of the court of inquiry, even though such courts did not conduct any form of trial. Their object was merely to gather the information necessary

---

[8] The Order of the Bath, hitherto consisting of one class only, was now divided into Grand Crosses, Knight Commanders and Companions. Several Company officers, including Ludlow, were made Companions in 1815.

to determine whether prosecution under the terms of military law was justified or not in a particular case. They passed no judgement and did not even give an opinion unless expressly ordered to.

The one appointed to examine the circumstances of the failures before Kalanga remains, alas, almost wholly mysterious. The meagre scraps of information concerning it which have so far come to light indicate that the court initially convened in January 1815, but was then adjourned on some point of legal procedure. It assembled again at Meerut, the following year, under the presidency of Jasper Nicolls, then Quartermaster of the King's Troops in India. The indications are that Hastings had had second thoughts concerning its expediency in the meantime. In October 1815, Sherwood had noted in his journal that 'Lord Hastings [was] aware now of his injustice, and appear[ed] to wish to forget it', and his contention is supported by the fact that the Governor-General had become especially anxious that the court should be held in secret. When Mawby agreed to secrecy, Hastings was very relieved.

The court, which began its sittings on 24 January 1816, was therefore closed from the outset. A search among the records in London and in Delhi has failed to uncover its proceedings, and its opinion, which was asked for, is not known. The court's minutes must have been voluminous, for, according to Chepmell, it was not until July that Hastings received them and 'determined to read them throughout', and with them is undoubtedly lost much valuable information concerning the strange history of Gillespie's last hours and the third failure to take Kalanga. All that is now known about the court is contained in the few sparse jottings made by Captain Chepmell in his diary. From these it appears that the inquiry began unfavourably for the Colonel and the regiment, but that there was a general sense of relief when Nicholls was replaced as President by Lieutenant-Colonel Need, another King's officer, in February. 'I feel glad of that circumstance, as I consider Nicolls a prejudiced man.' But it is possible to make a reasonably confident conjecture concerning the nature of the court's findings. It is known that Mawby did not suffer as a result of the inquisition. There is no record of a court martial, he was promoted major-general in 1819 and he died a lieutenant-general in 1851. It is therefore almost certain that the court exculpated him. Did it do more? Did it uncover unpleasant truths concerning Gillespie's mental state and conduct? Or had Hastings in that year's interval uncovered such truths himself, which made him regret his rash promise to scrutinize the behaviour of Mawby and the 53rd and anxious that the whole business should be brought to a conclusion as quietly and inconspicuously as possible? It is an interesting and possibly relevant fact that from about October 1815 Hastings's attitude towards Stamford Raffles began to change. In that month he recorded his official minute recognizing that Gillespie had been totally unjustified in traducing Raffles's moral character; and later his manner towards Gillespie's old adversary became almost gracious.

VIII

THE COLLAPSE OF THE EASTERN
OFFENSIVES

MAJOR BRADSHAW remained in possession of the twenty-two disputed villages on the frontier of Saran during the 1814 rains, when the rivers swirled down from the mountains clouded by millions of tons of silt, and flocks of aquatic fowl resorted to the flooded rice fields. He had with him three companies of sepoys, a detachment of the Champaran Light Infantry (a new local battalion) and about 150 troopers of Gardner's Horse, commanded by his young brother-in-law, Cornet John Hearsey. This small force was distributed about the village of Ghorasahan, where he had set up headquarters. Although fully twenty miles from the edge of the Tarai jungle, the site was very unhealthy; and during the steamy autumn warmth which followed the monsoon, the men became feverish and sickly. As soon as the waters had subsided, Bradshaw planned an attack on the enemy post at Bar-harwa, some dozen miles to the east, where Parsa Ram Thapa was encamped with 300 men. His object was to clear the approaches to the hills in preparation for the advance of the main army under Major-General Bennet Marley. Marley's force, assembling at Dinapur, was not expected to cross the Ganges until 15 November; and aware that a premature offensive would be risky, Bradshaw waited until the 17th before requesting the reinforcement which would enable him to put his plan into operation. Marley then sent forward two detachments. One, consisting of local infantry and pioneers, he dispatched under Major Roughsedge to occupy the frontier of the department of Tirhut, which adjoined Saran on the east; the other, comprising five companies of regular sepoys, went to join Bradshaw. But he warned Bradshaw not to advance too far, because the main army was not yet ready to march to his support.

Hastings planned that a chain of military posts should be installed in front of the passes into the hills. They would protect the occupied lowlands and preserve the army's communications with the plains. He intended that they should be established after the army had entered the mountains and claimed the main attention of the Gurkha commanders; but Bradshaw, now that his force was to be increased to battalion strength, became over-ambitious and determined to occupy the proposed sites at the same time that he attacked Barharwa. Instead of moving his force to the frontier along a single line, he decided to advance along three, which diverged and described an arc some forty miles wide at their northern extremities. While the right-hand detachment moved to Barharwa under Captain Sibley, the centre column under Captain Hay was to attack Baragarhi, a mud fort about twenty miles to the west, and the left-hand force, under Lieutenant Smith, was to march on Parsa, a ruined stronghold some twenty miles to the west again. This project was put into operation on the night of 24 November, after the junction of the reinforcement from Dinapur.

Sibley left camp for Barharwa at midnight, with 270 sepoys and Hearsey's *risala* of irregular horse. They marched silently and neared their destination, which was on the west bank of the Baghmati river, before daylight. A clammy counterpane of river fog lingered on the country: not high enough to cover the summits of the mango trees, but obscuring the surface of the ground. Sibley formed his detachment into three columns and attacked the Nepali encampment, taking the enemy completely unawares. They had no time to form and fired blindly through the matting of their huts. Parsa Ram Thapa emerged and engaged in personal combat with Lieutenant Boileau, wounding him by a sabre thrust in the thigh; but a quick-thinking sepoy, Rama Sahai Singh, immediately swiped at the Gurkha *Suba* from behind. When Parsa Ram turned to deal with this new opponent, Boileau brought down his sword and cleft the Gurkha's skull. All the principal Nepali officers were wounded and, deprived of leadership, the enemy troops scrambled back towards the Baghmati, hoping to escape by crossing it. But while the infantry had been attacking from the west, Hearsey and his horsemen had dashed round their northern flank, got between the encampment and the river, and sunk all their boats—a daring and dangerous move, which exposed them to the fire of their own comrades. The Nepalis gathered in great consternation inside the river bank, and then made for the jungle and the hills to the north. Again they were checked by Hearsey's men, who dismounted and blocked their path. Some threw down their arms and begged for quarter; others plunged into the deep icy river and were shot or

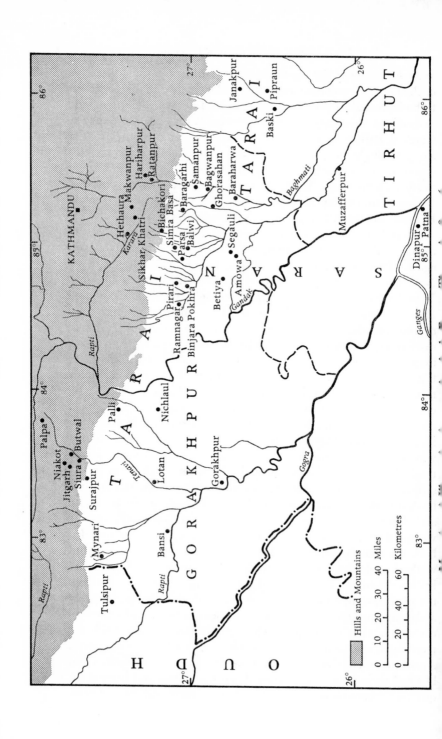

Hills and Mountains

Miles
0   10   20   30   40

0   20   40   60
Kilometres

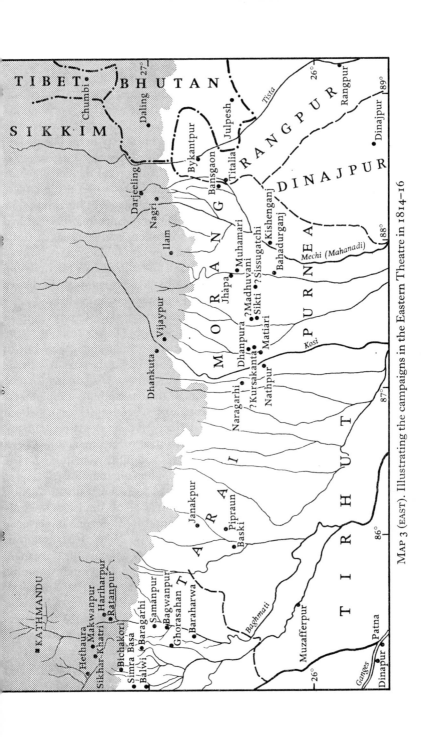

TIBET

BHUTAN

SIKKIM

Chumbi

Daling

Tista

26°

89°

RANGPUR

Rangpur

Dinajpur

27°

Bykantpur

Julpesh

Titalia

Bansgaon

DINAJPUR

Darjeeling

Nagri

Ilam

Muhamari

Kishenganj

Sissugatchi

Bahadurgan

88°

Mechi (Mahanadi)

M

O

R

A

N

G

Jhapa

?Madhuvani

Sikti

Matiari

Kosi

Vijaypur

Dhanpura

Dhankuta

?Kursakanta

Nathpur

87°

Naragarhi

T

A

R

A

I

Janakpur

Pipraun

Baski

PURNEA

TIRHUT

KATHMANDU

Makwanpur

Hariharpur

Hethaura

Sikhar-Khatri

Ratanpur

Bichakori

Baragarhi

Samanpur

Bagwanpur

Ghorasahan

Baraharwa

T

Simra Basa

Balwi

Baghmati

Muzafferpur

26°

Ganges

Patna

Dinapur

86°

MAP 3 (EAST). Illustrating the campaigns in the Eastern Theatre in 1814–16 drowned while trying to swim to safety. It was estimated that about fifty Nepalis lost their lives in this way alone. The total killed was reckoned at seventy-eight, and twenty-three were taken prisoner.

Among the latter was the *vakil* Chandra Sekhar Upadhyaya, who was captured early in the action. All the property in his possession, including the presents destined for the Governor-General, was seized as plunder and shared among the troops of the detachment; and Bradshaw, thinking that he might prove a useful diplomatic pawn, decided to retain Chandra Sekhar himself in his camp. The *vakil* earnestly assured him that neither he nor his masters had ever seriously expected a British invasion, and he begged to be allowed to write to the Raja to inform him of the gravity of his situation. Permission was granted, and under Bradshaw's invigilation he penned a forlorn dispatch, describing the calamity at Barharwa and counselling the Raja to open negotiations immediately.

But the durbar at Kathmandu, apprised of British reverses in Dehra Dun, was less pessimistic. Bhim Sen Thapa's reaction to the news of the attack on Barharwa was not to sue for peace, but to affect an attitude of high indignation. He shrilly resented Bradshaw's seizure of the *vakil* and his property, claiming that it constituted a scandalous violation of the basic ethics of diplomacy. Hastings dismissed these protestations. Chandra Sekhar had been informed of the nature of the relations between the two countries, apparently possessed no authority to treat for peace, and had been given ample time to withdraw to Kathmandu. By remaining on the frontier he had forfeited all right to diplomatic immunity.

Baragarhi, the objective of the centre detachment under Captain Hay, was about twelve miles in advance of Bradshaw's headquarters. It was a large rectangular mud fort, of some importance since it was the winter residence of the *Suba* of Makwanpur. Although it was known to be garrisoned by only fifty or sixty men, it was appreciated that its high ramparts and deep ditch would be formidable obstacles, and a field gun was placed at Hay's disposal. The route, though short, was intersected by numerous nullas, and it was not until eight in the morning that Hay reached the place. Its occupants were on the ramparts, apparently intending to resist, so operations were postponed until the six-pounder arrived. Meanwhile Hay parleyed with the *Faujdar*,[1] and while their leader was

---

[1] An official subordinate to a *suba*, combining the functions of magistrate and revenue collector.

thus engaged, all the Nepalis in the fort absconded by scaling the back wall. The gun was not necessary after all.

Lieutenant Smith, who marched to occupy Parsa, twenty miles to Hay's left, did not even see the enemy. When he arrived at the mud fort, after a march of twelve hours, he found its dilapidated works ghostly and abandoned—though spies soon brought word that there was a Nepali force lurking in the forest a couple of miles in front. With the capture of this post Bradshaw's plan was all but accomplished, and it only remained to tidy his row of advanced posts by moving forward two companies of sepoys from Barharwa, which was on a latitude somewhat behind that of the other two positions, to the village of Samanpur, which was more nearly aligned with them. This done, Bradshaw declared the Tarai of Saran to be occupied, and called on the inhabitants to submit to the Company's authority.

Despite its immediate success, the wisdom of Bradshaw's tripartite advance was very dubious. His three advanced posts— Parsa, Baragarhi and Samanpur—were widely separated; they had no support, because the main army had been delayed and had not yet even crossed the Ganges; and they were in continuous danger of attack from enemy bands prowling in the jungle. By setting up these positions at this stage in the campaign, he had exceeded the letter of his instructions and had, furthermore, infringed a regulation of 1806, which decreed that field guns should always be detached in pairs. There was a single six-pounder with each of the detachments in advance. Nevertheless, he and the officers under his command were publicly congratulated by the Commander-in-Chief on their success.

It was not long before the serious dangers of Bradshaw's arrangement became apparent. Early in December, Lieutenant Smith, in charge of the western post at Parsa, became positive that he was about to be attacked by a superior enemy force, and he hurriedly withdrew to join Hay. His arrival was timely, because on 7 December the pickets in front of Baragarhi were involved in a skirmish with the enemy, and three sepoys were killed. But as the main army was by then at last approaching the frontier, Bradshaw decided not to abandon any of his positions. He made a march along the frontier, re-deploying his force so that Captain Blackney was left in charge at Samanpur, Captain Hay at Baragarhi, and the post at Parsa re-established with a stronger force under Captain Sibley.

Then he formally surrendered his military command to Marley and turned southwards to meet the Major-General.

Major Bradshaw in Saran and Major Roughsedge in Tirhut having already deprived him of some 1,750 men, Marley's army was less than 5,000 strong when he finally left Dinapur. Of these approximately 900 were Europeans, comprising artillerists and the King's 24th Regiment of Foot.[2] To this army was assigned the most important role in the Governor-General's grand strategic scheme. It was to seize the enemy capital and impose those terms of submission which the Calcutta government had judged essential for its own security. The route of its advance was left to Marley's discretion; but it would be an important object in his operations to secure the three forts in the first range of hills which commanded the principal passes to the plains—Hethaura, Hariharpur, and Makwanpur.

The service now entrusted to you [wrote the Adjutant-General] is of a peculiarly important nature. We are about to engage in hostilities with a new power, whose insolence and aggression have defied us to arms. The maintenance of the established renown of our country in Asia, the future security of a vast proportion of our dominions, and the prevention of future wars of a similar character will greatly depend on a speedy and successful issue to the approaching contest. Of all the operations now in progress against Nepal, none can more effectively contribute towards bringing about such an issue than the accomplishment of the important and honorable part assigned to you in the general plan.

At first it was considered both impracticable and unnecessary to send heavy battering ordnance with Marley's column; but further information representing the road to Makwanpur to be less difficult than had been supposed and a prudent lesson being drawn, no doubt, from events in the west, a siege train was ordered from Cawnpore to Betiya. Marley was to use this if the need became apparent after he had entered the hills.

The supreme importance of his mission naturally caused Hastings to follow Marley's progress with special attention; but this was not the only reason for his scrutiny. While it is true that his choice of generals had been very limited, there nevertheless remained in Calcutta a very eligible officer, whom Hastings personally preferred to Marley but whom he had felt bound to pass

[2] Later the South Wales Borderers.

over because he was Marley's junior and not on the general staff. This was Major-General George Wood, known after forty-three years' prominent service in the east as 'the Royal Bengal Tiger'. His part in the capture of Java had been less conspicuous only than Gillespie's and had earned him a gold medal and the praise of the Prince Regent. He was a much more impressive figure than Marley, an obscure old general who had risen without drama or special distinction, merely as a result of the inexorable workings of the seniority system. Hastings was distinctly predisposed in Wood's favour. 'Let me assure you that your character is too well known to me for it to be possible that I should not have you in contemplation when I look forward to Staff appointments', he wrote to him in November 1814.[3] It seems certain that the principal command in Nepal would have been given to Wood had the Governor-General not been concerned to avoid an invidious supersession.

But if Hastings was not the man to allow personal predilections to outweigh the preference due to seniority, neither was he one of those men whose concern to act with scrupulous fairness makes them distrust even their own judgement where the object of their prejudice is concerned. On the contrary, his sympathy for George Wood made him eager to discover such lapses in Marley's conduct as might justify his replacement.

As luck would have it, Marley's army was detained at Dinapur for two weeks beyond the date fixed for its departure. Its supply of treasure was late in arriving at the rendezvous, and Marley did not care to march until he had the means of paying his men. Hastings chafed at the delay, complaining of Marley's dawdling, and asked George Wood to hold himself in readiness for immediate service. 'Wherever you may be placed, I can assure you of my full dependence on you.'[4] He obviously did not expect that it would be long before an opportunity to dismiss Marley presented itself.

Marley finally crossed the Ganges at the end of November, aiming to move to Baragarhi, the central point in Bradshaw's advanced line of defences. To save time, the field guns, stores and engineering equipment were sent directly to the western end of this line, by way of Betiya, because it was Marley's intention to enter the hills with his main force through the Bichakori pass, which was

[3] Printed in Mrs. F. M. Montague, *Memorials of the Family of Wood of Largo*. Both Marley and Wood were Company officers.
[4] Ibid.

just in front of Parsa. The army arrived at the southern bank of the Great Gandak on 6 December. Because the rains had been so late, the river was still about 100 yards wider than normal, and even the elephants could not ford it. As there were only seven or eight boats at the ghat, getting the army across might have taken many days had it not been for the ingenuity of the Field-Engineer, Captain Tickell, and the co-operation of a local indigo planter, Mr. Moran. With the help of large coils of rope, cast-iron weights, large slabs of rock from the indigo factory vat and plenty of manpower—all provided by Mr Moran—a long pier-head was constructed to join a bridge laid over the boats and the whole force with all its baggage and camp followers brought across the river in one and a half days. By 19 December it was encamped at Lautan, two miles from the forest and slightly west of Baragarhi.

Marley was preoccupied as he approached the frontier. News of the harassment of the advance posts convinced him that he must enter the hills quickly; but at the same time he was very reluctant to do this without the battering train, which would not arrive at Betiya for over a week. The root of his predicament was Bradshaw's premature establishment of the line of frontier posts. Marley felt that he had insufficient troops to reinforce them, and he would rather have protected the Tarai by advancing into the hills with his whole force and monopolizing the enemy's attentions. Bradshaw, however, having issued a proclamation to the border inhabitants which pledged them British protection, was now unwilling to have the posts withdrawn, and the Major-General was not resolute enough to contradict an officer whom he had been specially in-structed to consult. He therefore silenced his misgivings, hoping that the confident reports of the officers in advance were well founded, and allowed the posts to remain as they were pending the arrival of the battering train. They were to serve as bases for his projected three columns of invasion. But after he had entered the hills they were to be garrisoned by a levy of irregular militia.

On 30 December, when the heavy ordnance had at length joined the field train at Betiya and the whole of the artillery was preparing to move forward to Parsa, news was received from Captain Sibley, in charge of that post. He wrote that the enemy were gathered in some force in his front and seemed to be meditating an attack. The tone of Sibley's note was almost casual, and apparently he did not even request a reinforcement; but the Major-General's suppressed apprehensions at once revived, and he immediately sent four companies of sepoys to strengthen him. Under the command of Major Greenstreet, they left camp at three o'clock in the morning of 31 December.

Henry Sibley was brave and very cocksure. He was so confident of his ability to drub the Nepalis that when he received a note from Greenstreet on 31 December, informing him of the approach of the reinforcement, he did not even bother to send a reply. Greenstreet, who was as obtuse as Sibley was self-assured, consequently saw no reason to hurry, and halted on the road for the night.

Sibley's force consisted of about 360 men, including fifty of Gardner's Horse. Besides the six-pounder, he had a small one and a half-pounder mountain gun. Finding the mud fort of Parsa too small to accommodate all his men, he had neglected altogether to use this, and taken up a position farther north. His camp was spread along the western bank of a deep nulla. Serried sal forest enclosed it to the front and left. No situation could have been more manifestly perilous; yet Sibley had remained there for two weeks without taking any measures to make it more defensible. No trenches had been dug; no forest had been cleared. He had not even posted look-out men in the trees. The enemy had excellent cover to well within gunshot of the camp on both its northern and western approaches. The advanced pickets, in fact, were merely a few yards from the forest. The only precaution he had taken on the night of 31 December, when Lieutenant Smith warned him of an imminent enemy attack, was to put all his men under arms. He was too busy with New Year's Eve celebrations to do more.

What appeared to be myriads of Nepalis emerged from the jungle half an hour before daybreak on 1 January. Officers later swore that they had counted five battalions of regulars alone. There were also numerous elephants mounted with *jinjals* (large matchlocks on pivots, each throwing a two-pound ball). The main body swept round the left flank and attacked the British rearguard, which contained the officers' tents, the magazine and the bazaar, but which was protected only by the fifty irregular horsemen. These were soon overpowered, and the enemy rushed among the tents and grabbed the stores and ammunition. Simultaneously, other parties attacked the advance guard and inserted themselves between the right flank and the nulla. Smith was commanding the pickets in front, which were pelted with an obliterating fire. He called up the small gun, but the thing was of experimental design and the cartridge shells proved too large for the barrel. Only a few rounds had been discharged before the gun was overturned and crippled by a *jinjal* shot. Sibley, who had come forward to assess the situation, turned to hurry back to the main camp, which was being attacked from both flanks as well as from the rear, but he was wounded twice during his journey: first in the leg, and then much more seriously in the chest. He remained conscious, but incapable, and a sepoy ran forward to tell Smith that the command had devolved on him. On arriving back at the main camp, Smith found Lieutenant Matheson, the artillery officer, trying to clear the ground at the rear with the six-pounder. But the Nepalis remained inaccessible in the forest, and the shot merely ripped bark from the trees, while his own artillerists had no cover and were falling at an alarming rate. Seeing that the sepoys refused to advance and reoccupy the ground of the rearguard and that the pickets in front had been overpowered and were falling back on the main body, Smith decided that his only resource was to make a circle, and in this formation the force defended itself for another hour. The European artillerists and native lascars sweated courageously at the gun. Four Europeans of the detail were killed, and nine wounded. Matross William Levey was wounded twice, in the arm and leg; but he persevered until the priming pouch was blown from his side and he was forced to sit down, cramped with pain and weak from loss of blood. Matheson then seized the ramrod and the sponge staff and worked the gun himself, stoically assisted by a native lascar called Salari, whose hand and foot were lacerated. But after an hour all ammunition was spent, and with it all hope. Smith and Matheson, grimy with gunpowder, held a hurried discussion and agreed that they must withdraw to the old mud fort. Gun, baggage and stores were all abandoned. The Nepalis could have massacred the fugitives; but they were more intent on plunder. Sibley, who was still alive, had to be carried on the shoulders of four grenadiers. But there was no respite at the fort. It was full of Nepalis; and as a last resort, Smith ordered his men to retreat across the eastern watercourse. As the river was high and glacial, few of the enemy pursued and those of the British force who managed to swim to the eastern bank escaped. Smith himself could not swim, but two strong sepoys managed to bring him across. Sibley, like the rest of the helpless wounded, was abandoned. If his agonies were intense, they cannot have been long, because the enemy gave no quarter.

Early that morning, Major Greenstreet, ambling easily along the route to Parsa, was startled to hear the sound of heavy firing. He speeded his advance; but when within about three miles of the scene of action the sight of a horde of drenched and bedraggled survivors coming to meet him told him only too plainly that it would do little good to hurry now. Officers who came up warned him that his small force could do nothing against such a multitude, so he halted to receive the survivors and gave up the idea of marching to Parsa. Casualties were reckoned at 121 killed, 134 wounded and three missing.

When he received Greenstreet's report, Marley was shocked and alarmed. His depot and artillery train were actually on their way from Betiya to Parsa and unless swiftly intercepted might be attacked by the enemy or even led straight into the captured post by their unsuspecting officers. He wasted no time. Within a couple of hours the whole of the main army was on its way eastwards. Before he left Lautan the Major-General sent orders to Blackney, commanding the western post at Samanpur, and to Major Roughsedge, coming from Tirhut, to withdraw at once to Baragarhi.

Then came a second blow. Two hours after leaving camp the Major-General received a hurriedly scribbled dispatch from Lieutenant Strettel, Blackney's second-in-command. The detachment at Samanpur had been attacked and dispersed at five o'clock that morning. Strettel reckoned that the enemy strength had been 2,000 men and twenty guns:

Captain Blackney and all the officers of the wing did their utmost endeavours to bring our sepoys to the charge, which failed in every attempt from the very destructive fire which opposed them. It is with the utmost sorrow I am to mention, that after the action had continued about ten minutes with equal ardour on each side, we were deprived of the assistance and directions of Captain Blackney and Lieutenant Duncan (who, I fear, are both killed, having been very severely wounded and disabled). On the fall of these two gallant officers, the sepoys became quite dispirited, and began to retire with some confusion upon which the enemy advanced upon and destroyed our tents by fire. The village of [Samanpur], in which was the commissariat depot, was burnt in the commencement of the action by the enemy. Finding that the detachment had suffered most severely, added to the great numbers and strength of the enemy, it was judged most prudent to retire; and as the enemy had taken possession of the road to Baragarhi, we directed our course to [Ghorasahan], at which we have just arrived. I am unable to state the exact loss of the detachments, as the stragglers are coming in every minute.

Apart from the two officers, no men were listed as dead; but of the seventy returned as missing it seems few escaped alive, for when John Shipp visited the site of the engagement over a year later the ground was strewn with skulls, bones and even whole skeletons.

Assuming that the enemy had kept in reserve a force at least equal to each of those which had been detached to attack the out-posts, Marley, Bradshaw and Lieutenant Joshua Pickersgill, the Surveyor, agreed that the number of Nepali troops between the British army and Kathmandu must be something near 13,000; and there were in addition reports of reinforcements on their way from Tirhut and from the west. Wondering how he could possibly overcome such a force with the means at his disposal, Marley continued towards the high road linking Betiya to Parsa, and encamped between the two places to await the guns. On 3 January he sent his light infantry and pioneers north to Parsa, to bury the dead and bring away any wounded who were still alive. The remains of Sibley, of the European gunners and of the native Christian drummers were recovered and brought back to the camp, where they were buried with military honours. On the 4th reports were received from Major Mason, conducting the artillery train from Betiya, that enemy parties were hovering around him, and Marley quickly moved his force southwards to escort him for the rest of his journey. Much to his relief, he met the artillery without incident later the same day. On the 6th, the completed army moved forward again, and encamped about one and a half miles south of Parsa.

Hastings blamed no one but Marley for the calamities at Parsa and Samanpur.

While he was delaying at Dinapur [he wrote to Colonel McMahon] the country in his front was cleared for him by a successful attempt of Major Bradshaw's. Instead of profiting by the event and making rapid movement forward, he sends in advance two weak detachments. He stations them at forty miles asunder; and he leaves them without any support within twenty five miles of either. He remains utterly inactive in his retired camp for three weeks, during which term these two posts continued under the enemy's nose in the skirt of a forest without a work of any kind to cover them. At length the enemy appeared to have been shamed into the resolution of attacking these sacrificed parties.[5]

This was very uncharitable. Hastings knew full well that the advanced detachments had been stationed not by Marley but by Bradshaw, during the time of his independent command, and he omitted to state that the measure had received his own approval. He told McMahon that the affair was 'very vexatious, though nothing more', but the language in which he castigated Marley for it was quite out of harmony with such a judgement. The Adjutant-General was instructed to tell the Major-General:

Your reports . . . are in every point of view unsatisfactory. [They bear the appearance] of your not estimating these occurrences as they really affect the state and yourself. It seems at present as if you were not aware of the heavy responsibility attaching upon you for the loss incurred; nor do you intimate any sense of the mischievous consequences of this triumph given to the enemy, so . . . that a hope may be entertained of your striving instantly to counterbalance them by energetic effort.

Of the imprudence of making these detachments at all (unless suitably protected) no doubt exists in His Excellency's mind; but the the danger and [dis]advantage of extending and advancing them was greatly increased by your remaining inactive in a position so remote and from which no timely support could be given in the event of information that the enemy meditated an attack . . .

It was never the Commander-in-Chief's intention, nor agreeable to any of his instructions, that your force should be divided and dispersed over the Tarai. The Corps under your orders had a specific destination . . . A reserve follows you for the purpose of establishing posts, covering your rear, and protecting communications. There is therefore no call for . . . detachments. To an injudicious distribution His Excellency primarily attributes the disasters which have befallen these two detachments.

Scornful of the startling figures which had begun to appear in Marley's dispatches, Hastings warned him against overestimating the enemy's strength. The main army of the Gurkhas was known to be fully engaged in the west, and they had had neither the time nor the means to increase the force before Kathmandu. All this was sound enough. In fact, the enemy troops operating on this part of the frontier were probably not regulars at all. Both Parsa Ram Thapa and Krishna Bahadur Rana, the instigator of the attacks on

[5] Printed in Aspinall, *Letters of George IV*, ii, p. 15.

Marley's outposts, were *subas* (civilian revenue and judicial officers), who normally had only local militia and police under their authority. But the officers with Marley in the field remained unconvinced. To make matters worse, troops and camp followers began to desert in large numbers. The 1,000 militiamen raised by the Raja of Betiya had to be dismissed for unreliability. The other Company zemindar in the area, the Raja of Ramnagarh, refused to help, and became so evasive that he was suspected of conniving with the enemy. The Magistrate of Tirhut set out to raise 1,000 militiamen, but finally had to report that he had managed to enlist only seven.

The discouragements seemed unending, and Marley's sense of quandary bacame acute. It was clearly impossible for him to protect the Tarai and to advance to Kathmandu while his force remained so small. On Bradshaw's advice, he put the issue to his brigadiers. They both expressed the view that his army was inadequate for the calls on its strength which an advance as far as Kathmandu would entail. To protract the Tarai of Saran and Tirhut; to guard the grand depot at Betiya; to form smaller ones at Hethaura, Hariharpur and Makwanpur; and to furnish convoys for lines of communication would, they conceived, require all the 4,000 effective troops at his command even before provision was made for an advance from Makwanpur to the enemy capital. His own convictions thus fortified by their concurrence, Marley abandoned all intention of advancing beyond Makwanpur during the present season. He then withdrew his camp to Binjara Pokhra, fifteen miles south-west of Parsa, so as to be nearer his depot until reinforcements arrived. To lighten the artillery and commissariat departments considerable quantities of shot and engineering materials were sent to be lodged at Betiya; and as a measure of economy all the coolies of the engineering department, whose services would only have been required in the hills beyond Makwanpur, were dismissed and replaced by bullocks.

The Major-General's change of plan cost him much misgiving, despite the support which the opinion of his brigadiers afforded; but events of the subsequent weeks, before Hastings's response was known, must have satisfied him that had it been well founded. After Major Roughsedge had joined the main army in Saran, when there was not a single sepoy of the line in the whole of Tirhut, the Magistrate received a report from his frontier police that four Nepali regiments had arrived at Janakpur—the post in the Tarai

which Roughsedge had evacuated. Mr. Sealy trembled, and prepared to meet his doom. At his entreaty, Marley ordered Colonel
Gregory, who was at Dinapur gathering reinforcements for the
main army, to take an infantry battalion and two six-pounders into
Tirhut. Owing to desertion among his bearers and to the difficult
country ('no regular roads and nothing but rice fields') the forty-
mile journey to Muzafferpur, the civil station of Tirhut, took him
almost ten days. Sealy, meanwhile, became almost hysterical. Every
day brought fresh news of villages being pillaged and terrorized;
and his *thanadars* reported the strength of the Gurkha border force
first at 8,000, then 10,000. He made no attempt to assess the truth
of these accounts, which Gregory quickly realized were highly
exaggerated. There was indeed a Nepali force at Janakpur, which
he estimated at 5,000 or 6,000 men; but the frontier disturbances
were traceable to the activities of bands of five or six people, who
burnt villages and stole cattle. Even these incidents Gregory was
inclined to attribute to the zemindars themselves, who, he knew,
were not averse to destroying their own villages in time of war in
order to get their rent assessments reduced. Sealy disputed this;
but there is no doubt that the alarms derived more from instances
of banditry in one form or another than from acts of war. The Tarai
jungles were infested with fugitives from justice who took advantage of the general disruption to rustle and plunder. Even in the
district of Saran, where the main British army was encamped, the
Magistrate received daily accounts from his *thanadars* of villages
being fired and cattle driven off; and here the problem was complicated by a moral obligation towards the inhabitants, who had been
promised the protection of the Company's government. The
criminals and vagrants in its lowland territories were thus proving a
valuable additional resource to the Gurkha government. Their
activities were a harassing distraction to the main British army and
they confused the attempts of British commanders to estimate the
strength of their enemy. 'It is confidently asserted, and may readily
be believed', Bradshaw told Headquarters, 'that many of the
inhabitants of the lowlands joined in the attack on our troops at
Parsa.' It was undoubtedly the presence of these uncounted supernumeraries which created the impression of such a swollen enemy
force on this and other occasions. It should not be overlooked that
the collapse of law and order on the frontier was hastened by the
Company's own subjects and servants, who made private reprisals

against depredators from across the border. Cases were reported of *thanadars* having applied to indigo-planters for armed men to repulse marauders and conduct retaliatory excursions into the enemy's territory.

Marley, still hoping that he would be able to march as far as Makwanpur that season, worked hard to raise a corps of 2,000 militiamen, so that his regular troops might be relieved of the police duties which were at present detaining them at Betiya and on the frontier; but by the end of the third week in January not a single recruit had enlisted. He was therefore glad to take up the offer of Mr. McEntee, a local indigo planter, to raise 1,000 irregular infantrymen, and advanced him money for the purpose. The offer of Mr. Cracroft, an attorney of Ghazipur, to furnish a body of horse and foot was also accepted; and the Resident at Lucknow, the Agent at Benares and William Moorcroft were all asked to recruit men. These expedients were also frustrated. Mr. Elliot, the Magistrate of Saran, strongly objected to Marley's unorthodox measures and reported them to the government. Calcutta then censured Marley for employing such unsuitable agents as indigo-planters. The troops supplied by private individuals were ordered to be dismissed forthwith and the Collector of Bihar was instructed not to honour, for the time being, drafts on his treasury issued by Mr. Moorcroft.

But these were matters for the attention of Bennet Marley's successor. When Hastings heard of the Major-General's conference with his brigadiers, and of his resolution not to advance to Kathmandu, his patience was exhausted and he reckoned that he had more than sufficient justification for replacing him by George Wood. He complained to McMahon that Marley had countenanced 'every childish rumour about myriads of regular troops opposed to him' and 'terrified his officers (who supposed him to have correct information) by the exhibition of his own alarms.' Marley was directed to surrender his charge to George Wood and then proceed to Berhampur, to assume the command at that station and of such troops as it might be deemed advisable to assemble there in reserve for future objects. George Wood was at the same time appointed to the staff of the Bengal army. Elaborating the reasons for his dismissal, Hastings accused Marley of disobeying his instructions. It had never been intended that his force should protect the Tarai. The risk of enemy incursions had been appreciated and advisedly

incurred, in the hope that the advance to Kathmandu would distract the Gurkhas from such enterprise. For any consequences
resulting from the insufficiency of his force Marley himself would
not have been held responsible. The present commotion and
paralysis derived from his initial blunder of distributing his force in
weak and unsupported detachments. As for delaying to await the
junction of the heavy artillery, this had never been authorized. His
army had been furnished with special portable light artillery with
the express purpose of expediting its march to Kathmandu. The
battering train had been provided only as a reserve to be called on
in case of proven need. Subsequent investigation revealed a further
lapse of Marley's. It transpired that during the period between his
assumption of the command and the repulses at Parsa and Samanpur, the Major-General had never once inspected his division or
seen any corps of it under arms.

Marley was numbed by the news of his disgrace, and made
absolutely no attempt to defend himself. Appalled by the prospect
of public humiliation, his only wish was to go away and hide. He
told nobody about his dismissal; but rumours began to circulate
the camp, and soon the wretched officer could hardly bring himself
to show his face. On the morning of 10 February, his second-in-
command, Lieutenant-Colonel Dick, was astonished to learn that
the Major-General was not to be found and had left no indication
why or whither he had gone. He had issued only the briefest
morning order, directing that all reports of the camp were to be
made to Dick until further notice, and the Colonel could only
suppose that he had absconded, in a moment of mental abstraction.
What had in fact happened was that Marley's sense of humiliation
had finally become too much for him. Hearing of the approach of
George Wood, he had slipped secretly out of camp with the intention of meeting his successor at Betiya and surrendering his command as surreptitiously as possible. Hastings was flabbergasted, and
very nettled, by the news of Marley's extraordinary behaviour. He
was not persuaded that the Major-General was insane; but he did
not doubt that he was inexcusably insubordinate and criminally
irresponsible. Marley was removed from the general staff in Bengal,
where Ochterlony was appointed in his place; and at the same time
the station of Berhampur, to which he was banished and which,
being so near to Calcutta, was in the nature of a sinecure, was
annexed to the Presidency command and declared to be no longer

the headquarters of a general staff officer. By these two measures Hastings intended to

apprize all officers who may hereafter hope to attain [general] rank and the honorable distinction of the Staff, that it [was] not altogether a reward for length of service to be enjoyed in ease and inactivity . . . The liberal policy of the Court of Directors has not overlooked the claims of unemployed officers who are no longer capable of fulfilling the active functions of command. But the General Staff has high and arduous duties annexed to it, which must be faithfully and zealously discharged . . . The Commander-in-Chief will proceed to take into his earliest consideration the further course of military procedure which it may be necessary to pursue in the case of Major-General Marley.

No further measures were in fact taken. Marley's mansuetude prevented his ever attempting to exonerate himself publicly; but he wrote privately to Hastings, earnestly assuring him that his behaviour had been dictated not by contempt of authority but only by a sense of acute embarrassment. Hastings, while he had perhaps been indecorously eager to publicize the justification of his own conduct towards Marley, was not by nature vindictive; and as Marley's explanation implicitly admitted that justification, he professed himself satisfied with it and decided that the Major-General had already suffered punishment enough. Marley was never again employed either on active service or on the general staff; but he remained on the army active list as commandant first at Berhampur and then at Allahabad. Assured of a comfortable obscurity by the tender mercies of the seniority system, he was promoted lieutenant-general in 1821, and full general in 1838. He was then eighty-five years old.

Marley's was not the only head to roll. Shortly after his dismissal the timorous and credulous Mr. Sealy was relieved of his post because of his palpable 'unfitness for the charge of a frontier district in time of war'.

Major-General John Sulivan Wood[6] had been directed to advance through the district of Gorakhpur, along a route about eighty miles west of Marley's. He was to quit Gorakhpur town, his rendezvous, as soon as possible after 15 November and re-establish the Company's authority in the disputed frontier departments of Siuraj and

[6] No relation to George Wood.

Butwal. He was then to attempt to force or turn the Butwal pass and, should he succeed in entering the hills, to march to Tansing, the military station in Palpa province which had served as General Amar Thapa's headquarters. A full-scale invasion of the provinces of Palpa and Gurkha was not expected of him, because his resources (he had some 3,700 men and a few pieces of light artillery) were recognized to be inadequate for the penetration of such difficult country. His main objects were to create a diversion in favour of the army bound for Kathmandu and to help constrict the Gurkhas' channel of communication with their armies in the west.

John Wood was a King's cavalry officer. He was a pleasant man to have dealings with: modest and urbane. As a commander, his flair was for administration, and his weakness the usual concomitant of an over-fastidious mind—a lack of imagination. He was delayed at Benares until the middle of November while the commissariat searched for coolies for the public stores, and company commanders, whose responsibility it still was at this time, struggled to collect sufficient bearers for the doolies (hospital stretchers). Meanwhile, the Nepalis took the initiative and made menacing movements along the frontier of Gorakhpur, causing great commotion among the population. To stay the alarm, the Major-General ordered Captain Heathcote, who with five companies of sepoys had gone on to Gorakhpur in advance of the main force, to proceed northwards to Lotan, a village in the Tarai south of the Butwal pass. He found the going very heavy. While Saran, across the Gandak river to the east, was one of the most intensively cultivated and prosperous districts in the Company's dominions, Gorakhpur was one of the most wild and desolate. The whole area north of the district capital was a malarial wasteland of swamp and jungle. The frontier was lost in a wilderness of elephant grass and forest, which extended from the foot of the hills to within 300 yards of the sepoy cantonments of Gorakhpur town itself. At this time of the year, wide expanses of the country were waterlogged, and Heathcote had to make long detours.

Wood, with that part of his force which had been stationed at Benares, arrived at Gorakhpur on 15 November. Here he was joined by the King's 17th Regiment of Foot,[7] from Ghazipur, and a troop of the 8th Native Cavalry, from Partabgarh. A certain

---

[7] Later the Leicestershire Regiment.

delay was inevitable, because a lack of bearers meant that the stores and ammunition had to be transported from Benares by cattle; but John Wood was fanatically meticulous, and his insistence on having all his arrangements completed to the most intricate detail before moving increased the length of his stay at Gorakhpur from the expected week to a whole month. The inadequacies of his commissariat stimulated no talent for improvisation. Never was there a more helpless victim of the military system of supply, whose slow and ponderous machinery required weeks of precious time to complete the preparations which he regarded as the *sine qua non* of any military enterprise. He dallied for porters, even though he already had 1,000 by the end of November, and notwithstanding the Magistrate's assurance that a further 2,000 would be available once he had occupied the Tarai. In any case, porters would not be required until the army had actually entered the hills. By the end of the first week in December he had collected nearly 2,000, the medical authorities were satisfied that the climate of the Tarai was now safe and some 350 carts had arrived from Allahabad; but even then he did not move. He decided he must wait for the fifty elephants and five companies of infantry promised by the Nawab of Oudh, and was still dissatisfied with the state of his consignment of warm clothing. Only 2,300 woollen waistcoats and pairs of pantaloons had arrived and, as he disliked the idea of partial distribution, he set his commissariat to work to make good the deficiency. These, again, would be of no use at all until the troops had entered the hills. He assured the Adjutant-General that he was making the utmost effort to advance as quickly as possible, but explained that if he did not ensure that his arrangements were complete before leaving Gorakhpur he would only have to wait at the foot of the hills, consuming supplies which could not easily be replaced. It was typical of his thinking that the possibility of a problem concerning supplies outweighed the certainty of military advantage. By 14 December the native infantry from Oudh had at last joined; but the Major-General would have delayed even then, for the elephants, for more porters and for his chief surgeon, had he not received an urgent dispatch from Captain Heathcote.

This informed him that a force of Nepalis, estimated at 8,000, had come down in advance of Lotan and was preparing an attack for the night of 16 December. It left the Major-General no choice: he was compelled to act. A reinforcement was sent to Heathcote, and the rest of the army followed on the 15th. As it happened, there was no attack; so, instead of resuming his march, Wood waited at Lotan, which was still thirty miles from Butwal, for the bullocks with the commissariat and stores. They arrived on the fourth day, when Wood announced that he would move forward again—but *slowly*, so that the pace of the bullocks would be accommodated and the elephants on their way from Lucknow not be left too far behind. He took ten days over the journey to Siura, a distance of no more than thirty miles. Wood also had intended to establish three posts to protect the Tarai: Palli, in Butwal department, to his right; Lotan to his front; and Mynari, in Siuraj department, to his left. But these positions too were far-flung, covering a fifty-mile extent of frontier, and for this reason he had decided not to occupy them until his main force was menacing the foothill passes and engrossing the enemy's attention. When he left Lotan, he had sent Lieutenant Anderson to the west, with a force of about 700, to seize the ruined fort of Mynari; but on reflection it had seemed that his remaining force—twenty-six companies and a few guns—was insufficient to enable him to garrison Palli as well. Instead of sending a detachment to the east, he had therefore written to Bradshaw, asking him to send a force across the Gandak for that purpose. This now left all his remaining resources available for a concentrated attack on the Butwal pass.

The old and derelict town of Butwal was situated on the west bank of the Tenavi river, whose defile formed a passage for the main route to Palpa from the plains. The pass itself was protected by the fort of Niakot, which overlooked it from the heights a few miles north-west of the town. Originally, Wood had planned to besiege the fort by ascending the hills to its right and moving along successive peaks to attack from the west; but now he revised his tactics on the advice of his principal informant, a brahmin called Kanaka Nidhi Tewari. This man was a member of the family who had served as counsellors to the old rajas of Palpa, and he had been recommended to Wood by Francis Hamilton, whom he had assisted in the researches for his book on Nepal. Kanaka Nidhi said that the country to the west of Niakot was too inaccessible to make the Major-General's plan practicable, and that in any case there was no water outside the fort within a radius of three miles. He suggested that the force should instead turn the Butwal pass by advancing into the hills by a less known route to the east, occupy

Palpa, and then attack Niakot from the rear. Struck by the ingenuity of this idea, John Wood determined to adopt it and submitted
trustingly to the guidance of the brahmin. Kanaka Nidhi then
explained that there was a Nepali post at a place called Jitgarh,
which was at the southern foot of Niakot hill. It might perhaps be
more advisable to reconnoitre and attack this place from the plains
before moving round to take the main fort from behind. He
assured the Major-General that it was only a redoubt and would
give little difficulty, being in an exposed position at the far end of
some 700 yards of clearing in the forest.

Wood acquiesced without hesitation and on 3 January moved
northwards with the greater part of his army, leaving only five
companies and a gun to protect the camp at Siura. For a few miles
the march was along the eastern bank of the Tenavi. Just below
Butwal the army crossed the river and struck westwards through
thickets and jungle grasses on a route parallel to the skirt of the
hills. About two miles past the river a party under Major Comyn
turned right, climbed over the tumbled folds of the lower foothills
and made to turn the left flank of the post at Jitgarh. Wood and the
rest of the force continued westwards for another three miles, and
then turned into the glaucous recesses of the sal forest, which grew
thick where the foothills curved away to form an extensive bay.
Kanaka Nidhi directed the way forward for about two miles. The
march was very poorly organized. No light infantry flanking or
preceding parties were detached, with the consequence that the
General and the three companies of the advance guard were
startled to find themselves suddenly in a narrow glade, at the far
end of which, only fifty paces ahead, was a kind of wall, made of
large loose stones and almost concealed by grasses and creeper.
Wood was nonplussed. Immediately behind the structure the hills
rose up, crowned by the fort of Niakot, so it was impossible to go
farther; but the nature and location of the edifice ahead gave it no
resemblance to the one which had been described to him. He
summoned Kanaka Nidhi; but the brahmin, foolishly left unguarded, had vanished, and was nowhere to be found. There was
no sign of life ahead; but the disappearance of his guide made the
commander uneasy. He sent forward Ensign Stephens of the
engineers with a small party to reconnoitre. Stephens was soon
convinced that the place was empty, and was on the point of ordering his men to enter when there was a sudden familiar sound, as of

green wood split by burning. One or two men fell, but most of Stephens's party scrambled back to the body of the advance guard unhurt, because the enemy were aiming too high. John Wood was very cool and courageous. He marshalled the vanguard into formation, and ordered them to return the fire until the rest of the column and the guns should arrive. They fought at a great disadvantage. They were fully exposed, while the Nepalis were concealed by the jungle. Only occasional glimpses could be had of the enemy as they sidled round the flanks of the detachment. Bullets, fortunately badly aimed, sped in every direction. Wood himself was bruised on the chest by a ricocheting ball.

When the head of the main body came up, led by H.M. 17th, they approached the redoubt boldly, while the grenadier and two battalion companies of the 17th struck out to the right of it, herding enemy snipers before them up the steep flanking slopes of the bay. Captain Croker, who headed this group, killed Suraj Thapa, a Gurkha chief, in personal combat. His men successfully established themselves on the slopes in a position commanding the redoubt, which was meanwhile flushed of its inmates by Europeans and sepoys. All the officers and men realized that the Nepalis had lost their initial advantage, and they were confident of victory. But Wood was not happy. He could conceive success only in the terms of his own preconception. The sharp contrast between the Nepali post as he had envisaged it and as it really was, added to the unexplained elopement of Kanaka Nidhi, had disconcerted him and disposed him to expect failure, for victory in his philosophy was the fruit of carefully laid plans and the reward of accurately anticipating eventualities. He had no notion of improvised success. He turned helplessly to Colonel Hardyman and asked him what was to be done; and when Hardyman replied 'Support Captain Croker, or withdraw him', he took the line of least resistance and ordered a general retreat, convinced that this was the only way to avoid a 'fruitless waste of lives'. In fact the position could have been held and even advanced—perhaps as far as Niakot itself, which Major Comyn had successfully approached by the eastern flank. As it was, the retreat caused great danger and confusion. Most of the porters threw down their loads and fled, and the ammunition boxes had to be brought away by the soldiers. Even so the British casualties were only 119, of whom nineteen were killed, while it was calculated that the enemy had lost at least 500 killed and wounded.

But the Major-General's inopportune withdrawal gave the Nepalis the feelings of vanquishers. When Vazir Singh, the Gurkha commander, was later applied to for the dead and wounded, he replied in the insolent tone of a conqueror. 'I have issued orders to the troops of this victorious state not to molest your wounded men . . . any attempt to commit unjust aggression on this powerful state will be severely punished by its gallant army.'

Despite his assurance, many of the corpses brought into camp had been shockingly mutilated. The fate of Kanaka Nidhi remained unknown. 'If he is with the enemy, I can have no doubt of his treachery', wrote Wood, with exquisite inanity.

John Wood retreated first to Surajpur, a few miles south of Jitgarh; and then, when the water there had become contaminated, marched east, back to Lotan, where he arrived on 20 January. He was now firmly convinced that the Butwal pass was too strongly guarded to be penetrated by the troops at his disposal. Some reports represented the enemy force protecting it to be 16,000 strong, and he was gullible enough to allow such estimates to discourage him. Expectations of assistance from the exiled pretender to the throne of Palpa had, furthermore, ended in disappointment. It had become plain that he and his entourage had been too long from the hills and had too little notion of the precise sort of information required by military officers, to be of any use; while the royal family's erstwhile subjects were too awed by fear of Gurkha vengeance to rebel spontaneously. His original intentions completely upset by these frustrations, Wood tried to think of something else to do. He heard that the passes farther to his left—especially those west of Tulsipur, which debouched into the dominions of the Nawab of Oudh—were less carefully protected by the Gurkhas. He therefore decided to march to Tulsipur, by way of the department of Siuraj. Such a move could fulfil more than one purpose. The inhabitants of the western frontier of Gorakhpur were unsettled and affrighted, because Lieutenant Anderson's party had been recalled from Mynari (following reports that 3,000 Nepalis were about to attack it) and the reappearance of a British force would restore calm. It would also be possible to prevent the cultivation of the Tarai in that quarter, thus depriving the enemy of resources for a second campaign. The Tharus could be removed from the frontier and resettled in the waste areas of the Company's territory in Gorakhpur. Depopulation would hinder cultivation and would, besides, arrest the illicit trade in arms and military stores which was known to be conducted between northern Oudh and Nepal. These suggestions were approved at Headquarters and orders were issued that the rest of the 8th Native Cavalry should be sent from Partabgarh to Wood's camp, to assist their implementation; but despairing of ever seeing him accomplish that urgent punch into the enemy's flank which had been his assignment, Hastings had already resolved that the Major-General must be removed as soon as an opportunity arose —under the pretence of entrusting him with another command, if possible.

As John Wood prepared for his march to the west with his usual time-consuming fastidiousness, taking a week to complete arrangements for having his wounded sent to Gorakhpur, it began to dawn on him that he was being surrounded. No longer held in check by his presence before Butwal, the enemy had begun to move down on both his flanks. On his right, they were intruding from the north-east corner of Gorakhpur. There were no troops to hinder them, because Marley, his division already overworked, had been unable to spare men to garrison Palli. By the end of the first week in January reports had arrived from the police at Palli of Nepali incursions and looting; and before long similar dispatches were coming in from Nichlaul, farther south. Martin, the Magistrate of Gorakhpur, told Wood that if he moved westwards as planned, the enemy might well march in from the east and attack Gorakhpur town itself. Eight hundred of them, with two guns, were said to have arrived at Nichlaul. This was only forty miles north east of the district capital, where there were only 435 sepoys and three officers.

Simultaneously came alarming reports of Nepali intrusions on his left. Colonel Baillie, Resident at Lucknow, sent word that the enemy had occupied the passes in front of Tulsipur and were threatening to overrun the plains. There was an additional cause of apprehension in this quarter, because the allegiance of the Tulsipur Raja himself seemed uncertain. He had from the start shown little enthusiasm for the Company's cause, and even the promise that he would be restored to his old hill possession of Dang if he contributed to its success had failed to dissipate his scepticism. In his opinion the strength of European armies lay in their artillery and cavalry, and these arms, he predicted, it would be impossible to convey across the 'thick jungles, deep ravines and stupendous torrents' of Nepal. He had so far failed to respond to Wood's repeated appeals for a diversion in his quarter and had not even bothered to reply when Lieutenant Anderson, before quitting Mynari, had asked him for assistance. The Nawab of Oudh sent his vassal a sharp admonition; but meanwhile the Nepalis set about destroying the frontier posts in Siuraj and menaced the whole area north west of the British army with invasion.

Threatened from the front and from both flanks, John Wood's first concern was for the safety of Gorakhpur town, and he sent 1,200 men to reinforce the garrison there. But he could not decide what he should do next. To move westwards would expose the district capital to attack; to stay at Lotan and allow the enemy to plunder with impunity seemed equally ill-advised. Completely nonplussed, he appealed to Headquarters for fresh instructions to match his 'new and embarrassing situation'. Meanwhile, he resolved to make one of his favourite creeping marchs towards Bansi, twenty-five miles west, in the hope that he would receive the Commander-in-Chief's directions on the way.

Hastings's annoyance at this fecklessness was acute. In a very frosty dispatch, he made it clear that when the government entrusted an officer with a distant command, it did not expect to have to spell out instructions for every eventuality, but counted on that officer's own resourcefulness. In his view, all present embarrassments sprang from the Major-General's having allowed himself to be delayed for trivial reasons at the outset. He had thereby lost the initiative on which the whole success of the general strategic plan depended. He was told that his primary concern now must be the safety of Gorakhpur town. If he remained at Lotan, he was to organize the force in the capital into a mobile column able to strike at the enemy marauding parties—for although the Nepalis may well have had an appreciable force in his front, the demonstrations on his flanks were assuredly the work of small detachments intent on propagating an exaggerated idea of their own strength. If he advanced to the hills, he was to leave a strong force for the protection of Gorakhpur. But as Hastings had no real hope that the latter was the course which the Major-General would adopt, he instructed him to send the King's 17th Regiment into Saran forthwith, where George Wood would have better use for it.

John Wood left Lotan on 28 January and arrived at Bansi,

twenty-five miles to the west, on 3 February—having covered, on an average, between three and four miles a day. While he was at Bansi further troubling reports arrived from the east, where the town and *thana* of Nichlaul had been sacked. Then a torrential rain set in. It continued for several days, and so swelled the nullas and flooded the country that Wood declared that it would be impossible for him to move again until several days after it had ceased.

The weather cleared; but then more time passed while he waited for the 8th Native Cavalry, moving up from Partabgarh, and for reinforcements called from Lotan and Gorakhpur. It was not until 17 February that he finally struck camp. The old fort of Mynari was only twenty-five miles to the north, but it took Wood no less than twelve days to arrive there. Once in Siuraj, he began to devastate the country, destroying the crops on the ground and inciting the camp followers to pillage the hamlets, which had been evacuated on his advance. Within twelve days he had razed some two hundred villages and burnt immense stores of grain. Meanwhile measures were taken to re-settle, in the more southerly areas of Gorakhpur, the wretched Tharus who were deprived of their lands and homes by this odious but essential operation.

In the second week of March it became known that ill health among his men had compelled Vazir Singh, the local Gurkha commander, to retire from Niakot with six companies of his force and station them in the higher and cooler regions of Palpa. The news inspired Wood to contemplate another attempt on the Butwal pass. There were of course long delays before the thought was translated into action. He dallied first for Captain Robertson's force from Balrampur, and then for the contingent of Gardner's Horse which had been put at his disposal in place of the 8th Native Cavalry (now also sent into Saran). He found that he could not quit Siuraj until Gardner's Horse had arrived there, because, having inflicted havoc on the Gurkha territories in the area, it was necessary to leave cavalry to protect the Company's subjects from enemy reprisals. Unforeseen circumstances delayed the departure of Gardner's Horse from Cawnpore (their commander complained that when he joined them they were in a state of virtual mutiny) and they did not arrive on the frontier until 4 April. Even then they proved totally unsuited for their duties, because instead of allaying local panic they inflamed it by ransacking and looting themselves.

Wood did not arrive back at Lotan until 6 April. By then the healthy season was waning fast and the weather had become dangerously sultry. Yet still no sense of urgency spurred the ambling General's progress. He dithered at Lotan for three days and then, with twenty-four companies of infantry and 200 irregular horsemen, trudged north up the east bank of the Tenavi river. Now hindered by heavy artillery—he had two eighteen-pounders, sent from Gorakhpur, as well as four light pieces—he managed to cover only four miles a day. On the morning of 17 April, having suffered no molestation, despite the thickly wooded country, he arrived at a position on the river bank directly opposite Butwal town. There was some sporadic firing from one or two guns in Butwal, but these were soon silenced and it appeared that the town had been abandoned. Some carcasses were thrown, but these failing to set the town on fire Wood ordered a party of light infantry to cross the Tenavi and enter the place. They had waded half-way when renewed musketry fire from the town's defences wounded a few men and forced the others to withdraw. Wood's big guns gave short shrift to the Nepali sharpshooters, while his men still held their musket fire in reserve; but closer inspection had revived and confirmed the Major-General's conviction that the pass was impregnable. He therefore decided that his object had not, after all, been to force an entry to the hills, but merely to make a demonstration. Having thus retrospectively modified his intention to match his accomplishment, he called off the troops, limbered the guns and marched back to Siura, congratulating himself upon a success.

He lingered on the frontier for a few more weeks, but passed the time planning the distribution of his army for the monsoon. Hastings contained his displeasure, because he appreciated that by making Wood's instructions so imprecise he had disarmed himself in advance for the eventuality of the Major-General's incompetence. If Wood had abused the spirit of his orders, he could nevertheless claim that he had created that diversion which had been prescribed as the guiding principle of his operations. Hastings had been reluctant to shackle any of his generals with fussy directions, only to discover to his cost that to allow latitude for initative is to risk that it will, with impunity, be used for ineptitude. Wood combined a mania for method with such a lack of imagination that, after having spent weeks perfecting arrangements which could only have been of use in the mountains, he adhered slavishly to the letter of his instructions and never really made a serious effort to leave the plains.[8]

While John Wood crawled aimlessly up and down the frontier of Gorakhpur, to his right, across the river Gandak, in Saran, the main division of the army lay waiting at Binjara Pokhra for its new commander, Major-General George Wood. The area around the camp was by now a scene of absolute desolation. Independently of the depredations of the enemy, the presence of the British army of 5,000 and the attendant public servants and camp followers who swelled the total to nearly four times that number had been sufficient to lay waste the surrounding country over a considerable area. All the local inhabitants had fled and the deserted villages been torn down and used for firewood.

The new Major-General arrived at Binjara Pokhra on 21 February. He found the troops in good heart. Their appetite for action had been whetted by an exciting altercation with the enemy only the day before, at the village of Pirari, seven miles north. Five or six hundred Nepalis had attacked a reconnoitring party under Surveyor Pickersgill, only to find themselves routed by an opportune reinforcement from Binjara Pokhra. Almost 100 had been killed and wounded, at the cost of only eighteen British casualites.

George Wood was a bilious old officer, known as 'the Tiger' as much because of his growling and swearing as because of his courage. He abhorred risking his reputation, which he hoarded like a miser. When he examined Hastings's instructions, he at once smelt a rat. The Governor-General apparently required him not only to undertake a dangerous assignment, but also to bear the blame for any failure. Hastings had made it quite clear that Wood had been appointed in order to resume active operations; but his official instructions were very vague. Pointing out that the malarial season was expected to begin in the first weeks of April, the Adjutant-General merely *suggested* that an advance as far as Makwanpur might still be attempted. The final form of his operations was left to Wood's own discretion. To the Major-General,

---

[8] Wood was not again employed on active service, but this was probably no more than the inevitable consequence of his returning to Europe soon after the Nepal campaign, where the British army fought no wars in the remainder of his lifetime. There is no evidence that he had forfeited the confidence of the Horse Guards. He was promoted in lieutenant-general in 1819, and full general in 1836. When he died in 1851 he was Governor of the Tower of London.

this seemed to imply that if he did advance and his army was in consequence decimated by disease, his judgement would be pronounced faulty and himself be held responsible. Imputing his own cunning in matters concerning reputation to the Governor-General, he concluded that Hastings had advisedly made the instructions imprecise in order to insure himself against culpability in the event of failure. He immediately dropped any idea of taking his division into Nepal. He told the Adjutant-General that he could not advance. His discretion warned him that it was too late in the season to do so without endangering the health of his army. Instead, he said, he would devote his attention to expelling the enemy from their advanced positions on the plain.

Hastings seethed with indignation when he heard of this 'unfortunate and extraordinary decision'. Here was an officer who, having obviously been appointed in order to resume active operations and possessing the 'apparent means of inducing the enemy to submission in a month', was calmly prepared to subject the Company to the expense of six more months of inactivity and to afford the enemy time to strengthen their defences. Wood was sent a very angry rebuke, and left in no doubt that he would not be commanding the division in the campaign of the following season.

The Major-General thereupon lost his temper, and retorted that invasion had not been specifically enjoined because it was desired that all the blame for any failure should accrue only to himself. He was in effect accusing the Governor-General of moral cowardice and hypocrisy, and even the Bengal Tiger, when his passion had subsided, realized that this was going too far. Hastily, he wrote a private letter of apology to Hastings, asking that his indiscretions be forgiven and forgotten. But this letter which, far from evincing contrition, invoked the Governor-General's 'undeserved imputations' as the cause of his ill temper, instead of mollifying Hastings, made him furious. He disdained to be offended by insults whose vulgarity was now apparent even to their author; but he fulminated against the idea that his original imputations had been undeserved. He was so incensed that he waived protocol, sending Wood a reply over his own signature instead of the Adjutant-General's:

I had with great pain to myself been constrained to subject Major-General Marley to the disgrace of a removal from the command of the Saran Division . . . That fact alone was sufficient to point out to his successor that energy was expected and required of him. You were the person selected by me for the command; and when you were substituted for Major-General Marley professedly that you might repair the mischief entailed by his inactivity, I should have thought it an unworthy impeachment of your character had I by any special orders for exertion insinuated that you might not feel the necessity of it.

You assumed your command at a moment when the spirits of the enemy had been remarkably affected by the brilliant success of our irregular cavalry against a detachment of their infantry; you further found yourself strengthened, beyond any hope that had been held out to you, by the addition of the King's Seventeenth Regiment to your army. Every circumstance concurred to urge your attempting that impression stated in the letter of February 2nd as so important for the public interests.

Had you, in this situation, informed me that you deliberately weighed my representation of the benefits to be gained by inflicting a severe blow on the enemy, but that you thought they would [be] purchased too dearly by exposing the troops to a pestilential malady on penetrating through the forest, and that you would therefore limit your enterprises to . . . attacking the enemy in their several fortified positions on the plain, I should have had no impalatable remark to make. I should have lamented that you saw cause to forgo what appeared a most advantageous opportunity; but I should have given you credit for acting from an upright conviction of expediency, and I should have applauded you for the vigor with which you projected the expulsion of the enemy from the advanced stockades.

Nothing of this sort is even the most remotely intimated by you. . . . Do not deceive yourself. Your neglecting to give me, your Commander in Chief, whose other plans were to be modelled accordingly, satisfaction on that point, was no venial oversight. It was substantially culpable . . . My selection of you for the command manifested my opinion of your character and my personal disposition towards you. I must not, however, suffer my partialities to betray me into a parley with insubordination. I desire you as a soldier to say conscientiously how I, your General, ought to act in the case which I have detailed to you.

Hastings's anger was all the more intense because his information indicated that, had Wood taken the trouble to seek professional medical advice on the issue, he would have found that enough time still remained for him to penetrate as far as Makwanpur. If necessary a force could have been maintained there during the ensuing hot and rainy seasons; but the Governor-General's own persuasion was that this measure, in conjunction with Ochterlony's successes in the west, would have been sufficient to cause the Kathmandu government to sue for peace. Furthermore, the lower provinces of the Bengal Presidency had been mulcted of troops in order to reinforce Wood's division; and by the beginning of March an additional ten companies of infantry, a specially constituted eight-company battalion of sepoy grenadiers, and two King's regiments (the 14th and 17th Foot) had either joined or were about to join his force. These made a total of some 3,000 men, and brought the strength of his army to about 8,000. This, moreover, was exclusive of an extra battalion of native infantry which was sent to join Colonel Gregory in Tirhut. After all these detachments had been made, only 2,500 troops of the line remained in Calcutta for the duties of the Presidency and the lower provinces, and two battalions of the Madras army had to be moved up into Cuttack to relieve them of the pressure of duties on the southern frontier. The 8th Native Cavalry had also been sent from Gorakhpur to reinforce the Saran army; but on learning of Wood's supine disposition Hastings countermanded the order, deciding that the services of cavalry were too precious to be wantonly squandered.

Dispatches travelled very slowly then, so by the time Wood's quarrel with the Governor-General had reached its climax the plan which he had devised was already in operation and the season was too far advanced for alterations to be ordered. Having waited about two weeks for his force to assemble, Wood then proceeded to divide it. Roughly a half was left for the protection of the camp and of the depot at Betiya, while the rest, with six guns, was led on a hundred-mile march along the borders of Saran and Tirhut to clear the jungle approaches of enemy stockades and pickets—a measure which was, as far as the disgusted Governor-General could see, no less hazardous to the health of the troops than a penetration of the hills would have been.

The detachment, headed by George Wood himself, left Binjara Pokhra on 3 March. He planned first to oust the Nepalis from their post in the forest north of Baragarhi; but they heard of his approach and withdrew into the hills before he arrived. The defences of their position were then destroyed by Roughsedge, commanding at Baragarhi. Wood continued eastwards, past Samanpur. There was no road, and the pioneers had to make one for the carts and artillery as the army went along. High jungle grasses had to be cut away and innumerable channels of nullas filled with branches and bundles of grass to prevent the gun-carriages from sinking into the mud and sand. Each operation drew torrents of swearing from the General. At night, he pitched a very small tent in front of the whole army, so as to be first into the fray if the enemy attacked. As there were no other mounted troops with the force, the small band of Gardner's Horse, under jaunty Cornet Hearsey, had to control the baggage train the whole length of the way.

I scarce had a night's rest the whole way [grumbled Hearsey]. I did not know what it was to take off my clothes, long boots or sash at night, or to take any sleep. I was obliged to be on horseback at eleven p.m., guarding with my men the only road to prevent its being blocked by baggage. When the force moved I had to precede the column on its march, and to prevent the elephants, camels, bullocks and camp followers from obstructing it . . . I seldom got any food, except what I carried in my haversack, until 5 o'clock in the afternoon, and very frequently not then . . . I had all the arduous duties of baggage master to perform, and this disagreeable and incapable old general would not even enter my name in orders as 'Baggage Master' to increase my Cornet's allowance of pay.[9]

The army reached the Baghmati on 9 March, having ascertained that no Nepalis remained in the Tarai of Saran. Across the river, in Tirhut, the situation was the same as far as the neighbourhood of Janakpur. Rupitagarhi, three miles south of that place, was known to be occupied by an enemy garrison, reported by local inhabitants to be 12,000 strong. Hearsey wanted to gallop ahead and beleaguer the place until the rest of the army could move up to the attack; but Wood would not consent, and the enemy, hearing of his approach, made good their escape. Hearsey chafed that such a good opportunity had been lost. The Nepalis were known to be still at large in the neighbourhood, but instead of staying to seek them out, the Major-General, after only three days at Janakpur, turned about and marched all the way back to Saran, taking a route slightly south of that by which he had come. Colonel Gregory was left to deal with the enemy still remaining in the north-east corner of Tirhut. 'I swept the whole of the eastern Gurkha territory, destroying several stockades,' Wood later boasted. True, he fired the odd deserted enemy outpost; but he never saw a single Nepali and his main achievement was to exhaust his army and swell its number of sick.

Once back at Betiya, he busied himself with arrangements for the dispersal of his force during the rains. The native part of the

[9] Hearsey's 'autobiography' is printed in Pearse, *The Hearseys*.

army and the King's 24th were posted in selected positions at suitably retired distances from the forest, while the rest of the Europeans were remanded to cantonments. This accomplished, he hurried away to Dinapur, pleading ill health, but probably also because he wanted to avoid the indignity of being superseded at the start of the next campaign. Paris Bradshaw quitted the army on 14 April, and retired to the village of Segauli, where he built himself a bungalow for the monsoon.

Gregory, joined by his reinforcement from Calcutta, under Joseph O'Halloran, flushed the Tarai in Tirhut of the remaining pockets of enemy troops before settling his men at Nathpur, on the west bank of the Kosi, for the rains.

So ended the first campaign of the grand army. The Tarai of Saran and Tirhut had been cleared of the enemy, and the occasion taken to declare its annexation to the dominions of the East India Company; but such a timid intrusion into the Nepalese lowlands fell far short of the spectacular climax so confidently envisaged by Hastings. The army was hardly nearer Kathmandu than it had been five months earlier. All its time, though hardly all its energies, had been consumed in retrieving the consequences of an initial blunder. Hastings must himself bear a large share of the blame for the débâcle. He had switched commanders half-way through the campaign more in deference to personal partiality than to military judgement, and had thereby replaced an indifferent commander by one much worse. Marley had fumbled and hesitated, it is true; but it must be remembered that at the very outset of his command he had been upset by a double calamity for which he was not principally to blame, and that throughout he had been assisted by second-rate subalterns and misinformed advisers. His own tactical ideas had been perfectly sound, and it is quite possible that, had he been given an opportunity to collect his wits, he would have attempted that advance on Makwanpur which, had it been successful, would (as Hastings himself admitted) probably have brought the Gurkhas to their knees. Whether it would have been successful is another matter. The main pass, the Bichakori, was in fact impregnable, and it was only by extraordinary good luck that a vastly better general with a much larger army managed to turn it and reach Makwanpur the following year. Perhaps, in refusing to advance, Wood had done the right thing. But the fact remains that he had done it for entirely wrong reasons.

His fondly treasured reputation did not suffer. Together with Gillespie and Martindell he was gazetted K.C.B. in April 1815, and in 1821 he was promoted lieutenant-general. But during the remaining half-dozen years of his service life in India, Hastings never again gave him a field command.

There was one crumb of consolation for the Commander-in-Chief. Captain Barré Latter, entrusted with the defence of the frontier beyond the Kosi, surpassed himself. The Gurkhas had a major military station at Vijaypur, and it was feared that they would swoop down into the fen of reeds, brushwood and moist grasses that was northern Purnea. According to a knowledgeable brahmin prisoner, the enemy had some 7,000 musketeers and 5,000 archers in the eastern hills. To hold this force in check, Latter had only 1,200 men at first, and no more than 2,700 ultimately, of whom about half were irregulars of the new and untried Rangpur Local Battalion. On top of this, he found the civil authorities unhelpful and even downright obstructive. Mr. C. R. Martin, the Magistrate of Purnea, was so abusive and unco-operative that the government had to remove him, and his successor, Mr. Halhed, had no idea of how to behave in time of war. He inflamed the general agitation along the frontier by chasing up and down with two local indigo-planters and their henchmen, by sending peasants into Nepalese territory to recover property allegedly seized by the enemy and by propagating the most absurdly exaggerated estimates of the enemy's strength. He upset Latter's dispositions by detaining at Kursa Kanta a reinforcement destined for a threatened post at Sissugatchi. Yet despite these frustrations Latter managed not only to hold the Gurkhas in check, but also to wrest from them large segments of the Morang. He attacked their lowland posts at Dhanpura[10] and Jhapa, whence they withdrew eastwards across the Mechi to Bansgaon. This post was only a few miles north of Latter's own headquarters at Titalia. With the aid of a spyglass he was able to assess the strength of their accumulated forces as

[10] Koilia, or Koileah, is the name featuring in the MS dispatches, which corresponds to no name on available maps. It is clear, however, from references to its position, that this post was somewhere in the neighbourhood of modern Birathnagar and Rangeli. Kumar Swami, a Vijaypur brahmin captured in the Morang in February, referred to the same enemy post as being at Dhunpalna (*sic*, in *Enclosures to Secret Despatches from Bengal*, vol. 9, no. 394). It was there-fore probably at Dhanpura, marked just north of Birathnagar on Percival Landon's map.

something near 4,000. Early in March, Latter made plans to call in
all his detachments and mount a concentrated attack on Bansgaon;
but then, soon after noon on 8 March, all the troops there withdrew into the forest, apparently having decided that they were not
strong enough to resist a British attack. Almost the whole of the
Morang was now controlled by the Company.

The operations in Latter's quarter were all the more gratifying
to Headquarters because their effect was not confined to the lowlands. It was in the eastern hills that there at last occurred a stirring
among the mountaineers in support of the British effort. Not that
this co-operation came whence it had most confidently been
expected. The heirs of the quondam Makwanpur empire had
proved as ineffectual as all the other exiled hill chiefs, and the
rather naïve expectation of Hastings—who was imbued with
the legitimist ideas fashionable in contemporary Europe—that
the Kiratas would flock to the standard of their ancient princes had
proved sadly lacking in foundation. Bradshaw had sent the brother
of the surviving pretender to Latter's camp, but his efforts to raise
a force of Kiratas had proved as futile as Latter had predicted, and
he had been sent crestfallen back to Betiya. The hill chief who rose
to the occasion was the young Raja of Sikkim, who, with his old
Lepcha general, Lepcha *chagzod* (minister) and band of loyal
retainers, was still flouting the Gurkhas from Gangtok. Quite
spontaneously, the minister wrote to Latter, enclosing a letter from
his master to the Governor-General, suggesting that if the British
occupied themselves with conquering the lowlands, their men would
attack the Gurkhas in the hills. The only help they asked for was
gunpowder and musket flints. Latter eagerly responded. He sent
ten seers (about 20 lb.) of gunpowder and 200 flints, and advised
the Sikkimese leaders to direct their efforts against the fort of
Nagri. This was a stronghold in the hills about twenty-five miles
north of Titalia, in a position of great strength and traditionally the
residence of the headman of the Lepcha tribe. Yuk Namchu, the
brother of the Raja's minister, having died, this office was now filled
by the minister's young son who was kept as a virtual prisoner at
Nagri by his Gurkha coadjutor, Gentri Khatri. The Raja's emissaries had been confident that if Nagri was taken, all the Lepchas
with Gentri Khatri would desert.

At first, Latter had been keen to make plans for concerted
action with the Sikkimese, undertaking to attack Nizamtara while

they dealt with Nagri; but news of the reverses suffered by Marley's army caused him to abandon the idea, and he warned the Raja's agents that their people should only assault Nagri if they felt strong enough to succeed alone. Notwithstanding this caution, the Raja's minister insinuated himself into Nagri in the place of his son, who was spirited away to Gangtok, and then worked to undermine the Gurkha position from within, while the Raja's troops awaited their opportunity at a short distance outside. After his own successful advance on Nizamtara and Bansgaon, Latter encouraged the Raja to exploit this diversion to press home his attack. The Sikkimese army assaulted Nagri, but found itself outnumbered, the garrison having been reinforced by troops from Bansgaon. There was a contest which lasted three days, but little impression could be made with bows and arrows against Nepali firearms, and a request for assistance was sent to Titalia. At the beginning of May, Latter decided to make a personal inspection of the scene of operations; but his strength was already undermined by months of overwork, and now that the hot weather had arrived he swiftly fell a victim to some jungle fever or infection. He was forced to go to Rangpur to recuperate. David Scott, the Magistrate of Rangpur, assumed charge of the correspondence with the Sikkimese, and in July sent a consignment of muskets to the force before Nagri. He had heard that the Raja's army was now blockading the place, with the help of 200 soldiers from Tibet. Soon after, however, the rains set in, and the messenger sent with the muskets found that the besiegers had been forced to withdraw into the mountains.

So here too operations fizzled out; but enough had been achieved to compensate in some measure for the puny efforts of the generals in command of the two principal columns. It had been demonstrated that even the Gurkhas' regulars, on the plains at least, were far from formidable antagonists when confronted with well-armed troops incisively led and shrewdly disposed; and this made it doubly shameful that the main invading columns had been confounded by mere police and militia levies, supplemented by mobs of scavengers who were scarcely clothed, let alone armed.

IX

THE TRIUMPH OF OCHTERLONY

THE more westerly of the two 'divisions' formed to act in the western theatre of the war was commanded by Major-General David Ochterlony. Acting on what was the remotest periphery not only of the East India Company's possessions, but also of known southern Asia, its purpose was to attack the Gurkha field army under Amar Singh Thapa. This lay in the hill station of Arki, deep within the fastnesses of the freshly conquered Gurkha colonies between the Jumna and the Sutlaj. Hastings determined that the army must be destroyed, dispersed or compelled to surrender before it could move eastwards to assist the defenders of Kathmandu. Assuming that his tactics would be those of pursuit rather than of siege, the Governor-General did not anticipate that Ochterlony would need heavy ordnance; but his own discretion was to be the Major-General's guide in this matter.

Ochterlony's record was impressive. He had fought as a subaltern under Coote, in the Carnatic, where he had been captured and deprived of an eye. As a major, he had commanded a battalion under Lake in the Maratha campaign of 1803 and, after the capture of Delhi, had been appointed British Resident at the Mogul court. His defence of the city against Holkar had been brilliant and had checked the Maratha in the full swell of his jubilance after the discomfiture of Monson. But Ochterlony's military talent and instinctive flair for leadership were combined with a proneness to pessimism and an easily aroused sense of grievance. His removal from the Residency at Delhi by a Governor-General who wished to make room for a more senior civilian had left a permanent strain of bitterness in his character and heightened his sensitivity to adverse criticism. His appointment at Ludhiana, where he was Agent for relations with the protected Sikh states, dated from 1808. It had signalled fresh recognition of his talents and given him fresh interests; but he remained temperamental and difficult to deal with. In moods of enthusiasm he would show eagerness, independence and even arrogance; while in his melancholy or sense of discouragement he would descant on his own foreboding and make a parade of his despair.

Despite his previous keenness to march into the hills and chastise Amar Singh Thapa, he regarded the Governor-General's plan for a full-scale war against the Gurkhas with apathy and misgiving. He decided that the restoration of the hill chiefs (which he had himself previously advocated) was not a good idea after all, and he wrote at length to the government to 'deprecate the extension of an expensive and harassing protection to ingrates who, if relieved from their present oppressors, or restored to their ancient possessions will, by their own petty internal disputes in all probability furnish an endless source of trouble and vexation to the government which has exercised itself for their deliverance'. It was now his view that it would be much wiser to abandon the policy of restitution. 'If we do attack, it should be avowedly in the first instance to conquer for ourselves.'[1] He no longer had hopes of assistance from the exiled hill chiefs—'men who now literally subsist on charity'—and he began to disown his own earlier assessment of the enemy. There was no more mention of 'ill disciplined barbarians'; instead, he became cautionary and even grudgingly appreciative of the Gurkhas' qualities.

This change of attitude is not difficult to explain. Ochterlony disliked Hastings, for a start, and had been depressed by the departure of his old friend, Lord Minto. 'I do not like this new viceroy', he wrote confidentially to Metcalfe, the Delhi Resident, in January 1814. 'All noise and emptiness, like a drum . . . I believe the old one was worth a dozen such.' Secondly, he was disappointed for personal reasons with Hastings's arrangements for the invasion. He was fifty-six, and had been waiting for thirty-five years for an important independent command; and now, when a project he had made his own and which he was better qualified than any officer in India to conduct was at last put into operation, he found that he was assigned a subordinate role, as second-in-command to Gillespie, a King's officer nearly ten years his junior. His sourness is not to be wondered at. It typified the state of mind induced in many officers by the frustrations and humiliations of service with the Company.

There was no apparent reason why the Governor-General should have any special regard for Ochterlony. His promising youth was long past, and he had had no dazzling career in Java to renew his

[1] *Ludhiana Records*, pp. 392–3. See also Kaye, *Life of Metcalfe*, i, p. 386, fn.

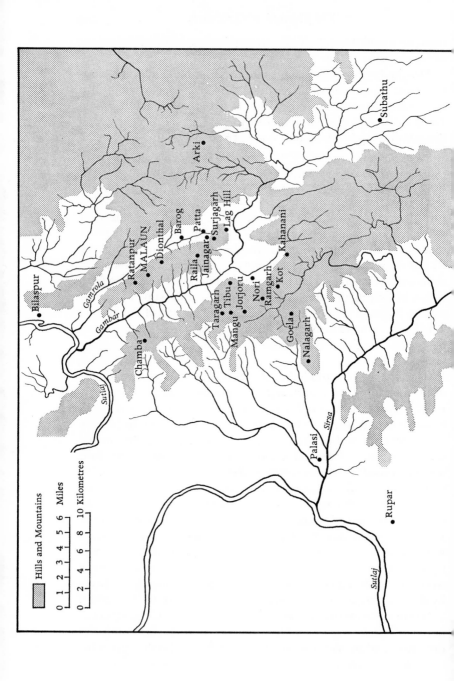

Hills and Mountains

Miles
0 1 2 3 4 5 6
0 2 4 6 8 10 Kilometres

Subathu

Arki

Barog   Patta   Surjagarh   Lag Hill
Ratanpur Dionthal   Kahanani
MALAUN   Raila Jainagar
                Kot
                Ramgarh Nori
Bilaspur   Taragarh Tibu Jorjoru
        Gamrola   Mangu
        Gambar   Goela
                            Nalagarh
Chamba

Sutlaj

Sirsa

Palasi

Sutlaj

Rupar

reputation. He was not on the Bengal general staff, and had for five years been absent from the main sources of influence and patronage, exercising a rather obscure political function at the very extremity of the Bengal Presidency. Hastings therefore felt no qualms about giving him a modest role. He was merely to occupy Amar Singh Thapa for a few weeks, until the second western division could join him. He was then to surrender his command to Gillespie. His army contained no European troops and, as Hastings for some reason reckoned that the scene of his operations presented 'comparatively fewer difficulties' than territory further east, he decided not to furnish him with 'the same description and extensive scale of equipment'. This seems to have meant that Ochterlony's men had to do without even warm clothing, because the records seem to contain no mention of their having been issued with pantaloons and waistcoats.

Ochterlony consequently had to pin all his hopes on the unaided merits of his sepoys and to rely on whatever extraordinary resources he could improvise himself. His force consisted of four and a half battalions of native infantry, two troops of native cavalry, two companies of pioneers and a company of foot artillery—making a total of between 5,500 and 6,000 men, including gun lascars and ordnance drivers, of whom only the commissioned officers and sixty-two artillerists were Europeans. He had in addition some auxiliaries provided by Ram Saran, the exiled Raja of Hindur (in whose old hill territories he was to operate) and by the lowland Sikh rajas under the Company's protection, among whom the Raja of Patiala was the most unstinting contributor. These amounted to about 4,000 men. His aggregate force therefore outnumbered that of his adversary, the total of whose army he estimated as 7,000 men, but which in fact was probably more like 5,000. The Sikhs were most impressive. With their tall athletic physiques, long glossy beards, multicoloured turbans, broad scimitars and proverbial matchlocks, they looked ready to eat the Devil. But it was doubtful that they would prove reliable in mountain warfare. Their traditional mode of combat was as free cavaliers, and they had no experience of fighting as disciplined infantry.

In addition to the troops, there were about 3,000 public servants and 6,000 camp followers, so the concourse which assembled at the town of Rupar, on the eastern bank of the Sutlaj below the foothills, finally comprised something in the region of 18,000 people. The number of servants was so relatively small because the lowlanders half dreaded and half revered the hills as the abode of the gods. They would not volunteer for service as coolies, and those impressed continually deserted. Anxious to avoid initial delays, Ochterlony made up his mind to use bullocks for transportation at the outset of his campaign, and his commissariat department collected 5,000 of these. He counted on being able to recruit porters, who would be essential in the difficult country of the interior, after he had entered the hills. Perspicaciously, he made up his mind to take heavy guns. Hastings, assuming that Amar Singh Thapa's first concern would be to rush his force to the defence of Kathmandu, had inferred that Ochterlony's operations would take the form of pursuit and interception; but Ochterlony himself was becoming increasingly convinced that his tasks would in fact be siege and dislodgement. 'It may be concluded', he wrote as early as August 1814, 'that either at the entrance of the Nalagarh pass, or in some chosen strong position on the way to Arki, [Amar Singh Thapa] will make his first and principal stand with every man he can collect and with every defensive art of stockade etc., which they have in use.' Making use of the latitude which the Governor-General had accorded him, he therefore decided to equip himself not (as had been recommended) for the pursuit of a mobile enemy, but for confrontation with a stationary one who would have to be expelled from hilly fortresses by shot and shell. Two eighteen-pounders, ten six-pounders, two heavy howitzers and two heavy mortars were summoned from the magazines at Karnal and Agra.

The army left Rupar shortly before the end of October. Its march lay north-eastwards. The mountains of Hindur stretched across its path in successive massive ridges, heaving progressively higher towards the farthest ranges of peaks, which glistened like freshly broken alabaster. Each ridge was buttressed by hefty spurs, which thrust at irregular intervals and haphazard angles into the interjacent valleys. Well within this immense and multiple barricade lurked the old Gurkha general: resolute, defiant, and at his ease. His defences at Arki were strong; the approaches well guarded; and his communications with his client state of Bilaspur, lying across the Sutlaj to the north-west, well secured. Its puppet Raja, Maha Chand, acting under the vigilant eye of Shiva Dat Rai, the Kaji's personal agent, had so far proved a complaisant ally. He was keeping the Gurkha army well supplied and had obediently complied with Amar Singh's request for 1,000 soldiers. Ochterlony arrived at Palasi, the lowland capital of the Hindur Raja, on 31 October, and halted a day to pay the troops and jettison superfluous baggage. On 2 November he resumed his march, striking due east along the route to Arki, through thickly tufted forest. Occasional glimpses could be had of the first range of hills and, on a high forward-jutting bluff before it, the fort of Nalagarh.

This was known as the key to Hindur. It was of irregular shape, matching the contours of the ground, and seemed like an excrescence of the rock itself. Its bastions and walls were high, with parapets, and punctured all over with loopholes; but it did not, on inspection, give an impression of great strength. The approaches, however, presented formidable difficulties. The only access was by a steep, narrow pathway, which was intercepted by numerous watercourses. These were now dry, but littered with boulders and obstructed by rocky projections. The whole ground was covered with a matted jungle of spiky bamboos. It was impossible to pitch camp any nearer than three miles from the fort, but Lieutenant Peter Lawtie, the Field-Engineer, immediately took a small party, by a widely circuitous route, to reconnoitre the adjacent heights. He found a site suitable for a battery near the ruins of the abandoned town of Nalagarh and only 225 yards from the walls of the fort, and this position was occupied the same night (2 November) by seven companies of sepoys under Lieutenant-Colonel Thompson. The Nepalis in the fort kept up a brisk fire from muskets and jinjals while the detachment prepared the ground, wounding a few men and killing a sergeant of pioneers. The following morning, while the battery was being constructed, the two eighteen-pounders and two six-pounders were moved from the camp by fatigue parties of sepoys. There had been no time to make a proper road, and it would have been impossible to drag up the heavy guns had it not been for the elephants. Ochterlony had been warned by native informants that the mountain paths were impassable for all four-footed animals save the hill pony; but when he heard that an elephant had once been sent as a present from Nahan, in Garhwal, to Basahar, he had reasoned that these beasts must be capable of manoeuvring the ground if carefully handled. The performance of the elephants on this occasion amply vindicated his judgement. The eighteen-pounder barrels, made of iron and each weighing over a ton, were too heavy to be carried on the backs of even these powerful animals; but wherever there was room two elephants followed each mounted gun and, at a command from the mahouts perched on their necks, bent their foreheads to the backs of the carriages and thrust the machines bodily up the slope, while the men at the drag ropes guided them along. When a wheel lodged in a rut or cavity, an elephant would either mould his trunk to the outer rim or entwine it around a spoke and lift the whole engine free with an impressive combination of finesse and strength. They showed little hesitation so long as low overhanging branches were cut away. The ordnance pieces were at the summit by dusk and in battery by eight o'clock the next morning, 4 November.

The hills reverberated and birds soared up as they opened fire. At first, the six-pounders wrought great havoc. The Nepalis had piled stones on their ramparts, ready to assail a storming party, and a few well-aimed balls sent the whole lot showering into the fort, lethal as grapeshot. But the walls themselves proved more resistant than had been expected. Although the eighteen-pounders were at reasonably close range, it took them twenty-four hours to hammer down sufficient fabric to make a breach. At about nine o'clock on the morning of the 5th, when preparations were at last being made for an assault, two brahmins appeared in the breach to parley. After some negotiation, the garrison surrendered as prisoners of war and relinquished their arms. A small outpost to the north-west capitulated at the same time, bringing the total of prisoners to ninety-five. These were sent to Ludhiana, escorted by one of the troops of native cavalry. So the first of Amar Singh's fortresses fell to Ochterlony—at the cost of much labour and patience, but with few casualties. Apart from the sergeant of pioneers, none of the British force was killed and only about half a dozen wounded.

The road to Arki meandered over the shoulder of the Nalagarh spur to a village called Goela, where it crested the first ridge of hills. From Goela, the road plunged 1,000 feet into the valley of a small river, and then climbed up the western flank of the second hilly range. This second ridge maintained a general altitude of between 4,000 and 5,000 feet above sea level, save opposite Goela, where there was a wide gash, 800 feet deep. Through this, like a very fine strand lost in the eye of a huge needle, threaded the Arki road. Guarding the gorge from its northern side, sprawling astride the crest of the ridge, was the fort of Ramgarh.

On the night of 4 November, Ochterlony had heard that the main body of Amar Singh Thapa's army had left Arki and its subsidiary post of Subathu and advanced to Ramgarh. Anxious to forestall any fresh advance, Ochterlony directed his reserve, commanded by Thompson, to move on immediately to secure the road in advance of Nalagarh. By the morning of 5 November Thompson had reached Bariyan, *en route* for Goela, without having encountered the enemy. Meanwhile Ochterlony lightened his column as much as possible, in preparation for his own advance. His heavy ordnance, however, he kept, persuaded that his forecast concerning the nature of the impending warfare had been confirmed. 'It would seem that the character and operations of the war should be changed', he told the Adjutant-General, 'and instead of being composed of small detachments with light artillery, our force should be concentrated on certain points; and however tardy their progress . . . [none] should move without a gun or guns sufficient to throw open these barriers . . . It is not my intention to relinquish the battering guns if any strength, labour or exertion can get them forward.' He resigned himself to a slow but sure advance. 'Manual labour, strength and perseverance seem our principal dependencies in these alpine regions. Our progress will be slow, but I trust it will be certain; and I hope His Excellency will approve a determination I have formed not to be hurried into any attempt that will occasion more eventual delay than the very tedious advance I now anticipate.'

Hastings had many faults as a Commander-in-Chief, but he was neither meddlesome nor dictatorial. Not being on the scene of action himself, he did not presume to question the decisions of deputies who were, provided always that those decisions were cogently argued and genuinely influenced by local circumstances. Privately, he was dismayed by the loss of speed which Ochterlony's proposals would entail; but having allowed the commander to use his own discretion and devise his own tactics, he did not now hesitate to honour the spirit of the permission. Publicly, he fully endorsed Ochterlony's argument.

So the pioneers set to work to prepare the road for two eighteen-pounders, four six-pounders and a couple each of heavy howitzers and mortars. They were diligently assisted by artisans and labourers supplied by the Raja of Hindur. Trees had to be felled and rocks blasted to clear the way. Labyrinthine pathways had to be widened, borders scarped, pot-holes filled, declivities banked and parapets raised to prevent the heavy engines from toppling over the brinks of precipices. The ordnance was got forward to Thompson's position at Bariyan by 10 November, and Ochterlony then prepared to follow with the line. Thompson again moved ahead of the main force and arrived at Goela at sunset on the 11th—which was none too early, because he disturbed a party of Nepalis who had already begun to stockade the position. He was now on the crest of the first ridge of hills. From Goela he could look across the valley to Ramgarh fort on the second ridge. Here lay Amar Singh Thapa, with the flower of his army—nearly 3,000 men, besides his Bilaspur auxiliaries. His dextrous soldiers had already been busy, stockading the spurs below and the heights adjacent to the fort, so that his position now straddled the gorge through which the road to Arki passed. Ramgarh guarded the passage from the north; while just over a mile south of it a peak called Kot, which was 200 feet higher again than Ramgarh, had also been occupied and fortified. Between these two posts were five stockades: four on the crest of the ridge, and one in the gorge astride the Arki road itself.

The Major-General arrived at Goela with the rest of the army on 12 November. It needed only a glance through his telescope to convince Ochterlony that the Gurkha's position was unassailable from the front and north; but it did seem that Kot stockade could be attacked by a force moving up the crest of the ridge from the south. The next day, therefore, he augmented the reserve and sent it across the valley and up the flank of the ridge to a settlement called Kahanani. This was on the crest of the ridge about two miles south of Kot, and was situated on ground broad enough to give sufficient camping space.

Thompson arrived there without mishap, and Field-Engineer Lawtie, who had accompanied the reserve, then embarked on an intricate inspection of the vicinity of the Gurkha position. Every night for a week he roamed into the rugged and uncharted crevices of the Ramgarh ridge, producing invaluable maps and sketches of country hitherto untrodden by Europeans. The front and southern flanks of Amar Singh Thapa's position he confirmed were inaccessible; but in the valley to the Gurkha's rear, on the other side of the ridge, he discovered the settlement called Nori. This was on an extensive plain, and Lawtie reckoned that an attack could be launched against Ramgarh from here. Ochterlony readily accepted his assessment, and resolved that the fort must be assaulted from behind.

Peter Lawtie was only twenty-four, and youth was no recommendation in an officer cadre where rank was determined by seniority. But Lawtie was a brilliant engineer, modest and charming, while Ochterlony was never one to suffer his feelings to be dictated to. He took to Lawrie at once, made him an A.D.C., and was happy to rely on both his professional skill and his friendship.

When he transferred his base to Nori, Ochterlony would, of course, considerably extend his line of communication and supply; but he did not reckon that this need increase significantly its vulnerability. He had already learnt, from studying the Nepalis' own tactics, how effective the stockade was as a mode of defensive war, and he shrewdly calculated that the enemy would hesitate to attack his detachments if these were defended after their own manner. Inevitably, more detachments would entail a dispersal of his army and reduce the number of men he could bring against Ramgarh; but he acted with the hope that the advantages of ground on the eastern side of the ridge would sufficiently compensate for this decrease by enabling him to bring his artillery into play. Even failing this, there would always be the advantage in the move that it would place the British army between Amar Singh Thapa and Arki, his main base, and thereby enable it to harass the enemy supply lines.

As a ruse designed to mask his main manoeuvre, he decided that, for the time being, he would leave his two eighteen-pounders and a couple of pieces of light artillery in the valley below the western approaches to Ramgarh, under the charge of a battalion of native infantry. A convenient position once established on the heights by an assault from the east, these could then either be brought through the Ramgarh gorge or taken up the western flank of the ridge and over the crest.

The most daunting obstacle to the main movement was the appalling difficulty of the road. It was as well that Ochterlony had prepared his men for the expenditure of 'manual labour, strength and perseverance', because the campaign could never have proceeded had the army given these qualities grudgingly. The pioneers had already been busy clearing the descent from Goela, and all the artillery was moved down to the valley by the evening of 7 November; but the route from there over the hump of the ridge into the valley beyond was still impassable for carriage cattle. Determined to economize every hour at his disposal, Ochterlony had each of the field-guns selected to accompany the principal force taken from its carriage and lashed to the back of an elephant. 7,000 coolies were put to work to drag the empty carriages and carry the ammunition. In this fashion the force and its ordnance were got as far as Thompson's position at Kahanani, on the crest, by nightfall on 19 November; and simultaneously the battering train, with a battalion of sepoys under Lieutenant-Colonel Adams, had made its way north up the valley to a site below the western face of Ramgarh. All the baggage and the bazaars were left temporarily at Goela, under the protection of a party of Patiala Sikhs, until the road to Kahanani had been made practicable. Fortunately, as the army had moved into the interior, certain of his old zemindars had joined the Hindur Raja, and these were now bribed to set their people working on the road. They worked hard, and by the evening of the 20th the stores and baggage had begun to arrive at Kahanani. The position here was meanwhile defended by an elaborate Gurkha-style stockade. But before the army could descend the eastern flank of the ridge and move to its new ground at Nori, this part of the route had also to be cleared. It was not until the 23rd that the movement was resumed, and not until the 24th that camp was finally pitched in the valley at the rear of Ramgarh.

The new position of the British army was a level plateau in the beautiful valley of the Gambar river, about one and a half miles north of and some 500 feet below the gorge of the Ramgarh pass. The valley was well watered, and richly wooded with shrubs and wild fruit trees. As soon as he had understood Ochterlony's intentions, Amar Singh Thapa had set his men to defend the eastern approaches to his position, so the spurs jutting into the Gambar valley were already pimpled with stockades and stone redoubts. Ochterlony had a battery for his field-guns constructed in front of the foremost enemy stockade by 26 November, and early that morning an attempt was made to bombard the structure. It soon became apparent that the guns were too far from and below their target. At about half-past nine, the Major-General asked Lawtie to reconnoitre the ground farther forward. The Field Engineer left the battery about an hour later, accompanied by 100 sepoys. The detachment proceeded towards a hill which had been designated as a possible site for a new battery. It had to pass through a small gully, and before this had been cleared enemy marksman opened fire from the heights on both sides. Lawtie thought quickly. The hill was not far ahead and, although it was crowned by an occupied stone breastwork, he judged that a rapid advance to assault it would involve no greater hazard than a retreat through the gully; while if the hill was gained, it would be a good position in which to await a reinforcement. He therefore divided his force and sent fifty men forward immediately to the attack. Ensign Symes led them up the hill to the breastwork, which they easily captured. They wanted to charge the stockade, which was about 300 yards behind, and took cover under the breastwork only after repeated urging from their officer. Meanwhile Lawtie came up with the remainder of the force, which he deployed to the right and the left of the position to ward off the snipers still on its flanks. After about ten minutes a crowd of Nepalis emerged from the stockade with drums, trumpets and colours, and bore down on the small party at the breastwork.

When Ochterlony heard the sound of firing, he immediately ordered forward a reinforcement under Lieutenant Williams; but, because of a cruel contretemps, its assistance came too late. Before the main body of the reinforcement could reach them, Lawtie's men were without ammunition and already in retreat. Cartridges were supplied in wooden boxes, which were like cigar cases joined end to end at their bases and designed to fit into the sepoys' leather ammunition pouches. The cartridges were pulled lengthwise from their tubular cavities by small tags. When all the cartridges in the one section of the box had been used, it had to be lifted from the pouch, reversed and re-inserted so that those in the lower tier were uppermost. But on this occasion the sepoys at the breastwork found that when their upper rows of cartridges had been expended it was impossible to lift the boxes from the pouches and get at those below. Variations in the climate had shrunk the leather or swollen the wood, or both. Fingers tugged and tore in vain. Emboldened by the slackening of their fire, the Nepalis came on faster. Even so, it was only when the accessible supply of cartridges had failed altogether and when the enemy were hardly twenty paces away that the party withdrew. With fire coming from both flanks and the rear, to which there was no means of replying, the retreat threatened to become a rout, and only the timely arrival of the bulk of the reinforcing party enabled Lawtie's men to complete it in reasonably good order. Williams lost his life while supervising the covering operation in the defile. Forty-one sepoys also were killed, and thirty-three injured.

Lawtie was full of praise for the courage of his men, and insisted that any blame for the reverse must attach to his own misjudgement. But Ochterlony reproached only himself, for having entrusted the operation to a weak reconnaissance party instead of making it a regular and concerted attack.

The repulse, although minor, had grave implications. It made it seem that the move to Nori had been unprofitable after all. While certain advantages of ground had indeed resulted from it, the detachments from Ochterlony's main force which it had demanded had none the less made it impossible for these advantages to be exploited. Furthermore, as the weeks slipped by it became increasingly apparent that the manoeuvre would produce only slow and uncertain effect by way of straitening Ramgarh. Amar Singh was now beleaguered on three sides, it is true; but his communications with the north were still secure and he continued to draw supplies from Maha Chand and Shiva Dat Rai in Bilaspur. Ochterlony had hoped that Raja Sansar Chand of Kotoch, the Gurkha's erstwhile rival contender for Kangra fort, would attack Bilaspur from west of the Sutlaj, and his failure to do so was the cause of fresh disappointment. Sansar Chand's military commander was, it will be recalled, an Irish deserter from the 8th Dragoons, calling himself O'Brien, who had professed to be willing to use his influence to help the British. At the beginning of November he had written to Ochterlony to assure him that Sansar Chand had placed all his troops in readiness to enter the war, whereupon Ochterlony had requested him to attack Bilaspur. But instead of allowing his army to march, Sansar Chand had sent his excuses, affirming that he dare not move it for fear lest Ranjit Singh (to whom he now professed allegiance) should attack his territories in its absence. Convinced that the Raja was merely prevaricating, Ochterlony had sent a letter to Ranjit Singh making it perfectly clear that his suzerainty over Kotoch was not questioned, and renewed his efforts to persuade O'Brien to co-operate. He had extended to him the promise of a free pardon, and the prospect of even further reward. But Ochterlony's letter found O'Brien flat on his back in an alcoholic stupor, and when he was sufficiently sober to raise the matter again with the Raja, the latter was enraged by this unauthorized correspondence with the British. The quarrel between the two men became very violent, and at the end of December O'Brien offered to desert with 1,500 men and eight pieces of ordnance in return for a free pardon for himself and 'a Nother

European', called Charles Macdonald. But then a month went by without further news, and in the meantime a dispatch from Headquarters instructed Ochterlony to use O'Brien as a free agent only as a last resort. Even then, while he was left free to resume attempts to influence the Raja through O'Brien, it was stressed that the Raja's co-operation would not be worth the ill will of Ranjit Singh. Thus discouraged on the one hand by hedging and hesitation in Kotoch, and inhibited on the other by doubts and second thoughts at Headquarters, Ochterlony finally concluded that it would be idle to hope for assistance from Sansar Chand's army, and resigned himself to fighting the war alone.

This was not the only source of disheartenment. Ochterlony was finding himself increasingly hamstrung by his lack of information. He knew almost nothing of the country in which he was operating, and local guides had absolutely no notion of accurate information. They reckoned distances, for example, in terms of the 'coss', which could mean anything between three-quarters of a mile and two miles; and they were incapable of descriptions of terrain which had any meaning in military terms. He was therefore entirely without the means of knowing what natural strategic advantages his position afforded. The exact location of Arki was unknown, and the number of forts and the nature of the routes between that place and Ramgarh only guessed at. He was circumscribed by uncharted territory and could not plan beyond the range of his telescope—which was not very far in country composed of mountains and glens, of which twice as much was always concealed as was surveyed from any single vantage-point. Then again, the proclamation inviting the co-operation of the hill chiefs and their people had produced only a very limited response, and not enough porters could be found for even the most essential purposes. Finally, there was the deeply disturbing knowledge that three attempts to take the contemptible hill fort of Kalanga had failed. News of the last repulse arrived on 2 December, just as Ochterlony was contemplating another attempt to gain an advanced position for his field-battery, and the information made him throw up the idea in despair.

During December the campaign remained in a state of impasse. It now seemed most unlikely that the projected joining of forces with the other western division would ever take place; but in his pessimism Ochterlony claimed that even with reinforcements he would be unable to do more than embark on the long and wearisome expedient of starving the Nepalis into submission. Despondency pervaded the British camp in these dull dank days about the winter solstice, when the mountains were half-dissolved in mist and human breath hung visible in the air. The sepoys began to fall ill, and by the middle of the month almost 600 out of 4,600 infantry were returned as sick. The nights were frosty, and many of the invalids were probably suffering from the effects of the cold, against which they can have had little protection if, as seems likely, they had not been supplied with warm clothing. But primitive sanitation must also have played its part in causing the general debility. When in the field, Indian armies, like medieval royal households, were compelled to keep moving in order to escape the diseases engendered by their own garbage; and now that the troops and all the attendants and followers of the army had been using them for a month, the various camp sites around Ramgarh must have been like open latrines. Seeing the sickness and dejection of his men, Ochterlony was oppressed by qualms and dark presentiment. He began to think that the Bengal sepoys were physically incapable of withstanding the duresses of mountain warfare, and he doubted that success was even possible.

A reinforcement of a battalion of sepoys (the 2nd/7th, 'one of the finest in the service and nearly complete') had been promised Ochterlony soon after the outset of the war, and would have reached him early in the campaign had its progress from Lucknow not been delayed by civil disturbances in Moradabad. It was not until the third week in December that the corps, commanded by Lieutenant-Colonel Lyons, finally arrived below Ramgarh. Here it relieved Adams of the eighteen-pounders and escorted them over the ridge, arriving in the main camp at Nori on 27 December. At about the same time two field-howitzers and four light mortars, all with collapsible carriages of the type which Hastings had personally designed, arrived from Cawnpore.

Ochterlony's effective regular infantry force now stood at about 5,000, of whom just over 3,000 were in the main camp at Nori, and he felt strong enough to try to close the northern gap in his encirclement of Amar Singh Thapa's position.

On the crest of the ridge, about four miles north of Ramgarh, was a fort called Mangu, possession of which would, Ochterlony reckoned, serve his purpose well. It was approached by a two-mile-long spur, which jutted from the ridge into the Gambar valley and which was defended by a stone redoubt called Tibu at its eastern end. Soon after dusk on 27 December, Thompson left Nori with fourteen companies of sepoys, 1,000 auxiliaries, two six-pounders and two howitzers to occupy this spur and attack Mangu.

The night was fine, and the distance not great; but the ground was so broken and inhospitable that it was eight o'clock the next morning before Thompson began to climb the flank of the spur. He reached the crest with his advance about 700 yards in front of Tibu, and was at once assailed by musket fire from a party of the enemy which had emerged from the redoubt and advanced to a position near the end of the spur. He immediately ordered his advance guard to turn left and repel this party, which they did, driving the Nepalis back along the crest of the spur and into the redoubt. The post itself, he decided, was too strong to attack without artillery, so he waited for the gun-bearing elephants to arrive before resuming operations. At about four in the afternoon the two six-pounders opened fire at 500 yards, but made little impression. Thompson decided that the battery must be pushed nearer, and he asked the pioneers to make extra fascines and gabions.

By now, however, Amar Singh Thapa had fathomed Ochterlony's intentions, and he determined to bring every man he could spare into an effort to dislodge Thompson. During the night he withdrew all his troops from the stockades south of Ramgarh and moved them into fresh positions on the crest of the ridge to the north. He transferred his own headquarters to Mangu. About a quarter of an hour before sunrise on 29 December, the largest force of Nepalis so far seen, estimated at between 2,000 and 2,500 men, streamed out of Mangu and came in full career towards the peak on which the British camp was perched, at the eastern extremity of the spur.

There followed a ferocious and confused engagement, which lasted for nearly three hours. The enemy, sword in hand, attacked Thompson's position with reckless disregard for the impracticability of its approaches. It seems, indeed, that it was to the general inaccessibility of their ground and the command it gave them over the various assailing detachments, that Thompson's party owed their deliverance. The mere sight of the *khukuris* again made the sepoys pusillanimous, and they refused to parry them with bayonets. Several fled in terror, and were ripped to shreds by the flashing enemy knives. But because almost all the directions of their assault could be enfiladed by musketry, few Nepalis actually reached the camp and great numbers were killed and wounded in the attempt. The main party grimly persisted in their effort to scale an escarpment raked by fire from above, but were finally forced to retreat bearing many wounded and leaving sixty dead. It was estimated that the total of their casualties must have reached 250 wounded and 150 killed. Thompson had nine men killed and forty-four wounded.

As soon as it got dark the Nepalis in the intermediate redoubt at Tibu abandoned their posts and retired to Mangu. It was immediately occupied by Thompson's light infantry pickets, who discovered that it had been so deeply excavated as to be virtually impregnable by artillery.

Amar Singh Thapa had suffered a repulse, but he had nevertheless successfully forestalled Ochterlony's attempt to turn his northern flank. By abandoning his posts to the south of Ramgarh and establishing new ones to the north, he had in effect shifted his position farther up the ridge, so that it still outreached Ochterlony's in the direction of the Sutlaj and the crucially important area of Bilaspur. He might thwart further attempts to outflank him simply by repeating the manoeuvre. The contest would then develop into a race to the north, in which Ochterlony could have no hope of overtaking his adversary, because every step forward would manifoldly increase his difficulties of communication and supply. The road even to Tibu was impracticable for bullocks and, although only three miles long, required three and a half hours' marching even under the most favourable conditions. The troops there had no tents, and the officers only small canvas shelters open at both ends. Ochterlony could now have bombarded Ramgarh from the south, since all its outlying positions on that side had been evacuated and he already had a post at Kahanani on the crest—but this would have done no good. The effect would still only have been to drive the elusive Gurkha farther up the ridge towards the impenetrable wilderness of Bilaspur, and a decisive issue to the campaign would have been as far off as ever.

So it seemed that there was deadlock. Assault was futile; blockade impracticable. The contest threatened to become a war of attrition in which time was on the side of the enemy. There is no need to explain what would have been the reaction of Martindell or John Wood under circumstances such as these. Ochterlony was just as liable as they were to express a sense of helplessness; but the difference was that with him it was no reflection of real incapacity. It was only a plea for sympathy. Ochterlony had rich reserves of talent which were released by adversity and stimulated by the solicitous attention of his superiors; and now that his difficulties were most complex and the despondent concern of his Commander-in-Chief most gratifying, he revealed his full brilliance as a strategist.

All the while he remained in his present situation, Amar Singh Thapa was immune from assault and straitenment. The only way to destroy his immunity was therefore to draw him into another position, where he would be deprived of his *a priori* advantage of unrestricted access to the north. Behind Ochterlony's camp at Nori, parallel to but yet higher than the Ramgarh ridge, lay a third range of hills, dominated by the fortress of Malaun. That, Ochterlony decided, was where he wanted the Gurkha. Lawtie set to work, and after a month of crippling exertion had collected enough information about the layout of the Malaun ridge to enable his commander to devise a bold and ingenious plan.

Ochterlony's idea was to seal the eastern, southern and northern approaches to this ridge, inveigle Amar Singh Thapa into quitting the Ramgarh range and concentrating his army in Malaun, and then attack the cornered Nepalis as opportunity might best dictate. The crucial assumption in the plan was that Amar Singh could be induced to move to Malaun, and at first glance it seems that Ochterlony was so sanguine as to expect his adversary to walk into what would obviously be an ambush. But in fact the plan's mechanism would be less apparent than that. The move to block the northern end of the Malaun ridge would not take place until the Kaji had actually entered Malaun fort. In its first stages Ochterlony's manoeuvre would bear the appearance simply of a preparation to attack Malaun from the east, which it was hoped would cause the Kaji to move all his men to defend the fort. Here Ochterlony was gambling on Amar Singh's concern for his treasure and his youngest son and kinswomen, all, as was known from intercepted letters, left in Malaun. However, there was the possibility that he would guess Ochterlony's ultimate intentions and march immediately to Bilaspur to protect the source of his supplies and conserve his access to the north. The plan was therefore designed to accommodate this eventuality. While the main force and the auxiliaries moved, under Ochterlony's own command, round the southern end of the Malaun ridge and up into the Gamrola river valley on its eastern side, Colonel Arnold was to be left with the force at Tibu to see how the Gurkha reacted. If he moved across the Gambar and entered Malaun, Arnold was first to expel any remaining detachments from the Ramgarh range, then move up the Gambar valley to the town of Bilaspur in the plain beyond its northern end, overawe the Raja and secure a position on the northern extremity of the Malaun ridge. If, on the other hand, Amar Singh marched north to Bilaspur, Arnold was to follow. Ochterlony planned to have a force moving northwards up the Gamrola valley simultaneously, so that when the Nepali army arrived at Bilaspur it would be caught in a pincer movement by a pursuing column and one emerging from the eastern side of the ridge. The enemy would be forced into an engagement on a plain, where all their best-tried tactics would be useless.

The operation was set in motion on 16 January, and in one swift movement Ochterlony successfully accomplished his own manoe-uvre. He crossed the Gambar river south from Nori, continued round the southern end of the Malaun ridge, turned north into the Gamrola valley and finally halted near the village of Barog, which was on a latitude slightly south of that of Malaun fort itself. Lieutenant Ross, with 2,000 Hindur auxiliaries, then continued up the bank of the Gamrola for Bilaspur. The Hindur troops, used to this sort of ground, covered the distance in a trice, relishing the opportunity of dealing a blow at the Bilaspurians, who were their mortal enemies. They occupied the Bandela heights, which over-look the town of Bilaspur, and then moved on to attack a force assembled under Shiva Dat Rai himself. This they triumphantly dispersed. Trembling for his life, Raja Maha Chand scuttled across the Sutlaj, convinced that his capital was about to be sacked by the Hindur troops, who were baying for blood. But Ross had strict orders to restrain his men from inflicting this final indignity. In Ochterlony's view, consigning the town to destruction would have been both repugnant to humanity and contrary to policy. He was relying on its granaries to replenish Arnold's stock of provisions, which was sufficient only for a week; and he was besides anxious to coax Maha Chand into actively supporting the British, which might be done it they showed themselves to be forbearing deliverers, but not if they descended on him like butchers.

Meanwhile, back in the Gambar valley, Arnold had awaited the reaction of Amar Singh Thapa to Ochterlony's movement. As had been anticipated and hoped, the Kaji's immediate concern was for the safety of his treasure and family. As soon as he perceived the direction of the Major-General's march, he reduced the garrisons in Ramgarh and three other main positions along the ridge to a company each, gathered his men about him, quitted Mangu and hurried across the valley to Malaun. It now only remained for Arnold to complete the British ambush of that place by joining Ross at Bilaspur. On 18 January he sent men to occupy the deserted fort at Mangu; then, leaving Lieutenant-Colonel Cooper with the heavy guns and a force of sepoys to reduce Ramgarh and the remaining occupied posts on the ridge, prepared to march north up the Gambar valley.

It was at this stage that the whole plan was menaced by disaster. That brisk advance on Bilaspur which Ochterlony had prescribed for Arnold's force became in effect an agonizing crawl. First the march was delayed by desertions among the coolies and porters; and then the route up the left bank of the Gambar river, over the spreading feet of the spurs which buttressed the western face of the Malaun ridge, was found to be atrocious beyond anything that local informants had implied. Finally, to fill the cup of frustration and disappointment, the weather turned viciously wintry. A heavy fall of snow obstructed the march for two days and made the road to Bilaspur even more inhospitable; and when the sepoys at last moved on, they trudged through lashing sleet and freezing slush. Nepali snipers still prowling on the Ramgarh ridge added to their tribulations. Ochterlony, tired and trembling for the success of his plan, began to show signs of strain. He became edgy and peevish, and carped at Arnold for petty things—such as the style of his reports. These unforeseen difficulties turned his plan into a dangerous gamble. All the while the British army remained into two unconnected sections, divided by a ridge in the possession of the enemy, its vulnerability was extreme. Had Amar Singh Thapa decided to attack, the odds would have been heavily in his favour. Ochterlony, having noted the Gurkha's persistent reluctance to take the offensive, had incurred this as a calculated risk; but he had not reckoned on such a prolongation of the enemy's advantage, which obviously made it more likely that that advantage would be perceived and exploited. These three weeks were Amar Singh's time of both great danger and supreme opportunity. A plan was in operation whose completion would ensure his defeat; but until it was complete, he derived overwhelming benefit from the movements Ochterlony had been compelled to make. Inaction was bound to have disastrous consequences; whereas action would offer the possibility of decisive victory. Luckily for Ochterlony, Amar Singh did not act, and thereby forfeited his claim to be a good general as opposed to merely a brave soldier and patriot. Either his mind was too slow to follow Ochterlony's intentions, or he failed to appreciate that his fortresses could not withstand the British artillery. Arnold marched on without molestation, save that offered by sporadic discharges of musketry from the Ramgarh ridge. He reached the northern end of the Malaun range by the second week in February and established himself in a position within three miles of Bilaspur. His men were exhausted and wretched, but the turning-point in the campaign had been passed.

Now that Arnold's force was safely in the vicinity of Bilaspur, only a few of Ross's auxiliaries were needed on the Bandela heights, so Ochterlony transferred the greater part of the Hindur troops, together with all the pioneers and 200 sepoys, to Cooper, still at Nori. Cooper then made preparations to eject the troops which Amar Singh Thapa had left in the main forts on the Ramgarh ridge.

There were still Nepali garrisons in Ramgarh fort itself, and in the less elaborate stone sangars at Jorjoru, Taragarh and Chamba, which were widely spaced along the crest of the ridge farther north. Ramgarh contained about 100 men; Jorjoru about 160; and the others about 100 each. Cooper first concentrated on getting a position on the crest between Ramgarh and Jorjoru. Lawtie and 600 auxiliaries left camp to climb the ridge in the small hours of 12 February. The ground was rough, steep and hard with frost; but this was the Hindur soldiers' own country, and they had reached the crest by daylight, unseen by the enemy. They took up a position about 750 yards north of Ramgarh.

Soon members of the garrison were seen scurrying among the clutter of huts and ramshackle outworks under the walls of the fort, intent on protecting their three guns, which were in a stone emplacement in front of the northward-facing main gateway. A party advanced, *khukuris* unsheathed, as if to give battle; but the Hindurians immediately riposted with a menacing movement forward, striking up their own martial tune. The Nepalis thereupon halted and, taking cover behind rocks and bushes, resorted to sniping. The guns in front of the gateway were also occasionally discharged; but their shot, of which the heaviest was only 3 or 4 lb., invariably went wide. By four in the afternoon Lawtie had coaxed up an elephant with a six-pounder strapped to its back, and he set up the gun to give cover to the pioneers who were now on the crest busy constructing two batteries—one for mortars at 300 yards, and one for the eighteen-pounders at between 500 and 750. Meanwhile parties of auxiliaries took possession of all the pinnacles between Ramgarh and Jorjoru. All had been stockaded by the Nepalis, who, on evacuating them, had left the defences conveniently intact. Several reinforcements were sent from Nori, and by nightfall 1,200 auxiliaries were posted along the heights.

The batteries were ready by ten o'clock the next morning, and work was begun on preparing a road for the eighteen-pounders from Nori to the crest of the ridge. The pioneers dug, blasted, felled trees and built parapets all through the day and night, while the six-pounder and two small mortars already aloft maintained a slow and regular fire to prevent the enemy from removing their guns from the emplacement. The eighteen-pounders were trundled from the park at Nori at noon on 14 February, with three complete companies—270 men—assigned as a working party to each. Yard by yard they were hauled up the 1,200-foot ascent. Only a third of the distance was covered that day, and not until ten o'clock on the morning of the 15th was the first piece in battery. It was aimed at the Nepali gun emplacement. An hour later it discharged its first ball with an explosion that was heard thirty miles away, in Nahan. Fifty rounds had been expended by one o'clock, and two of the enemy guns buried under a pile of rubble. One embrasure was still intact; but the Nepali artillerists were so encumbered by masonry and continuing fire, that they could make no use of the cannon inside. The second eighteen-pounder arrived in battery at three in the afternoon. Both guns were then aimed at the wall of the fort itself, but before they opened the garrison was given a chance to surrender. Liberal terms were offered, because Ochterlony, anxious not only to spare the lives of his own men, but also to increase the difficulties of supply in Malaun, had instructed that the garrison of each fort was to be allowed to join Amar Singh Thapa with all its arms and property. The Ramgarh garrison nevertheless rejected such terms, and prepared to resist a storm. Stones were gathered and piled in heaps on the bastions, ready to be rolled down on an assaulting party.

At dawn on the 16th the same terms were again offered and were again rejected. Consequently, at eight o'clock, the heavy guns were reopened. Two hundred rounds were discharged before any effect was noticeable. Then the walls began to split, loose stones began to tumble and crumbled mortar began to cascade. Still the solid iron balls thumped into the flank of the fort—50, 100, 150 more. Suddenly, at three in the afternoon, with a loud roar and a rushing sound the whole curtain opposite the battery collapsed into a single heap. At last there was a breach; but it was not wide enough to storm. The shot flew on, now fragmenting the ragged fringes of the gap and shaking down great masses of masonry both outside and inside the fort. To intensify the destruction shrapnel shells were occasionally fired from the six-pounder.

Great commotion was now visible in Ramgarh. At four o'clock a messenger appeared in the breach waving a white flag. The guns were silenced while he discussed terms with Lawtie. Finally, at sunset, after a long conference, a treaty was signed. The garrision of Ramgarh was permitted to march to Malaun with all its arms, colours, musical instruments and public and private property, including cannon; and it was agreed that all belongings which could not conveniently be carried away at once should be preserved until they could be sent for. In return, the Subadar commanding consented to try to persuade the garrison of Jorjoru to surrender on the same terms. He was as good as his word, and that fort capitulated at noon the following day.

Thus two formidable strongholds were captured without the loss of a single life—virtually, in fact, without a single casualty, because the only wounded man in Lawtie's force was a Sikh auxiliary who injured himself while attempting to plunder some caves. The Field Engineer had managed the whole operation with tact, judgement, and unflagging endurance. After the treaty was signed he quitted the battery for the first time in seventy-two hours.

At Headquarters, everyone was relieved to hear of the fall of Ramgarh, and Hastings paid handsome tribute to Ochterlony's enterprise and to the 'cheerful patience' shown by his sepoys under such abnormal stresses. But the success did not dispel his misgivings. He remained convinced that the rains would set in before the war in this quarter had reached a conclusive issue. On the scene of operations, the way of thinking of one person at least was in harmony with the Governor-General's—and that was Amar Singh Thapa. Never for a moment did he relax his posture of self-assurance. The attitude of his own government, supine and disposed to sue for peace after the loss of Kalanga, exasperated him and made him even more defiant. Seeing that the administration in Kathmandu, having committed the initial error of provoking the war, was now contemplating the even greater blunder of a premature and disastrous peace, he envisaged himself as the sole remaining cantilever of the Gurkha empire: its isolated guardian, appointed by the gods to fight not only a strong enemy without, but also weak and foolish ministers within, and preserve it inviolate. On 23 December the Raja had sent Ranjor Singh, Amar Singh Thapa's son (who was, it will be remembered, defending Jaithak), a letter enjoining him to treat for peace. He was authorized to surrender all the disputed lowlands. If that was insufficient to buy peace, he was to offer as well the whole of the Tarai and Dehra Dun; and if this was still not enough, he might cede in addition all the mountainous country from Dehra Dun to the Sutlaj.[2] Ranjor sent a copy of this missive to his father, who agreed to negotiate on the basis of the surrender of the disputed lowlands, but flatly refused to offer more. This was tantamount to saying that he would fight on regardless of instructions from Kathmandu, because, having already tried to propitiate the British with them and failed, he knew full well that his terms would never end the war. The further concessions he emphatically deprecated, since in his view they were as extensive as the worst sacrifices that defeat could entail, which it would be shameful to offer before defeat was even a reality. On 2 March he sent the Raja a long reply (which, being intercepted by the British, never arrived in Kathmandu). It was a mixture of cantankerous reproach, grim warning and urgent reassurance. He upbraided him for his folly in instigating a war for trifles; warned that appeasing the British by such large concessions would merely inflame their cupidity (he advised the Raja to ponder the fate of Tipu Sultan of Mysore); and bade him take heart, for the East

[2] The instructions are summarized in Amar Singh Thapa's reply of 2 March 1815 to the Raja. This letter was intercepted and is to be found printed in its entirety in several places, e.g.: *P.R.N.W.*, pp. 553 et seq.; J. B. Fraser, *Journal of a Tour*, Appendix V; H. H. Wilson, *History of British India*, vol. ii, Appendix A; Prinsep, op. cit., vol. i, Appendix B. A MS. version is in Home Misc., vol. 653, ff. 179, et seq.

India Company was not invincible—as was clearly proved by its
failures at Bharatpur—and the Sikhs and Marathas were but
waiting for a Gurkha victory as the signal for joining a grand
coalition against it.[3] He counselled conciliation of the brahmins as
a means of mollifying the gods and suggested that the Raja, acting
in his capacity as loyal vassal of the Emperor, invoke the aid of
China by representing the British intention to be the conquest of
Tibet.

It was a stirring exhortation: the war speech of an informed
rhetorician, rich with that speciousness which a dextrous manipulation of historical references and a cunning presentation of enticing
possibilities can give. Amar Singh had in fact received no indication that the Sikhs were prepared to join the Gurkhas. Ranjit Singh
had made it clear that he would not ally himself with them while
his relations with the British remained friendly; but the Kaji, himself an opportunist *par excellence*, obviously believed, and perhaps
with reason, that if the British were brought to the point of submission an entirely new political situation would arise which such
opportunist powers as the Sikhs, the Marathas and even the
dynasty of Oudh would be unable to resist exploiting to the detriment of the Company.

Convinced that the defeat of Ochterlony was not only essential
for the preservation of the Gurkha empire, but also the means of
creating a situation which would favour its expansion, he refused
to allow himself even to contemplate failure, and stifled symptoms
of it with the tyranny of a religious bigot whose creed is assailed.
The Ramgarh garrison had their ears and noses cut off as a punishment for unjustified surrender, and the castellan was shackled with
irons. The Subadar in charge of the force would have been sum-
marily executed had not Bhakti Thapa, the Kaji's more humane
principal lieutenant, interceded on his behalf. It would be a mistake
to think that Amar Singh Thapa was wilfully deceiving himself. He
had been informed of the dispatch of a large reinforcement from
Kathmandu, said to amount to twenty-seven companies of 100
men each. This was known to have almost reached Kumaun, and
he confidently expected that it would join him in Malaun within a
few weeks. He judged that when it arrived he would have enough

[3] The expression he used was 'the Chiefs of the Deccan'. It is unlikely that
he was referring to the state of Hyderabad. Deccan is probably used in its
general sense of 'south' here, the reference being to the Marathas.

men to launch a decisive counter-attack against Ochterlony. Meanwhile, he made a determined effort to redeem the worst consequences of the capitulation of Ramgarh by reinforcing the troops still in Taragarh and Chamba.

When he heard of the arrival of these extra men, Cooper, hitherto occupied in strengthening the defences of Ramgarh, which now replaced Nalagarh as the principal British depot, made preparations for reducing the two remaining forts. The eighteen-pounders bombarded Taragarh for more than twenty-four hours without making a breach. At daybreak on the 12th it was discovered that the fort had been evacuated during the night. When Cooper's men occupied it, they found that the wall facing the battery had been lined, so that the total thickness was twelve feet at the bastions and sixteen feet at the curtain.

It now only remained to reduce Chamba, six miles still farther north. The auxiliaries under Lawtie pushed forward to take up a position about 350 yards before the fort, and the pioneers set to work yet once more to make a road. The Bengal Pioneers or Sappers were not without their critics. They were said to have malingered in Java, and to have refused to bury the dead. But there is no indication that indolence or caste-consciousness ever affected their performance in any of the Nepal campaigns. In fact, they were a mainstay of Ochterlony's effort. By 16 March an eighteen-pounder had been set up before Chamba, and it opened fire at half-past eleven. This time the effects were swift. After only an hour one complete bastion had been reduced to rubble, and the garrison surrendered. There were only fifty men in the fort, the rest having already absconded. So greatly did they dread the wrath of their commander, that they begged for quarter as prisoners of war, which was granted. Seeing that they remained very apprehensive lest in his vindictiveness the Kaji should make their families atone for the capitulation, Cooper agreed to continue firing blank cartridges, so that Amar Singh should not guess what had occurred, while two of their number went to Malaun to bring away the prisoners' women and children.

So were the enemy dislodged from their last footholds on the Ramargh ridge. Only small detachments of auxiliaries were needed to man the captured fortresses, and the 1,100 regulars under Cooper were made free to assist Ochterlony's measures against the main Gurkha army in Malaun.

When Amar Singh Thapa realized that Chamba had surrendered and its garrison defected, he was enraged. To give vent to his vexation and to reanimate his troops, whose morale was flagging under the inertia caused by Ochterlony's blockade, he at last made up his mind to take the offensive. But he planned only a token attack, whose virtue was sure success rather than tactical purpose. He selected as his prey not one of the detachments of regular troops in the Gamrola valley, but a party of Sikh auxiliaries who had taken post on the western flank of the Malaun ridge, above the Gambar river. Late on 19 March, he sent a party of 400 men from Malaun. They crept towards the unsuspecting Sikhs in the half-light of the evening, and then lay quiet until the moon had gone down. 300 Sikhs were in an outwork and some 900 below, in the main stockade. The Nepalis assaulted in three groups, screaming their war cry. There was a noise like that of ripping tarpaulin as the first body discharged a volley; then the second and third attacked the outpost and stockade simultaneously. The Sikhs, taken completely unawares, made only feeble efforts to defend themselves. Those in the outpost were literally made mincemeat of, and only sixty survived. In the stockade there was pandemonium, and all the occupants fled, long hair loose and streaming.

But this cheap triumph can have caused only transitory exultation among the troops in Malaun, because it had no important long-term consequences and was not dazzling enough to disguise the grave portent of other events to the north, south and east. Slowly, a cordon was tightening around them.

Maha Chand of Bilaspur, at last convinced that the grand Gurkha vessel was doomed, had lowered himself hurriedly into the modest lifeboat proffered by the British. For a fortnight he had resisted Ochterlony's summons to change his allegiance, hoping to barter his support against a recognition of his claim to the Twelve Lordships; but at the end of February, hearing of Arnold's advance towards his capital and aware of the new posture of affairs, he had attached himself 'heart and soul to the British Government' in return for a *sanad* which confirmed to him only the territories which he then possessed on the eastern bank of the Sutlaj. He became a protégé of the East India Company, but was exempted from tribute. When he received news of the Raja's tergiversation, Shiva Dat Rai fled across the Sutlaj into the territories of Ranjit Singh, and Amar Singh Thapa's remaining influence in Bilaspur was destroyed. He lost the services of his 1,000 Bilaspur auxiliaries, while Arnold's force was furnished with plentiful supplies and given access to the stronghold of Ratanpur, which was on the Malaun range and barely two miles north of Malaun fort itself. The Kaji's passage to the north was at last stopped, and the co-operation of O'Brien, who still had not sent Ochterlony a final reply, was made a matter of little consequence. This was just as well, because it seems that that extraordinary character had composed his quarrel with Sansar Chand and given up the idea of deserting. Probably, in one of his few moments of sober reflection he had realized that he would have made a poor bargain by exchanging the princely powers, the unlimited liquor and the copious harem which he enjoyed in Kotoch for the dubious advantages of a free pardon from the Governor-General.[4] On 1 April, Amar Singh Thapa's access to the south was also blocked. On that day, Colonel Cooper, with the troops from the Ramgarh ridge, occupied a hill on the southern end of the Malaun range. In its new position his force was only a mile or two below Surjagarh, the fort south of Malaun which was occupied by Amar Singh's best officer, Bhakti Thapa. Meanwhile, in addition to his accumulating advantages of ground, Ochterlony had begun to derive great benefit from his own corps of Nepalis. This was composed of deserters and prisoners of war. At the beginning of April there were 324 of these in the British camp, and they had quite won over the Major-General by their sunny nature, their industry and their eagerness to gratify. He resolved to form them into a separate battalion of three companies. 'I shall with the sanction and approbation of His Excellency call it the "Nasiri [friendly] Paltan" and consider myself their commandant and patron. These trifles have great weight; and I must confess myself sanguine in my hopes of their not discrediting my favour.' It was this body which formed the nucleus of the regiment later called the 1st Gurkha Rifles.

The steady trickle of deserters from Amar Singh Thapa's camp was a sure indication that the policy of blockade was beginning to have an effect. Time, however, was running short. By early March the pear trees in the Gamrola valley were already in blossom. The Himalayan spring, in the urgency of its parturience, had pushed winter violently aside; and within a couple of months it too would

---

[4] When William Moorcroft visited Kotoch in 1820, O'Brien was still in the Raja's employ.

be unceremoniously displaced by the rains, when all military operations would be impracticable. Determined to deprive his adversary of the advantages of such respite, Ochterlony devised a complex and daring maneouvre, which, if successful, would give him a position on the Malaun ridge from which he could hammer the fort into submission. As soon as he had finished his work in the vicinity of Ramgarh, Peter Lawtie began making an intricate reconnaissance of the hills around Malaun. Ochterlony afterwards acknowledged that it was entirely to his 'intelligent mind, diligent inquiry, and personal observation' that he owed the information essential for the construction of his plan.

The Malaun ridge rises four and a half thousand feet above the level of the sea and two thousand above the Gamrola stream, which flows in a deep channel along its eastern base. The spine of the ridge is narrow and jagged. The ground falls steeply from it, in places precipitously, to swell out into broad spurs, on whose level ledges stand little hamlets. Scraggy vegetation sprouts here and there; but generally the slopes are arid, gaunt and brutally scarred by water-worn furrows. On a commanding height towards the northern extremity was the stone fort of Malaun: long, with square bastions, and deprived of apparent height by the massive proportions of the rock on which it sprawled. The cantonments were outside the fort —a clutter of huts huddling under its eastern walls, protected by a semi-circular stockade. Bhakti Thapa's headquarters were about four miles farther south, in the fort of Surjagarh. The Nepali forces were concentrated in and about these two centres. Stockades and redoubts, scattered over the different levels of the ridge, clustered around them like electrons around nuclei. But the two configurations did not meet. Between their outer orbits on the crest there was a vacant space, called Raila Peak by the British.

Equipped with a thorough knowledge of the ground, Ochterlony completed his plan. Although it involved several simultaneous movements, it was basically very simple. His aim was to establish two positions on the crest of the ridge: one at Raila, to hold Bhakti Thapa at bay; and one on a vacant site within the system of defences around Malaun, south of the fort and separated from it by two intervening stockades. For easy identification, this site was labelled Dionthal.

Starting from different positions in the Gamrola valley, three columns were to advance up the eastern flank of the ridge on converging lines, finally to meet at Raila Peak. At the same time, two columns were to leave the valley from points farther north and converge on Dionthal. Such were the main movements of the plan. But in addition, in order to distract Amar Singh Thapa's attention from the columns advancing to Dionthal, a feint attack on the Malaun cantonments was organized. One party was to advance on them from the Gamrola valley, while another approached from the north, so that the two lines of attack were at a right angle. The northern column was to come from Colonel Arnold's position at Ratanpur, and would have to cross the thousand-feet-deep ravine which separated that fort from Malaun.

All these movements were to begin on the morning of 15 April, at a prearranged signal. This was to be given by the central column of the Raila operation, when it had reached its destination.

The Raila operation was accomplished without a hitch. The three columns which were to converge on Raila can be labelled the left (southernmost), the central, and the right.

The central column moved first. Led by Lieutenant Fleming, it quitted the village of Patta in the valley late on the night of 14 April. It consisted of 1,100 men, and included 300 of the Nasiri Battalion under Lawtie. This was the first occasion when 'Gurkha' troops went into action as British mercenaries, and they immediately impressed their officer by the closeness of their files and their perfect silence, both maintained over even the most difficult ground. The column reached Raila Peak at one o'clock in the morning of 15 April, having encountered no opposition, and made the signal flare. This was answered from a hill in the rear of Ochterlony's camp, and the other columns immediately moved. On the right, Major Innes with the Grenadier Battalion and two six-pounders moved from headquarters and ascended to Raila 'in admirable order'. The left-hand column, led by Lieutenant Hamilton, moved from a small village called Jainagar on the lower slopes of the ridge below Surjagarh. It was composed of troops from Cooper's post at Lag Hill, at the extreme south of the ridge, who had moved to their starting position during the night. The column was fired on from an enemy stockade as it marched up the flank of the ridge; but the men pressed on in perfect composure and reached the summit without mishap. Meanwhile Raila Peak had been stockaded by a group of pioneers, enthusiastically assisted by the Nasiris, who seemed oblivious of the musket fire from the fort.

The Dionthal operation was the focus of Ochterlony's plan. Two columns marched up to the site: Major Laurie's on the right (400 auxiliaries), and Colonel Thompson's on the left (1,300 regulars, 300 auxiliaries, and two six-pounders). The heads of the columns arrived at Dionthal almost at the same time, but the guns still lagged a long way behind. A patter of firing to the north telling him that the diverting columns had begun their work, Thompson mustered his three companies of light infantry and, leaving the rest of the combined columns under Laurie to wait at Dionthal for the guns, marched boldly northwards up the crest of the ridge to seize a position for a battery nearer Malaun. Enemy musketeers, sniping from behind rocks and bushes, tried unsuccessfully to check him. But as he approached the nearer of the two stockades which commanded his path to the fort, a party of Nepalis threw themselves from it with *khukuris* drawn. The sepoys, steadfast enough under invisible musket shot, shrank at the sight of knives whose lightest stroke drew blood. They greatly outnumbered their antagonists; but their officers cursed and cajoled in vain. They would not use their bayonets. Breaking formation, they fell over themselves in their anxiety to get back to Dionthal, where Laurie and his men were luckily prepared to cover their retreat. The Nepalis did not attempt to assault the Dionthal position, but took cover behind rocks and trees and began sniping. The pioneers worked feverishly to raise a breastwork; but enemy marksmen were everywhere and because of the ruggedness of the ground had cover to within twenty yards of the position. Soon the sepoys were visibly flagging, ammunition and water were getting low, the six-pounders still did not arrive and pioneers were being picked off at an alarming rate. Crichton, the Surgeon, could not cope with all the wounded, and made an urgent request for assistance. Thompson feared that he would be unable to strengthen his post sufficiently to withstand the attack which he was sure must come during the night. Ochterlony was in agonies of anxiety, and told him to fight to the last man. If his position was lost, the whole plan would be wrecked. During the afternoon the Major-General withdrew two companies of infantry from Raila and transferred them to Dionthal; and Ram Saran, the Raja of Hindur, provided men to replenish the depleted ranks of Thompson's pioneers. Nevertheless, for the rest of the day it remained touch and go whether the force at Dionthal would be able to hold its position. The elephants carrying the six-pounders arrived on the crest late in the afternoon, but there were only eight European matrosses to serve the guns, and before long one of these had been wounded. At dusk Thompson was still in possession of his ground, but the hours of darkness were a time of terrible suspense. All the troops knew that the worst was yet to come, because it was certain that sooner or later the Nepalis would make a full-scale attempt to dislodge them.

It was a mercy that the diversion had long averted from Thompson's detachment the brunt of the Nepali resistance.

Captain Charles Showers, who led the column from Ratanpur, was an earnest young officer who combined magnificent courage and chivalry with a puritanical sobriety. He had sworn that he would never accept a challenge to a duel, and always said that he trusted to his profession to provide him with a more appropriate claim to the title of soldier.

At the head of the battalion (the 1st/19th Native Infantry) of which he had assumed the command at the outset of the war, he marched from Ratanpur early on the morning of 15 April. He had first to descend the slopes which plunge into the ravine between Ratanpur and Malaun, and then cover the long and difficult ascent to the Nepali cantonments. Its climb took his column by an enemy stockade, which was on a ledge to its left, about 100 feet below Malaun fort. This was passed without incident; but at about half-past ten, when the force was half-way between the stockade and its objective, a party of the enemy issued from the cantonments and came down to the attack. Showers, seeing that they were numerically considerably inferior to his own column, commanded his men not to load but to scatter the pack with their bayonets. The first part of his order they obeyed. The second part they did not. Showers had forgotten what had been demonstrated time and time again: that the Bengal sepoy's musket was his fetish. His men hung back, chilled with fear. Striving to inspirit them by his own example, Showers drew his sword and ran forward alone, outstripping even his orderlies. A Gurkha officer came towards him. Showers coaxed him forward with taunting gestures, and soon had him on a desperate defensive. Then, with a sudden vigorous lunge, he killed the Gurkha. As he struggled to pull out his sabre, he swayed under the weight of the corpse, which was on higher ground. Seeing him encumbered, the Nepalis sprang forward and stabbed him to death. Horrified, his sepoys receded. The enemy took up the pursuit, gaining confidence as the momentum of their descent increased. Some sepoys turned about and ran; and as others followed their example the retreat became a general flight down the crumbling contours of the gorge. Not until they reached the plateau of a small village 1,500 feet below did Lieutenant Rutledge, on whom the command had devolved, manage to halt and rally the men. Once they had had time to load their muskets they became more amenable, and responded obediently when Rutledge ordered them to chase the enemy back up the hill. Colonel Arnold had been watching operations from Ratanpur, and when he saw Showers killed and his men routed, he immediately ordered forward a third column of diversion. In a stockade called Tipnu, on the eastern side of the ridge below Ratanpur, there was a party of Sikh auxiliaries and a Subadar's party of regulars. Arnold directed these troops to advance on that enemy stockade below the cantonments which Showers had passed on his ascent. This they did with exemplary enthusiasm. The Subadar was killed; but the leader of the Sikhs, Ghoshi Ram, led the party right up to the stockade and would probably have entered it had not some of his men wavered at the last minute. Rutledge's fresh advance to their right now afforded this party support and cover for its retreat.

Meanwhile, farther south, Captain Bowyer, leading the second diverting column from the valley floor, had reached Malaun village, which was about 1,000 feet below the fort. At about eleven o'clock came news of Showers's death and the overpowering of his column. Bowyer persisted at his post for another hour and then, deciding that action against the Malaun cantonments with his limited resources alone was bound to be abortive, he ordered a withdrawal to the Tipnu stockade. The retreat was performed with field-day precision, one half of the detachment retiring to a rear position and the remainder then following under cover of its fire. It was during their retreat that the sepoys of this detachment finally derived support from the other diverting column, Arnold having ordered Rutledge to incline to his left to help cover Bowyer's movement. The detachment finally reached the Tipnu stockade with no more than fourteen casualties.

Despite their failure to penetrate the enemy cantonments, the diverting columns had fulfilled their main purpose. For several crucial hours during the morning they had almost monopolized Amar Singh Thapa's attention and thereby greatly lessened the opposition with which the Dionthal columns had had to contend. But their achievement had been costly. In an army in which their importance was so exceptional and their numbers so inadequate, the loss of any European officer was no light matter; but when the officer was 'most zealous, brave, and excellent', which is how Ochterlony described Showers, the loss was especially grave. However, Showers had proved his merit as a soldier, even in the estimation of his enemy. In the East, it is a gesture of respect for a brave foe to cover his remains. When the bearers went up the next day to retrieve Showers's body, they found it laid on a bed of leaves, wrapped in fine cloth.

Thus ended the grand concerted manoeuvre of 15 April. When night fell Amar Singh Thapa was brooding within the walls of Malaun, conscious that he had reached the most critical emergency of his career. If the British were not expelled from the post they had gained at Dionthal, Malaun must be either strangled or bombarded into submission. Early in the night, Bhakti Thapa decided that his own post, Surjagarh, must be sacrificed in an attempt to preserve his chief's headquarters. Prevented from attacking Thompson from the south by the intervening British post of Raila, his force was of no more use to Amar Singh than a severed limb. He therefore mustered his men and, proceeding stealthily below the crest on the western flank of the ridge, made for Malaun. He hoped to pass Innes's and Thompson's posts unobserved, or at least unimpeded. But his design had been anticipated, and Lieutenant Murray, in charge of the Hindur auxiliaries at Raila, had placed himself and his men in a position commanding the Gurkha's route. Falling pitilessly on their inveterate enemies, the Hindurians turned Bhakti's progress to Malaun into an ungainly tumble.

Bhakti Thapa was the bravest officer in the Gurkha army, and the most popular. When he arrived in Malaun, Amar Singh appointed him to lead a dawn attack against Thompson's position. He assigned to his command the élite of his army: 2,000 warriors, all in scarlet broadcloth. It is said that Bhakti delivered his son into the Kaji's care, and solemnly swore that he would return victorious or remain dead on the field. Shortly after four o'clock on the morning of 16 April, having adjured his two wives to be prepared to sacrifice themselves on his funeral pyre, he led his men from the fort. Silently, they took up positions on the narrow ledges around Dionthal, clustering thick as bristles on a hairbrush.

At a given signal they attacked, with a satanic din of war-cries and trumpets. Musketeers opened fire from close range on the northern front and both flanks of the post at Dionthal, but their main offensive was directed against Thompson's two six-pounders. Bhakti knew that if he could but silence these, the proven superiority of his men in close combat would be decisive. The guns had been placed in embrasures commanding the smooth ground on the western side of the position, which was the only approach free of natural impediments. Naked *khukuris* in the right hand, loaded muskets in the left, the Nepali assaulting party surged out of the darkness, straight towards the cannon. There was a vivid flash, a crash, and red-hot blasts of grapeshot dispersed them. So many Nepalis were killed and crippled that their charge could not be completed, and Bhakti was forced to withdraw the party to make good the losses. There were only seven British gunners. They worked with fanatical haste to recharge the pieces, but were falling one after another under the fire of the encircling enemy snipers. Again the Nepalis charged; and again the hilltop shuddered and flared briefly into brilliance as they were blown away from the mouths of the guns. Their defiance of these impassive artefacts had an ecstatic nobility. Still once more the Gurkha chief rallied and re-formed his men. Behind him, on a hill within musket range of Dionthal, was Amar Singh Thapa himself. He stood conspicuously by a stand of colours, urging on his troops. Again Bhakti Thapa ordered his men to charge the guns, and again they obeyed magnificently. In the British battery Lieutenant Cartwright of the artillery now had only one gunner undisabled, and with him was loading one of the pieces himself. The other was being served by Lieutenant Armstrong of the pioneers and Lieutenant Hutchinson of the engineers, with the help of two pioneer sergeants. Before the next discharge could be made, one of the sergeants spun away, shot through the head. It seemed, for a second or two, that the battery was lost. But then, when the Nepalis were only yards away, the guns finally recoiled and disgorged, and swept them flat. Thwarted in this design, yet still sustained by his adamantine courage, Bhakti Thapa collected the remnants of his storming column and marched them over the crest to the eastern flank of the ridge, with the intention of assaulting the British position from that direction. Here Major Laurie and the Hindur Raja's auxiliaries were posted with a body of sepoys in a small outwork. Thompson decided that this was the moment to counter-attack, and he ordered Laurie's detachment to make a sortie with swords and bayonets. If the sepoys had misgivings, the Hindur troops had none. They rushed among Bhakti's men, and the sepoys, inflamed by their example, followed close after. For nearly two hours, the enemy disputed every yard of ground. Masses of combatants ebbed and flowed in the slow straining rhythms of battle. No advantage was gained by either side until suddenly, when light was beginning to turn the gunsmoke yellowish grey, it was as if an invincible weariness quelled the Nepalis. In trance-like abjection, they began to retire. The Hindur troops followed up their advantage, and accomplished a massacre just as the sun was rising.

Amongst the grisly debris littering the windswept crest was the corpse of a Nepali in the full-dress uniform of an officer. It was brought into the camp at Dionthal for identification, and the Nasiris sorrowfully confirmed that it was that of Bhakti Thapa. The reason for his men's sudden surrender to despair in the middle of the battle was now apparent. Ochterlony ordered that the body be covered with shawls, and sent with an escort to Malaun. That night, as Charles Showers was being buried with military honours in the valley, there was a bright glow on the heights. It was Bhakti Thapa's funeral pyre, into the flames of which, in full sight of the British troops on the ridge, the Gurkha hero's distraught widows flung themselves.

When the muster roll was called, it was found that Thompson's force had suffered 253 casualties—but of these only 30 were fatal. Amar Singh's losses were much greater. 150 dead were left on the field alone, and it was reckoned that his total casualties must have reached at least 500.

But the Gurkha Kaji had lost more than his best officer and a quarter of his army. He had never commanded the affections of his men; and from this time he was deprived even of their loyalty. Large numbers deserted every day, despite his brutal efforts to prevent them. To add to his troubles, the expected reinforcement from the east had been detained in Kumaun by Brahma Shah and did not now seem likely ever to arrive in Malaun. Then another of his subject allies, the Vizir of Basahar, defected to the British. This minister, who had formed a part of Amar Singh's retinue since the subjugation of cis-Sutlaj Basahar in 1811, had come into Ochterlony's camp to proffer his allegiance even before the battle of

Malaun, and on 13 April had left to promote rebellion in his own country. Within a few weeks news arrived from William Fraser that the Nepali occupationary force in Basahar, led by Kirti Rana, had been attacked and dispersed. Meanwhile, Ochterlony's cordon round Malaun had continued to tighten. One by one all the enemy posts around Malaun surrendered and were occupied, and work began on clearing a way for heavy ordnance. On 7 May two brass twelve-pounders, strapped to elephants, arrived on the crest.

As the situation outside Malaun became so ominous as to leave no room for hope, the spirit of mutiny increased within. When they saw the arrival of the twelve-pounders, all his principal sirdars, or lieutenants, presented Amar Singh Thapa with an ultimatum. They demanded either food for their men, or some decisive line of conduct. But Amar Singh, powerless to attack again, yet withheld by stubbornness and pride from opening negotiations for surrender, refused to stir from a state of taciturn inactivity. Peevishly, he ordered his officers to await events; but they had no patience for futile temporizing. They gathered their men, amounting to nearly 1,600, left the fort and pledged their allegiance to the British. To Amar Singh's army, reduced already to half its original 4,000 by casualties and desertions, this was the death blow. The old man in Malaun now had about him only 250 fighting men. At last he sent an ungracious note to Ochterlony, demanding to know his wishes; but the Major-General replied that according to usage all proposals must come from him. Thereupon the Kaji relapsed again into sullen silence, struggling with his pride and—who knows?— perhaps still clutching at the hope of a last-minute intervention by Ranjit Singh. It appears that he made another application to the Sikh about this time; but Ranjit, while confessing himself surprised at the swiftness of his defeat, had too many problems of his own to help redeem it.

By 9 May emplacements for the twelve-pounders and mountain howitzers had been constructed within battering distance of the southern aspect of the fort, and on the following morning, at seven o'clock, the pieces opened fire. The bombardment continued all day, save for a few intervals during which notes were exchanged. The effect of the twelve-pounders was perceptible, but slow; and the mountain howitzers, because of the flimsiness of Hastings's collapsible carriages, tumbled over like toy cannon every fourth round or so. Ochterlony therefore decided that he must bring up the eighteen-pounders; and it was the sight of fatigue parties labouring up the flank of the ridge with these instruments of sure destruction that finally wrung from Amar Singh Thapa a surly concession of defeat.

His youngest son, Ram Das, came to tell the British that his father was willing to negotiate on the basis of the surrender of the fort; and in reply Ochterlony offered liberal terms. Malaun and all the forts west of the Jumna, including Jaithak, were to be evacuated, and such members of their garrisons who did not choose to take service with the British would be allowed to march unmolested back into the eastern provinces of Nepal with all their private property. In addition, Amar Singh Thapa and his kinsmen would be permitted to march with all their arms and accoutrements. Ochterlony's forbearance is all the more apparent when it is recalled that he and his army, according to the usages of war, were entitled to the contents of Malaun (which included the Kaji's reputedly immense store of treasure) and of all the other captured forts as prize money. His motive in conciliating the Gurkha was to induce him to use those powers, which he was known to possess but which he not so far exercised, to negotiate for a general peace treaty. His hopes in this direction, however, were thwarted by Hastings, who had other plans. Brahma Shah, governor of Kumaun, and a known opponent of the Thapa administration in Kathmandu, had signified his desire to the Gurkha negotiator. The Governor-General reckoned that he would be both more amenable and more sincere as an agent than Amar Singh Thapa, and fancied that if the Thapas were denied the prestige attaching to the conclusion of a satisfactory peace treaty, their ruin, already half-assured by the disastrous issue of the war, would be completed, and the way prepared for a return to power of the pro-British Panre party. Ochterlony was therefore informed that the settlement with Amar Singh should embrace no more than the conditions of the latter's own immediate surrender.

Smarting with chagrin and humiliation, Amar Singh resigned himself to relinquishing the territories which it had taken him a decade of hard campaigning to acquire. He was not noble in defeat. At the last minute, a letter arrived from Brahma Shah, who was ignorant of the latest developments in the west, announcing his own capitulation and advising Amar Singh to follow suit. The Kaji thereupon insisted that a clause be inserted into Ochterlony's convention, stating that he agreed to its terms only at the behest of the governor of Kumaun; and when informing the Raja of his capitulation, he expressly stated that he had agreed to it on the authority of Brahma Shah's letter. It was a shabby stratagem, dictated equally by vanity and malice. It was calculated not only to remove the obloquy attaching to his own defeat from himself, but also to transfer it to his hated political enemy.

So he left Malaun, body ailing and mind poisoned by wormwood, and made his way slowly back to Kathmandu. The empire which he had laboured so long to build had collapsed around him, and the army which he had so proudly and magisterially led had rejected him to serve his enemy. No fewer than 2,000 Nepali soldiers had elected to stay with the British.

As for Ochterlony, he had snatched celebrity while on the brink of obscure old age. From being one of the least known he had become one of the most famous of Bengal officers and an acknowledged favourite of the Governor-General. It had been intended that he should return to his old command at Allahabad at the conclusion of the campaign; instead it was Marley who was banished to that obscure backwater, vacating a place on the general staff which Ochterlony was appointed to fill. In a flattering dispatch from Headquarters, he was asked to proceed to Nahan and assume command of the division under Martindell; but it so happened, as we have seen, that Jaithak surrendered before this appointment became operative.

Ochterlony had, together with Gillespie, Martindell and George Wood, been gazetted K.C.B. early in 1815, before news of his success reached England; and when the Court of Directors of the East India Company heard of the resounding victory that he had achieved, they supplemented the award with a pension of £1,000 a year, 'to enable him to live in a style commensurate with the dignity bestowed on him by the Prince Regent'.

Ochterlony's satisfaction was great; but it was not complete, for the comrade he had come to love like a son never knew of the victory for which they had both worked so hard. The death of Peter Lawtie of a typhus infection, only a few days before the surrender of Malaun, cut him to the quick. He requested all the officers of his division to wear mourning for a month—a gesture unprecedented for someone so young.

It was by the division from which least had been expected that most had been gained. Hastings was right to attribute the victory above all else to Ochterlony's brilliant quality as a commander—but in what, particularly, did that quality consist? A list of his merits would include all those of a good general—imagination, opportunism, courage, audacity and caution, compounded in exactly the right proportions. But more than in any of these, his quality consisted in that perspicacity which had enabled him to foresee the necessity of guns, and in that calm patience and dogged determination which had enabled him to eschew flashy exhibition of prowess and concentrate with absolute seriousness on making use of them. Without the use of artillery he could not have won the contest. Of that there is no doubt.

His infantry had been poor. The Bengal sepoys had made a show that compared very unfavourably with that of their antagonists. There had been, as ever, individual instances of bravery and hero- ism; but time and time again they had demonstrated that in the particular art of close combat which mountain warfare demanded they were quite unable to match the courage and skill of the men against whom they were pitted. An anonymous civilian[5] who accompanied the expedition was appalled by the lack of confidence, the trepidation and the apathy which he had observed on their part. It caused him to draw some alarming conclusions concerning the worth of the Bengal army. 'They turned', he wrote, 'almost uniformly from the contest before a blow had been struck, under the influence of a moral impulse which deterred them from proving the badness of the ground and the inferiority of the bayonet.' And again: 'The physical mass of the army bent or broke like a useless weapon whenever a blow was to be struck.'

These are severe strictures and perhaps, in his desire to shock the authorities at home from their complacency, he exaggerated

---

[5] Author of *Military Sketches of the Goorkha War* (p. xiv). W. G. Hamilton has suggested (*J.U.S.I.I.*, xli, no. 189: Oct. 1912, p. 456) that this was Captain Edmund Cartwright, Ochterlony's Major of Brigade. This is certainly not so. The author, in his preface, distinctly states that he is a civilian and that he returned to England six years after the war. Cartwright is disqualified on both counts. It is possible that the author was Ochterlony's own Eurasian son, R. P. Ochterlony. He held an official position as Assistant to his father until July 1815, so it is more than likely that he accompanied him during the first cam- paign. He announced his intention of resigning his post in July 1815, but could have accompanied his father *ex officio* on the second expedition in 1816. See *Ludhiana Records*, pp. 135, 349, 458, for references to this person.

somewhat. It is a fact that his accounts of engagements tend to differ from those contained in official dispatches, in that they present a much less flattering picture of the behaviour of the sepoys. This could be partly tendentious denigration; but, on the other hand, it could be because his view, as a civilian, was less clouded than that of the army officers, whose partiality and complaisance were the subject of more than one commentator's criticism. But the essential truth of his complaint is indisputable. It is attested by Ochterlony's own views, and by his consistent avoidance of full-scale infantry engagements. Infantry had never formed the spearhead of his offensives. There had been no escalades, and the foot soldiers had played a secondary role in the capture of every fort. The most important attribute throughout had been his artillery.

But it was not only the particular and local circumstance of the poorness of his infantry which had induced Ochterlony to rely most heavily on his guns. He had discovered principles which enjoined their use in mountain warfare in general.

The first of these principles was that in mountain warfare it was much less important for an invader to equip himself to pursue than to equip himself to dislodge his enemy. It had been assumed by many, including the Governor-General, that the Nepalis' main advantage would be their mobility. The premise which underlay Hastings's planning was that his divisions would have to deal with an elusive antagonist. He had expected Amar Singh Thapa to try to move either eastwards, or northwards, across the Sutlaj, and had thought it likely that the main Kathmandu army would try to escape to the west. For this reason, he had urged his commanders to make lightness and mobility their primary attributes. But Ochterlony had doubted, from the outset, that this was accurate reasoning. He had therefore equipped himself to fight a static, fortified enemy; and the event had completely vindicated his policy. It had transpired that in practice the Gurkhas treated as their main asset not their elusiveness, but their inaccessibility. They had shown themselves very unwilling to budge from positions they had occupied, and only abandoned them as a last resort. It was his under-estimation of the advantages which defenders derive from mountain topography which had caused Hastings to suppose that the Gurkhas would try to concentrate their forces. Unlike Ochterlony—and Napoleon—he failed to realize that in mountain warfare the attacker is at a disadvantage, since his main task must be to oust his adversary from positions which are virtually immune to assault.[6] It was the Nepalis' reluctance to move, their stolid defence of every yard of ground, which had rendered artillery indispensable. Even with the best soldiers in the world, it seems unlikely that Ochterlony could have taken their hill forts without it.

The second principle which Ochterlony had discovered and illustrated was that in mountain warfare the delays which artillery causes need not increase the likelihood of the invaders' being attacked. It was commonly believed then, and later, that they must. Twenty-five years after the Nepal War, Sir Jasper Nicolls sent a body of infantry to force the Khyber pass without guns, arguing that they would delay the column and increase its exposure to fire. Yet if there was one precept for which military theorists were beholden to Ochterlony it was that in mountain war such delay was no liability, because the invader can partake of his adversary's principal advantage—inaccessibility. By adopting the mode of defending advantageous ground with stockades—an expedient entirely novel in the Bengal army—he had virtually eliminated the risk of counter-attack. Only twice during the whole campaign had detachments of his army had to sustain a major offensive while waiting to bring guns into play—at Tibu and at Dionthal—and on both occasions they had been saved by a combination of natural and artificial defences.

On the occasion of the Gurkhas' defeat, 'a prominent native' is reported to have remarked to a Bengal staff officer: 'Of what use is it to fight with the English? Beaten or successful, they are always conquerors!'[7]

It is easy to see what he meant. It had not been granted to any of the British divisions to deserve success; but they had nevertheless won, because it had been in the power of Ochterlony's guns to command it.

---

[6] Napoleon wrote as follows on the subject: 'Dans la guerre de montagnes, celui qui attaque a du désavantage . . . Dans la guerre de montagnes, obliger l'ennemi à sortir de ses positions pour attaquer les vôtres, c'est ce que nous avons dit être dans le génie et dans la bonne conduite de cette guerre . . . Ne jamais attaquer les troupes qui occupent de bonnes positions . . . mais les débusquer en occupant des camps sur les flancs ou leurs derrières.' (Quoted by Hough, *The Englishman*, 16 Oct. 1846.)

[7] Quoted in the *Asiatic Journal* for May 1816, p. 428.

X

THE CONQUEST OF KUMAUN

HASTINGS'S original strategy included an attack on Kumaun. He appreciated that its position on the west bank of the Kali river would make this province a foothold and base for any reinforcements which Kathmandu might send to the western theatre of the war, and the incentive to invade it was the more especially strong as it promised to succumb very easily. The number of troops in Almora, the capital, was estimated by reliable informants as between 300 and 600 only; and the disaffection of Brahma Shah, the Gurkha governor, was well known at Headquarters. Francis Hamilton, Hyder Hearsey and William Fraser were all of the opinion that he would forswear his allegiance to the Thapa government in Kathmandu if sufficient inducement was offered. It was therefore determined that while Hyder Hearsey was busy raising the corps of irregulars which was to help effect military occupation of the province, overtures should be made with a view to encouraging the Gurkha to apostatize. He was to be offered a *jagir* (estate) under the protection of the Company—possibly in the Gurkha province of Doti, on the eastern bank of the Kali, of which his brother, Hasti Dal, was at present governor.

Thomas Rutherfurd, the Assistant-Surgeon at Moradabad, who had extensive interests in Kumaun hemp, rather fancied himself as a diplomat. Without any authorization from the government, he sent an agent to Brahma Shah and invited him to join the British cause. Rutherfurd's efforts were not appreciated at Headquarters. Much to his disappointment, he was scolded for meddling and told that it was not the Governor-General's intention to appoint him Political Agent for the affairs of Kumaun. Hastings, deeming it 'advisable that the conduct of this important branch of our measures should be vested in an individual of more approved talents, judgement, and political experience', selected the Honorable Edward Gardner[1] for the post. Gardner was William Fraser's fellow Assistant at the Delhi Residency. Like his colleague, he

[1] Not Gardiner, as given in the *D.N.B.* (s.v. William Linnaeus Gardner).

permitted himself eccentricities. In common with Hindu and Muslim society, he wore immense whiskers and abjured pork and beef; but his equable temperament and courtly manners made him better suited to diplomacy than was Fraser. He had a flair for oriental languages, and had qualified with distinction in Persian and Hindustani at the College of Fort William in 1802. Reaching Moradabad in the middle of November 1814, Gardner made his own soundings and discovered fewer encouraging signs than he had been led to expect. Brahma Shah's enigmatic reception of Rutherfurd's agent had, it was true, evinced a certain indecision; but other intelligence represented the Governor to be raising troops and making preparations for resistance. Gardner was personally inclined to discredit reports of the Gurkha's infirm loyalty, but he suggested that it was possible that the presence of Amar Singh Thapa's officers was preventing him from divulging his true disposition. He recommended that some form of military demonstration be made at once against Kumaun, as a means of provoking Brahma Shah into disclosing his true sympathies.

But the calamities in Garhwal meant that all available regular troops were now occupied, and Hastings did not at this stage contemplate sending irregulars alone into Kumaun. Early in December, however, his tour of the upper provinces brought him to Moradabad, and Gardner, who was very keen to satisfy the expectations of military assistance which had been aroused among the recalcitrant inhabitants of Kumaun, was able to exert direct persuasion on members of the Governor-General's suite— especially on John Adam, the Political Secretary, who was a personal friend. Perhaps even more decisive was the presence at Moradabad of Lieutenant-Colonel William Gardner, Edward's cousin. This was a remarkable character. Beginning his military career in the King's service, he had served under Hastings (then the Earl of Moira) at Quiberon, in 1795. Some time afterwards he had quitted the King's army in order to try his fortune as a freelance in India. He had entered the service of Holkar, the Maratha prince of Indore, and when on a mission to Cambay had sought and obtained the hand of the thirteen-year-old Begam, thereby becoming brother-in-law to Hyder Hearsey. After a quarrel with Holkar, in which he made to cut the Maratha down, he had fled

Edward Gardner was a brother of Alan, 2nd Baron Gardner—see Lady Nugent's *Journal*, ii, pp. 6, 9.

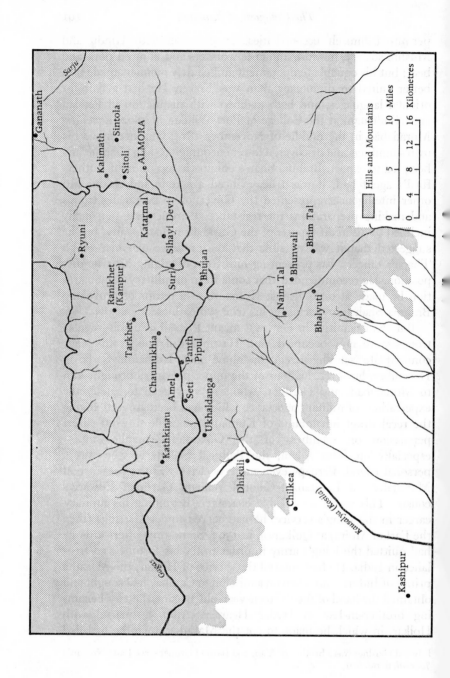

from Indore and taken service with Amrit Rao, adoptive brother of the Peshwa of Poona. Gardner made a spectacular escape from the clutches of this prince in 1804, when he clambered down a fifty-foot precipice, swam a river in full flood and disguised himself as a grass-cutter in order to join Lord Lake. He had been in the Company's employ ever since, latterly as the commander of the corps of irregular horse which bore his name, though he was only a pensioner and his rank was purely nominal, or local.

William Gardner was in very easy circumstances in 1814, enjoying, by special dispensation, possession of the considerable estate near Agra which had been bestowed on his wife by the Emperor of Delhi; and he had no material object to seek in the command of an expedition into Kumaun. But he was still only in his early forties, and had far from exhausted his superabundant energy. Hastings, for his part, admired the experience and expertise of the eighty or so ex-Maratha officers now on Company pensions, and respected the patriotic motives which had induced them to forsake positions of great power and remuneration and join the British in 1804. He was always pleased to grant them some favour in return. It was no doubt this disposition, together with characteristic feelings of generosity towards an old fellow campaigner, which caused him to change his mind and consent to a 'hazardous' military expedition, which was cast more in the old Maratha then the modern Company mould. Gardner, assisted by such of the ex-Maratha officers as appeared eligible, was permitted to raise a corps of 3,000 irregular infantry from Rohilkhand. This, together with Hearsey's corps, was to commence the invasion of Kumaun, pending the availability of a supporting force of regulars. Gardner was to be furnished with a couple of six-pounder field guns, a few elephants and Mr. Rutherfurd as chief medical officer, commissary, postmaster, chief of intelligence and general factotum.

Hastings was right to describe it as a 'hazardous effort'. The martial populace of Rohilkhand consisted of Afghan immigrants, mostly of Pathan extraction, who, although individually intrepid, were instinctively cavalry rather than infantry soldiers, were not susceptible to discipline and unlike Hindus, were not renowned for loyalty to their salt.

There was no shortage of volunteers. Both Gardner and Hearsey recruited in the neighbourhood of Rampur, the estate of a semi-independent Muslim nawab, whose capital was the resort of the thousands of Pathans who came down from Afghanistan every year in search of employment as mercenaries. By the beginning of January 1815 Gardner had collected 1,600 men. Soon after, he was joined by the body of Pathans who had taken service with the Gurkhas at the outbreak of the war, and these swelled his corps to a number in excess of its permitted limit. The 500 surplus troops were put at the disposal of the exiled Raja of Doti, who, it was decided, should be encouraged to make a diversion into his old territories. This would prevent Hasti Dal from crossing the Kali and going to the assistance of his brother in Kumaun. As an extra insurance against this eventuality, it was arranged that Hearsey's force should move up the western bank of the Kali and secure the ghats. Harak Deva Joshi arrived at Gardner's headquarters at Kashipur early in January. At the invitation of Edward Gardner, who was struck by his intelligence and persuaded that his local knowledge and influence could be turned to good account, he agreed to accompany the expedition.

Gardner left Kashipur on 11 February, after having been delayed first by lack of porters and then by tempestuous weather. His advance to Almora, over snow-covered hills and through dark and dripping deodar forests, was arduous, but largely uneventful. Always remembering that the morale of a force such as his could not survive the shock of a defeat, his constant concern was to avoid direct confrontation with the enemy and proceed by outwitting rather than by thrashing them. Never did he take unnecessary risks for the sake of personal glory. He constantly (though unsuccessfully) urged Hearsey to attack Almora from the east while his own activities distracted Brahma Shah's attentions to the west, and did not covet that opportunity for himself.

The main trade route to Almora from the plains followed the Kosila river, which approaches Almora from the south-west. In order to confound the enemy, Gardner decided to take a longer and much more difficult subsidiary path, which stretched across country by way of Ranikhet and Ryuni and approached Almora from the north-west. As soon as he learnt of the direction of his march, Brahma Shah sent about 1,500 men, almost the whole of his force, to oppose Gardner at Ranikhet. This is a small shrine, situated at the northern end of a long mountainous ridge which rises some 6,000 feet above the sea and stretches like a natural barrier across the western approaches to Almora. Gardner deftly foiled this attempt by sending a lightly equipped detachment, comprising almost half his force and led by Mohan Singh, a native officer of his own corps of horse, to turn the southern end of the ridge and occupy a summit called Sihayi Devi, which lies between Ranikhet and Almora. Fearful of being cut off, the Nepalis abandoned their positions on the ridge and hurried back to Almora, leaving the northern route open again. Despite assurances to the contrary from the guides, this path proved too difficult for the elephants. Gardner had to leave them and have the guns dragged by teams of hillmen from Rutherfurd's commissariat establishment. The force left Ranikhet on 25 March, and took until late on the 29th to cover the sixteen-odd miles to Katarmal. This is a hill on the western bank of the Kosila, almost facing Almora, which is on the eastern bank. It was occupied by an enemy force when Gardner approached, but they decamped during the night of 28 March.

Having secured a position whence he could effectively impede all Brahma Shah's contacts with the west, Gardner was content to beleaguer Almora until the regulars came. His magnanimity was appreciated at Headquarters, and Hastings commended him for 'so generously spurning the temptation of assaulting the city before Colonel Nicolls should come up, and availing himself (though at the hazard of the public interest) of what might have proved a brilliant opportunity for himself'. Before long there was evidence to show that his blockade, in which the local landholders and peasants enthusiastically co-operated, was very effective. Spies, deserters and intercepted correspondence all told the same story. The Nepali troops were without pay and so straitened for provisions that they were having to plunder the adjacent villages. Most of its civilian inhabitants had abandoned the town—in response to Brahma Shah's orders, according to one report.

The main source of disquiet at the British headquarters was the various rumours to the effect that Brahma Shah's second brother, Hasti Dal Shah, had crossed the Kali and was on his way to Almora with a large additional reinforcement. At first there was little fear that he would be able in any event to reach the capital, because Hearsey was known to be operating in eastern or Kali Kumaun with the express purpose of preventing such a juncture; but on the night of 5 April a *feu de joie* was fired from a fort on the Almora ridge, which informants said was in celebration of a victory gained by Hasti Dal over Hearsey on 2 April. The worst fears were confirmed the next day, when Edward Gardner received the following note from Brahma Shah:

You will have been informed that my brother Hasti Dal, being on his march hither from Doti, met me on the road after crossing the Kali, with Mr Hyder Hearsey who, having opposed and engaged him, was wounded and made prisoner. My brother has sent for surgeons to attend him; and Mr Hearsey having observed that his own medicines were best suited for the cure of his wounds, my brother has sent for his private servants and his own medicines, and has kept him comfortably accommodated near himself.

Hyder Hearsey's background was similar to Gardner's, but he had nothing like the same ability and modesty as a commander. Among other functions, he had fulfilled that of lieutenant to George Thomas, the Irish adventurer who was for some years at the end of the eighteenth century the ruler of his own private empire in Sirhind. It had been largely owing to Hearsey's bad judgement that Thomas's army, of which he was in effective command while Thomas himself was prostrate from the effects of alcohol, was defeated by the forces of his rival Perron at Georgegarh in 1801. He was very flamboyant, and struck people as boorish. 'Very ingenious, but uneducated' was Lady Nugent's opinion. He made no secret of the contempt in which he held the Gurkha army. Hearsey had had three months in which to raise and train his corps, as opposed to Gardner's one; but even with this advantage, he was unable to draw from his men a performance that bore comparison to that given by the force under his brother-in-law.

He was instructed to force the Timla pass, which led into eastern Kumaun from just north of Pilibhit, and then secure possession of the ghats on the Kali, so as to prevent Hasti Dal's crossing the river from Doti. But from motives of vanity, of revenge against the Gurkhas for the rough treatment he had suffered with Moorcroft in Garhwal in 1812 and, no doubt, of inspiring in government a gratitude which would cause it to favour his claim to Dehra Dun, Hearsey privately made up his mind to widen his operations and win greater *éclat*. Instead of devoting his resources to guarding the river ghats, the function for which they were intended, he undertook the siege of forts in the interior as well, thereby frittering away his troops and making them insufficient for either purpose. He paid no heed to Gardner's anxious dispatches, which stressed that the securing of the Kali ghats was his essential object, and after occupying Champawat, the old capital of Kumaun, he turned his main attentions to besieging Katalgarh. It was a senseless undertaking. Katalgarh, five or six miles to the north, was the strongest fortress in Kumaun. Its position precluded its being completely surrounded, while Hearsey had few men and not a single gun.

At the beginning of March, the greater part of Hearsey's force was distributed between Brahmadeo, at the foot of the Timla pass, the forts at the top of the pass, Champawat and Katalargh. He spared only the remainder, amounting to hardly 300 men, to guard the river ghats. Ignoring all directions to divert his own troops for the purpose, he asked government to organize a separate incursion into Doti in order to contain Hasti Dal.

On 31 March, intelligence was received by Hearsey, then at Champawat, that 500 of the enemy had crossed the Kali about fourteen miles upstream and, harassed by a body of local troops, was attempting to make a stockade on the western bank. His guide, knowing that this part of the country was the stronghold of the Phartiyal faction, propitiated by Brahma Shah and implacably opposed to Harak Deva Joshi, warned the Captain that this was probably a ruse and advised him not to engage the force. But Hearsey fancied he knew better, and in a fit of irritation sent the guide to Katalgarh in order to be rid of him. He marched that night with 270 men, and reached the scene of action the next morning. Judging that the enemy could not be driven back without a reinforcement, he sent to Katalgarh for 400 extra troops. That evening the scorned guide's warning was only too well vindicated. It was learnt that at three o'clock in the afternoon Hasti Dal had taken advantage of Hearsey's preoccupation to cross the river below the scene of the engagement with a force reported to be 1,500 strong. Hearsey at once marched his force south again, in a desperate bid to intercept the wily Gurkha. Hot with haste, tired, and thirsty, and with no ammunition save that which they had in pouch, they finally accosted the enemy early on 2 April at Khilpati, about five miles north east of Champawat. The battle was fierce, and Hearsey's men had soon expended all their cartridges. The Captain was severely wounded in the thigh, and when he fell all his men fled. Most were cut to shreds by pursuing Nepalis. It is a tradition in the Hearsey family that Hyder would have been decapitated as he lay on the field, had it not been for the timely intervention of Hasti Dal. The two men were not strangers. Hearsey had met Hasti Dal when on an official expedition, whose purpose was to survey the upper reaches of the Ganges, in 1808. According to the family story, that encounter had been the occasion of his saving the Gurkha from being killed by a wild bear. Hasti Dal now recognized his deliverer and repaid his debt of gratitude.

In view of Hearsey's failure, it was lucky that a reinforcement of regular troops was already on its way to join Gardner. In Hastings's view, the collapse of the British offensive in the eastern theatre had made the possession of Kumaun indispensable. Once the Gurkhas had been relieved of the threat of an attack on Kathmandu, it was essential to prevent their diverting their unexpectedly available reserves of manpower to bolster the defensive in the west. Acting on this conviction, Hastings had, early in March, requested Lieuten-ant-Colonel Nicolls, a King's officer of the 14th Foot, to prepare for active service. The force which could be put at his disposal was very modest. It consisted of two battalions of native infantry, a detachment consisting of flank (grenadier and light) companies from Dehra Dun, four six-pounders, two small mortars and a few pieces of heavy artillery. According to paper estimates, the strength of the infantry was 2,035 men; but these took no account of men sick and 'on command' (detached on extra-regimental duties), and the number which actually took the field with Nicolls did not exceed about 1,300. Of these, only thirty artillerists were European.

Nicolls wasted no time at Moradabad, his rendezvous. His force was barely half-assembled by the end of March, and no word had been received from Captain Leys, commanding the detachment from Dehra Dun. Nevertheless, the Colonel marched on the 29th with two six-pounders and a vanguard of three companies, leaving the remaining segments of his column, with the rest of the ordnance and the elephants, to make their own way into the hills. There had been no time to acquire and distribute greatcoats, long pantaloons or tents, and the men were going to have to improvise protection against the cold with their *kamals* (blankets). It had been impossible to collect an adequate number of hill porters, and the arrangement had to be made whereby all spare provisions and supplies were left in a depot at Dhikuli. It was hoped that porters sufficient for moving these forward would be enlisted later. Meanwhile the sepoys had to carry their own equipment and five days' provisions, which together weighed little less than eighty pounds. Nicolls had had to choose between two evils—delay or a deficient commissariat; and although he had decided that the former was the greater, he never lost sight of the insufficiencies he had been unable to remedy before marching. Although spring was well advanced, the weather remained capricious in the hills and there were periods of heavy rain. Anxious to provide against the worst discomforts of these and of the monsoon season proper, which was expected in a few weeks, the Colonel asked for greatcoats and pantaloons for the men, which the Adjutant-General promised would be provided. News of the defeat of Hearsey's detachment made Nicolls fear that the local populace might cease to provide victuals should his own column suffer any mishap, and he made an urgent request to the Magistrate of Moradabad for 1,000 bearers, to bring up supplies from the depot.

The Magistrate, Mr. Oldham, had to impress men for the service, paying them an advance of one rupee in return for a promise not to run away for twenty-five days. Needless to say, most of them pocketed their rupees and absconded even before they had reached Dhikuli. The lack of means of bringing forward his provisions remained a major problem for Nicolls throughout the campaign.

He reached the camp before Almora with the advance on 9 April, and the other sections of his force, including the artillery, arrived at various intervals over the next ten days. The new arrivals, who, with camp followers, numbered more than 3,000 souls, had soon consumed available stores of grain, and poor Rutherfurd was at his wits' end to feed the army. One observer wrote that 'not unfrequently the men, after toiling all day over the hills, had no better evening fare awaiting them than a few ears of wheat, which happened to be ripe, gathered in the fields, [and] roasted over a fire.'[2]

Jasper Nicolls, who was only thirty-seven, was an officer who had partaken to the full of the opportunities for military experience available during the years of the Revolutionary and Napoleonic Wars. He had served with distinction in the West Indies, in the Peninsular, in Hanover and at Buenos Aires, and had returned for

[2] *E.I.U.S.J.*, vol. iii, 1834, p. 249.

a second spell in India in 1813, when he assumed the staff appointment of Quartermaster-General to the King's Troops. Lean, dark-eyed and prematurely balding, he was, unless roused, a man of tact and delicacy of feeling. He was at great pains to spare Gardner any sense of embarrassment at having been superseded, and treated him in all things as an equal. But he had no sympathy for the errant Hearsey. 'I have never approved of Captain Hearsey's grand views and great extension of his force', he grumbled to the Adjutant-General on receiving news of the calamity in eastern Kumaun; 'but I arrived too late to confine his exertions.' He did not estimate the consequences of the defeat lightly. 'We may fairly suppose that the enemy's defence of the capital will [now] be greatly prolonged', he told the Magistrate of Moradabad. For his own part, Hearsey detested Nicolls until the end of his life, and ever afterwards insisted on disparaging his achievement in Kumaun.

On the evening of 12 April, guns were fired from Almora in salute. There was no doubt in the British camp that this signalled the arrival of the triumphant Hasti Dal with his prisoner. Intelligence reports represented his force to be no greater than 300 to 400, of whom only between 125 and 175 had matchlocks. This suggests either that Hasti Dal had left the greater part of his men in Kali Kumaun, which seems unlikely, or that estimates in Hearsey's camp had been wildly exaggerated. Informants from the fort assured Gardner that the total force at Brahma Shah's disposal did not exceed 2,000 men, and that they were all 'distressed for want of provisions and rather down in the mouth, the few remaining inhabitants running off for want of food'.

On April 22, when his column, including the two iron twelve-pounders and the two eight-inch mortars by which he set great store, was at last complete and when he was waiting only to improve his stock of provisions, Nicolls heard from Rutherfurd that Hasti Dal had left the ridge before Almora with 200 or 300 men, and was making for Gananath. This was a mountain about fifteen miles north of Almora, between the Kosila and the Kali. The Colonel, knowing that Rutherfurd's intelligence was not always reliable, doubted that the Gurkha could in fact have made such a rash move; but subsequent information confirmed the news, and Nicolls could only assume that Hasti Dal had gone to meet the ammunition and treasure expected from the west. In fact, as was afterwards learnt, his only concern was to retain possession of the northern perganas of

Kumaun, in order to safeguard communications with Kathmandu.

Nicolls acted quickly. At midnight, Major Patton was sent in pursuit with ten companies of infantry, a company of irregulars and a day's supply of victuals. After a hot and thirsty march, he caught up with his prey on a conifer-clad ridge near Gananath and, at the cost of only two of his own men killed and twenty-six wounded, took about eighty enemy lives. Hasti Dal's was among them. He was shot through the temple and died on the way back to Almora.

Although his provisions were still seriously inadequate, Nicolls decided that he must take the tide at the flood, and attack Almora before the enemy had time to recover from the shock of this reverse.

Almora was a small town by European standards, but ranked as considerable in the north Indian hills. It stretched for about three-quarters of a mile along the crest of a mountain ridge, in a north-west—south-east direction. There was one main street, naturally paved with slaty rock and lined with houses. These had open ground floors of whitewashed stone, fitted out as shops, and wooden upper storeys. There were two citadels. One, Fort Almora, was in the centre of the ridge. The other, then called Lal Mandi, but later renamed Fort Moira in honour of the Governor-General, was at its southern extremity. They were not impressive, being little more than glorified circular sangars, constructed of unhewn stones embedded in clay. Their walls were not above about eight feet in height, but the scarped knolls on which they stood increased their elevation considerably. A narrow col ran to the west, connecting the Almora ridge with a parallel range, which rose from the eastern bank of the Kosila. This range formed a natural bulwark against attack from west of the river, and was sprinkled with stone breast-works. The most considerable of these was at the northern extremity on the pinnacle called Sitoli. It formed Brahma Shah's principal outpost, and seemed almost immune to attack. The ground fell steeply from its walls, and a mountain slightly to the north, called Kalimath, overlooked the position and commanded the approaches to it. In general aspect, the landscape here was rather bleak. The highest reaches of the mountains were then devoid of trees, and their stony sides were cut into terraces to make more room for cultivation.

The five flank companies under Captain Leys returned from Gananath at nine o'clock on the morning of 25 April, and four hours later Nicolls launched an attack against the enemy outposts on the Sitoli range. He marched in person at the head of the flank companies and the 1st/4th Native Infantry, with the aim of establishing a position on the northern end of the range and expelling the Nepalis with mortar fire. Gardner advanced with the irregulars on a parallel line to his right, directing his effort against the defences on the southern part of the range. Those who remained in camp at Katarmal watched the columns march down together, and found it a stirring spectacle.

But the road was rough and narrow, and made it impossible for the columns to remain compact. As soon as he had crossed the Kosila, here a small mountain stream with deep pools and fordable shallows, and reached a small level spot on its eastern bank, Nicolls halted for about half an hour to allow the men to collect and to re-form his column. He asked his two artillery officers to give the enemy a few shells. A howitzer was unloaded and mounted within five minutes; but appearances were deceptive, and the enemy breastworks were found to be much too distant for the shells to have any effect. Then came the order 'Move on!', and the long climb up the flank of the Sitoli range began. It took two hours to reach the crest. As Nicolls's troops got nearer, a gun opened on them from the breastwork most immediately above, but the hill was too steep for it to bear with any accuracy. By comparing their height with that of some enemy soldiers who had earlier been standing outside them, Nicolls had been able to ascertain that the breastworks rose no more than four or five feet above the ground. This fact, and the eagerness of his men, determined him not to wait for the mortars, but to take the positions by *coups de main*. Appreciating that the flank companies must be tired after their recent exertions, he put the 1st/4th Native Infantry in front. Led by Lieutenant Wight, one group of four subalterns and some sepoys with fixed bayonets dashed at the first breastwork. It was about four feet wide, with an embrasure in the centre, cut to within about two feet of the ground. As the barrel of the enemy gun obstructed this, only one person could enter at a time. Wight was first in. He was immediately cut down, and lay dangerously wounded; but another officer, clambering after, saved him by felling his adversary with a swingeing blow. The Nepalis were overpowered within three minutes. Abandoning the gun, they left their position by the rear, which was open, and fled down the opposite side of the ridge.

The two breastworks to the left were carried almost simultaneously. His bravery in one of these encounters earned a sepoy named Dokal Singh special mention in Detachment Orders as 'a hero, who, though wounded in five places, refused, when lying disabled on the ground, to surrender his musket to several of the enemy, who would have wrested it from his hands'. The flank companies, under Leys, now reaching the crest of the ridge, Nicolls directed them to pursue the ejected enemy. They promptly divided, and hounded them by five different routes down the eastern side of the range. Meanwhile the 1st/4th easily ousted the occupants from the four or five breastworks to the north, including that on Sitoli mount itself. The enemy post on Kalimath was thus completely cut off from Almora. Gardner's men seized the three breastworks on the southern end of the crest at about the same time.

This was the first time that Nicolls had commanded native troops in action, and their bravery had made the occasion unforgettable for him. 'I congratulate His Excellency the Commander-in-Chief', he wrote to Headquarters, 'on the glorious result of the noble exertions of the troops, whom it will be a source of pride to me, to the end of my life, to have commanded'. More than anything else, the behaviour of the sepoys on this occasion demonstrated the decisive influence of the presence of an adequate number of European officers. Because the column had been disorganized by the badness of the road, almost all the officers were in front when the engagement began, and there were five subalterns with the party which attacked the first breastwork alone.

The Sitoli range once secured, an advance party was pushed across the connecting col to the northern end of Almora ridge. Headquarters were established in a quadrangular fort, about sixty yards square, which had been abandoned by the enemy.[3] About 250 men of the 1st/4th and flank companies were then sent southwards into the town itself. They occupied a pagoda, called Dip Chand temple, and set up two howitzers on its terrace. The first shells were fired at about six o'clock. They were aimed at Fort Almora, which was 300 yards farther south, beyond the Raja's palace.

Meanwhile, all was quiet on the Sitoli range. Then, at about eleven o'clock, the Nepalis still at Kalimath attacked Lieutenant Costley and the eighty sepoys on Sitoli mount. A local story is that

[3] Later called St. Mark's Tower.

they covered their advance with a drove of cattle carrying firebrands on their horns. Nicolls immediately sent a reinforcement of about 150 sepoys under Lieutenants Browne and Whinfield to aid the overwhelmed party. Gardner, who was with Nicolls at headquarters, volunteered to go with them, taking Mohan Singh and a company of irregulars. The reinforcement met Costley and his men at the foot of Sitoli mount, fleeing before the Nepali onslaught. Browne, Whinfield and Gardner then drove the enemy at bayonet point back up the hill. So ferocious was their offensive, in which they did not fire a shot, that Sitoli had been retaken in ten minutes. But the Nepalis would not concede defeat, and contested the post stubbornly throughout the night. The British officers and their native troops, with equal pertinacity, refused to yield, and three charges were repulsed. The valour of Browne and Mohan Singh was especially conspicuous. In honour of the former, the hill was later named Mount Browne; and the latter was presented with the sword which Hastings had entrusted to Nicolls with the instruction that it was to be given to the sirdar of Gardner's levy who proved himself most worthy. 'He headed three successive and successful charges of the Pathan levies', ran his citation, 'and taught the Gurkha chiefs that at night, their favourite hour of conflict, and with the sword, their favourite weapon, they were unequal to face our gallant troops with any hope of success'.

The noise of battle from Sitoli acted as a summons to the enemy in Fort Almora, who attempted to dislodge the advanced post and battery at Dip Chand temple. They made a sortie and sprinted up the main street of the town. The wall of the temple enclosure was only five or six feet high. This they lobbed stones over, with leather slings, and tried to vault. Several were shot or bayonetted on the wall, and one was killed actually inside the enclosure. The rest were beaten off. Work meanwhile continued on the placing of eight-inch mortars, and these opened on the fort about midnight.

The night was murky, and it was impossible to distinguish objects even at ten yards' distance. Throughout, the repetitive crepitation and orange flashing of musketry continued, and there was incessant skirmishing, which added considerably to the casualties on both sides. It was reckoned that many of Nicolls's losses were caused by his own men, firing blindly. Early in the morning of 25 April, Lieutenant Tapley, at Dip Chand temple, lost his life. Each time an enemy party had been repulsed, he insisted on going outside the wall of the enclosure 'to watch when they were coming again'. Lieutenant Field, commanding the post, repeatedly urged him not to expose himself so needlessly; but his warnings were ignored, and about two o'clock Tapley was shot by a musketeer in one of the houses which overlooked the temple.

Mental strain and hunger made the night seem interminable. Nicolls was restless with worry; but when at last the hills were streaked with light, all his positions were still secure, and the Nepalis slunk back into their lairs. The British commander's first concern now was for the comfort of his men. Remembering that they had not eaten for twenty-four hours, he mustered a group of his own servants and some coolies, and personally visited each post with bread and butter and bottles of warm tea for the officers, and gram and sweetmeats for the sepoys. As he spoke little Hindustani he asked Lieutenant Hay to tell the men how pleased he was with them. Needless to say, Jasper Nicolls was ever afterwards a favourite of the Bengal army.

At about half-past eight, when extra cartridges had arrived from Katarmal, operations were resumed. Field was directed to take his party from the temple down the main street of the town and seize the palace, which intervened between his present position and Fort Almora. It was a spacious, square, upper-storeyed building, surrounded by an eight-foot stone wall. The Nepalis in the place peppered his men with bullets, but they vaulted the wall, entered the building and ran up the main staircase. Eight or ten of the enemy were shot or bayoneted; the rest fled down a back staircase and escaped to the fort. Field waved his cap as a signal and Bell and Wilson of the artillery brought down a couple of six-pounders. They knocked embrasures in the rear wall of the palace compound, which was only about seventy yards from the fort, and set up a battery.

Meanwhile, the mortars at Dip Chand temple had continued to fire, and despite the great distance, several shells landed in the fort. Soon large numbers of the enemy were seen leaving the place by a door in the eastern wall and making for Lal Mandi fort behind. Nicolls ordered Lieutenants Field and McGregor to try to enter while the enemy were coming out. The two officers took a small party of sepoys and ran up the side street which led to the entrance; but on reaching it they found that the enemy had been leaving through a wicket, which was slammed shut as they approached.

They could not force it open and, being showered with stones and shot from the walls of the fort, were compelled to withdraw.

The contest, however, was all but over. Brahma Shah had neither enthusiasm nor energy for further defiance. He had never understood the expediency of the war; and now that his troops were hungry, unpaid and increasingly disgruntled, he saw no merit in prolonging it by futile self-immolation. Having made as honourable a resistance as his means permitted, he resolved, in consultation with his chief officers, that it was his duty to end the contest on the most favourable terms that he could get. At the end of March, Edward Gardner had offered him and his men a safe conduct to the eastern bank of the Kali in return for the surrender of the capital. At nine o'clock on 26 April, he sent a note to the Political Agent, under a flag of truce, requesting a suspension of hostilities on the same terms. Nicolls and Edward Gardner had no inclination to flaunt their victory by demanding stiffer terms, and William Gardner was sent to meet Brahma Shah and negotiate the surrender. There was some delay before a convention was signed, owing to the Gurkha's insistence that the troops originally intended for Amar Singh Thapa's army in the west should be allowed to continue their journey; but finally, on 27 April, realizing that the Colonel was adamant in his refusal, he gave up this condition and agreed to release Hearsey and withdraw with all his men to the eastern bank of the Kali within ten days. On the 28th, Nicolls and Edward Gardner paid Brahma Shah a visit, and the reasons behind his concession became clear. He wanted to retain control of negotiations for a general peace, and had 'projects of inducing the British Government to assist the Raja's party in regaining their power and overturning that of the Thapas'. Gardner felt bound to decline discussing such issues at this stage; but he found it impossible not to feel considerable sympathy for this tall, stout, affable Gurkha, whose looks belied his seventy years, whose nervous speech impediment somehow removed all doubts concerning his sincerity, and whose competent Hindustani made it possible to address him with reasonable ease and informality.

On the night of 31 April, Brahma Shah quitted Almora, taking with him such of his army as had remained loyal. This must have included the great majority of his regular troops, because only the irregular Kumauni soldiers had taken service with the British—and even they did not number more than about 300.

As the news of the surrender of the capital spread through Kumaun, the other Gurkha garrisons scattered throughout the province spontaneously capitulated. Edward Gardner thereupon declared the territory annexed to the dominions of the East India Company, and assumed the functions of civil administrator. The cost of the acquisition had not been great. British casualties during the operations of 25 and 26 April did not exceed 50 killed and 161 wounded; and the total of casualties for the whole campaign was not greatly in excess of those figures.

Nicolls attributed his success to 'the daily miracle of feeding the troops in such a poor country' and to 'the efficient service of our eight-inch mortars', which 'considerably hastened' the fall of Almora. The latter conviction confirmed Ochterlony's experience of the necessity of heavy artillery in mountain warfare and makes it all the more surprising that Nicolls, when Commander-in-Chief, sent a column to the Khyber Pass without guns. The response of the sepoys under his command appears to have been far more impressive than that of those under the other commanders of the war, Ochterlony included; but it must be remembered that the Kumaun detachment had been in the hills for barely a month when its first and only major engagement took place—a month, moreover, in which the weather had been at its kindest. The other two divisions in the western theatre had had to endure all the rigours of a mountain winter.

Considering their notoriety, and the circumstances under which they had been raised, the performance of Gardner's corps of Pathans had been nothing less than remarkable. More than anything else, this had been a testimony to the talent and personality of the man who commanded them. He had transformed untamed brigands into disciplined, tractable and steadfast soldiers. No one else could handle them. No sooner had Gardner returned to the plains than the Pathans, left in the hills to garrison the various acquired strongholds, again reverted to an unruly rabble. They deserted in droves, helping themselves to Rutherfurd's stores of grain and terrorizing local villages. Nicolls fully appreciated the measure of Gardner's contribution to the success of the campaign. With characteristic generosity, he made his acknowledgement the subject of a separate dispatch to Headquarters; and on his recommendation Gardner's monthly pension was raised from 300 to 1,000 rupees.

XI

INTERLUDE

DURING the hot and monsoon seasons of 1815, the troops acting in the eastern theatre had the unenviable task of defending the frontier of the newly acquired territory in the Tarai and the Morang. Time hung heavy on their hands, because the Nepalis knew better than to enter the region at this deathly period of the year; but casualties in these divisions were nevertheless greater than they had been during the whole period of active operations. The prevalent symptoms—violent fever and delirium—indicate that the principal malady was malaria; but its effects were complicated by all the various disorders caused by primitive sanitation, contaminated drinking water and the well-intended but horrifyingly unscientific antics of contemporary surgeons. John Wood's division was distributed between three posts on the border of Gorakhpur. By the middle of May more than 1,200 men were sick, and had had to be withdrawn. There being no hospital in Gorakhpur town, they were lodged in the bullock sheds, which can hardly have hastened their recovery. H.M. 24th Foot was the only European regiment on the frontier, the others having been remanded to cantonments. They were posted at Amowa, just south of Segauli. 135 men out of 751 were seriously ill in June, and between the end of March and the beginning of September sixty died. At Nathpur, farther east, Colonel Gregory was in charge of some 2,500 native infantry. In the middle of August his force was in 'a dreadful sickly state'. 'In less than a month', he wrote, 'I lost four European officers; nearly 300 men are absent on sick certificate, and an equal number are now in the hospital; and the men who have recovered from the Tarai fever have not yet regained their strength, and are perfectly useless . . . added to which I have only one medical man in charge of the sick of two and a half battalions.' This last fact may have been less a liability than he thought.

While the troops suffered, the diplomats talked. Serious negotiations began at the end of May, and lasted until the end of the year.

During the latter half of his tour of the upper provinces, and in the first months after his return to Calcutta in October, hardly a week passed without the Governor-General's receiving a formidably bulky dispatch concerning peace discussions, and without his dictating an equally elaborate one in reply.

A few days after Brahma Shah had crossed the Kali and entered Doti, he was joined by his surviving brother, Rudra Vir, who was governor of Sallyana province, beyond Doti to the east. William Gardner, who had escorted the garrison of Almora to the river, met Rudra Vir and had a long informal conversation with him. During the course of this, it became clear that great political significance attached to the selection of a Nepalese negotiator. The Gurkha assured Gardner that 'whoever was charged with arranging a treaty with the British Government would hereafter have the greatest weight in the Nepal councils.'

There were three contenders for the commission. They were Brahma Shah; Gajraj Misr, the erstwhile guru of the royal family, who had approached the Governor-General with an offer to mediate; and Amar Singh Thapa. Hastings, having no wish to increase the political influence of the last, did not contemplate negotiating through him; but he was prepared to conclude a treaty with whichever of the two other parties offered the indemnification he demanded. He reasoned that if either of them was deputed to treat, it must be with powers to grant all the territorial sacrifices he required, because the durbar at Kathmandu was not ignorant of their scope. Bradshaw, in his exchanges with Chandra Sekhar, the captured *vakil*, and with Gajraj Misr, had made it known that the Company would insist on retaining all the lands it had conquered, and would demand a treaty which guaranteed it compensation for the cost of the war and security from fresh aggression. If either of the two contenders, therefore, offered less than the decided price, it could only be in order to increase his own prestige and influence. It followed that acceptance of a reduced offer would be tantamount to abetting the ambitions of a particular individual or political party, and such behaviour was, in Hastings's view, beneath the dignity of the Company. But neither of the Nepalese agents understood that this was the British attitude. As they saw it, the prime purpose of the Company must be not territorial indemnification, but the establishment of an influence in Kathmandu. This was why Gajraj Misr emphasized that it was his especial desire to recover the office of royal guru and exercise it under the protection of a British Residency; and why Rudra Vir Shah urgently stressed to Gardner that their securing the peace negotiation would enable his brother and himself to overthrow the low-caste usurping Thapas, whom he contemptuously referred to as 'Khasias', and re-establish the power of their own party, which had always been the pro-British one. Neither seems to have taken the British demand for indemnification in territory seriously at first, and the two governments negotiated at cross purposes for many months.

Because he was the first to secure the appropriate authority, negotiations were begun with Gajraj Misr. Since the palace revolution of 1803, this brahmin had been living in exile at Benares, on the proceeds of a *jagir* provided by the Company. Motivated partly by a desire to reingratiate himself with the durbar and recover his lost position, and partly by a genuine concern to open the Raja's eyes to the peril of his situation and save his kingdom from destruction, he had offered his services as a mediator. Both governments had welcomed the tender. Hastings had recalled his previous adherence to the pro-British party in Kathmandu and his efforts to promote the success of the Kirkpatrick and Knox missions; and the durbar was anxious to employ an agent who was in favour with the British and able to inform it of the true nature of the Governor-General's conditions of peace. In response to an invitation from the Raja, he had left for Kathmandu early in May, accompanied by Chandra Sekhar Upadhyaya, whom Bradshaw had repossessed of his private property in order to foster an auspicious atmosphere.

Both men returned to Bradshaw's headquarters at Segauli on 18 May. Gajraj Misr produced an authorization under the Raja's red seal, and declared that he was empowered to accept whatever terms the victors in their mercy might require. But, confident in his assumption that what the Company really sought was the institution of himself as guru in Kathmandu, Gajraj had given the durbar to understand that the price in territory would not, when it came to the point, be as high as had been threatened; so when Bradshaw informed him that the Gurkhas were required to relinquish all colonies west of the Kali and the whole of the Tarai and Morang, he was aghast and incredulous. He was forced to confess that he had no mandate to accede to such stringent demands, and asked to be allowed to make further reference to Kathmandu. Hastings, on the other hand, was disposed to think that he must have received plenary powers with his commission, and that he was bargaining well within their limit with a view to improving his personal standing. He therefore retaliated by ordering a suspension of negotiations in this quarter and informed Edward Gardner that he might begin discussions with Brahma Shah.

The Shah brothers were desperately eager to be acknowledged as negotiators by the British. Brahma had been edgy and nervous ever since his capitulation, because he dreaded the effects at Kathmandu of Amar Singh Thapa's misrepresentations. It had taken all the kindly expostulation of William Gardner to induce him to cross the Kali and enter Nepalese territory once more. On Edward Gardner's advice, he had applied to Kathmandu for authority to treat, and while waiting to know the result of his solicitation had been in such a state of agitation (earnestly affirming that if he failed to be appointed negotiator he could expect nothing but death from the despised 'Khasias') that William Gardner had been moved to compassion. At his suggestion, Brahma and his brother were offered the chance to seize the Gurkha province of Doti and rule it as Company protégés. But they had declined the invitation, Brahma's reason being that he could not endanger his many relatives still within the reach of the Thapas.

On 4 July, Brahma Shah informed Edward Gardner that he had received a favourable answer from Kathmandu, and the following day Edward Gardner's own instructions to open negotiations arrived. Brahma being ill, it was Rudra Vir Shah who crossed the Kali to confabulate. He was more aggressive and stronger-willed than his brother, and when he heard Gardner's demand for the whole of the Tarai he flatly refused to entertain such a sacrifice. With great emphasis he told Gardner that he was authorized to cede no more than the western hill provinces, and that the Tarai was the most vital source of the wealth of his state. Take away the lowlands, he insisted, and national penury would ensue. Unconditional powers to treat subsequently arrived, but Rudra Vir refused to change his attitude. He had several more interviews with Gardner, some of them in company with his brother, and at all of them he reiterated the same arguments in a tone increasingly acrimonious. At the last he became almost violent. He informed the Political Agent

that others might negotiate on these grounds; but that for himself he would not accept of a commission for that purpose . . . That it was what would never be consented to at Nepal, and was a subject, in fact, he had received no orders or authority to treat of . . . That if this point were insisted upon, it would occasion a popular war in which every subject of Nepal would personally engage; that hitherto many of the chief people had kept aloof through party feelings and disapprobation of the contest the Thapa faction had involved them in; but no sooner should it be known that we insisted on the dismemberment of the whole Tarai, than all party faction would be forgotten in the general cause, and everyone unite in the general defence.

Even the normally mild and timid Brahma Shah was infected by his brother's vehemence, and met all Gardner's remonstrances with steady pertinacity.[1]

Such a reaction was not, in fact, unreasonable. The Tarai estates were the main source of income for the Gurkha government and nobles, all other land being assigned to the army in lieu of payment. But Gardner knew nothing of this, and was convinced that all these protestations were subterfuge; that the Shah brothers were holding in reserve concessions which they had been authorized to make, in the hope of securing a cheap peace. This would not only enhance their political prestige; it would also, in the case of Rudra Vir, at least, who possessed extensive estates in the Tarai, preserve personal interests. Hastings was of the same opinion, and he agreed that Rudra Vir probably greatly exaggerated the importance of the lowlands in the national economy. Nevertheless, if the Gurkha's demurring had failed to persuade him that a relaxation of his demands concerning the Tarai was necessary in order to secure a settlement, it had convinced him that such a relaxation would make the settlement, once concluded, more permanent. Above all else, he was anxious to avoid extorting from the Gurkhas a treaty which they would dishonour as soon as his back was turned. Events during the early period of the Bengal army's preoccupation in the mountains had, to his mind, presented a striking portent of the situation which might arise if the British challenged the Maratha powers of central India before the Gurkha threat had been exorcised. There had been simultaneous and ominous stirrings among all the Company's potential antagonists. Ranjit Singh, had, in November 1814, marched his army to precisely that point whence he had intended to cross the Sutlaj in 1808, while the whole British force on the east bank of the river consisted only of the two squadrons of

---

[1] *P.R.N.W.*, pp. 802–9.

native cavalry at Ludhiana. Sindhia, the Maratha Raja of Gwalior, had taken the first step towards a revival of the Maratha confederacy, by concluding an alliance with Berar in contravention of the treaties of 1805. Amir Khan, the leader of the Pathan mercenaries of central India, had collected an army said to be 30,000 strong on the borders of Jaipur, in Rajputana, only twelve marches from Delhi, while Sir William Keir Grant, commanding the remainder of the 2nd (Meerut) Division of the Field Army, had little more than a single battalion of native infantry with which to oppose him. Disquieting reports had arrived from the north-east to the effect that Gurkha *vakils* had been received in Bhutan, and that Bhutanese troops were accumulating in the passes of the Bhutan-Nepal boundary. Finally, the long-truculent King of Burma had been known to be watching events in India with interest, and to have made secret communication with Nepal. 'The cloud which overhangs us is imposing', the Governor-General had noted in his Journal; and Metcalfe, surveying the scene from the Delhi Residency, had been convinced that the end was at hand. 'I, who have always thought our power in India precarious, cannot help thinking that our downfall has already commenced.'[2] So pressing had been the emergency, that urgent requests for European troops had been sent to Ceylon, the Cape of Good Hope, Mauritius and even to England.

During the ensuing months the immediate crisis, it was true, had passed. Ranjit Singh had been distracted by a recrudescence of his quarrel with the Amir of Kabul; Sindhia's generals had fallen to fighting among themselves; Berar had been effectively overawed by the dispatch of an army of observation, 10,000 strong, from Madras to the northern border of the dominions of the Nizam of the Deccan; and apprehension concerning the intentions of the Deb Raja of Bhutan had been dissipated. Relations with this last monarch had, in fact, become so promising that the British authorities were disposed to think, for the moment, that they had found a new ally rather than a new enemy. He had most convincingly disavowed inimical intentions, and had agreed to an exchange of *vakils*, whose purpose was both to settle the boundary disputes between the Company and Bhutan, and to afford a medium for British explanations concerning the war to the Chinese authorities in Lhasa.

[2] Kaye, *Life of Metcalfe*, i, 402.

But, however transitory, these menaces had buttressed the Governor-General's conviction that there existed an incipient danger of collaboration among the native states which must be nipped in the bud by the establishment of an effective British hegemony, and his main concern throughout the negotiations with Nepal was to secure a peace which would indispose the Gurkhas to re-enter the conflict when British energies were absorbed in central India. To make this object sure, he now realized that he would have to make concessions; but he equally realized that the concessions must be granted from a position of strength—that is to say, after the Gurkhas had eaten humble pie and agreed to the terms originally proposed. To grant concessions before they had avowed submission would, by giving an impression of weakness, merely whet their appetite for revenge. As a reward, therefore, for submission, Gurkha nobles nominated by the durbar were to be offered either *iagirs* in the Tarai or pensions, for life.

Hastings had no serious apprehensions that the Gurkhas would reject his terms of pacification; but he nevertheless took the precaution of ordering preparations to be made in every department for a renewal of the war.

It soon seemed that his optimism was justified. No sooner had they learned of the collapse of negotiations in Brahma Shah's quarter, than Bhim Sen Thapa and the Raja hastened to reopen the communication through Gajraj Misr. Wrote Bhim Sen to the guru: 'All our hopes rest on you. This state will agree to whatever you may do, and I charge myself with the ratification of it . . . Bring the subject to a conclusion by whatever means it can be effected, consistently with the public interest and your own reputation.' Towards the end of August, Chandra Sekhar, who had gone to Kathmandu to report the negotiations with Bradshaw in greater detail to the durbar, returned with more letters for Gajraj Misr. Their tone was in harmony with that of the previous one. Wrote the Raja: 'The country towards Kumaun in the west, and the Tarai, have lately been conquered by the British Government. With regard to those conquests, whatever may be the result of your negotiation will be approved by me.' Wrote Bhim Sen: 'The sentiments of the *Bharadars*[3] to the west are these: "If, for the sake of peace, you will give up to the British Government our territory

---

[3] Title given to the twelve most senior officers in the realm, members of the council of state.

hill and plain, east of the Sutlaj to Kumaun, we will not be parties
to such a policy. Rather than with our hands and voice surrender
that territory, we consent to sacrifice our lives in it." But the sentiments in this quarter are, that with regard to our territory west of
Kumaun and the Tarai, which have lately fallen into the hands of
the British Government, whatever you shall do or say, we will
advocate the same before the Raja, and obtain a confirmation of it.'[4]
Gajraj Misr showed these letters to Bradshaw, whom they satisfied
that the last impediment to peace had been removed. The Governor-
General was of the same persuasion. He forthwith ordered the
discharge of the extra troops who had been enlisted for the war
emergency, and shortly afterwards commissariat preparations for
renewed hostilities were countermanded.

The tone of the letters from Kathmandu was a source of great
relief to Hastings. In his view it was sufficiently humble to constitute that submission which he had required as the precondition
of concessions, and he now felt able to demonstrate his generosity,
conciliate the Gurkhas and bring the whole business to a close. In
government circles, uneasiness at the prospect of another campaign
was growing. Edmonstone and the Council, in Calcutta, had become so hostile to the idea that they had publicly dissociated themselves from the Governor-General's conditions of peace and
counselled 'a relaxation of our demands to the extent solicited by
the Court of Nepal'. Hastings was furious because, after a previous
unbroken silence which he could not but interpret as assent, they
had chosen to register disagreement in an official dispatch, thereby
evading responsibility for measures which had not even been the
subject of discussion between them and himself; but although he
took exception to the mode of their dissent, there is no doubt that
he felt the force of its content and was becoming aware that by
insisting on indemnification he was perhaps prejudicing the success
of the main purpose of the Gurkha war. Consequently, now that he
was offered the opportunity to modify his original terms without a
blatant sacrifice of dignity, he did not hesitate to grasp it. Bradshaw
was instructed to alter the draft of the treaty so that it provided for
the retention by Nepal of all the lowlands as far west as the Gandak
river which were at present unoccupied by the British; the grant of
pensions for two lives to selected nobles; and the relinquishment of
the demand for the surrender of the Gurkha official responsible for

[4] *P.R.N.W.*, pp. 824–6.

the atrocities in Butwal in 1814. Thus revised, the treaty[5] was not thereafter altered; but Bradshaw was given latitude to modify it still further. Should he judge that such concessions would be the means of averting its rejection, he was to commute the pensions for *jagirs*, tenable for one life, in the Tarai east of the Rapti river, and to delete the article stipulating an exchange of Residents.

The new draft was submitted to Gajraj Misr. Despite the apparent plenitude of his mandate, he refused to sign it until he had made further reference to Kathmandu. His reluctance was probably not completely unexpected at Headquarters. Edward Gardner had been having more conference with Brahma Shah, who was informed of events at Kathmandu, and he had reported that according to the Gurkha there was no real authority behind the guru's commission. Still, it seems, British demands for territorial compensation were not taken seriously at the durbar. The Gurkhas were hoping that a show of willingness to make sacrifices would prevent their actual extortion, and the guru was chary of using an authority which he was only meant to flourish. His fresh application to Kathmandu elicited an answer which manifestly perturbed him, and which he refused to show Bradshaw. After some prevarication, he offered to sign the treaty provided the temporary pensions were exchanged for a permanent restitution of lands of equivalent value in the Tarai east of the Gandak. Bradshaw refused, and Gajraj pleaded for time to consult the durbar once more. But the British agent was adamant and told him (presumably having judged that the further concessions he was authorized to offer would not alter the guru's attitude) that he was at liberty either to sign the treaty as it was, or to terminate negotiations and withdraw to Kathmandu. Gajraj Misr chose the second alternative and left Segauli, with Chandra Sekhar, on 3 November. On departing, he assured Bradshaw that he would return within twelve days with the Raja's acceptance of the peace terms, or not at all.

This was a grave setback, and Hastings ordered a resumption of the commissariat preparations which he had suspended in September. Sir David Ochterlony was requested to assume command of the main division as soon as George Wood had absented himself on sick leave; Jasper Nicolls was asked to hold himself in readiness to proceed to Sitapur and lead a column into the hill provinces west of Kathmandu; and a corps of observation was ordered to be assem-

[5] See Appendix 1.

bled at Lautan, on the frontier of Butwal, under Major-General John Wood.

It was Hastings's professed belief that this show of determination would bring the durbar to its senses. Bradshaw was authorized to make yet another concession, if it appeared that it would tip the balance in favour of peace. As the final extremity, short of war, the Company would agree, in so far as it could do so without dishonouring assurances of protection given to the inhabitants of the Tarai, to restore permanently estates in the lowland tract between the Kosi and the Gandak instead of granting pensions.

It was the end of the month before Gajraj Misr and Chandra Sekhar arrived again at Bradshaw's headquarters. They had letters for the Political Agent and for the Governor-General from Bhim Sen Thapa and the Raja. These contained no concrete proposals, but their tone seemed not to admit a doubt concerning the durbar's final resolution to accept whatever terms the British would impose. Gajraj Misr was importunate, but as he did not again mention the commutation of pensions, Bradshaw did not raise the subject and confined his assurances to general promises to use his limited influence in favour of the Raja's hopes and expectations. Gajraj Misr then agreed to sign the treaty. The ceremony took place on 2 December. Two copies were signed. One was then sent to Calcutta, for ratification by the Governor-General in Council, and the other to Kathmandu, for ratification by the Raja of Nepal.

Hastings breathed again. Once more the commissariat officers were instructed to 'discharge all establishments and discontinue all expenses' connected with preparations for renewed hostilities. A special Council was summoned for the purpose of ratification, and the signed treaty was hurriedly sent back to Bradshaw. But the months of hesitation, protest, and indignation on the part of the Gurkhas had not been without their effect on the Governor-General. He realized that the treaty had been wrung from an unwilling and unconsoled foe, and appreciated that it was therefore liable to be disavowed at the first provocation. Motivated by this fear, and also by the consideration, prominent after the recent sufferings of the troops, that its climate would make the Tarai more a liability than an asset, he now framed more concessions. These were to be offered as 'a gratuitous and liberal relaxation from conditions already acceded to', after the ratified copies of the treaty had been exchanged. As a substitute for pensions, Bradshaw was to grant permanent estates in the originally disputed Tarai as far west as the Rapti. Hastings would probably have gone even further and offered estates in the Tarai west of the Rapti, had he not already earmarked that territory for a special purpose. The Nawab of Oudh had been persuaded to 'volunteer' to lend the Company two crore (20,000,000) of rupees—equivalent to £2,500,000. This had formed Hastings's war fund. He now planned to liquidate half the loan by granting the Tarai on the Oudh border to the Nawab. Even the prospect of mollifying the Gurkhas could not deter the Governor-General from this project, which, for personal reasons, he contemplated with great satisfaction. Edmonstone had been sending to London what Hastings considered to be mischievous complaints concerning the expense of the war, and discharging half the Oudh loan in this manner would enable him to claim that the war had not, in fact, cost the Company a single shilling.

The ratified Nepalese copy of the treaty was confidently awaited; but time slipped by and it was not brought. Then, only a few days before the interval fixed for its receipt had expired, events took a dramatic turn. Hot with haste, the son of Chandra Sekhar arrived from Kathmandu with a message for Gajraj Misr. It was from Bhim Sen Thapa, who warned the guru that there had been a hitch. Amar Singh Thapa, summoned to endorse the treaty, had arrived in Kathmandu with his judgement, it seems, still warped by acerbity, and was striving to incite the chiefs of state to reject it. He had virulently attacked the clause relating to pensions, and stigmatized those willing to receive them as potential puppets of a foreign power. In order to allay the scruples he had aroused, Bhim Sen needed a firm assurance that, after the treaty had been ratified, the pensions would be exchanged for territory. Considering that this was a situation which called for the revelation of the special concession which he held in reserve, Bradshaw promised the messenger, the guru, and Chandra Sekhar that such a modification would subsequently be sanctioned. Chandra Sekhar's son then returned to Kathmandu, followed on 28 December by Gajraj Misr and Chandra Sekhar, who went to receive the ratified instrument.

These were the last dealings they had with Bradshaw. Early in January 1816 he was relieved of his functions as Political Agent. Ochterlony was henceforth to exercise both military and political authority. At the same time, Hastings privately determined that Bradshaw should be removed from his post of Head Assistant at the

Lucknow Residency as soon as a favourable occasion arose.[6] His conduct had been a cause of dissatisfaction for some time. As administrator of the occupied Tarai, he had insisted on having soldiers preserve the crops from possible enemy raids against the advice of officers commanding on the frontier, who, remembering the unfortunate result of his dispositions the season before, were strongly averse to detaching small unsupported bodies of troops. In addition, his manner as negotiator had been high-handed and hectoring. The occasion of his dismissal was a quarrel with Ochterlony. Bradshaw complained that Ochterlony was supercilious, and Ochterlony accused Bradshaw of being obstructive. There was a measure of justice in both charges; but Bradshaw's stock was by now too far fallen, and Ochterlony's was too high, for there to be any doubt about whom Hastings would support. Bradshaw received the news of his supersession with a very bad grace. He adhered to an absolutely literal interpretation of his instructions, and thereby kept Ochterlony in the dark concerning the state of negotiations until the last possible minute. It is unlikely that Bradshaw's shortcomings had caused any serious damage to the negotiation; but it is indisputable that his replacement by Ochterlony, who, with his insight into and sympathy for the oriental character was an incomparably better diplomat, was a salutary change.

On 23 January, Gajraj Misr returned crestfallen from Nepal and told Bradshaw that he had not got the ratified treaty. In his absence adverse councils had prevailed, and the durbar now demanded that the whole of the Tarai between the Gandak and the Kosi be substituted for the proposed pensions. He was referred to Ochterlony, who informed him that he might return either to Kathmandu or to Benares, as best his fancy dictated.

There is no reason to question the essential truth of the reason given by Chandra Sekhar's son for the treaty's failure to gain

---

[6] A private letter from Richard Strachey to John Adam, dated 16 Dec. 1815, concerning the post of Head Assistant at Lucknow, has this pencil note jotted in the top left-hand corner: 'to be considered when Bradshaw is removed'. See I.O.L. MSS EUR/D/585, f. 161. Bradshaw returned to England on furlough when his dismissal from the Lucknow Residency was announced (probably in 1817) in order to protest before the Court of Directors. His representations were successful, and he returned to India in 1821 to assume the post of Resident. But he never reached Lucknow. He died at Patna the same year. It was rumoured at the time that he had been poisoned with diamond dust at the instigation of the Nawab of Oudh. See Pearse, *The Hearseys*, pp. 218–20; Hodson's *List*, Part 1; Political Letter from Bengal, 4 May 1822.

acceptance in the durbar. Information obtained by Edward Gardner confirmed that Amar Singh Thapa had been summoned to Kathmandu on business of state; and Chandra Sekhar, on his return from Nepal in August, had told Bradshaw that the Kaji, bitterly opposed to the terms of peace, had been recalled to court. Amar Singh Thapa's counsel must have been the weightier because, by a freak of circumstance similar to that which had obtained on the eve of the war, his avowed political enemies, the Shah brothers, were in fundamental agreement with it. The '*Bharadars* to the west' mentioned by Bhim Sen Thapa probably included Brahma and Rudra Vir Shah, as well as Amar Singh Thapa. So much would seem to be indicated, at least, by the tenor of their representations to Gardner, and by the fact that neither again gave any cause to suppose that his allegiance to the durbar was shaky.[7] Bhim Sen Thapa himself appears to have been an unstable and ineffectual figure at this critical juncture of his country's history. The instructions sent to Ranjor Singh Thapa after the fall of Kalanga, enjoining an attempt to secure peace by extensive sacrifice, show that he was still far from defiant and resilient in the face of defeat, so his professed desire for an acceptance of the treaty had therefore probably been sincere. But he was very impressionable. Thus while the moderating influence of Gajraj Misr prevailed, he had been disposed to throw himself on the mercy of the conquerors; but after the return of his uncle, now the elder statesman of Nepal and the symbol of her resistance, he had neither the self-possession nor the prestige to prevail against his fiery exhortations.

Amar Singh's belief in miracles had been strengthened by adversity. He clung to the idea that China might be induced to help, even though repeated applications to the Imperial authorities in Lhasa had failed to evoke any sympathy. It is known that an application for aid had been sent to Lhasa, for the purpose of being forwarded to Peking, by the Nepal Raja early in 1815. It had been couched in the form of an accusation against the British, the gravamen of which was that they were seeking to force a passage to Tibet. Accounts differ concerning the fate of the petition. When

---

[7] It is known, from various casual references, that Brahma Shah remained in the west as governor of Doti province. See, for example, Richard Strachey to John Adam, 19 November 1816: I.O.L. MSS EUR/D/585, f. 212. Rudra Vir's subsequent career is so far unknown. It is probable that he remained governor of Sallyana.

the two Chinese *Ambans* in Lhasa wrote to the Rangpur Magistrate later in 1816, they haughtily scorned the idea that they should ever have sent such a contemptible missive into the august presence. 'What has befallen us that we should communicate the unsuitable petitions of the Gurkha Raja, or of anyone else to the Emperor, or to trouble His Majesty with such misrepresentations?'; and, in a letter later intercepted by the British Resident, the Nepal Raja complained that no attention had been paid to his petition, which had been returned from Lhasa. But other sources and subsequent events show that this apparent indifference was mere dissimulation. The *Ambans* had, in fact, secretly forwarded copies of the application to the Emperor, together with the Rangpur Magistrate's explanation of British procedure. The result had been a refusal to aid the Gurkhas; but the Emperor had nevertheless felt the need to investigate the whole situation in the Himalayas a little more thoroughly, and he had ordered an agent, called Shee Chan Choon in the English records, to advance from Peking to the southern frontier of Tibet with an army said to number thousands. But nothing was known of this in Nepal when the treaty was rejected. The Emperor had ordered the Lhasa authorities not to divulge their communication with himself—probably because he did not want to encourage the Gurkhas in their conflict with the British.[8]

It appears from the report of Kishen Kant Bose, Company *vakil* in Bhutan, that Nepalese attempts to acquire the support of the Deb Raja had been no more successful. A Gurkha ambassador resided at the court of Bhutan and special messengers had, in addition, been sent there from Kathmandu late in 1814. But Kishen Kant found no evidence to suggest that there was any formal alliance between the two governments. His suggestion was that the Deb Raja was detaining the Gurkha agents only in order to make the British more tractable in the matter of his border disputes with Company zemindars. A Gurkha embassy was sent to Burma, either later in 1814 or early the following year, which must have seemed more promising, because Anglo-Burmese relations had been disturbed ever since 1785, when the King of Burma had conquered Arakan and made his territories contiguous to those of the Company; but there is no doubt that, in so far as Amar Singh

---

[8] Sec. Cons., 25 Nov. 1815, no. 24; 16 Mar. 1816, no. 51; 22 June, no. 30; 13 July, no. 17; 27 July, no. 12; 10 Aug., no. 15. See also E. H. Parker's article in *Imperial and Asiatic Quarterly Review*, vol. vii, 1899, p. 178.

322 Interlude

Thapa and the Gurkha durbar were induced to reject the treaty by promises of co-operation, it was the machinations of Sindhia, the Maratha Raja of Gwalior, which were their main source of encouragement. Information obtained by the British in the latter half of 1815 showed that Amar Singh Thapa's expectations of assistance from the Marathas were not entirely fanciful. The British newswriter at the court of Ranjit Singh reported that Sindhia had sent *vakils* to try to persuade the Sikh leader to help the Gurkhas and thus contribute to the success of a grand plan for the conquest of Hindustan; and in September 1815 British informants in Benares reported the passage through the city of a messenger from the Gurkha *vakil* at Gwalior. He was carrying a letter, from Sindhia to the Nepal Raja, which information represented as 'of a nature inimical to the negotiations now pending between the British and the Nepal states, urging the latter to spin out time by negotiation and not to make peace, in which case they would be assisted by the Marathas'.

True, there had been such promises before, which had not been kept; so perhaps the Gurkha nobles did not really have much faith in Sindhia. But even if they did, the receipt of such assurances was probably less the cause than the occasion of the rejection of the treaty. It seems unlikely that a majority in the durbar was reconciled to it. Rudra Vir Shah's attitude had been unequivocal, and no doubt typical. 'He acknowledged', Gardner had written, 'that if the war were prosecuted it might terminate in their ruin; but that the result was in the hands of Providence and that they would stand the hazard of the issue.'

Hastings had therefore accomplished only half his aim of leaving a substantial and conciliated Gurkha state. By merely disfiguring instead of crippling Nepal he had incensed her leaders without making them incapable of retaliation. It had become clear that a greater demonstration of his strength was necessary if the Gurkhas were to appreciate the measure of his leniency. But he had reason to be grateful, at least, that the incompleteness of his policy had been made apparent while there was still time for further measures. The Gurkhas could have lulled him into a false sense of security by ratifying the treaty and then rejecting it at a later opportunity more favourable to themselves, on the ground that it had been extorted under pressure—an expedient at which nations professedly more civilized and sophisticated have not baulked. Pride, fortunately, has many aspects. Stubbornness, ungraciousness and intolerance are among them; but so is honesty. 'Lands transferred under a written agreement cannot again be resumed', Amar Singh Thapa had written in his intercepted letter to the Raja of March 1815.[9] If negotiations for peace collapsed because of his adherence to this principle, at least the collapse contained a promise that peace, once attained, would not be destroyed by guile.

[9] *P.R.N.W.*, p. 554.

XII

THE FINAL CAMPAIGN

HASTINGS saw no reason to change his plans for the main invading division. Captain Casement, who had been in charge of the guides and intelligence department of the main force during the first campaign, had assured him that Marley's instructions, had they been carried out, would have produced success. No new information had come to light which suggested that any of the recommended passes across the foothills was impracticable. The only new idea, adopted at Casement's suggestion, was that one of the columns of the main division should advance from Ramnagarh into the Rapti valley, considerably to the west of Kathmandu, which was reckoned to be 'the interior Tarai of Nepal'. Otherwise Ochterlony's instructions were the same as Marley's: to penetrate the foothills below Kathmandu; to occupy the three forts of Hethaura, Makwanpur and Hariharpur within the first range of hills; and then, if submission was still delayed, to advance into the Nepal Valley and attack the Gurkha capital itself.

It was already very late in the cold season, and only two clear months remained for military operations. In 1814 Francis Hamilton had written to the Political Secretary: 'It cannot be too earnestly recommended that the troops should reach the approaches to Kathmandu by the 1st of December, so that they may have time before the return of the unhealthy season, which often begins by the 1st of April, and usually by mid-May.' If Ochterlony was to remain true to the lessons of his first campaign, he would have to ensure that he always had heavy artillery at hand to dislodge the Nepalis from roosts on ridges and pinnacles. But whereas, in the previous year, he had had six months at his disposal, he now had only slightly more than that number of weeks. His well-tried tactics of slow but sure advance would now be inapplicable. Somehow, he was going to have to combine heavy firing power with exceptional mobility. It was an almost absurd task that he had been set, because the two requirements were obviously incompatible.

Hastings compensated for Ochterlony's lack of time by increasing his division to four brigades—a total of almost 20,000 men—and no fewer than eighty-three pieces of ordnance. The nucleus of the force was composed of men who had served in the eastern divisions during the first campaign; but the additions were drawn, wisely, not from corps tired after serving in the western theatre, but from those which had either remained in the interior during the previous year or recently arrived from Mauritius. No troops had been sent from England in response to the Governor-General's request. Some had been on the point of embarking, but had then been retained because of minatory events in Europe. Hastings had himself rescinded his requisition for troops from the Cape and Mauritius as far back as May, when the situation in India had become less disquieting; but the order had arrived too late to have effect in Mauritius, and troops from the island had disembarked at Calcutta in August 1815. Among them was H.M. 87th, the Prince's Own Irish Regiment of Foot,[1] which was now ordered to the frontier to join Ochterlony's division. Sir David had besides two other King's regiments: the 24th Foot, which had formed part of the main eastern division the previous year, and the 66th Foot,[2] up to strength after the recent arrival of three companies from Ceylon.

But even this force, which was almost equal in size to the original four divisions in combination, did not satisfy Hastings. Determined that prolonged resistance by the Gurkhas must be prevented, he prepared to overwhelm them with a human avalanche. On Ochterlony's left, John Wood, reprieved from threatened supersession by present necessity, remained in charge of the division he had commanded the previous year. Now 5,000 strong, with a small artillery train, this was to complete the occupation of the Tarai north of Gorakhpur, thereby creating a diversion in favour of the principal operations and, if circumstances permitted, to advance to Palpa, Tansing and the provinces immediately west from the Nepal Valley. On Wood's left Jasper Nicolls was to march into Doti, now the most western Gurkha province, with 6,500 men and 20 pieces of ordnance. Edward Gardner was to accompany him and make another attempt to buy the allegiance of the Shah brothers with promises of the independent sovereignty of the territories they administered. Nicolls's advance was to be supplemented by a thrust from Kumaun, organized by Lieutenant-Colonel Adams, to the flank of the enemy positions in the west.

[1] Later 87th Royal Irish Fusiliers.   [2] Later the Royal Berkshire Regiment.

Finally, at the other extremity of the line of operations Barré
Latter, now recovered, was to resume command at Titalia. His
function, as before, was to be essentially defensive; but he planned
to encourage the Sikkimese to renew their siege of Nagri. Altogether, some 35,000 men of the regular army and more than 100
pieces of ordnance would take the field for the second campaign.

It is a wonder that the main division was ever mobilized in time.
The commissariat officer at Dinapur, after having received four
sets of instructions in six months, alternately ordering and counter-
manding the resumption of preparations, can hardly have known
whether he was coming or going. In response to orders of 11
December, all extra field establishments of coolies, bullocks and
carriage cattle had just been discharged again; and now yet a fifth
set of instructions enjoined the immediate recruitment of carriers
and cattle sufficient for an army of 20,000 men and 80 guns. Fortunately, followers had been so recently dismissed that large
numbers of them were still at Dinapur, and by dint of great energy
on his own part and of unstinting co-operation on that of the
Dinapur commissariat and the Magistrate and Collector of neighbouring Patna, Ochterlony was able to send the artillery train
across the Ganges on 13 January. He followed them north, with
H.M. 24th, on the following day. Because the expense would have
been so enormous and because peace had, until very lately, seemed
likely, no pantaloons had been prepared for the sepoys this season,
and only the Europeans were provided with tents. Arrangements
for the comfort of the native troops being so inadequate, it was in
one sense lucky that the worst of the winter was past.

The rendezvous for Ochterlony's division was near Balwi, a
hamlet on the frontier of Saran about six miles from the edge of the
Tarai forest. Troops had been accumulating there since the end of
November, and the normally desolate area had become transformed into a sprawling, teeming shanty town, clamorous with all
the noise and bustle of an Indian military encampment. Both
officers and men were in good spirits. Sickness had declined with
the hot weather and provisions were plentiful. 'As one proof of the
goodness of our fare', wrote Walter Henry, Surgeon to H.M. 66th,
'I may mention that at the mess we had green peas in abundance,
that had been carried in baskets on men's shoulders, all the way
from Dinapur.' The troops were regularly turned out an hour
before dawn and kept under arms until it was light; but the enemy

made no attack, so the days were free to be devoted to the amusements of the camp—the bazaar, the nautch girls, the jugglers, the musicians, the performing bears and monkeys, the wonder-workers and the edifying spectacle of *sadhus* deformed by expiatory contortion. The European officers would take their fowling-pieces and ride out to shoot mallard, teal, widgeon and snipe.

Ochterlony planned to divide his force and cross the foothills (here called the Churia range) at three points. The central column, under his own direction, would comprise the third and fourth brigades, consisting of H.M. 87th and seven and a half battalions of native infantry—about 9,500 men, including the gun lascars and ordnance drivers. This would force the Bichakori pass, which was known to be defended, and advance to take Hethaura and Makwanpur. Thirty miles to the west, Lieutenant-Colonel Nicol, of H.M. 66th, was to lead the second brigade, consisting of his own corps and four native battalions and totalling about 5,000 of all ranks, into the Rapti valley by way of Mahajogi, and then march east to join Ochterlony. Colonel Kelly, in charge of the first brigade, would operate with H.M. 24th Foot and 4,000 natives on a line some thirty-five miles to Ochterlony's right. He was to march up the ravine of the Lakanda nulla, an eastern tributary of the Baghmati, and deal with the fort of Hariharpur.

On 3 February, Ochterlony led the third and fourth brigades forward some six miles to Simra Basa, on the edge of the forest. Here he had a strong stockade constructed, designed as the second heavy artillery depot. At seven o'clock on the morning of the 9th, the column began to move from Simra Basa with four six-pounders and four three-pound mountain guns. Striking north, the advance guard led the way through matutinal mists into the primeval jungle of the Tarai.

It seemed certain that they must meet resistance. No territory lent itself better to defence. Sal and sissu trees of huge girth and height, draped with weird vegetation, utterly still, and receding ever farther like the reflections in facing mirrors, shut out the sunlight, stifled every echo and confused all sense of direction. For nine miles the army crept up the western bank of a dry river channel, encumbered by dense tropical undergrowth. The pioneers often had to clear a passage by chopping and firing, and then the screams of startled parakeets broke the silence; but there was neither sight nor sound of enemy soldiers. The march was twelve miles long, and it was not until late in the afternoon that the vanguard reached Bichakori, a hamlet of about a dozen huts in a clearing under the foothills. Camp was pitched in the dry bed of a nulla, whose channel farther up formed the Bichakori pass. Ochterlony was astonished that he had been allowed to come so far unmolested.

He remained at Bichakori for five days, gathering information about the enemy defences in the pass and seeing to the fortification of a large, square, brick building, which was apparently a caravansary. This he had decided to use as a depot and hospital. The information of scouts and spies concerning the obstacles in the Bichakori pass allowed only one conclusion. Despite all the assurances of the Commander-in-Chief, it was impregnable. Enemy preparations had turned it into a death-trap. But Joshua Pickersgill, now acting Quartermaster, told Sir David that there was an alternative route across the Churia range slightly to the west, which was 'unguarded and practicable, though difficult'. It was a passage well known by smugglers, and seems to have lain about half way between the Bichakori pass and the modern road from Amlekhganj. Satisfied that Pickersgill must know what he was talking about, after spending months surveying the border country, Ochterlony decided to try to penetrate by this passage with the third brigade and then, by attacking the Gurkha defences in the Bichakori pass from the rear, open the main route for the fourth brigade and the heavy guns. He commanded the operation in person and moved from camp when the moon rose, at nine o'clock at night on 14 February. He had two six-pounders, carried by elephants, and 3,000 men. Tents at Bichakori were left standing, and immediately occupied by men of the fourth brigade, in order to conceal the movement.

Ochterlony's detachment followed the dry channel of the Bali river. Where this began climbing into the hills, its banks were steep and rugged, thick with overhanging trees which trailed long tresses of wild ginger. In the deep colourless night, it seemed like the entrance to a cavern. The men moved in files, with the silence of a funeral procession. The only sounds were the thudding of axes, as the pioneers moved trees grown or fallen across the path, and the crashing of a distant cataract. Above, fractured turrets of rock were transformed by the moonlight into mythological sculpture. After five or six miles the path branched off into the ravine of a narrow watercourse, whose bed was hard and flinty. White baboons peered from the foliage, causing hearts to pound; but there was no enemy to be seen. When dawn broke, the men were aching and parched with thirst, but, feeling the brisker air of the mountains, they knew that the march must be almost over.

Almost; but not quite, and the part remaining was ten times more difficult than all the rest. The incline of the path suddenly increased sharply, as the channel of the watercourse began to climb a steep 300-foot cliff-face. For the moment, Ochterlony was sure that they could not continue. Angry and disappointed, he rebuked Pickersgill for having misled him. Pickersgill remonstrated and said that if he thought that, he should go back; but he urged that if the passage was cleared the enemy would be bound to evacuate the Bichakori pass, to escape being attacked from behind. Ochterlony knew that the season was already too far advanced for the campaign to be halted and replanned, and that to postpone it until the following year would involve crippling expense and imponderable political consequences. He therefore wasted no more time by arguing, but took a deep breath and gave the order to move on.

The scree was so steep that the men had to haul themselves up by means of bushes and branches. The Major-General, who had walked every yard of the way to encourage his troops, was helped up by the artillerists, who tied their sashes together to make a life-line. While the main body of the brigade was negotiating this stretch of the pass, the advance moved on in search of water and eventually bivouacked in a small wooded valley near a running stream, about five miles farther north. The last of the rearguard did not join them until nine that night—fully twenty-four hours after leaving Bichakori. By now the men were a sorry sight. Their clothes had been torn to tatters and their toes protruded from lacerated shoes. But nothing could dampen the spirits of the 87th, who were up in the trees and lopping off branches almost as soon as they had arrived. Then they set to work building huts for their officers, themselves, and 'Sir David Maloney'. The bivouac was on a small hill, protected by an arc of outlying pickets. The Major-General and the men remained without tents for four days, until the baggage had been brought through the pass. They were even without food until the morning of the 16th, when the first supplies of liquor and biscuit arrived. Outwardly, Ochterlony remained buoyant and good-humoured; but inwardly he was still numbed by dreadful uncertainty, because even all his previous experience of hauling artillery over mountains could not persuade him that it was possible to bring the elephants and the guns over that last stretch of the pass.

As had so often been the case in his first campaign, it was to the virtuosity of his pioneers that he owed the achievement of the seemingly impossible. Commanded by Captain Baines, they laboured from late on 15 February until early on the 17th, and turned the ascent into a rough flight of steps. First, the hill was cut away and made less steep; then trees were felled, and laid transversely up its whole length. His mahout coaxed the first elephant to try the ascent with a six-pounder strapped to his back; but it was too steep for him to be able to balance with this extra weight. There was a moment of acute suspense as he swayed, trumpeted, and almost toppled over; and there was nothing for it but to remove the gun. Both animals then ascended—slowly, and never taking a step before testing the strength of the tree trunk or projection in front. The guns had to be dragged up by hand, mounted on their carriages. The hill was made, as far as possible, a succession of direct ascents. Next, fox wedges were driven into the bank on either side, and down the centre of the path. Pulleys were attached to the side fixtures, and ropes from each side of the gun carriage passed through them. Working parties then descended, pulling the ropes, and the gun moved upwards for a few yards. As soon as it had reached the level of the pulleys, the machine was made fast by tying its preventer rope to one of the central wedges, and preparations were made to repeat the process higher up. A subaltern of artillery sat astride the gun to direct the operation. In this way both the six-pounders were hauled up the slope, followed on subsequent days by the bullocks and tumbrils with the ammunition and stores.

Describing his manoeuvre in a dispatch, Ochterlony wrote that the assurance he had received that the pass was practicable had been 'founded on an erroneous estimate of our resources, powers, and means'. He added: 'that the movement had been effected is to be ascribed to great good fortune, as well as to the most persevering labour, the greatest exertion, and most persevering fortitude.' It was chillingly obvious that had the enemy learnt of his manoeuvre in time to interrupt it, they could have inflicted an historic extermination. There is no doubt that Ochterlony would never have attempted the manoeuvre had he been aware of the difficulties. It was not in his nature to gamble with catastrophe. For once, he had acted without good information, and had come near to paying dearly for his ignorance.

During the night of 16 February, the enemy detachments in the Bichakori pass learnt that Ochterlony had turned their position, apparently by some magic. Unnerved, they at once withdrew to join the main Nepali force before Makwanpur. When Lieutenant-Colonel Burnet heard of this, early on the morning of the 17th, he had brought the fourth brigade as far as the lower reaches of the Bichakori pass. He now sent forward a party to seize the top.

It was plain that the enemy had placed their greatest faith in the impregnability of this passage. As well as constructing three stockades, each immensely strong, they had heaped rocks and stones on surrounding eminences, ready to be rolled down on the invaders, and had even poisoned the mountain pools, using some toxic plant. Five elephants of Burnet's detachment bellowed and shrieked with agony after drinking, and had to be destroyed. Ochterlony's breathtaking movement, by nullifying all these elaborate precautions, threw the Gurkhas off balance. It was an eventuality for which they were psychologically unprepared, and they never recovered sufficiently to make the most of the advantages they still retained.

Burnet was now delayed for nearly a week, engrossed by the formidable task of bringing the artillery, including two eighteen-pounders from the depot at Simra Basa, through the Bichakori ghat. Ochterlony did not wait for the fourth brigade to join him, but resumed his march to Hethaura as soon as he had learnt on 15 February that the main pass had been secured.

His route lay north eastwards, over open, gently rolling country, intersected by watercourses and powdered with early spring flowers. The march could not be hastened, because the path was narrow and much prickly brushwood had to be cleared away. Slightly to the south of Hethaura the Karara river, a branch of the Rapti, flowing from the east, crossed the route. The buildings of Hethaura could be seen on its northern bank. They consisted of two converted and fortified caravansaries, rather like the one at Bichakori but larger and stronger. The river was forded without difficulty, and the light company of the 87th pushed on to beleaguer the enemy posts. There were soldiers in the buildings, but they offered no resistance, and fled into the forest at the rear on the approach of the British force. Ochterlony remained encamped at

Hethaura for over a week, while one of the caravansaries was converted into a depot, and it was here that Burnet's brigade and the battering train finally caught up with him.

On 25 February, Sir David received a visit from Chandra Sekhar Upadhyaya, who earnestly assured him that the treaty had been ratified, and was now at Makwanpur, in the possession of Bhaktawar Singh, brother of Bhim Sen Thapa. Bhaktawar was ready to surrender it, and was only waiting for the arrival of Gajraj Misr, whom the Raja had summoned from Sagauli. Ochterlony sternly declined to allow his advance to be delayed, and said that he must have the treaty in his own hands before he could enter into discussions and grant an armistice. Secretly, he wished that he was able to believe Chandra Sekhar, because the moment seemed propitious for a lenient peace, and he viewed the prospect of a prolonged campaign with weariness and misgiving. 'Protracted war', he told Headquarters, 'can only produce enormous expense, which the most successful results cannot indemnify, but may as in our western provinces, burden us with territory without revenue, and with troops without resources to maintain them.' But he dared not trust the Gurkhas until he had irrefragable evidence of their sincerity. It could well be that they were temporizing, with a view to halting his operations until the hot weather compelled him to withdraw on their own terms. When he left, the *vakil* said that he would do everything in his power to bring Bhaktawar Singh into the British camp that same day; 'but', remarked the Major-General, 'it seem[ed] impossible to place any dependence even on assurances which seem[ed] dictated by self-interest.'

Nothing more had been heard by the morning of 27 February, when Ochterlony's arrangements at Hethaura were complete, so he ordered camp to be struck. Seven companies of native infantry were posted to guard the depot, and at seven o'clock the rest of the combined third and fourth brigades moved westwards for Makwanpur. The third brigade, under Ochterlony, led the way, while the fourth, with the heavy ordnance, followed. The distance was only about six miles, but there were extensive tracts of woodland to be crossed, in which Ochterlony insisted on probing his way with the utmost circumspection. So it was three o'clock in the afternoon before the first troops arrived before the fort of Makwanpur.

They found themselves in an exquisite valley, which was bisected by the Karara. On the southern bank of the river there were broad green pastures, inclining gradually to the stream. To the north the ground rose more sharply and culminated in a hefty ridge of sandy hills, some 1,500 feet high. It was a different world from the Tarai. Foliage had lost its waxy patina, trees and grasses moved and breathed, partridges and woodcocks flickered through the sunlight, and the water was transparent.

The army encamped in a long line of deserted huts on the northern strand of the river, which were apparently enemy summer quarters. All the Gurkha forces were now concentrated in and about Makwanpur, a fortress in itself unimpressive but situated in a position of great strength. It was on a high and steep hill beyond the eastern extremity of the ridge of cliffs. The main enemy outpost was a small village of about twenty huts, called Sikhar Khatri, which was at the western end of the ridge slightly below the crest. It was connected to Makwanpur by a road which ran eastwards along the crest of the ridge, dropped to cross a considerable indentation and then, at a point about one and a half miles from the village, turned sharply to the north. A large stockade straddled the road about a mile beyond the turning, and the eminence carrying the fort of Makwanpur rose just behind it. West of the hollow, the ridge was bare; but its eastern half was covered with luxuriant deciduous forest.

When day broke the next morning, there was no sign of the enemy colours and troops which had thronged Sikhar Khatri the afternoon before. Ochterlony had not yet formed his plan of action and had reckoned on waiting for the arrival of Colonel Nicol and the second brigade, whom latest dispatches reported to have successfully penetrated to the Rapti valley and to be only two or three days' marching from Makwanpur, before starting operations. But his instinct prompted him to grab the abandoned site. He reckoned that he might be able to turn it to good account subsequently, and thought that in any case it would afford a good view of the enemy's defences. Three companies of sepoys and forty men of the 87th were instantly sent up the ridge to seize the village.

Once they were ensconced among the huts, Captains Tickell and Pickersgill took a small escort and went out to reconnoitre the road along the crest. The party had occupied two more breastworks to the east of the village, and had crossed the hollow and entered the forest beyond, when, at about half-past twelve, a substantial enemy force emerged from the woods below and began to ascend the northern side of the ridge. Their intention was obviously to cut off the reconnoitring party from Sikhar Khatri. Seeing that it was already too late to regain the village, Tickell, Pickersgill and their party made their escape by clambering down the southern flank of the ridge and making for the main camp. Before they had got far, the enemy were swarming on the crest, and eight sepoys were killed and one wounded by a spray of musket shot. The Nepalis then turned their attention to the British in front of the village. They made *khukuri* charges against the two advanced positions, overwhelming them and forcing their inmates back to Sikhar Khatri. Here the troops were rallied by Lieutenant Tirrell, the Adjutant of the Company's Marine Battalion,[3] who, intent on gaining experience of active service, had obtained leave from his corps and arrived in camp only a few days before. The enemy, now seen to be a good thousand strong, surged up to the hamlet from four different directions successively, but each onslaught was repulsed by what one observer called the 'astonishing intrepidity' of the young Lieutenant and his men. Ochterlony, who was watching the engagement from the main camp below, ordered a reinforcement, consisting of a full battalion of native infantry and the light company of the 87th, to speed to Tirrell's assistance; but the path to the village was half a mile long, and very steep and strangled. The men could advance only slowly, and in single file. Tirrell was dead before they could reach him. But the troops of the reinforcement compensated for their tardiness with their fortitude. Imitating the enemy's style of combat, they covered the last stretch of the ascent not in formation, but in an extended line, so that they could take advantage of the irregularities of the ground. Resolutely, they inched their way up to the village, nudging the Nepalis forward almost at point-blank range. But then trumpets pealed in the main stockade, and 2,000 more of the enemy, with several small guns, poured along the crest of the ridge. Realizing that the Gurkha commanders were, for some reason, making a major issue of retaking a post which they had recently spontaneously abandoned, Ochterlony threw a further battalion of sepoys, four more companies of the 87th, and two six-pounders on elephants into the conflict. As this second reinforcement was moving up to the village, under Lieutenant-Colonel Miller, Ochterlony turned out his line and commanded the artillery to play on the enemy troops as they

[3] The 1st Battalion, 20th Regiment of Native Infantry.

advanced along the crest of the ridge. Their commander immediately retaliated by turning his own guns on the British camp. Ochterlony's tent was pitched well within their range, and his flag and the red and white plumes of his and his staff officers' cocked hats were conspicuous targets. The Major-General only narrowly escaped death when a shell exploded near him, killing the servant who was holding his inkpot.

The action was now a battle. Miller determined to try to rout the Nepalis from the village with a bayonet charge. The Europeans of the 87th led, and among them was Ensign John Shipp, an irrepressible Englishman who was one of that rare breed of officers who had won their commissions from the ranks. Soon he was engaged 'hammer and tongs' with Krishna Bahadur Rana, the Gurkha *Suba* who had been responsible for the attacks on Parsa and Samanpur the previous season.

He was a strong, powerful man [wrote Shipp], protected by two shields, one tied round his waist and hanging over his thighs as low as his knees, and the other on the left arm, much larger than the one round his waist . . . He cut as many capers as a French dancing master, till I was quite out of patience with his folly. I did not like to quit my man, so I tried other extremities; but he would not stand still, all I could do. At length I made a feint at his toes, to cut them; down went his shield from his face, to save his legs; up went the edge of my sword smack under his chin, in endeavouring to get away from which he threw his head back, which nearly tumbled off, and down he fell.

The enemy flinched under the impact of the assault, and recoiled beyond the hollow. Miller's men streamed into the village and formed a convex line round its eastern approaches; but the enemy rallied once they had crossed the hollow and formed a corresponding line on its opposite brink, which outflanked the British on either side. Thus deployed, they maintained a stubborn fire and even brought up a gun to the edge of the hollow. Miller thereupon called for his own six-pounders, but an accident had delayed one of the elephants and only one gun was at hand.

It was now late in the afternoon, and Ochterlony realized that Miller must have yet more men if he was to finish the action before sunset. The Nepalis were astonishingly resilient; but they had been fighting without respite for the whole afternoon, and when the 2nd/8th Native Infantry, fresh and unscarred, joined the conflict, the scale was turned decisively against them. Under Major Nation, the 2nd/8th made a bayonet charge along the crest of the ridge, across the hollow and up its eastern slope. Their assault was furious and irresistible. Milling in confusion, the Nepalis blew up their ammunition and threw their advanced gun into the hollow. Then they retreated eastwards along the ridge, to the shelter of their main stockade. They left hundreds behind, strewn all over the ground. In the hollow, their dead and wounded lay in masses, and John Shipp's last impression, before the light failed, was of hacked and bloody bodies in a pit, some squirming, some jerking, and some attempting to rise, and falling back again.

The British casualties were 45 killed, 175 wounded and 2 missing. The enemy were reckoned to have lost 800 killed and wounded. The gun they had abandoned was later recovered from the bushes in the hollow, and was found to be 'of beautiful construction, and equal to our mountain ordnance, being in every point exactly similar'.

The Gurkha effective force now amounted to just over 2,000 men, all of whom were jaded and dejected. Taking account of the detachments made to guard the depots along his line of communication, Ochterlony had some 6,000 fighting men at his disposal, of whom about 2,500 were still untried. His artillery, the arm which had proved decisive in his first campaign, had hardly yet been used; and a couple of days later, on 2 March, Nicol arrived from the west with the second brigade and thirteen pieces of ordnance, consisting of twelve-pounders, six-pounders, mortars, howitzers, and light mountain guns. But for all this, he knew that the odds were not so overwhelmingly against the Gurkhas as appearances suggested. They still held the eastern and strongest part of the ridge, where their main defences were intact; and a powerful and insidious agent was working in their favour among the British ranks—dysentery. It was spreading quickly, and every day Ochterlony became more anxious to end the war and quit the hills.

Spurred on by his commiseration, by that vague distaste which, for all the personal prestige he had gained from it, the war against Nepal never ceased to inspire in him, and by the knowledge that time was running short, the Major-General intensified his efforts to bring the confrontation to a conclusive issue. On 3 March, H.M. 66th Foot, which had arrived with Nicol the day before, a battalion of sepoy grenadiers and four elephants with two field guns were sent to the captured village. From there they advanced along the crest of the ridge, crossed the hollow and pushed forward to a point only about 800 yards from the principal enemy stockade, while all the troops remaining below made a parallel movement along the valley, so as to be able to provide support in the event of an attack. A temporary redoubt was built for the guns, pending the construction of a battery, and a road begun from the camp for the eighteen-pounders.[4]

The same day, Ochterlony received a letter from Bakhtawar Singh. It explained, in the urbane understatements of a practised diplomat, that he had intended to send the ratified treaty on 28 February, but that 'owing to the unexpected occurrence of your troops having ascended the hills, and the conflict that ensued . . . a delay of two or three days was occasioned.' He now requested permission to send Chandra Sekhar to the British camp with the treaty.

The Gurkhas had at last decided to submit—but not solely as a result of their repulse from Sikhar Khatri. The last straw had been news from the east, as yet unknown to Ochterlony, that Kelly, leading the first brigade, had reached Hariharpur, attacked it from the west and compelled the Gurkha garrison of 1,000 men, under Ranjor Singh Thapa, the hero of Jaithak, to flee.

Ochterlony now found himself in a dilemma. Instructions from the Governor-General enjoined him to alter the treaty and insist on the unconditional surrender of the whole of the Tarai 'in the event of a renewal of hostilities unaccompanied by the early submission of the enemy'. Obviously, surrender after a full-scale engagement could not be qualified as 'early'. On the other hand, his own strong wish was for an acceptance of the treaty as it stood. He wanted to forgo the tiresome process of renewed negotiation, which would not only retain his ailing army in the hills, but might, in the event of a fresh collapse, compel it to reduce Makwanpur and even march against Kathmandu. He resolved the problem with a typically imaginative compromise. He received Chandra Sekhar the following afternoon, but at first declined to accept the treaty and roundly harangued him for the 'duplicity, folly, and perfidy' which had

---

[4] Shipp (pp. 204–5) says that a cannonade was begun. Either his memory deceived him, or he was heightening his narrative, because there is no mention of any guns actually having opened in any contemporary account. Generally speaking, his book is enjoyable, but often exaggerated, and occasionally quite fanciful. Eighteen-pounders become twenty-fours; and when describing the enemy casualties (of whom official reports reckoned 128 to have been killed), he says 'eleven hundred were committed to the grave'!

marked every stage of the durbar's conduct. The unfortunate *vakil* wilted before this tirade and made no attempt to defend his government. Almost cringing with contrition, he pleaded the youth and inexperience of the Raja and humbly begged Sir David to be merciful, as became the powerful. Ochterlony, still feigning reluctance, said that he feared the displeasure of the Governor-General, who was determined to inflict condign punishment, and agreed to accept the treaty only if it was accompanied by a written declaration, signed by Chandra Sekhar and Bhaktawar Singh, which registered unconditional acceptance of the stipulated terms and disclaimed all hope of subsequent modification. Eagerly, the *vakil* promised that this should be provided, and hurried away. Work on the road still continued, and Tickell selected a sight for a breaching battery only 500 yards from the principal stockade. Chandra Sekhar returned at about half-past two the next morning, 5 March, when the eighteen-pounders were actually in position before the stockade, and laid the required declaration before the Major-General. Satisfied that, after such an overt signal of humility, the British government could grant the original terms of pacification without losing face, and secretly deeply thankful for that satisfaction, Ochterlony received the copy of the Treaty of Segauli which had been signed by the Raja, and surrendered that ratified by the Governor-General in Council.

So the war with Nepal came to an end. That it had not led to the extirpation of the Gurkha dynasty was due in the last analysis to Ochterlony's integrity and humanity. Had avidity for the fabled treasure of Kathmandu outweighed his desire for a politically expedient peace and his solicitude for the health of his troops, he might, both in perfect consonance with his instructions and with confidence in his own superior strength, have demanded terms so severe that the enemy would almost certainly have rejected them and enabled him to march against their capital. Hastings was out of patience with the Gurkhas and had made it plain that his own preference was the subversion of their government; while the Major-General, following the successes of Nicol and Kelly, had at his command between 12,000 and 14,000 effective men and a formidable array of artillery. In the army, hopes of prize money had been high, and the troops were disgruntled that an early peace had thwarted their expectations; but the temptation of private fortune never seems to have influenced their leader.

When Ochterlony told Chandra Sekhar Upadhyaya that he feared the displeasure of the Governor-General, he had not been bluffing, because he was still not sure that his compromise would satisfy Hastings. 'I am in a terrible fright lest Lord [Hastings] should be angry', he wrote to Metcalfe a few days after the conclusion of peace; 'but new negotiations, with the necessary cessation of hostility, were in my mind worse than the acceptance of the old, ready cut and dry.' However, he need not have worried. The Governor-General was grateful that his initiative had made extreme lengths of chastisement unnecessary and in his relief he even indulged a little humour at the expense of George Wood, then recuperating from jungle fever (*awl*): 'Ochterlony has done admirably', he wrote to Jasper Nicolls. 'I fear Sir George Wood will die of the owl when he hears to what profit less time than he had at his disposal has been turned!'

So swift and incisive had been Ochterlony's advance, that the separate divisions under John Wood, Jasper Nicolls and Colonel Adams had hardly begun to move at the time of the Gurkhas' capitulation. Only in the extreme east had there been time for any collateral operations, where the Raja of Sikkim and his generals had again acted as enterprising and plucky allies. They had even sent troops beyond the Mechi river and occupied the abandoned Gurkha posts at Ilam and Phae Phae. Latter had invited the Gurkha *Suba* of Nagri, Genti Khatri, to desert to the British. Peace had been made before his answer was received; but it was an answer which made it clear that he would never have contemplated such a step.

Ochterlony emerged from the war in a blaze of glory. He was fêted and toasted all over India. In December 1816, he joined the few Company officers who had been created baronets and became the first among them to receive the Grand Cross of the Order of the Bath. When bestowing these decorations, Hastings told him that Company officers had now at last come into their own: 'You have obliterated a distinction painful for the officers of the Honorable Company, and you have opened the door for your brother officers in arms to a reward which their recent display of exalted spirit and invincible intrepidity proves could not be more deservedly extended to the officers of any army on earth.'[5]

This proved an accurate prognosis, because Company officers were thereafter decorated by the Crown with fair frequency. But

[5] *East India Military Calendar*, i, p. 368.

their merits, however outstanding, never became sufficient to secure them the reward of promotion. When he died, nine years later, Ochterlony was still only a major-general.

Nevertheless, he had become a legend in the Bengal army, and for years afterwards hill chiefs and sepoys alike spoke fondly and in wonder of 'Loney Ackty' and his eighteen-pounders. In his last years, he discharged the combined functions of Resident in Delhi, Malwa and Rajputana, and many tales were told of his wealth, his princely hospitality, his harem and his vast entourage. He became a last lingering example of the old 'nabobs' of the East India Company, whose mode of existence was a happy compromise between oriental and western styles and who exercised an almost viceregal authority. Before his death, opinion was already running strongly against such licence, and Amherst, who became Governor-General in 1823, was not so prepared as Hastings had been to let Ochterlony have his own way. The old Major-General quarrelled bitterly with the new authorities in Calcutta and soon resigned with his pride irreparably injured. He died in 1825—of a broken heart, according to his friends.

These last nine years were perhaps Ochterlony's most conspicuous, but it is doubtful that they were his best. If he has a place in the pantheon of the early heroes of British India, it is less because of his achievements in peacetime than because of his leadership in war. As an administrator, he lacked the breadth of vision and the penetration which emotional and scholastic commitment to India gave men like Malcolm, Munro, Metcalfe and Mountstuart Elphinstone. He moved among the Sikhs and the Rajputs for many years, but no romantic imagination was ever stirred, no intellectual curiosity awakened. In spirit, he remained a conscientious and upright European civil servant, seeking only the applause of his seniors in Calcutta as the final authentication of the worthiness of his opinions and conduct. He was unable to draw sustenance from deep personal convictions and weather the storm of official castigation in a determination to earn the approbation of a higher tribunal. Ochterlony came to despise Tod, who was his Assistant in Rajputana, precisely because of the latter's emotional involvement with the Rajput past and his apparent indifference to the esteem of his superiors.

Cunningham, in his *History of the Sikhs*, indirectly criticized Ochterlony for his shortcomings as a provincial governor, but he also acknowledged his merits as a soldier. 'Sir David Ochterlony', he wrote, 'will long live in the memory of the people of northern India as one of the greatest of the conquering English chiefs; and he was among the very last of the British leaders who endeared himself both to the army which followed him and to the princes who bowed before the colossal power of his race.'

That is no shameful epitaph.

PART III

EPILOGUE

FOR a few anxious months, it seemed that the victory over Nepal was going to cost a serious confrontation with China. Late in May, Shee Chan Choon, the Emperor's special envoy, arrived in Lhasa with his army. He sent a letter, by way of Sikkim, to Captain Latter, explaining that he had come to investigate the situation in the Himalayas and would shortly arrive at Tingri, a pass on the Nepal–Tibet border. The agent of the Sikkim Raja told Latter that his army was commanded by five generals and amounted to between 12,000 and 16,000 men. 'You can safely assure His Lordship', wrote Latter to the Political Secretary, 'that the Chinese vizir is an officer of high rank, and that the army which is under him has actually come from China.' At about the same time, the envoy informed Bhim Sen Thapa of his arrival and required a deputation of senior Gurkha officials to wait on him. The Prime Minister replied that the Gurkhas had been forced to submit to the English, who had deprived them of all their old provinces, and that an agent was being sent to explain at greater length. 'Pacify and talk smoothly to the Raja Lama,[1] the Shee Chan Choon and the Ambans', he instructed his agent, 'to draw down their compassion and favour on us, and return with suitable answers.'

Such was the situation when Edward Gardner arrived in Kathmandu as British Resident, at the end of June. He soon learned how matters stood, both from his spies and from Chandra Sekhar and Gajraj Misr, who acted as go-betweens for himself and the durbar. From these last two he received news of the death of Amar Singh Thapa at Nilkanth, a shrine five days' journey north of the capital, where, they hinted, he had been engaged in negotiations with the Chinese. Gardner did not doubt the substance of their intelligence, but suspected, probably with reason, that they

---

[1] i.e. the Dalai Lama?

were exaggerating the Chinese menace in order to alarm the British and induce them to relax the terms of the treaty.

But then affairs suddenly began to look critical. The durbar received a note from its agent at Tingri, stating that the Chinese envoy had left Lhasa and marched south to Digarché and advising that *vakils* and presents be sent to him at once. Shaken to find that the Chinese were apparently sincere, the Gurkhas abandoned all ruses. Gajraj Misr and Chandra Sekhar implored Gardner to advise them, and begged to know what the attitude of the British government would be in the event of hostilities. The Resident, realizing that their apprehension was real, became very uneasy himself.

Early in December, the durbar received further news that some Imperial troops had advanced to the Kirong pass, by which the Chinese had invaded Nepal in 1792. Shee Chan Choon had remained at Digarché at the instance of the Lama and officers of Tibet, but would not hesitate to move forward if the expected deputies did not quickly arrive. In desperation, the Gurkhas sent three senior *Bharadars* to the envoy, with instructions to reiterate Nepal's allegiance to the Emperor and to inculpate the British as aggressors.

The Calcutta government was determined to avoid a rupture with China at all costs. A detailed explanation of British policy was sent to Lhasa through Sikkim and Gardner was instructed to adopt an attitude of strict neutrality. He was to withdraw to India immediately if hostilities ensued. The view in Calcutta was that the Residency was not worth the resentment of China and that even the extension of Imperial hegemony over Nepal, while regrettable, would not be sufficient to justify a quarrel with Peking.

Fortunately, the cloud passed. The Chinese envoy received the Governor-General's explanations shortly before the arrival of the Gurkha deputation, and professed himself completely satisfied. His mind at rest, he would, he replied, duly forgive the Nepalese Raja for his transgressions. The Gurkha deputation was received at Digarché, and treated with great indignity. But that was as far as the envoy's chastisement went. The *Bharadars* returned to Kathmandu humiliated, but unscathed and much relieved.

On receiving the Governor-General's assurances, Shee Chan Choon remanded his troops to China; but the matter did not quite end there. The Gurkha representations and the establishment of the British Residency in Kathmandu had combined to engender a lingering mistrust in the envoy's mind, and he politely requested that the Residency be withdrawn. Calcutta expostulated, pointing out that some restraining influence over the Gurkhas was necessary, and agreed to recall its own agent only if the Chinese sent a replacement. The reply was that it was not the custom of the Imperial court to depute ambassadors, and with that the incident was closed. The Chinese had maintained a temperate, if haughty, tone throughout; but their sensitivity concerning their interests in Tibet had been sufficiently obvious to cause the British to make their own presence in the Himalayas as inconspicuous as possible for the time being.

The business of implementing the Treaty of Segauli was impeded by evasion and chicanery on the part of the Gurkhas. Gajraj Misr, still secretly convinced that the British would be prepared to sacrifice important acquisitions in return for an influence in the Kathmandu durbar, had assured the Prime Minister that if he was reinstated as Raj Guru he would be able to secure retrocession of the Tarai and abolition of the Residency. Bhim Sen thereupon reinvested him with his old office and had the Raja inform Lieutenant Boileau, Acting Resident pending Gardner's arrival, that the durbar now confidently awaited the indulgences promised by Colonel Bradshaw. The truth was, of course, that Gajraj Misr's was now a correct calculation of the ulterior concern of the Governor-General who, although rather reluctant to forgo the Residency, still intended to exchange the stipulated pensions for extensive tracts of the Tarai in order to ensure the goodwill of the durbar. Gardner was obliged, as a matter of principle, to secure strict adherence to the letter of the treaty before he broached this subject; but he was enjoined to proceed with 'the utmost conciliatory and temperate . . . tone of conduct . . . and the greatest care to avoid everything capable of being misinterpreted to the disadvantage of the British Government or [hazarding] the interruption of the growth of that confidence which it is the hope of the Governor-General in Council will arise between the two governments after the irritations arising from past events shall be allayed'. Pleading various excuses, the Gurkhas delayed evacuation of the lowlands for some weeks; but finally, seeing that Gardner was adamant and also, it seems, receiving a warning from their *vakil* at Gwalior that no help could now be expected from

Sindhia, they ordered their troops to be withdrawn and negotiations concerning the demarcation of a permanent frontier began.

By December, a settlement had been made. The British government surrendered, in commutation of the pensions, the whole of the occupied Tarai between the Kosi in the east and the Rapti in the west, with the exception only of areas which had been the subjects of dispute before the war. The Tarai west of the Rapti was retained to be made over to the Nawab of Oudh in extinction of half his loan. The new boundary was then surveyed and marked with pillars of masonry.

The Treaty of Segauli set Nepal firmly apart from the native states of whom the British demanded tribute, feudal obligations and abstention from foreign relationships in return for protection. The only permanent liability with which Nepal was encumbered, apart from amity with the British and the acceptance of their Resident, was forbearance to employ Europeans.[2] The British, for their part, undertook to protect the Gurkha dynasty neither from external nor from internal aggression. This meant that the position of the Resident in Kathmandu was fundamentally different from that of Residents elsewhere, whose obligations to uphold native governments drew them increasingly into the sort of political interference which they were, paradoxically, required to eschew. He was, in fact, an ambassador, whose professed impartiality was not liable to redound to the existing government's advantage. Thus was Nepal defined as a sovereign state outside India—a status which she still retains.

It did not always seem that that status would survive. Hastings's hope for a cordial relationship with Nepal was not immediately realized. The death of Guru Gajraj Misr, while on an embassy to the Governor-General in 1817, removed a salutary influence from the durbar and for many years thereafter intrigues in Kathmandu remained a cause of constant concern at Calcutta. While Nepal escaped the anomalies which caused the collapse of the subsidiary system and the annexation of Indian states, it was not spared the sort of scrutiny which fears inspired by Russian ambitions caused British statesmen to bestow on states beyond the Indus; and for some time in the 1830s and 1840s it seemed that Nepal must fall a victim to the same policy which led to the expedition to Afghanistan and the annexation of Sind and the Punjab. It was not until the

[2] Nepal was not bound to abstain from foreign relationships until 1839.

two rival parties, the Panres and the Thapas, had finally destroyed each other in a gory political struggle, which lasted for a decade from the fall of Bhim Sen Thapa in 1837, that a firm tradition of Anglo-Nepalese alliance was established. Only then did a minister emerge, called Jung Bahadur Rana, who abandoned imperial ambitions and made friendship with the British the keystone of his policy.

Although Hastings forsook the style of treaty dear to Wellesley when dealing with the truncated state of Nepal, his settlement of the hill states from which the Gurkhas had been expelled bore the clear imprint of Wellesley's influence. The Governor-General's policy was 'to restore the ancient chiefs in all cases in which special reasons did not exist against it', and then afford them protection in return for feudatory obligations—such as submission to the Company's arbitration of disputes, the furnishing of troops when requisitioned and the provision of a free passage for merchants. These principles were applied to Sikkim, whose Raja was restored to all his old hill territories east of the Mechi river, and to all the hill states west of the Kali river except Kumaun, which remained annexed to the Bengal Presidency. Hastings's extreme reluctance to burden the Company with direct responsibility for remote hill territories made him unwilling to disqualify any chieftain, and in the event not even the Thakurs of Bhagat and Kionthal, two of the Twelve Lords who had refused to renounce their allegiance to Amar Singh Thapa, were completely excluded from the benefits of his scheme, though the greater part of their patrimonies was sold to the lowland Sikh Raja of Patiala. In cases of escheat, it was planned to transfer the lapsed estates to neighbouring chieftains.[3] Some reinstated sovereigns were required to cede small portions of territory, which the British wished to retain either for strategic reasons or as payment for subsidiary forces. Thus Malaun, in Hindur, and Subathu, in Kionthal, were both kept as British fortresses. The restored Raja of Sirmur, infant son of Karman Prakash, was compelled to cede Kayarda Dun and accommodate British garrisons in Jaithak and Nahan; and the Raja of Garhwal was deprived of Dehra Dun and all lands east of the Alaknanda river.[4] Hyder Hearsey was

---

[3] The only territory of any note involved was the thakuri of Pandur, which was transferred to Kionthal.

[4] William Fraser was made Commissioner for the Settlement of Garhwal. His function was the same as that of Residents at native courts on the plains—guidance without excessive interference.

naturally vexed on discovering the government's intention to annex Dehra Dun. Flourishing his title deeds, he pushed himself forward as zemindar and proprietor and proposed that he farm the revenues. He based his claim on the principle that 'a king or raja expelled by force loses no rights or pretensions', which was absurd and which the government justifiably rejected. As far as it was concerned, the Garhwal heir had sold to Hearsey something which he no longer possessed.

It was intended that political relations with Bhutan should cease after the war, and the native agent sent by the Magistrate of Rangpur was recalled. But demarcation squabbles and border raids kept the two governments quarrelling for many years, until in 1865 a war was undertaken against Bhutan in circumstances similar to those which had led to the invasion of Nepal half a century before.

The annexations in the western Himalayas were justified by Hastings on strategic and economic grounds; but their greatest significance in the history of British India was to pertain to neither of these considerations. In a letter to Jasper Nicolls, dated Almora, April 1816, Captain Raper wrote: 'I think in the course of a year or two . . . this place will become a fashionable resort in the hot weather.' He thereby prophesied a phenomenon which ultimately transformed the whole of the social life of the British in India. Recognizing the value of the place as a sanatorium, the government had before long built special hospital bungalows in the vicinity of Almora, and the hill station was thus born. Obscure mountain hamlets near the battlefields of the Nepal War became, within the space of a quarter of a century, as well known as Calcutta, Delhi, Bombay and Madras. Such were the village of Mussoorie, only a few miles north-west of the spot where Gillespie fell in 1814; the spa called Naini Tal in Kumaun; and the hamlet of Simla, in the mountains just north of the scene of Ochterlony's final combat with Amar Singh Thapa in 1815. When Lord Amherst moved to Simla for the hot weather in 1827, he began a custom that soon transformed it into the bustling summer capital which Kipling immortalized in *Plain Tales from the Hills*. The contribution which the hill stations made to the consolidation of British rule in India must have been considerable. By providing such a respite from the devastating climate of the plains as had hitherto been obtainable only from a voyage home, they made India more accessible to

Europeans than it had ever been before and helped make European family life possible.

The hill stations were a legacy of the Nepal War which the British retained until they left India, 130 years later. Another legacy of that war they did not relinquish even then, and have still. This is the 2nd, King Edward VII's Own, Gurkha Rifles—a regiment raised in 1815 as the Sirmur Battalion.

By the time the war in the west ended, in 1815, about 4,650 soldiers of the Gurkha army had deserted and sought service with the Company in response to the invitations of the British commanders. It was the Governor's-General intention to group these men into provincial battalions: some for the occupation of the acquired hill territories, and some for the use of the restored mountain chiefs. The available soldiers in Nahan and Hindur greatly exceeded the estimated need; so, as Hastings was anxious to honour the pledge of employment which all the deserters had been given, he was compelled to reject Ochterlony's plan for a single regiment of two battalions and order the embodiment of three battalions, each consisting of eight companies of 120 privates. They were denominated the 1st and 2nd Nasiri Battalions and the Sirmur Battalion. A similar corps was organized in Kumaun and called the Kumaun Battalion. To each was attached a European commandant and adjutant, and the monthly pay of each private was five and a half rupees less off-reckonings. The uniform of the four corps was to be 'clove green jacket without facings, red cuffs, collar and trimmings.'[5] The value of these new battalions was quickly made apparent. The regular sepoys detested the climate of the hills, and it was not long before sickness and desertion were seriously depleting the ranks of those in Kumaun. At first, the Governor-General was not disposed to humour this dislike, because in his view, 'it would not . . . be wise or politic . . . to unaccustom the native troops altogether to hill service.' But by the middle of 1816, he had relaxed this attitude and found it expedient to replace a part of the regular infantry stationed in Kumaun by the 2nd Nasiri Battalion.

---

[5] The strength of each battalion was to be allowed to diminish to 100 privates per company, by the effect of retirement and casualties. The 2nd Nasiri Battalion was absorbed into the 1st in 1829, and the corps became the 66th Native Infantry in 1850, when the name 'Nasiri' was given to another, non-Gurkha, battalion.

It should be noted that these four corps were originally modelled on the pre-war provincial battalions (see above, p. 96), but in contemporary correspondence the designations 'provincial' and 'local' seem to be used interchangeably.

The 'Gurkhas' have become legendary by virtue of their service with the British, but it was in fact a long time before the British made use of them. Successive Commanders-in-Chief in India recognized the potential worth of the hill corps, but fear of offending the high-caste sepoys, parsimony and prejudice against short men long operated to prevent their being brought into the regular army, while distaste for the idea of employing mercenaries precluded their being replenished or supplemented with bodies of recruits from Nepal proper. The Sikhs were far more enterprising than the Company in this regard. Ranjit Singh had followed the progress of the war with close interest, and the resistance offered by the Gurkha army to the British convinced him of the importance of skilled infantry. Almost as soon as hostilities were over he had Shiva Dat Rai (Amar Singh Thapa's old mentor—now a refugee in Sikh territories) send an agent across the Sutlaj, who was to try to entice the men of the 2nd Nasiri Battalion to forsake the Company's service for his own. This particular design was unsuccessful, despite his offer of high pay; but Nepali mercenaries did enter his army in increasing numbers as time went on. They even included Bal Bahadur Singh, the hero of Kalanga. To this day, the Nepali word for mercenary is *lahuré* (one who goes to Lahore). Most hill corps in the Company's service had to make do with inferior status and the same miserable pay for fifty years. It was only in 1861, after they had shown steadfastness during the Mutiny of 1857, that the hill corps (save the Nasiri Battalion, made regular in 1850) were finally brought into the line and that the prejudice against mercenaries from among the tribes of Nepal was abandoned. Now called Gurkha regiments, the original number had been increased to ten by 1947, of whom four, including the Sirmur Battalion under its modern title, remained with the British Army. The others became part of the Army of the Republic of India.

Hastings did not receive many thanks for his victory over the Gurkhas, because he had influential detractors in the Court of Directors. The Court was required by the Board of Control to approve his dealings with Nepal in principle, but its Chairman, Charles Grant, a venerable figure with immense experience of Indian affairs, was too implacable an opponent of Hastings's martial pretensions to neglect to find some way of deploring the scale of the war. Under his guidance, the Court resumed its favourite theme and complained of the enormous expense involved, which it attributed to the Governor-General's elaborate strategy. A second campaign might have been avoided, it insisted, had the British force not been divided into so many small columns initially.

This was a common criticism, and it almost certainly originated with Nugent, who had arrived back in England still harbouring his grudge, and ready to support Edmonstone's lamentations about expense with on-the-spot recrimination. Hastings had no difficulty in confuting the Court, because the war had, in fact, been conducted with remarkable economy. The expenditure incurred during the first campaigns had been scarcely more than a third of the original estimate, considerably less than the charges involved in either of the campaigns of 1803–4 and 1804–5, and less than a third of the expense of any former war in India for a corresponding length of time. In any case, the total cost of the war, which was roughly estimated at six and a half million rupees,[6] was more than covered by the half of the Oudh loan which was to be liquidated with acquired territory.

The Court was obliged to modify its attitude. It conceded that the arrangements for the final campaign had been 'very judicious, both in a military and in a political point of view' and expressed its satisfaction at the economies which the commissariat had realized. But no real gratitude lay behind its formal phrases. Besides the intense distaste of men like Grant for all acquisitive enterprises, there was a general apprehension in London lest Hastings's policy should embroil the Company with China—if not directly, then in the long run, by making the British territories contiguous to those of China in an area where the frontier was almost bound to be a cause of altercation.

While the Directors were eager to expatiate on the ruinous expenses created by the war, they were by no means ready to adopt those measures which it had plainly indicated would lead to long-term economies. Still paralysed by a petty cash mentality, they remained incapable of balancing immediate sacrifices against the prospect of ultimate gain. Hence, although they recognized that the commissariat had saved considerable expense, they refused to allow that department to profit by its recent experiences and perfect its organization. Hastings warned that 'satisfactorily as the duties were

[6] See Appendix A to the copy of Hastings' *Summary* printed in the volume of *Papers Respecting a Reform in the Administration of the Government of his Excellency the Nawab Vizier* (1824).

fulfilled, the machine was evidently too feeble.' He continued: 'the individuals whom I temporarily lent to the commissariat, though deserving of applause for zeal and activity, were avowedly ignorant of details, and might have been found deficient had the enemy been skilful enough to comprehend the consequence of intercepting convoys.' He therefore proposed increasing the permanent staff of the commissariat by five officers, making a total of twenty-four. The Directors refused to sanction the increase, and complained that they saw no reason why it had ever been necessary to add to the original staff of eight. Fearful lest such augmentations should lead to understaffing in the regiments, they commanded that 'the utmost attention be paid to confining the number of officers employed on the commissariat both in peace and war, within the narrowest practicable limits.' At the same time, they prescribed measures designed to stifle the department's independence. Normally, all applications for government funds in Bengal had to be screened by the Military Board. This was a committee of the seven senior staff officers of the Bengal army, to whose 'unbiassed opinions' the Court professed itself 'accustomed to look with confidence in all cases of military expense', but which, in the opinion of a later Governor-General, Dalhousie, 'managed everything and marred everything', It had been intended in Calcutta that the Commissary-General's operations should be facilitated by allowing him to submit his applications for money through the Military Auditor-General; and it had been reckoned that, as his own department would therefore not be liable to the scrutiny of the Board, he might, in recognition of the importance of his office, be given a seat on that body. But the Directors objected. They did not understand the commissariat to be independent of the Board at all. Not only did they take exception to his having a seat on that body; they furthermore instructed that he was to have no official status whatever. In 1817, they directed first that the Military Board make an annual report on the commissariat's accounts, and then that the Commissary-General be made directly subordinate to the Board, through which he was thenceforth to submit all his applications for funds. The consequence of all this jealous restriction was that the commissariat never became capable of fulfilling its functions. In 1824, Sir Edward Paget, the new Commander-in-Chief, complained, very much as Horsford had done ten years before, that 'the efficiency of the army would be destroyed were the troops taught to depend on the commissariat for the carriage of their private baggage.'[7]

It was the branch of the army concerned with guides and intelligence whose reputation had been ruined by the war. Instances of its inefficiency were manifold and almost every calamity of the war was caused in some measure by its failings. Treacherous guides had taken Gillespie's columns astray at Kalanga and led John Wood into a trap. No guide had been provided for the party with Richards's spare ammunition on 26 December 1814, and no messengers had been posted along his route. Inaccurate intelligence had upset Martindell, confused Marley, terrified the frontier magistrates, caused Hastings to pronounce negotiable a pass that was in fact a death trap, and led Ochterlony into a defile from which he had emerged only by miraculous good luck. Again, the basic mischief was stinginess. An army gets only the intelligence it pays for. The King's army had recognized this and set up a special fund called secret service money, and general officers were allowed to account for its disbursement on oath, without divulging the names of informants. In India, there was no separate intelligence organization. Securing information and guides was a function of the Quartermaster-General's department, which was allowed so little money for the purpose that no useful spy could be induced to sell his services. During the war in the Carnatic in 1780, when a man, at the risk of his life, had brought Sir Hector Munro information concerning the position of Colonel Baillie's detachment, Sir Hector had given him sixteen shillings. The situation was still much the same sixty-six years later, when one Bengal officer complained: 'In India, you can . . . easily get intelligence if you pay well; but no man will risk his life for 16 shillings . . . It is probable that for every rupee we save by low payments, we lose hundreds or thousands of rupees and many valuable lives.'[8]

With regard to the size of the army, even the Directors were compelled to admit than an increase was necessary; but, concerned above all else with immediate economy, they allowed only 'the establishment of provincial corps to a certain limited extent', and the formation of 'some local corps in the hilly districts lately acquired from Nepal'. They sanctioned the augmentation proposed

---

[7] Quoted by Barat, *Bengal Native Infantry*, p. 203.

[8] *The Englishman*, 30 Oct. 1846. The (anonymous) author was Major William Hough.

by Hastings for the corps of irregular horse only on the condition that no additions were made to the regular cavalry. His three extra regiments of regular infantry they regarded merely as temporary expedients for the emergency of the Nepal War. 'We therefore trust that no impediment will arise to their being disbanded at an early period.' Their wish was never acted on, because war with the Marathas and their Pindari henchmen had broken out before the dispatch reached India; but from then on the use of *ad hoc* local and provincial bodies of troops as cut-price substitutes for new regular battalions became well established. The army grew mainly by means of them, and within a decade there were something like thirty battalions of irregular infantry and eight regiments of irregular cavalry in Bengal.

This method of augmenting the military establishment had one grave disadvantage: it made the shortage of European officers even more acute, because each irregular corps required between two and eight officers of the line. The experience of the Nepal War, combined with the effects of this new drain on the army's contingent of regimental officers, led critics to press for an increase in their number, and in 1825 the Calcutta government made a formal request to that effect. But the Court had no intention of nullifying the economies realized in one sector by increasing expenditure in another. It insisted that any deficiency in the number of regimental officers was caused only by the indiscriminate allotment of military men to political functions, and it stubbornly refused, until the very end of its existence, to authorize any significant increase.

War is bound to expose weaknesses in any military organization; but the dismissal, for professional ineptitude, of three out of the four Company major-generals employed in the invasion of Nepal indicated nothing less than the fatal deficiency of the Company's method of promotion. Yet no attempt was ever subsequently made to remedy even the worst abuses of the seniority system by making retirement compulsory or financially enticing, or both, at a suitable age. Until the Mutiny of 1857 there remained 'brigadiers of seventy, colonels of sixty, and captains of fifty'—to say nothing of generals of eighty-five, like Marley. Lord Roberts wrote in his memoirs:

It is curious to note how nearly every military officer who held a command or a high position on the staff in Bengal when the Mutiny broke out, disappeared from the scene within the first few weeks, and was never heard of officially again. Some were killed, some died of disease, but the great majority failed completely to fulfil the duties of the positions they held, and were consequently considered unfit for further employment. Two Generals of divisions were removed from their commands, seven Brigadiers were found wanting in the hour of need, and out of the seventy-three regiments of Regular Cavalry and Infantry which mutinied, only four commanding officers were given other commands, younger officers being selected to arise and command the new regiments.[9]

It was not only that seniority promotion made responsible officers old and tired; it also completely divorced rank from merit and made the whole military hierarchy ridiculous. By the time he died, Ochterlony had been superseded in rank by both the officers (Martindell and George Wood) whom he had been appointed to replace in the war of 1814-16.

Other lessons of the war were disregarded because of a callous concern to preserve vested interests. Perturbed to hear of the part which the sepoys' cartridge boxes had played in the defeat of Lawtie's detachment on 26 November 1814, Hastings and the Military Board turned their attention to improving the design of this article and requested the Court to send no more from England. The Directors made no reply to this communication, but, eighteen months later, informed the Calcutta government that they had been disturbed by a private report concerning an engagement in the late war, in which 'a party of infantry were cut off under a Captain Williams . . . owing to the cartridges sticking in the pouch boxes'. They had, they explained solicituously, 'deemed the rumour to be of sufficient importance to enquire whether any such incident did occur and, if so, the grounds from which it appeared to proceed'. Would it be preferable, they wondered, to send tin cartridge boxes in future? 'This article of military store has at different times led to much discussion and engrossed much more of the time of our survey department than any other.' In reply, Calcutta patiently reiterated its wish that all such consignments from England be stopped. 'This article of military equipment . . . can at all times be prepared here at trifling expense, of a quality equal to those sent from Europe . . . We understand that a cartridge box on an improved plan, particularly calculated for the service and climate of India, has been prepared by the commissariat and approved by His

9 *Forty-One Years in India*, i, p. 436.

Excellency the Commander-in-Chief.' But the Court had no intention of transferring any of its contracts for military stores from England to India and, Calcutta having intimated that the substitution of tin for wood would not solve the problem, it simply continued to send boxes of the old type. They were still in use twenty years later, when a writer in *The East India United Services Journal*[10] complained: 'The "office men" by whom these things have been regulated continue to issue these worse than useless, because dangerous equipments.' He stated that they had become so disreputable, that the sepoys in action at the final siege of Bharatpur in 1826 had carried their cartridges loose in their pouches. All the boxes had been left in a pile under the protection of a sentry, to be replaced when the fighting was over.[11]

Circumstances made it easy for the Court to be remiss towards its armies. It was very difficult for the Directors to share the sense of urgency which caused men on the scene to place such importance on efficiency in their military arrangements. Most had never been to India, and they formed their policies in the remote calm of East India House, with its solid furniture and imperturbable clocks, from the evidence of long copperplate dispatches and complacent newspaper reports that had taken five or six months to arrive. In such an atmosphere private ideals, mania for economy and fear of strengthening the hands of the Company's critics by infractions of the spirit of Pitt's India Act were bound to get more attention than the local realities of Indian politics. Even the memory of the American experience was insufficient to awaken the Directors to the possibility of their Indian possessions being lost. It is noteworthy that even Hastings, a soldier who had been directly involved in the struggle to retain the American colonies, had, earlier in his career, been as ready as anyone to condemn the military pretensions of Indian statesmen. It was only when he arrived in India that his views changed and he became the most martial of them all. But news of the worst calamities of the Nepal War still failed to trouble the Court's equanimity. 'The only objects which, *in our situation of*

[10] Vol. iii, Aug. 1834.
[11] Military Letter to Bengal, 22 Mar. 1816; Military Letter from Bengal, 27 Sept. 1816, para. 125; Mil. Cons., 13 Sept. 1816, nos. 41, 42; anecdotes entitled 'From my Notebook': *E.I.U.S.J.*, vol. iii, Aug. 1834, p. 91. By 1846 the design had been changed to 'a tin with three divisions, to contain ten rounds each, and a wooden former to rest on the tin, to contain twenty-six rounds more': *The Englishman*, 30 Sept. 1846.

pre-eminent power maintained by most expensive establishments, could render a war proper with the poor and mountainous country of Nepal, were the preservation of our honour and the integrity of our territories',[12] it pronounced with unshakeable self-assurance, at the end of 1815. Yet it was, in fact, precisely the lack of pre-eminent power which that war had by then served to demonstrate. Although members of the government in India argued whether pre-eminence was necessary, none of them ever pretended that it actually existed. They were too close to the evidence to delude themselves so far. The Bengal army had proved itself so inadequate, in one way and another, for the type of war it was fighting, that other frontiers had had to be denuded in order to reinforce it and urgent recourse had to other colonies for extra British troops. When success was finally achieved, every nerve was strained and every resource exploited. There was no power in reserve, because Europe was again in ferment and no troops could be spared from home. Had the Sikhs and the Marathas, or either, joined their strength to that of the Gurkhas, it is hardly debatable that the British would have been expelled from northern India.

The reality was not, then, a pre-eminence of power; and in so far as there was a balance of power, it was a fortuitous one, maintained by political events outside British control. The British victory against Nepal was not the ineluctable, predetermined consequence of British might. It was not achieved by the crude appurtenances of power—by numbers, wealth, weapons and superior military organization—alone; but by these plus good luck and the extraordinary ingenuity, dynamism, devotion and courage of a handful of European officers. An anonymous civilian[13] who accompanied Ochterlony on both his campaigns reckoned that the officers had been the saviours of the army. 'The General owed the execution of his designs entirely to the unyielding resolution and ability of the officers, qualities which were auspiciously manifested when they had to keep their ground or throw up fortifications in the face of a victorious enemy.'

He ascribed the unsteadiness of the sepoys to fundamental defects in the native character. They had no notion of disinterested honour and were deficient in mental energy. He drew the inference that more European officers were essential, as the only source

[12] *P.R.N.W.*, p. 548. My italics.
[13] Author of *Military Sketches of the Goorkha War*.

whence they could imbibe such qualities. This is, of course, an unsound diagnosis. It was afterwards estimated, by a reliable judge,[14] that in addition to sustaining some 3,000 battle casualties, the Bengal army had lost about 2,000 men as a result of sickness and desertion during the Nepal War. This indicates that lack of training for such a novel type of warfare and the demoralizing influence of inadequate clothing, sanitation, equipment, shelter and what Hastings himself called the 'constant, harassing and unmilitary duties imposed on them even in times of peace', were the real causes of their infirmity. The presence of British officers was not, therefore, a panacea for the army's ills; but there is no doubt that the example of the best of them was still of immense importance as a palliative.

To modern eyes, these officers seem half unreal, archaic figures. This is bound to be so, because theirs is a lost experience and theirs were ambitions and principles that have lost their power to inspire. Wars are no longer fought without maps, scientific medicine, knowledge of hygiene, specially adapted clothing and food, organized intelligence, radio and aircraft, on peripheries of the known world; and few honest soldiers now see the battlefield as a source of honour and glory. These terrible stresses and these old-fashioned ideas played havoc, no doubt, with weak personalities; but in the best officers they seem to have stimulated qualities whose value is eternal. These men became sublimely brave, and capable at once of the leadership that makes men devoted and the chivalry that gives even war nobility.

The Nepal War marks the beginning of the final stage in the history of the Bengal army. It was a stage marked on the one hand by the struggle to rationalize the army's internal structure, and on the other by its increasing involvement in difficult and distant operations. The Nepal War, which was the first 'frontier' war in the history of British India and thus a foretaste of the sort of service which the sepoys would increasingly have to undergo, served to demonstrate the sort of leader which that army now required. But it also served to demonstrate that such was not the sort of leader that the system was geared to produce. The most successful commanders in the war—Ochterlony, Nicolls, and William Gardner— were not products of the East India Company's system of military promotion. Ochterlony was a junior general officer who would never

---

[14] Major William Hough, writing in *The Englishman*, 27 Oct. 1846.

have had an independent command had it not been for Gillespie's unexpected death; Nicolls was a King's officer; and Gardner was a freelance. It was the least successful commanders who had owed their advancement to the system.

This inchoate army never resolved its problems. Each step in the process of rationalization was more painful, until finally the attempt to introduce the Enfield rifle with a new type of cartridge led to the disastrous mutiny of 1857. Journeys to distant theatres of war, the inevitable consequence of the extension of British dominion, became causes of unrest and rebellion. These ills could not be controlled and contained, because, as the need for it increased, so the palliative of good leadership grew weaker. At regimental level, officers tended to get fewer, less able and, because of changing social conditions in India, increasingly out of touch with the men. The holders of high command continued to be enfeebled by age and mental exhaustion. The causes of the destruction of the Bengal army in 1857 are manifold and complex; but its essential precondition was undoubtedly the destruction of that army's best asset— the European officers whose claim to authority rested less on the mechanical workings of a promotion system or on any sense of racial superiority than on real ability and an unconscious but exemplary achievement in the field of racial partnership. The names of these men have been forgotten, and their graves are often untraceable; but they did exist, and it is fitting that they be summoned from the shadows.

APPENDIX 1

TREATY of PEACE between the HONOURABLE EAST INDIA COMPANY AND MAHA RAJAH BIRKRAM SAH, Rajah of Nipal, settled between LIEUTENANT-COLONEL BRADSHAW on the part of the HONOURABLE COMPANY, in virtue of the full powers vested in him by HIS EXCELLENCY the RIGHT HONOURABLE FRANCIS, EARL of MOIRA, KNIGHT of the MOST NOBLE ORDER of the GARTER, one of HIS MAJESTY's MOST HON-OURABLE PRIVY COUNCIL, appointed by the Court of Directors of the said Honourable Company to direct and control all the affairs in the East Indies, and by SREE GOOROO GUJRAJ MISSER and CHUNDER SEEKUR OPEDEEA on the part of MAHA RAJAH GIRMAUN JODE BIKRAM SAH BAHAUDER, SHUMSHEER JUNG, in virtue of the powers to that effect vested in them by the said Rajah of Nipal,—2nd December 1815.

Whereas war has arisen between the Honourable East India Company and the Rajah of Nipal, and whereas the parties are mutually disposed to restore the relations of peace and amity which, previously to the occurrence of the late differences, had long subsisted between the two States, the following terms of peace have been agreed upon:—

ARTICLE 1st.

There shall be perpetual peace and friendship between the Honourable East India Company and the Rajah of Nipal.

ARTICLE 2nd.

The Rajah of Nipal renounces all claim to the lands which were the subject of discussion between the two States before the war; and acknowledges the right of the Honourable Company to the sovereignty of those lands.

ARTICLE 3rd.

The Rajah of Nipal hereby cedes to the Honourable the East India Company in perpetuity all the undermentioned territories, viz.—

First.—The whole of the low lands between the Rivers Kali and Rapti.

Secondly.—The whole of the low lands (with the exception of Boot-wul Khass) lying between the Rapti and the Gunduck.

Thirdly.—The whole of the low lands between the Gunduck and Coosah, in which the authority of the British Government has been introduced, or is in actual course of introduction.

Fourthly.—All the low lands between the Rivers Mitchee and the Teestah.

Fifthly.—All the territories within the hills eastward of the River Mitchee including the fort and lands of Nagree and the Pass of Nagarcote leading from Morung into the hills, together with the territory lying between that Pass and Nagree. The aforesaid territory shall be evacuated by the Gurkha troops within forty days from this date.

ARTICLE 4th.

With a view to indemnify the Chiefs and Barahdars of the State of Nipal, whose interests will suffer by the alienation of the lands ceded by the foregoing Article, the British Government agrees to settle pensions to the aggregate amount of two lakhs of rupees per annum on such Chiefs as may be selected by the Rajah of Nipal, and in the proportions which the Rajah may fix. As soon as the selection is made, Sunnuds shall be granted under the seal and signature of the Governor-General for the pensions respectively.

ARTICLE 5th.

The Rajah of Nipal renounces for himself, his heirs, and successors, all claim to or connexion with the countries lying to the west of the River Kali and engages never to have any concern with those countries or the the inhabitants thereof.

ARTICLE 6th.

The Rajah of Nipal engages never to molest or disturb the Rajah of Sikkim in the possession of his territories; but agrees, if any difference shall arise between the State of Nipal and the Rajah of Sikkim, or the subjects of either, that such differences shall be referred to the arbitration of the British Government by which award the Rajah of Nipal engages to abide.

ARTICLE 7th.

The Rajah of Nipal hereby engages never to take or retain in his service any British subject, nor the subject of any European or American State, without the consent of the British Government.

ARTICLE 8th.

In order to secure and improve the relations of amity and peace hereby established between the two States, it is agreed that accredited Ministers from each shall reside at the Court of the other.

ARTICLE 9th.

This treaty, consisting of nine Articles, shall be ratified by the Rajah of Nipal within fifteen days from this date, and the ratification shall be delivered to Lieutenant-Colonel Bradshaw, who engages to obtain and deliver the ratification of the Governor-General within twenty days, or sooner, if practicable.

Done at Segowlee, on the 2nd day of December 1815.

PARIS BRADSHAW, Lt.-Col., P.A.

Received this treaty from Chunder Seekur Opedeea, Agent on the part of the Rajah of Nipal, in the valley of Muckwaunpoor, at half-past two o'clock p.m. on the 4th of March 1816, and delivered to him the Counterpart Treaty on behalf of the British Government.

DD. OCHTERLONY,
Agent, Governor-General.

APPENDIX 2

In 1814 the East-India Company's Bengal army was composed of:

Corps		Total all ranks	
European	Engineers	31*	
	Horse Artillery	312	
	3 battalions of Foot Artillery	1,761	
	1 regiment of European Infantry	1,103[1]	
	Total European contingent		3,207
Native	1 battalion of Native Foot Artillery (*Golandaz*)	952	
	45 Companies of Gun Lascars	2,975	
	8 regiments of Native Cavalry	4,512	
	27 Regiments of Native Infantry (including the Marine Regiment)	52,880*	
	Pioneers	728	
	Miners	131	
	Ordnance Drivers	2,860*	
	Total native army		65,038
	Grand Total	68,245	

The figures are those given in Gov. Gen. to Vice-Pres., 9 Feb. 1815: Secret Consultations, 21 March 1815, No. 1., para. 88, except those marked*, which are taken from the General Abstract Return of H.M. and the Hon. Company's European and Native Troops Serving under the Presidency of Fort William, 13 Jan. 1812: Nugent MSS, ff. 108–9. These figures have been used where Hastings's estimate takes account of increases made for the purpose of the Nepal War. The above therefore represents the peace establishment of the regular army in 1814. The Pioneers and Miners were in fact a single corps, having been designated since 1808 as the Corps of Pioneers or Sappers. Supplementary bodies, counted as part of the Bengal military establishment but not liable for general service, were the Governor-General's Bodyguard and the Residency escorts at Hyderabad, Poona, Berar and Gwalior.

[1] This appears to be an underestimate. Cf. below, p. 92.

The irregular corps were as follows:

Ramgarh Local Battalion	989*
Hill Rangers	354*
Skinner's Horse	1,000
Gardner's Horse	1,000 (approx.)
Delhi Najibs	1,000 (approx.)
Calcutta Native Militia	1,824
6 Provincial Battalions	6,481
European Invalids	31c
Native Invalids	1,732
Total	14,690

Figures are taken from Gov. Gen. to Vice-Pres., 9 Feb. 1815: loc. cit., para 88, except those marked* which are taken from Nugent's Return, Nugent MSS., ff. 108–9 (in the case of corps increased by Hastings for the Nepal War) and that for Gardner's Horse, which is unaccountably omitted in Hastings's list.

King's and Company's Troops:
(a) In 1786 the total (to nearest half-thousand) of the Company's regular troops in Bengal and Madras was — 70,000 ⎫
The total of King's troops — ⎬ ratio 13:1
in same was — 5,500 ⎭
(Source: Ross, *Cornwallis Correspondence*, vol. i, p. 329)

(b) In 1811–14 the total of regular troops in Madras was — 77,500
(Source: *Mins. of Ev.*, 1832, Sec. 5, p. 194).
The total of King's forces in same was — 12,000
(Source: Nugent MSS., f. 25)
Therefore total Company troops in same was — 65,000 — 65,000
Total Company regular troops in Bengal — 68,000

Therefore, total Company
regular troops in Bengal
and Madras was   133,000 ⎤
Total King's troops   ⎬ ratio 8:1
in same   17,000 ⎦
(Source: Nugent MSS.,
f. 25).

APPENDIX 3

A Note on Official Sources

Hastings was away from Calcutta, on an official tour of the upper provinces, during the first phase of the war; but, desiring to supervise the campaigns and their concomitant diplomacy personally, he had correspondence concerning the war conducted from his itinerant Headquarters. This meant that much correspondence received by the Vice-President in Council,[1] at Fort William, for the Records, consisted of duplicates of dispatches received and sent by the Secretary to Government in the Secret Department (John Adam) and the Adjutant-General (George Fagan), both of whom accompanied Hastings in his dual capacity of Governor-General and Commander-in-Chief.

Sometimes duplicates of dispatches sent to Headquarters were directed to Calcutta, for the information of the Vice-President, by their authors; on other occasions, however, the latter made no duplicate, but left the copying to the clerks at Headquarters. Letters therefore arrived in Calcutta from two sources: from Headquarters, in which case they would be in batches with a covering letter; and from the individual authors, when they came in singly. In Calcutta, they were recorded on the appropriate set of Consultations, in the order of receipt. Letters sent to Headquarters were for the information either of the Governor-General, in which case they were addressed to the Secretary in the Secret Department, or of the Commander-in-Chief, when they were addressed to the Adjutant-General. In the first weeks of the war, these two officials sent their duplicates separately to Fort William, where the Governor-General's correspondence was recorded on the *Secret Consultations*, and the Commander-in-Chief's on the *Military Consultations*. Once operations were actually under weigh, dispatches concerning them, which as a matter of form were always addressed to the Adjutant-General, for the information of the Commander-in-Chief, naturally became of great concern to the Governor-General as well. Therefore, it was the custom for the Adjutant-General, as soon as he had received a dispatch from the field, to send a copy of it to the Secretary in the Secret

---

[1] The Vice-Presidency in Council was an office which existed only during the periods of a Governor-General's absence from the seat of government in Calcutta. During the period of Hastings's tour of the Upper Provinces it was filled first by Nugent and then, after Nugent's departure in December 1814, by Edmonstone.

Department for the information of the Governor-General. It was then left to the Secretary to send a further copy to the Vice-President in Council at Fort William. The result of this system was that most of the duplicates of dispatches from the field arriving in Calcutta came from the Secretary in the Secret Department, and were accordingly entered on the *Secret Consultations*.

The practice of conducting correspondence from Headquarters worked well for most aspects of the war, because Headquarters were nearer the scene of operations than Calcutta. For other areas, however— e.g. the north-east border—Headquarters were too distant, and dispatches were accordingly addressed to the Acting Secretary to Government in the Secret Department, or to the Acting Adjutant-General, in Calcutta, for the information of the Vice-President in Council; then a duplicate of each dispatch, and of the reply to it, were sent to Headquarters. In these cases, the Vice-President in Council issued instructions according to his discretion, pending advice from Headquarters. These original dispatches, and copies of their replies, were entered on the *Secret Consultations*; and copies of dispatches addressed to other secretaries were also entered there, so that a reasonably comprehensive view of operations and diplomacy was to be found on one set of records.

Once the Governor-General had returned to Calcutta, this separate direction by the Vice-President ceased, and all dispatches were addressed for the information either of the Commander-in-Chief or of the Governor-General in Council. Important correspondence continued to find its way into the *Secret Consultations*, because the Governor-General in Council continued to be informed of the Commander-in-Chief's dispatches in the way described above.

Duplicates of all Bengal records were sent regularly to London, and copies of most of the correspondence relating to the Nepal War are to be found on the *Secret Consultations* and the *Military Consultations* in the records section of the India Office.

During the period of Hastings's tour, official letters giving a general account of the war were sent both by the Vice-President in Council, and by the Governor-General, to the Court of Directors in London. At first, letters from the Vice-President in Council were classified either as 'Political' (open letters addressed to the general court and relating to military events), or as 'Secret' (addressed to the Secret Committee of the Court, and dealing with diplomacy). Later, this division was abandoned, and Secret Letters, beginning with that of 21 June 1815, contained both military and diplomatic intelligence. This practice was continued after Hastings's return to Fort William, and letters concerning the war, whether from the Governor-General or the Governor-General in Council, continued to be addressed to the Secret Committee.

These letters from Bengal nearly always contained numbered enclosures, which were copies of dispatches recorded on the various series of Consultations, selected with a view to illustrating the observations in the main letter. Sometimes the letter was no more than a few lines, accompanying a large number of enclosures selected and arranged to give a narrative of events by themselves. This was generally the nature of letters from the Vice-President in Council and from the Governor-General in Council. Letters from the Governor-General, on the other hand, tended to be much longer. Hastings's Secret Letter of 2 August 1815, for example, has 322 paragraphs, and contains no enclosures.[2]

When they arrived in London, these letters were included either in the series of records called *Political Letters from Bengal*, or in that called *Secret Letters from Bengal*, according to their classification. Any enclosures, however, were scattered, and recorded in various places. The enclosures to the Governor-General's Secret Letters were sometimes bound with the letters themselves; enclosures to other Secret Letters were included in the series *Enclosures to Secret Letters from Bengal*; and yet others went into the *Home Miscellaneous* series.

All open dispatches sent to India required the separate approval of the Board of Control (in the case of secret dispatches this was automatic because they were drafted in consultation with the President of the Board). When the Directors sent the first draft of an open dispatch to the Board for its approval, it was accompanied by copies of the correspondence on record which had given rise to the letter. These copies comprised a *Board's Collection*. Enclosures to Political Letters concerning the Nepal War therefore often found their way into *Board's Collections*.

When it is recalled that sets of all Consultations were automatically sent to London, it will be appreciated that it is not impossible, or indeed unusual, in the case of secret correspondence, for copies of the same document to be found in four different places in the London records, viz: with a letter from the Governor-General in *Secret Letters from Bengal*; in *Enclosures to Secret Despatches from Bengal*; in *Home Miscellaneous*; and in *Secret Consultations*. In addition, the inefficiency of the clerical departments in Calcutta sometimes resulted in two or even three enclosures to a letter being copies of the same document. Political enclosures can usually be found in the series *Board's Collections*, as well as on the *Political Consultations*.

The volume of printed documents called *Papers Respecting the Nepaul War*, published by order of the Court of Proprietors in 1824, contains (with many mistranscriptions) letters sent to and from London between

---

[2] Dalhousie's famous 'monster' Minute on Oudh of 1855 (75 paragraphs) is tiny in comparison.

27 December 1814, and 6 August 1816. The enclosures to the Governor-General's letters from the upper provinces are given complete; but this is not the case with letters from the Vice-President in Council and the Governor-General in Council. Those that are printed follow the haphazard sequence of volumes 643 to 656 of the *Home Miscellaneous* series—but there are extensive omissions. Volume 649, containing enclosures to the Political Dispatch of 20 February 1814, is not included. Nor are volumes 651 to 654, which contain many of the enclosures to the Secret Letter of 21 June 1815; and selections only from volumes 655 and 656 are given.

This printed volume therefore needs to be supplemented from the manuscript records. The unprinted parts of the *Home Miscellaneous* volumes mentioned above fill some gaps; but many of the 400 enclosures of the Secret Letter of 21 June 1815 (making, with sub-enclosures, some 1,500 letters) still remain unaccounted for. More of them are to be found in volumes 5 to 9 of *Enclosures to Secret Despatches from Bengal*; and where the enclosures themselves are untraceable, recourse has to be had to the *Secret Consultations*. Fortunately, it is possible to discover which letters constituted the missing enclosures from the list given in the printed volume. All extra correspondence relating to the war which was not transmitted to London in the form of enclosures is to be found on the *Secret Consultations* and the *Military Consultations*.

In one case, the text of a letter (as opposed to enclosures) has been bowdlerized in the printed volume. Paragraphs 263–7 of Hastings's Secret Letter of 2 August 1815, which relate to Marley's misconduct and removal, have been omitted. Documents relating to this affair have also been removed from the series *Enclosures to Secret Despatches from Bengal*. The full account is to be found only in the MS. version of Hastings's letter, in *Secret Letters from Bengal*, and on the *Secret Consultations*.

BIBLIOGRAPHY

I. MANUSCRIPT SOURCES

(a) *India Office Records: Commonwealth Office, Orbit House, Black-friars Road, London*

Secret Letters from Bengal.

Military Letters from Bengal.

Military Letters to Bengal.

Enclosures to Secret Despatches from Bengal.

Bengal Secret and Political Consultations.

Bengal Political Consultations.

Bengal Military Consultations.

Home Miscellaneous Records.

Personal Records.

Maps and Plans.

(b) *India Office Library Manuscripts, Commonwealth Office, Orbit House, Blackfriars Road, London*

The Raffles Collection: MSS./EUR/C/34.

Special Military Collections: L/Mil/5/391.

The Papers of Lt.-Col. John Lewis Stuart: MSS./EUR/D/668.

Letters to John Adam and Charles Ricketts: MSS./EUR/D/585.

The Moorcroft Papers: MSS./EUR/F/38.

The Stubbs Papers: MSS./MISC/348/MR.

MS. History of Sikkim, compiled by Their Highnesses the Maharaja Sir Thutob Namgyal and Maharani Yeshay Dolma of Sikkim in 1908: MSS./EUR/E/78.

'Regimental Histories of the Indian Army': a bibliography by M. A. Myers, 1957: MSS./EUR/C/142.

(c) *Library of the Royal United Services Institution, Whitehall, London*

The Correspondence of Sir George Nugent: MM/181, and folder marked 'Maps and Plans'.

(d) *The University Library, Cambridge*

The Ludlow Papers: MSS. AD 7450/1 and AD 7450/2.

(e) *Public Records Office, Chancery Lane, London*
Private Out-Letters of the Commander-in-Chief: MSS./WO/3/610.

(f) *National Army Museum, Camberley, Surrey*
The Papers of Sir Jasper Nicolls (unclassified).

(g) *Regimental Museum of the King's Shropshire Light Infantry, Copthorne Barracks, Shrewsbury*
Transcriptions by W. Rogerson of the private journals of Captain Henry Sherwood and Captain Charles Chepmell.

(h) *Library of the Royal Artillery Institution, Woolwich, London, S.E.*
'Memoirs on Artillery, Referring to the Present Establishment of that Arm in the Bengal Presidency', by Major-General Sir John Horsford, K.C.B., 1801 and 1816: Ms./15.

(i) *Library of the Royal Army Medical College, Millbank, London*
MS. notebook entitled 'Remarks and Observations on the Health of Troops and Meteorological Observations', among the papers of John Francis Smet, Surgeon to H.M. 8th Dragoons.

(j) *National Archives of India, Janpath, New Delhi*
Bengal Annual Military Statement, 1813/1814, 1814/1815: 2861/68/R.

2. OFFICIAL PUBLICATIONS

Papers Respecting the Nepaul War, Printed for the Court of Proprietors of the East India Company: London, 1824.

C. U. AITCHISON, *A Collection of Treaties, Engagements and Sanads Relating to India and Neighbouring Countries*, volume XIV, revised edition: Calcutta, 1929.

Political Missions to Bootan: Bengal Secretariat Office, Calcutta, 1865.

Minutes of Evidence taken before the Committee of the Whole House and the Select Committee on the Affairs of the East India Company: ordered by the House of Commons to be printed, 1813.

IIIrd and IVth *Reports* from the Select Committee of the House of Commons on the Affairs of the East India Company (1811–12).

Minutes of Evidence taken before the Select Committee of the House of Commons on the Affairs of the East India Company . . . 1832: Printed by order of the Court of Directors, 1833.

Report on East India Affairs from the Select Committee of the House of Commons, 1832.

The Marquis of Hastings' Summary of the Operations in India, with their

Results, from the 30 April 1814 to the 31 January 1823: General Appendix 11 to the *1832 Report*.

Events at the Court of Ranjit Singh 1810–1817: Punjab Government Records Office Monograph no. 17, edited by G. T. Garret: Lahore, 1939.

Selections from the Punjab Government Records, Volume 2 (*Records of the Ludhiana Agency, 1808–1815*): Lahore, 1911.

Army Lists

Selections from the Records of the Government of Bengal, vol. xxvii: Calcutta, 1857 (articles by B. H. Hodgson, entitled 'On the Aborigines of the Sub-Himalayas'; 'On the Origin and Classification of the Military Tribes of Nepal'; 'The Route from Kathmandu to Darjeeling'; 'Letter to the Political Secretary to Government . . . 1831'; 'The Trade of Nepal'; 'On the Law and Legal Practise of Nepal'.)

The Panjab States Gazetteer, vol. viii (*The Simla Hill States*): Punjab Government Press, Lahore, 1911.

The East India Register, for 1814 (Second Edition).

Historical Papers Relating to Kumaun, 1809–1842, edited by B. P. Saksena: Government Record Office, Allahabad, 1956.

A List of Inscriptions on Christian Tombs or Monuments in the Punjab, North West Frontier Province, Kashmir, and Afghanistan, compiled by Miles Irving: Punjab Government Press, Lahore, 1910.

Biographical Notices of Military Officers and Others Mentioned in Inscriptions on Tombs and Monuments in the Punjab, North West Frontier Province, Kashmir and Afghanistan, by G. W. De Rhé-Philippe: Punjab Government Press, Lahore, 1912.

3. PERIODICAL AND NEWSPAPER ARTICLES

CARDEW, F. G., 'Major-General Sir David Ochterlony, Bart., G.C.B., 1758–1825', *Journal of the Society for Army Historical Research*, vol. 10: London, 1931.

CARNATICUS (pseud.), 'A General View of Our Indian Army', *Asiatic Journal and Monthly Register*, vol. xi, no. 65: London, May 1821.

CHATTERJI, N., 'Lord Hastings, Colonel Baillie, and the Oudh Loans', *Journal of the Uttar Pradesh Historical Society*, vol. i, part 1: Lucknow.

HAMILTON, W. G., 'Ochterlony's Campaign in the Western Hills', *Journal of the United Services Institute of India*, vol. xli, no. 187: April 1912.

——, 'Some further Notes on Ochterlony's Campaign', ibid., no. 189: Oct. 1912.

——, 'The Campaign in Kumaun', ibid., vol. xxxii, no. 153: Oct. 1903.

HOUGH, MAJOR WILLIAM, series of articles (published anonymously) on the history of the Bengal army in *The Englishman and Military Chronicle*: Calcutta, Sept.–Oct., 1846.

HEARSEY, H. (Ed.), 'The Journal of Gholaum Hyder Khan', *Asiatic Journal and Monthly Register*, vol. xviii, part 1: London, 1835.

IMBAULT-HUART, CAMILLE, 'Histoire de la Conquête du Nepal par les Chinois, 1792; Traduit du Chinois . . .', *Journal Asiatique*, 7e série, vol. xii: Paris, 1878.

LAMB, ALISTAIR, 'Tibet in Anglo-Chinese Relations, 1767–1842, Part 1', *Journal of the Royal Asiatic Society*, Parts 3 & 4: London, 1957.

——, 'Tibet in Anglo-Chinese Relations, Part 2', ibid., Parts 1 & 2: London, 1958.

MACDOON SHARPSHOOTER (pseud.), 'Some Account of the 15th . . . Bengal Native Infantry', *East India United Services Journal and Military Magazine*, vol. iii: Calcutta, 1834.

MAJUMDAR, D. N., 'Some Aspects of the Cultural Life of the Khasa of the Cis-Himalayan Region', *Journal of the Royal Asiatic Society of Bengal* (Letters), vol. vi: Calcutta, Nov. 1944.

MOORCROFT, W., 'A Journey to Lake Manasarova in Undes, a Province of Little Tibet', *Asiatic Researches*, vol. xii: Calcutta, 1816.

NICOLLS, JASPER, Letter to the Editor, *Asiatic Journal and Monthly Register*, vol. xviii, part 1: London, 1835.

NOEL, E., 'The Marquis of Hastings and the Nipal War of 1814–1816', *United Services Magazine*: London, Mar. 1913.

PARKER, E. H., 'Nepal and China', *Imperial Asiatic and Quarterly Review*, 3rd Series, vol. vii: London, 1899.

PARRY (pseud.), Letter to the Editor, *East India United Services Journal*, vol. viii: Calcutta, Apr. 1936.

RAPER, CAPTAIN F. V., 'Narrative of a Survey for the Purpose of Discovering the Source of the River Ganges', *Asiatick Researches*, vol. xi, Calcutta, 1810.

SARKAR, S. C., 'Some Notes on the Intercourse of Bengal with the Northern Countries in the Second Half of the Eighteenth Century', *Proceedings of the Indian Historical Records Commission*, vol. xiii: Calcutta, Dec. 1930.

TRAILL, G. W., 'A Statistical Sketch of Kumaun', *Asiatic Researches*, vol. xvi: Calcutta, 1828.

——, 'A Statistical Report on the Bhotia Mehals of Kumaun', ibid., vol. xvii: Calcutta, 1832.

Miscellaneous news items and reports in:

Asiatic Journal and Monthly Register, vols. i & ii: London, 1816.

Calcutta Monthly Journal, vols. xxv-xxviii: Calcutta, Dec. 1814–Apr. 1816.

Calcutta Review, vol. xii: Calcutta, 1849.

East India United Services Journal, vols. iii & viii: Calcutta, 1834 and 1836.

Gentleman's Magazine: London, Mar. 1817.

4. OTHER WORKS

ANON., *Military Sketches of the Goorkha War in India in the Years 1814, 1815 and 1816*: London, 1824.

ANON., *Memoir of Sir R. R. Gillespie*: London, 1816.

ANON., *Sketches of India, Written by an Officer for Fireside Travellers at Home*, second edition: London, 1824.

ASPINALL, A. (Ed.), *The Letters of King George IV, 1812–1830*: Cambridge, 1938.

ATKINSON, C. T., *Regimental History of the South Wales Borderers, 1689–1937*: Cambridge, 1937.

ATKINSON, EDWIN T., *The Himalayan Districts of the North West Provinces of India*: Allahabad, 1884.

AUBER, PETER, *Analysis of the Constitution of the East India Company*: London, 1826.

BADENACH, WALTER, *An Inquiry into the State of the Indian Army*: London, 1826.

BARAT, AMIYA, *The Bengal Native Infantry, Its Organization and Discipline 1796–1852*: Calcutta, 1962.

BASHAM, A. L., *The Wonder that was India*: London, 1954.

BASTIN, J. (Ed.), *The Journal of Thomas Otho Travers, 1813–1820*: Singapore, 1960.

BOULGER, DEMETRIUS CHARLES, *The Life of Sir Stamford Raffles*: London, 1897.

BUTE, THE MARCHIONESS OF (Ed.), *The Private Journal of the Marquis of Hastings*, London, 1858.

CAMMAN, SCHUYLER, *Trade through the Himalayas*: Princeton, 1951.

CAMPBELL, GEORGE, *Modern India: A Sketch of the System of Civil Government*: London, 1852.

CANNON, RICHARD, *Historical Record of the 53rd or Shropshire Regiment of Foot*: London, 1849.

——, *Historical Record of the 8th or King's Royal Irish Regiment of Hussars*: London, 1837.

CARDEW, F. G., *A Sketch of the Services of the Bengal Native Army*, revised edition: Calcutta, 1903.

CAREY, W. H., *The Good Old Days of Honorable John Company*: Calcutta, 1906.

CHAUDHURI, K. C., *Anglo-Nepalese Relations from the Earliest Times of the British Rule in India till the Gurkha War*: Calcutta, 1960.

CLARK, T. W., *Introduction to Nepali*: Cambridge, 1963.

COMPTON, HERBERT, *A Particular Account of the European Military Adventurers of Hindustan*: London, 1892.

COOMARASWAMY, ANANDA K., *The Arts and Crafts of India and Ceylon* (reprint): New York, 1964.

CRAWFORD, D. G., *A History of the Indian Medical Service*: London, 1913.

CUNNINGHAM, J. D., *History of the Sikhs*, Indian reprint: Delhi, 1955.

DESGODINS, C. H., *Le Thibet, d'Après la Correspondance des Missionaires*, deuxième édition: Paris, 1885.

Dictionary of National Biography.

The East India Military Calendar, London, 1823.

EMBREE, AINSLEE, *Charles Grant and British Rule in India*: London, 1962.

FORTESCUE, J. W., *A History of the British Army*, vol. XI: London, 1930.

FRASER, J. B., *Journal of a Tour through Part of the Snowy Range of the Himala Mountains and to the Sources of the Rivers Jumna and Ganges*: London, 1820.

——, *Military Memoir of Lieutenant-Colonel James Skinner*: London, 1851.

GLEIG, G. R., *Memoirs of the Life of the Right Honorable Warren Hastings*: London, 1841.

GORER, GEOFFREY, *Himalayan Village, an Account of the Lepchas of Sikkim*, 2nd edition: London, 1967.

GREENBERG, MICHAEL, *British Trade and the Opening of China, 1800–1842*: Cambridge, 1951.

GREY, C., and GARRETT, G. T., *European Adventurers of North India*: Lahore, 1929.

HADOW JENKINS, L., *General Frederick Young*: London, 1923.

HAMILTON, C. J., *The Trade Relations between England and India*: Calcutta, 1919.

HAMILTON, FRANCIS BUCHANAN, *An Account of the Kingdom of Nepaul and of the Territories annexed to this Dominion by the House of Gurkha*: Edinburgh, 1819.

HAMILTON, WALTER, *Gazetteer of Hindustan and the Adjacent Countries*, second edition: London, 1820.

HART, LIDDELL, *The Ghost of Napoleon*: London, 1933.

HARVEY DARTON, F. J. (Ed.), *The Life and Times of Mrs Sherwood*: London, n.d.

HEBER, R., *Narrative of a Journey through the Upper Provinces of India*: fourth edition: London, 1829.

HENRY, WALTER, *Events of a Military Life*, second edition: London, 1843.

HODSON, V. C. P., *A List of the Officers of the Bengal Army, 1758–1834*: London, 1927–46.

HOUGH WILLIAM, *The Practice of Courts Martial and other Military Courts*: Calcutta, 1834.

——, *Political and Military Events in British India from the Year 1756 to 1849*: London, 1853.

HUC, E., *Souvenirs d'un Voyage dans la Tartarie, le Tibet, et la Chine, Pendant les Années 1844, 1845, et 1846*: Paris, 1850.

HUTCHISON, J., and VOGEL, J. PH., *History of the Panjab Hill States*: Lahore, 1933.

ILBERT, COURTENAY, *The Government of India*, second edition: Oxford, 1907.

JACKSON, MAJOR DONOVAN, *India's Army*: London, 1940.

JNAVALI, SURYA VIKRAM, *Amar Singh Thapa 1748–1816*: Darjeeling, Samvat 2000.

KAYE, J. W., *The Life and Correspondence of Charles, Lord Metcalfe*: London, 1854.

——, *Selections from the Papers of Lord Metcalfe*: London, 1855.

——, *Lives of Indian Officers*: London, 1867.

——, *A History of the Sepoy War in India*, seventh edition: London, 1875.

KELLY, SOPHIA, *The Life of Mrs Sherwood*: London, 1854.

KINCAID, DENNIS, *British Social Life in India: 1608–1937*: London, 1938.

KIRKPATRICK, W., *An Account of the Kingdom of Nepaul*: London, 1811.

LANDON, PERCIVAL, *Nepal*: London, 1928.

LAWRENCE, H. M., *Essays Military and Political, Written in India*: London, 1859.

LEE-WARNER, SIR WILLIAM, *The Life of the Marquis of Dalhousie*: London, 1904.

LEVI, SYLVAIN, *Le Népal: Etude Historique d'un Royaume Hindou*: Paris, 1905–7.

LI, TIEH-TSENG, *Tibet, Today and Yesterday*: New York, 1960.

LORRAINE PETRE, F., *The Royal Berkshire Regiment*: Reading, 1925.

LOW, C. R., *Life and Correspondence of Field Marshall Sir George Pollock*: London, 1873.

MACKENZIE, ALEXANDER, *The History of the Frasers of Lovat*: Inverness, 1894.

MALCOLM, SIR JOHN, *Political History of India*: London, 1826.

MARKHAM, C. R. (Ed.), *Narratives of the Mission of George Bogle to Tibet and of the Journey of Thomas Manning to Lhassa*: London, 1876.

MARON, STANLEY, ROSE, LEO, et al., *A Survey of Nepal Society*: Human Relations area Files, South Asia Project, University of California, 1956.

MARSHALL, P. J., *Problems of Empire: Britain and India 1757–1813*: London, 1968.

MARTIN, SIR J. RANALD, *The Sanitary History of the British Army in India, Past and Present*: London, 1868.

MARTIN, R. MONTGOMERY (Ed.), *The Despatches, Minutes, and Correspondence of the Marquess Wellesley*: London, 1836.

——, *China: Political, Commercial, and Social*: London, 1847.

MONTAGUE, MRS. F. M., *Memorials of the Family of Wood of Largo*: London, 1863 (privately printed).

MORSE, H. B., *The Chronicles of the East India Company Trading to China 1635–1834*: Oxford, 1926.

MURRAY, R. H., *History of the 8th King's Royal Irish Hussars*: Cambridge 1923.

NORTHEY, W. BROOK, and MORRIS, C. J., *The Gurkhas: Their Manners, Customs, and Country*: London, 1928.

NUGENT, MARIA, LADY, *A Journal from the Year 1811 to the Year 1815*: London, 1839.

OLDFIELD, HENRY AMBROSE: *Sketches from Nipal*: London, 1880.

PARKS, MRS. FANNY, *Wanderings of a Pilgrim in Search of the Picturesque*: London, 1850.

PARLBY, CAPTAIN S., *The British Indian Military Repository*: Calcutta, 1823.

PEARSE, COLONEL HUGH, *The Hearseys: Five Generations of an Anglo-Indian Family*: London, 1905.

PETECH, LUCIANO, *Medieval History of Nepal* (Serie Orientale Roma, vol. x): Rome, 1958.

POSTANS, T., *Hints to Cadets*: London, 1842.

PRINSEP, HENRY, T., *History of the Political and Military Transactions in India during the Administration of the Marquis of Hastings*: London, 1825.

PRYME, JANE TOWNLEY and BAYNE, ALICIA, *Memorials of the Thackeray Family*: London, 1879 (privately printed).

ROBERTS OF KANDAHAR, LORD, *Forty One Years in India*: London, 1897.

ROSS OF BLADESBURG, MAJOR, *The Marquis of Hastings*, Oxford, 1900.

ROSS, CHARLES (Ed.), *The Correspondence of Charles, First Marquis Cornwallis*: London, 1859.

ROUIRE, D., *La Rivalité Anglo-Russe au XIXe Siècle en Asie*: Paris, 1908.

Royal Military Calendar, third edition: London, 1820.

RAM, SITA, *From Sepoy to Subadar*, translated by Lt.-Col. Norgate, third edition, edited by D. C. Phillot: Calcutta, 1911.

SHAWE, W. B., *History of the Second Regiment of Bengal Native Light Infantry*: Julpigoree, 1872.

SHIPP, JOHN, *Memoirs of the Extraordinary Military Career of John Shipp*, A New Illustrated Edition with an Introduction by H. Manners Chichester: London, 1894.

SINHA, N. K., and DASGUPTA. A. K. (Eds.), *Selections from the Ochterlony Papers in the National Archives of India*: Calcutta, 1964.

SLEEMAN, W. H., *Rambles and Recollections of an Indian Official*: London, 1844.

——, *A Journey through the Kingdom of Oude in 1849–50*: London, 1858.

SPEAR, PERCIVAL, *The Nabobs*: Oxford, 1932.

STUBBS, F. W., *A History of the Bengal Artillery*: London, 1877.

SUTHERLAND, LUCY, *The East India Company in Eighteenth-Century Politics*: Oxford, 1952.

TUCCI, G., *Preliminary Report on Two Scientific Expeditions in Nepal* (Serie Orientale Roma, vol. x): Rome, 1956.

TURNER, R. L., *Comparative and Etymological Dictionary of the Nepali Language*: London, 1931.

TURNER, SAMUEL, *An Account of an Embassy to the Court of the Teshoo Lama in Tibet*: London, 1800.

TWEMLOW, GEORGE, *Considerations on Tactics and Strategy*, second edition: London, 1855.

WAKEHAM, ERIC, *The Bravest Soldier: Sir Rollo Gillespie, 1786–1814*: London, 1937.

[WALLACE, LIEUTENANT]. *Fifteen Years in India, or Sketches of a Soldier's Life*: London, 1823.

WATKINS, WALTER KENDALL, *The Scotch Ancestry of Major-General Sir David Ochterlony, Bart., a Native of Boston in New England*: Boston, 1902 (privately printed).

WEBB, E. H., *A History of the Services of the 17th (the Leicestershire) Regiment*, second edition: London, 1912.

WELSH, COLONEL JAMES, *Military Reminiscences*: London, 1830.

WHEELER, J. TALBOYS, *A Short History of India and the Frontier States of Afghanistan, Nipal and Burma*: London, 1880.

WHITE, GEORGE FRANCIS, *Views in India, Chiefly Among the Himalaya Mountains*: London, 1837.

WILLIAMS, G. R. C., *Historical and Statistical Memoir of Dehra Doon*: Roorkee, 1874.

WILSON, H. H. (Ed.), *Travels in the Himalayan Provinces of Hindustan and the Panjab by William Moorcroft and George Trebeck from 1819 to 1825*: London, 1841.

——, *The History of British India*: London, 1845.

WILSON, MINDEN, *A History of the Behar Indigo Factories*: Calcutta, 1908.

WOODYATT, NIGEL, *Regimental History of the 3rd, Queen Alexandra's Own Gurkha Rifles*: London, 1929.

WRIGHT, DANIEL (Ed.), *History of Nepal*, Indian reprint: Calcutta, 1958.

WURTZBURG, C. E., *Raffles of the Eastern Isles*: London, 1954.

YOUNG, H. A., *The East India Company's Arsenals and Manufactories*: Oxford, 1937.

INDEX